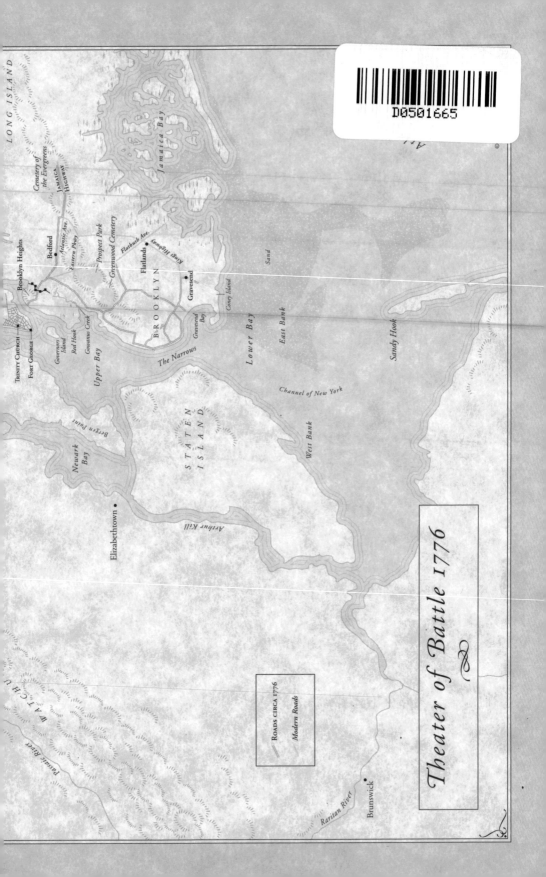

LONG ISLAND

Jamaica Bay

BROOKLYN

Cemetery of
the Evergreens

JAMAICA HIGHWAY

Bedford

Atlantic Ave.

Eastern Pkwy.

Prospect Park

Greenwood Cemetery

Brooklyn Heights

Flatbush Ave.

Kings Highway

Flatlands

TRINITY CHURCH

FORT GEORGE

Governors Island

Red Hook

Gowanus Creek

Upper Bay

Gravesend

Coney Island

The Narrows

Gravesend Bay

Sand

Lower Bay

East Bank

Sandy Hook

Channel of New York

Bergen Point

Newark Bay

STATEN ISLAND

West Bank

Elizabethtown

Arthur Kill

WATCHUNG

PASSAIC RIVER

ROADS CIRCA 1776

Modern Roads

Raritan River

Brunswick

Theater of Battle 1776

D0501665

THE BATTLE FOR
NEW YORK

THE BATTLE FOR
NEW YORK

The City at the Heart of the
American Revolution

BARNET SCHECTER

Walker & Company

New York

This book is dedicated to my parents,
Jerrold and Leona Schecter,
and my grandparents,
Edward Schecter and Miriam Goshen Schecter,
and
Barnet Protas and Belle Rubens Protas,
for whom New York was a key to the continent

Copyright © 2002 by Barnet Schecter

First published in the United States of America in 2002 by
Walker Publishing Company, Inc.
Published simultaneously in Canada by Fitzhenry and Whiteside,
Markham, Ontario L3R 4T8

For information about permission to reproduce selections from
this book, write to Permissions, Walker & Company, 435 Hudson
Street, New York, New York 10014

The images on the pages noted have been reproduced from the following
sources: Pages 12, 14, 47, 49, 70, 89, 99, 122, 176, 198, 211, 233, 238, 251,
252, 256, 270, 337, 341, and 349: New York Public Library. Pages 22, 33, 55,
228, 264, 278, 283, 295, and 340: Collection of The New-York Historical
Society. Page 29: Raising the Liberty Pole, The Old Print Shop, New York,
NY. Page 30: Courtesy of South Street Seaport. Pages 38 and 376: The
Museum of the City of New York. Page 57: Metropolitan Museum of Art,
New York, NY. Page 59: Courtesy of the U.S. Naval Institute; C. Corbett,
1777. Page 83: Courtesy of the Wadsworth Atheneum. Page 103: From the
original painting by Mort Küntsler, *Reading the Declaration of Independence*
© 1979 Mort Küntsler, Inc. www.mkuntsler.com. Page 105: Courtesy of the
U.S. Naval Academy Museum. Pages 119, 127, 151, 160, and 163: Courtesy
of The Brooklyn Historical Society. Pages 120, 180, 189, 311, 354, and 364:
Courtesy of The Library of Congress. Pages 144, 145, 146, and 147: Weapons
of the American Revolution, researched and compiled by Harold L. Peterson.
Page 173: U.S. Navy Submarine Warfare Museum. Page 290: William L.
Clements Library.

Library of Congress Cataloging-in-Publication Data
available upon request: ISBN 0-8027-1374-2

Visit Walker & Company's Web site at www.walkerbooks.com

Book design by Ellen Cipriano

Printed in the United States of America
2   4   6   8   10   9   7   5   3   1

Acknowledgments

First, I would like to thank Ramsey Walker, who called my attention to the intriguing story of Mary Murray's cocktail party for the British generals during the invasion of Manhattan and started me on the path to writing this book. He also introduced me to George Gibson, the president and publisher at Walker & Company, whose great patience, dedication, and editorial skill enabled me to develop the book to its full potential. A residency at Yaddo at the beginning of the project provided the ideal creative environment that I have tried to approximate in the city ever since. Polly Passonneau, William Petrick, Peter Brightbill, and Sloan Walker all read early drafts of various chapters and offered suggestions and encouragement. Michael Shafer also offered indispensable advice and support during the writing process. William Parry, Edward O'Donnell, Patricia Bonomi, Sloan Walker, and Andrew Page all read the penultimate draft of the manuscript and provided valuable criticism. I would also like to thank my agent, Sabine Hrechdakian, at the Susan Golomb Literary Agency.

In my research, many individuals and institutions were helpful. I would like to thank the staffs of the New York Public Library, the New-York Historical Society, the Pierpont Morgan Library, the Museum of the City of New York, Columbia University Library, and the Old Stone House Historic Interpretive Center; Sara Cashen of the Westchester County

Department of Parks and Recreation; David Osborn, site manager at the St. Paul's Church National Historic Site; Jonathan Kuhn at the New York City Department of Parks and Recreation; Richard Mooney; William Parry; and the late John Gallagher, author and tour guide. Dr. Laurence Simpson, president of the Sons of the Revolution in the State of New York, generously shared both his knowledge and the resources of the Fraunces Tavern Museum. Linda Johns tirelessly researched the illustrations for the book. At Walker & Company Michele Amundsen, Marlene Tungseth, Beth Caspar, and Krystyna Skalski also deserve my thanks.

I am grateful to Robert Boynton, David Rothenberg, Danielle Smoller, Peter Marcotullio, Martha Cooley, Caroline Harris, Michael Miscione, Kate Hartnick, and Sara Levine—friends and colleagues who have supported my work over the years. At Yale, Jaroslav Pelikan encouraged my interest in history, and I also had the privilege to study with Edmund Morgan and David Brion Davis. A Beinecke Memorial Scholarship for graduate study also supported my last year at Yale. Last but not least, I offer thanks to my parents, for imparting their love of history and for their extraordinary support, encouragement, and wisdom.

Contents

THE BATTLE FOR
NEW YORK

Prologue: Rethinking New York City's Place in the American Revolution

~⌒~

After the commencement of hostilities in 1776, New York being situated near the centre of the colonial sea-board, and readily accessible from the sea, was selected by the enemy as a principal point for their future operations." So began a front-page column in Walt Whitman's *Brooklyn Daily Eagle* on August 27, 1846, the seventieth anniversary of the Battle of Brooklyn, the first major clash in the contest for New York during the American Revolution.* Whitman himself introduced the historical account with his impassioned annual plea for the nation to commemorate, with the same fanfare as the Fourth of July, the anniversary of "that sad and yet most glorious Day for America, and for human freedom."[1]

Whitman's ancestors lived on western Long Island during the Revolution, and his grandmother told him tales of rapacious British invaders and defiant American patriots clashing on the wooded hills and lush farmland that became the city and later the borough of Brooklyn. One of Whitman's granduncles fought and died in the battle on August 27, which began a military campaign lasting almost three months. The British captured New York, but

---

*It was called the Battle of Long Island at the time, when Brooklyn was the name of a township and a tiny village in Kings County. The modern name for the battle reflects that the action took place across the entire area of today's borough of Brooklyn. See Stevenson and Wilson, *The Battle of Long Island,* ("The Battle of Brooklyn"), p. 3.

maintaining control of it for the next seven years in large part cost them the Revolution.

"See—as the annual round returns the phantoms return / It is the 27th of August and the British have landed," Whitman later wrote in his famous poem "The Centenarian's Story," in which he conjured a conversation between a Revolutionary War veteran and a young Union Army volunteer in the first year of the Civil War. Soldiers drill on a bright day in Fort Greene Park, and the veteran suddenly remembers the real fighting he took part in eighty-five years earlier on the same hills:

Aye, this is the ground,
My blind eyes even as I speak behold it re-peopled from graves,
The years recede, pavements and stately houses disappear,
Rude forts appear again, the old hoop'd guns are mounted,
I see the lines of rais'd earth stretching from river to bay,
I mark the vista of waters, I mark the uplands and slopes;
Here we lay encamp'd, it was this time in summer also.

The Declaration of Independence had been issued by Congress on July 4 and read to George Washington's army in New York on July 9, 1776. Whitman's centenarian continues: "'Twas a bold act then—the English war-ships had just arrived, / We could watch down the lower bay where they lay at anchor, / And the transports swarming with soldiers."[2]

Having succumbed to the American siege of Boston six months earlier,* and having regrouped in Halifax, Nova Scotia, the British saw New York as the key to subduing the rebellion. New York's strategic location secured one end of the Hudson River, and they expected their northern army, descending from Canada, to hold the other. Control of the Hudson, they anticipated, would sever the mid-Atlantic and southern colonies from New England.

Adding to New York's strategic value, the size and location of the harbor had also made the city a vital center of trade in the British Empire. It kept the profitable sugar islands of the British West Indies supplied with food, allowing them to devote more land to their cash crop. Ships left New York laden with wheat, rye, and corn; bread, butter, and cheese; pork, beef, and lamb; apples,

---

*After the clashes at Lexington and Concord on April 19, 1775, the British had been besieged in Boston until St. Patrick's Day, 1776.

peas, onions, and pickled oysters. They returned with holds full of sugar, molasses, hides, lumber, and silver. They also brought "bills of exchange," credits that enabled New York's merchants to buy manufactured goods from Britain. New York's merchant ships also sailed to Africa, where they traded rum and British manufactures for slaves to be sold in the West Indies.[3]

Until 1763, Britain had looked the other way as New York's merchants grew rich on illegal trade with the Dutch and French West Indies.*[4] The added wealth went back to Britain in the long run, because it enabled New York to improve its balance of trade and continue to buy manufactured goods and luxury items from Britain. (British laws prohibited the colonists from developing their own factories.) The landed and commercial aristocracy of the colony thrived within the mercantilist, imperial system.

Until the troubles began in Boston in 1775, New York had also been the British military headquarters in America and consequently home to a large population of royal functionaries. By 1776, New York felt comfortable and familiar to them, offering the perfect mix of urban and rural pleasures: a cosmopolitan town with a full schedule of glittering social events either at the fine houses and taverns or at the exquisite country estates a short carriage ride to the north. When the ministry in London dispatched the British fleet and the army to New York during the summer of 1776, it was on the assumption that the city and its environs were full of loyalists ready and waiting to hand the city over to the king's forces. The British commanders in chief, Admiral Richard Howe and his brother General William Howe, counted Americans generally as their friends, ever since the government of Massachusetts funded a monument to their older brother, a popular officer who led both British and provincial troops in the Seven Years' War. The Howes hoped the massive show of force in New York would help them negotiate a peaceful settlement of the American rebellion.

Over the summer of 1776, the British accumulated in New York's harbor the largest expeditionary force in their history prior to the great embarkations

*With the end of the Seven Years' War in 1763, the British began looking for ways to cope with the enormous war debt. The conflict began in North America as the French and Indian War in 1754, with the British and the American colonists pitted against the French and their Native American allies. In 1756, Britain officially declared war on France and the conflict spread to Europe, Africa, and the Philippines. In this second phase, called the Seven Years' War, the British drove the French from North America. Unlike most colonial wars of the seventeenth and eighteenth centuries, which began in Europe and spread outward, this contest reversed the pattern and reflected America's growing importance on the world stage (Faragher, *Encyclopedia,* pp. 147–148).

and landings of World Wars I and II.[5] Four hundred and twenty-seven ships carried 34,000 professional soldiers and seamen—roughly the population of Philadelphia, then the largest city in the colonies.[6] In addition to the combined total of 1,200 cannons projecting through the square gun ports of the battleships, the holds of the supply ships were packed with "an artillery more considerable than was ever brought before into the field," according to a British admiral on the scene. These transport vessels, also loaded with vast quantities of munitions, horses, and provisions, were "not to be counted," their masts "appearing as thick as trees in a forest."[7]

The British armada reached full strength in mid-August and landed troops on Long Island on the twenty-second. Washington's army of 23,000 poorly trained and ill-equipped troops was reduced by sickness and spread out in a precarious defensive line from New Jersey to Long Island via Manhattan. The Battle of Brooklyn, five days later, was the first battle ever fought by the United States as an independent nation.[8] It was also the largest battle of the Revolutionary War when measured by the number of participants.[9] Washington's baptism as the commander of an entire army was undeniably a disaster; the Americans were soundly defeated on the twenty-seventh, and the Revolution could easily have ended there had it not been for the Howes' failure to follow up their victory, and the intervention of the weather, which helped Washington carry out a miraculous escape to Manhattan.

The campaign in New York continued over the next three months with battles at Harlem Heights, Pelham Bay, White Plains, and back on Manhattan at Washington Heights as the Howes repeatedly failed to encircle the Americans. Most of Washington's army ultimately escaped across the Hudson to New Jersey, and the British settled into New York City, their goal all along, though some among them realized that a crucial opportunity had been lost. The Howes controlled all of Manhattan, but their three attempts to encircle the Continental Army had consumed the whole summer and fall, and the conditions that gave the British such an enormous military advantage in New York would not come again.

The Continental Congress had felt that New York, the second-largest American city, should not be given up without a fight, or the damage to American morale might prove fatal to the cause of independence. Once the city had been lost, Washington and Congress spent the rest of the war trying to get it back, while the British remained equally obsessed with protecting it as the hub of their operations.

Comfortably ensconced in New York, the military regime turned the city into a vortex of corruption and brutality that depleted Britain's financial resources and its moral authority; as the war progressed, the city became a trap for the British in more ways than one. When the French joined the American cause and naval warfare became an important element of the Revolution, the British discovered that the city's enormous and spectacular harbor was the worst possible location for a naval base.[10] The treacherous sand bars at Sandy Hook bottled the fleet up at critical junctures in the war as it waited for the wind and tide to cooperate.

The unique topography of the New York area also played a decisive role in shaping the strategy and tactics of both sides. Since New York City consisted of merely 4,000 wood and brick buildings covering less than a square mile at the southern tip of the island,[11] Manhattan retained most of its primordial landscape. To the north, two main dirt roads, a few cross roads connecting them, and some country lanes traversed a sparse patchwork of farms and villages scattered amid wooded hills and rocky outcroppings, salt marshes and streams.[12]

The entire area was then, and remains, an archipelago, its islands and peninsulas, rivers, channels and straits, creeks and inlets formed by the advance and retreat of a glacier.[13] The underside of the thick, heavy ice sheet raked the flat terrain some 50,000 years ago, carrying rocks and soil forward while leaving behind new troughs and valleys. Where the glacier stopped, it deposited the rocks and soil and created a terminal moraine—a line of hills that runs lengthwise across the middle of Long Island and continues on the southern part of Staten Island. The portion of this ridge at the western end of Long Island includes the hills of today's Prospect Park and was called Gowanus Heights.

When the climate became warmer, about 17,000 years ago, these hills trapped the melting ice, and the New York area was submerged under glacial lakes. Several thousand years later, the water broke through the hills, creating the Narrows (between Staten Island and Brooklyn)* and draining the landscape. However, as temperatures increased, approximately 9,000 years ago, rising sea levels sent water coursing back up through the Narrows, flowing into the depressions that the glacier had excavated and establishing New York's waterways: Upper New York Bay, the Arthur Kill, the East River, the Harlem River, Long Island Sound, and numerous smaller creeks and inlets.

*The strait now spanned by the Verrazano Narrows Bridge.

Below the Narrows, the Lower Bay connected to the Atlantic Ocean through the gap between Coney Island and Sandy Hook. A wide sandbar extended almost continuously between these two points, leaving only a few narrow channels by which ships could enter the port. The only other access to New York from the Atlantic was farther north, through Long Island Sound. Here, too, ships had to pass through a narrow strait—Hell Gate— an aptly named, rocky passage at the western end of the Sound where it meets the East River, and where the colliding currents, at that time, created roaring whirlpools.[14] Native American lore recalled that towering ancestors used to cross the treacherous channel on foot by stepping from rock to rock.[15]

To Native Americans, *Manna-hata* meant "hilly island,"[16] a characteristic that today is mostly confined to the rock formations in Central Park and the northern reaches of the borough, above West 110th Street. However, many of the area's physical features are still visible, despite the overlay of asphalt and concrete, of brownstones and skyscrapers, that obscures the battlefield in our midst. Fortunately—in a city famous for obliterating its past—the motivated tourist can also follow a trail of relics and reminders in all five boroughs and Westchester County that tells the forgotten tale of American heroism embedded in the defeat at the hands of the British: historic villages, houses, and churches; bronze plaques, gravestones, and colonial mile markers on the routes of the armies. In Green-Wood Cemetery, Prospect Park, the Cemetery of the Evergreens, Westchester County, and Washington Heights, one can walk on the very hills where the battles took place.

The tour at the end of this book offers surprising contrasts between old and new: a walk beside a picturesque salt marsh in the shadow of the New England Thruway, leading to a stunning eighteenth-century fieldstone church preserved in an industrial zone at the northern edge of the Bronx; George Washington's headquarters in a farmhouse dwarfed by a cement factory in Westchester County; a bronze plaque in the middle of Park Avenue at Thirty-seventh Street, marking the site of a mansion on a rural estate where Mary Murray served cakes and Madeira to the invading British generals and, according to legend, delayed them long enough to save thousands of American troops. These markers and structures set in the densely developed urban fabric can evoke the patchwork of fields, hills, and marshes as it appeared in the eighteenth century. Like the centenarian in Whitman's poem, one may feel the battle "pouring about me here on every side."

Whitman's fictional centenarian may have stood for the granduncle he never knew. Fortunately, many of the real participants on both sides of the battle for New York—from privates to generals, politicians to clergy—left diaries, letters, and memoirs. Excerpts of these materials are reproduced here, just as they were written, and they make vividly clear what it was like to live through the ordeal. Standing out among the original sources, the remarkable diaries of William Smith Jr., a lawyer, judge, and adviser to New York's governors, trace his odyssey from early days as a recent Yale graduate and Presbyterian propagandist against the city's Anglican, mercantile elite, to his middle years as a prosperous and increasingly conservative lawyer calling for reconciliation and reform to preserve the British Empire. Unable to remain a neutral, Smith slid by degrees into the loyalist camp, and by the war's end, he was in exile, never to see his native New York again. He embodies the painful dilemma that New Yorkers and all Americans faced, of choosing between the security of membership in a united empire and the uncertainties of independence and freedom.

Unlike Smith, the leaders of the Sons of Liberty, including Isaac Sears, were merchants who had risen from humble origins by making fortunes in the Seven Years' War. They galvanized the city's disenfranchised working class with calls for open resistance to the Crown—for radical measures that included mob violence—and kept the protest movement alive for a decade until the mounting conflict verged on war. They hounded New York's loyalists, whom they accused of conspiring with the royal governor and the mayor to hand the city over to the British. The radicals' words are preserved in the handbills they gave out at mass meetings on the Common* or at the Exchange on the waterfront.

Once the war came to New York, American recruiters plucked fifteen-year-old Joseph Plumb Martin from his grandparents' farm in Connecticut and sent him to the trenches, where he persevered all the way to Yorktown. His sardonic memoirs describe combat, hunger, exposure, and tedious weeks of inactivity on the front lines and reveal that a sense of humor was essential to his, and no doubt to many of his less eloquent fellow soldiers', survival.

---

*The wedge of land now occupied by City Hall Park and the converging traffic lanes of Broadway and Park Row.

Martin's commentaries echo those of General Henry Clinton, who was frustrated with the cautious, slow-moving William Howe. Clinton served for three years as Howe's second-in-command and then replaced him as the British commander in chief in 1778. He constantly and correctly disagreed with Howe's tactics, and his narrative, written after the war, is a revealing blend of impressive military achievements, thinly veiled critiques of other commanders, and abundant self-justification that also displays his single-minded concern, verging on paranoia, for holding New York City throughout the war.

As with all defining moments in history, the battle for New York hinged on both courage and human frailty: General Howe's infatuation with an American femme fatale, his young mistress, Elizabeth Loring, became a popular explanation for his halfhearted, sluggish pursuit of the rebels. The loyalist judge Thomas Jones declared that "as Cleopatra of old lost Mark Antony the world, so did this illustrious courtezan lose Sir William Howe the honour, the laurels, and the glory of putting an end to one of the most obstinate rebellions that ever existed."[17] As another historian later quipped, "The success of American arms owed a heavy debt to the success of hers."[18]

Because of its geography, its culture, its people, and its hold on the imagination of eighteenth-century military strategists, New York was, without exaggeration, the pivot on which the entire Revolutionary War turned.[19] The Revolution, John Adams famously wrote, was won first in the "minds and hearts of the people."[20] In the battle for New York, the struggle on this interior landscape—the difficult and, in some cases, agonizing choice between king and country in the conscience of each individual—had its roots in political and religious conflicts that dated back to the founding of the colonies, and which came to a head in the 1750s.

For all of the New Yorkers, like William Smith and his circle, or Isaac Sears and the other leaders of the Sons of Liberty, who had participated in the city's prosperity during the 1750s, and who sought to limit the scope of Britain's authority in the 1760s, a defining moment on the long road to revolution was the Stamp Act crisis of 1765. Britain's obstinacy served to reveal who was a radical, a moderate, and a conservative, and to test the extent to which each camp was willing to go in defending American rights. For a brief moment, however, in November of that year—after New York's polite petitions to the king, the House of Lords, and the House of Commons were ignored—the city's residents, dockhands and merchant princes alike, came together and took to the streets.[21] Just as the Stamp Act crisis is traditionally identified as the start of the American Revolution, the first skirmish in the battle for New York may properly be dated to November 1, 1765—eleven years before the arrival of the British fleet—when the mutual resentment between the people of the city and British authority erupted as street theater and then escalated into rioting against government targets.[22]

The story of the contest for New York provides a fixed point, a compass for orienting oneself amid the many disparate theaters and battles of the long, complex war. Because both sides remained focused on New York, even as engagements unfolded elsewhere, the ongoing battle for the city helps clarify the major turning points of the American Revolution, from Trenton and Saratoga to Yorktown and beyond—to the final departure of British forces from the United States in 1783. A reassessment of New York's role casts the Revolution itself in a clear new light.

CHAPTER I

The Bastions of Authority

$\sim$

The night of Friday, November 1, 1765, was moonless and still. At the southern tip of Manhattan, two restless mobs surged through the dark streets of New York, lighting their way with lanterns, torches, and the glow of 500 candles. During the day the hated Stamp Act had taken effect, and New York City shut down. Residents deserted the streets and closed up their shops, while in the tense quiet the equally detested Lieutenant Governor Cadwallader Colden prepared for the outbreak of violence that promised to accompany his enforcement of the new tax.[1]

In his forty-four years as a royal official in New York, Colden had antagonized the colonists at almost every turn while failing to win more than tepid approval from his superiors in London. For the previous two years, residents had anxiously awaited a successor to the last royal governor, Robert Monckton, while Colden filled the vacancy.[2] In this latest crisis, the stubborn seventy-seven-year-old lieutenant governor asked that marines from the British warships in the harbor take up positions inside Fort George at the foot of Broadway.*

Instead of cannonballs, the fort's guns were loaded with canvas sacks of small lead and iron balls called grapeshot—far deadlier against a crowd at close range. Two guns were wheeled up against the inside of the fort's wooden gates in case demonstrators broke through, while others were aimed up Broadway.

*Where the Customs House now stands, below Bowling Green.

View of New York City from the harbor, 1764.

Colden in turn was warned that if the soldiers opened fire, he would pay with his life; the death threat, posted in the Merchants' Coffee House during the day, was delivered to the gates of the fort at dusk.

Inside the fort, a ton and a half of specially marked paper, parchment, and vellum awaited distribution to City Hall,* the courts, lawyers' offices, printing houses, and retail stores, among other enterprises that required paper to conduct business. The embossed square stamp on every sheet constituted a tax that would be added to the price Americans paid when they bought a newspaper or almanac, for example, or when they needed a legal document, such as a marriage or liquor license. For the first time, the Crown attempted to reach beyond tariffs for regulating trade within the empire and imposed a tax that invaded the daily life of every American.[3]

Adding to the burden, the Currency Act of the previous year had abolished colonial paper money as legal tender, even though it was badly needed as a medium of exchange. Despite the shortage of hard currency, the new law required that the stamp tax be paid in silver. Prime Minister George Grenville's new program for taxing the colonies was ostensibly for their own protection: Britain, heavily in debt from the Seven Years' War that had ended in 1763, needed the colonists to defray the cost of defending vast territories on their own frontiers that had been won in the struggle against France. New York's econ-

*Federal Hall now stands on the site of the old City Hall at Wall and Broad Streets.

omy, meanwhile, was in the depths of a postwar depression; when the military contracts and British soldiers disappeared, the boom years of the 1750s came to an end.

When the stamped paper first arrived toward the end of October, an angry mob of 2,000 people had stood on the wharf to prevent the ship *Edward* from unloading its cargo. However, Colden had tricked them by sneaking the stamps into the fort at night. On Thursday, October 31, more than 200 New York merchants struck back with the first act of open rebellion in the American colonies: They gathered at George Burns's City Arms Tavern, five doors up from the fort on the west side of Broadway, and signed an agreement to boycott British goods until Parliament repealed the Stamp Act.[4] Merchants in other colonies soon committed themselves to similar nonimportation pacts.

As night fell on November 1, a huge crowd formed, this time on the Common. The demonstrators included day laborers, shopkeepers, tavern owners, blacksmiths, carpenters, and seamen as well as wealthy merchants. They placed a paper effigy of Colden in a chair and one of the seamen carried it on his head. Cheering loudly at each corner, the mob set off down Queen Street.* When they reached the house of James McEvers at Wall Street, they gave him three cheers for giving up his post as stamp distributor for New York. Then they proceeded to the fort, broke into the coach house, and stole Colden's carriage. With the effigy of the lieutenant governor seated inside, and one man with a whip acting as the driver, the crowd pulled the coach around the city. At the corner of Water and Wall Streets, they were cheered by patrons of the Merchants' Coffee House. As more people joined the parade, it turned up Broadway and headed back to the Common. By this time the second crowd was coming down Broadway carrying a movable gallows from which they hung another effigy of Colden. The dummy held paper in its hands, representing the stamp tax, while the devil, hanging next to him, instructed his disciple.

The combined mobs—with 2,000 marchers, the coach, and gallows—became a grand procession that returned to the fort, where they threw bricks and stones over the walls, pounded on the gates with clubs, and taunted the troops to fire. When it seemed that the marchers were about to crash through the gates and storm the fort, their leaders intervened and restrained them. As Colden and his entourage watched from the ramparts, the mob regrouped at

*Now Pearl Street.

Cadwallader Colden

Bowling Green across the street. Right under the muzzles of the fort's guns the unruly crowd tore down the wooden fence around the lawn and used it to make a bonfire of the effigies, the gallows, and the costly carriage.

However, the climax of the night's violence was yet to come. As the mob stoked the funeral pyre, some of the protesters slipped away to Major Thomas James's mansion. James was the artillery officer in charge of the fort who had promised publicly to cram the stamps down New Yorkers' throats with the end of his sword. In response, a rumor circulated that he was to be buried alive. James had leased Vauxhall, an elegant estate overlooking the Hudson River between Chambers and Warren Streets at the northern edge of the city. The detachment of rioters chased off the fifteen soldiers standing guard and ransacked the house. Mahogany tables, silk curtains, featherbeds, mirrors, and china were all heaped on a bonfire while the mob raided the wine cellar and drank or destroyed more than nine casks of liquor. They kept going until four in the morning, destroying the valuable library and every other room in the house, as well as the gardens and summerhouses outside. Carpenters with crowbars and hammers smashed the windows and doors, including their frames, leaving only the mansion's shell intact. Having trampled the wealth and ostentation of Vauxhall, the rioters moved on to attack what they deemed to be nests of sin and corruption: several brothels that catered to British soldiers.[5]

With daylight came the pealing of all the city's bells, as the rioters exulted and ended their rampage with a final flourish. In a city less than a square mile in area, with twenty-two churches and a skyline dominated by steeples, the din was inescapable. Captain John Montresor, the chief engineer who had prepared the fort to maximize the raking fire of its guns, wrote disgustedly in his journal: "The mob got the permission to toll the Bells of the several Churches, meetings and other houses of worship except the Churches of England, which they broke into and tolled the bells at half after nine."[6]

Like Montresor, the city's wealthy merchants, including those who participated in what began as a nonviolent protest, were appalled by the sacking of Major James's mansion. New York's commercial aristocracy feared that its own property would be next. While these patricians resented British attempts to tax them without their consent and thereby curb the power of the provincial legislature, through which they exerted their influence, they also feared mob rule and the leaders they saw as demagogues inciting a social revolution within the province. Similar riots had broken out in other American cities earlier that year, and some members of New York's elite believed that a civil war across the entire continent was not far off. Ultimately, the wealthiest merchants' interests lay with Britain's commercial empire, and most of them would become loyalists when events forced them to choose.[7]

The Churches of England that the rioters broke into, like Fort George, were bastions of royal power in New York City. The 175-foot steeple of Trinity Episcopal Church at Broadway and Wall Street towered above the rest of the skyline. The lavishly decorated interior, and the expensive carriages lined up waiting for their owners on Sundays, also proclaimed the wealth and influence of Trinity's Anglican congregation. Anglicanism was the official, established religion in England, and while its members in New York made up only 10 percent of the population, they included the governor, the lieutenant governor, most of the royal Council, and many members of the Assembly, as well as numerous wealthy merchants and landowners from old established families. Anglicans of modest means attended one of two other churches in less desirable locations: St. George's Chapel, near the stench of a tannery, or St. Paul's Chapel, six blocks north of Trinity, on the edge of a slum that housed the city's sex industry.[8]

By the 1760s, New York had already acquired its modern reputation as a cosmopolitan center catering to every human desire—from the spiritual to the carnal.[9] It had the most religious diversity of any city in America and also the most brothels. New Yorkers even had a sardonic nickname for the neighborhood where the sacred and profane overlapped. Because the Anglican Church owned most of the land north of St. Paul's Chapel and west of Broadway, the district—with its hundreds of prostitutes—was slyly dubbed the "Holy Ground." The concentration of brothels near the church was also convenient both to nearby King's College* and to the barracks of the British soldiers across Broadway on Chambers Street. Prostitution rose sharply in New York at the end of the 1760s and in the early 1770s as a decade of economic hard times took an especially high toll on single women who had no other means of support.[10]

The sources of the city's ethnic and religious heterogeneity were much older. New York inherited the richness of its urban culture from seventeenth-century Amsterdam, which was one of Europe's most vibrant and cosmopolitan cities because it sheltered a wide array of religious dissidents fleeing Spanish oppression in the southern provinces of the Netherlands. When the Dutch West India Company founded a trading post on Manhattan in 1624, it was called New Amsterdam, and its laws guaranteed freedom of worship to anyone who wished to live there and help the company make a profit in the fur trade. The city's success rested on these two mutually reinforcing pillars: unfettered commerce and freedom of conscience. However, this ideal of tolerance did not extend to the Native Americans just outside the city, many of whom were butchered in clashes with Dutch soldiers.[11]

When the British seized New Amsterdam in 1664—and renamed it New York in honor of its new ruler, James Stuart, the duke of York—they granted religious freedom to the Dutch inhabitants. A little more than a century later, waves of immigration had brought more nationalities and religions to New York than to any other American city. Besides the English and Dutch, there were French, German, Scottish, Irish, Swedish, and Portuguese residents as well as African slaves. Most ethnic groups introduced their own religious denomination into the city's mix of Anglicans, Quakers, Presbyterians, Dutch Reformed, Methodists, Moravians, Lutherans, Baptists, German Calvinists, Anabaptists, Huguenots, Sephardic Jews, and Catholics.[12] Hence the twenty-two houses of worship, half of which were either built or renovated during an upsurge of religious fervor in the quarter century leading up to the Revolution.[13]

British toleration of diversity did not mean equality, however. As the Anglican Church guarded and expanded its own power, it sought to curb the

---

*King's College became Columbia University in 1784 and moved to West 116th Street in 1897.

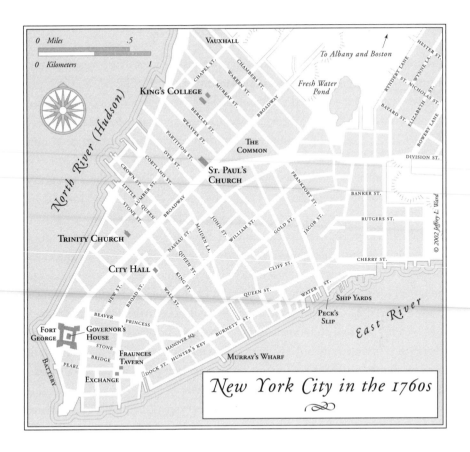

0 Miles .5

0 Kilometers 1

North River (Hudson)

VAUXHALL

To Albany and Boston

HESTER ST.

CHAPEL ST.

CHAMBERS ST.

WARREN ST.

MURRAY ST.

BROADWAY

Fresh Water
Pond

KING'S COLLEGE

BERKLEY ST.

WEASYES ST.

PARTITION ST.

DYES ST.

THE
COMMON

ST. PAUL'S
CHURCH

FRANKFORT ST.

RYNDERT LANE

ST. NICHOLAS ST.

WYNNE LA.

BAVARD ST.

ELIZABETH ST.

BOWERY LANE

DIVISION ST.

BANKER ST.

RUTGERS ST.

© 2002 Jeffrey L. Ward

CORTLAND ST.

CROWN ST.

LITTLE LUMBER ST.

QUEEN

STONE ST.

BROADWAY

JOHN ST.

WILLIAM ST.

GOLD ST.

JACOB ST.

TRINITY CHURCH

NASSAU ST.

MAIDEN LA.

QUEEN ST.

KING ST.

CLIFF ST.

CHERRY ST.

CITY HALL

NEW ST.

BROAD ST.

WALL ST.

QUEEN ST.

WATER ST.

SHIP YARDS

PECK'S
SLIP

East River

BEAVER

PRINCESS

FORT
GEORGE

GOVERNOR'S
HOUSE

STONE

BRIDGE

FRAUNCES
TAVERN

HANOVER SQ.

BURNETT ST.

DOCK ST.

HUNTER'S KEY

MURRAY'S WHARF

BATTERY

PEARL

EXCHANGE

New York City in the 1760s

growth of the dissenting churches. Nonetheless, Presbyterianism gained many adherents in the 1740s by attracting ethnic and religious groups that fervently opposed the English and Anglicanism, among them Scottish and Scotch-Irish immigrants, New England and Long Island Puritans, Dutch Reformed Converts, and individuals of mixed Dutch and Scottish descent.[14]

The Presbyterian-Anglican rivalry was inextricably enmeshed with the Byzantine world of New York politics. The dominant pattern in this mosaic of intermarriage and political alliances between New York's patrician families was the contest between the commercial and landed interests. Among the American colonies, the emergence of equally powerful "merchant" and "country" elites was unique to New York because its rivers and harbor supported trade while large estates could be carved out of the vast hinterlands.

James De Lancey, who dominated city and provincial politics as acting governor for most of the 1750s, led a coalition of the city's wealthy, and mostly Anglican, merchants that included three other families at its core—the Schuylers, the Philipses, and the Van Cortlandts. (James De Lancey's father, a French Huguenot, had converted to Anglicanism to solidify his social position in New York.) Also in their orbit were the Stuyvesants, Waltons, Bayards, and De Peysters.

An alliance of landed interest groups gathered around the Livingston and Morris families—headed by Robert Livingston Jr. and Lewis Morris Jr.—and competed fiercely against the De Lanceyites for votes and influence. Presbyterians for the most part, the Livingstonites were vocal opponents of the Anglican Church and hoped to threaten its supremacy by gathering all of New York's dissenting churches under their banner.[15] The two factions also disagreed on issues like taxation, since the De Lanceyites' fortunes stemmed from trade, while the Livingstons and their allies were primarily landowners and lawyers. These distinctions were not absolute, however: The leading merchants also invested in land, while the landed families could not sustain their opulent lifestyles solely by leasing farms on their vast estates and had to involve themselves in commerce to some extent.[16]

In this oligarchic society, the great families exerted their political influence through a system of voice-vote elections, which denied voters the protection of a secret ballot. The tenant farmers on the manors along the Hudson and the middle-class artisans who made up the bulk of voters in New York City were equally susceptible to intimidation, because their loyalty could be monitored by the powerful landlords and merchants who controlled their livelihoods.

In the 1760s, however, a significant increase in political activity among artisans and other manual workers (called mechanics) started to transform this feudalistic, deferential relationship. In October 1765 during the Stamp Act crisis, New Yorkers became freemen in record numbers in order to obtain the vote.* In the years leading to the Revolution, freemanship allowed all classes of citizens to participate in elections, and almost all white males gained the vote.[17] Gradually, elected officials became more accountable to a broader constituency.

The voters of New York City and county sent four representatives to the provincial Assembly, a legislature consisting of twenty-seven members from the colony's various counties, towns, and manors. The Assembly met in the

---

*Eligible voters were either freemen (white men who paid a onetime fee for being a retailer or artisan in the city, holding office, and voting) or freeholders (white males with an estate worth more than forty pounds) (Tiedemann, *Reluctant Revolutionaries,* p. 27).

city, where its power was checked by the governor's Council: twelve royal appointees chosen by London to advise the governor on policy and pass on legislation sent up by the Assembly. The decisions of the governor and his Council in turn were subject to approval or veto by Britain's Board of Trade. In bestowing the prestigious Council seats, along with enormous land grants, the British government expected to secure the allegiance of key figures from New York's elite and consolidate royal power in New York.[18]

With the Anglicans—the De Lanceys and their allies—occupying many of these influential positions, religious tensions became embroiled in New York politics. In the struggle for control over King's College in the 1750s, the Anglicans succeeded in extending their control over the school's leadership and religious services, while the Presbyterian Livingstonites tried to ensure that it was denied public funding. The Anglicans retaliated by opposing a charter of incorporation for the city's Presbyterian Church. The Anglican campaign to have a bishop appointed for the colonies accordingly drew fire from the Presbyterian faction.[19]

In this running battle—waged with newspaper editorials, broadsides, pamphlets, and magazines—William Livingston, William Smith Jr., and John Morin Scott led the Livingston party and served as its chief propagandists. The three young firebrands, still in their late teens and known as the Whig "Triumvirate,"* had graduated from Yale University and were clerks in the law office of Smith's father, William Smith Sr., who gained renown when he helped defend the printer John Peter Zenger in the historic libel case of 1735 that vindicated freedom of the press.

Before joining Smith's firm, William Livingston had clerked for James Alexander, Smith's partner in the Zenger case. James Alexander's son, William, studied law in his father's office and also participated in the "Whig Club" that formed around the Triumvirate. It was not all high-minded political discussion. William Smith Jr. described the club's initial weekly meetings at the King's Arms as "soaking at Tavern with a set of noisy Fops." After numerous toasts to their political heroes, they found relief from the drudgery of the law office by smashing windows and setting fire to the ponytails of their victims' powdered wigs.[20]

It was during this clerkship in the 1750s that a lifelong enmity began between William Smith Jr. and the grasping, vindictive Cadwallader Colden.

---

*In English politics a Whig was a member of the opposition in Parliament, while a Tory supported the king. In America the terms were later applied to patriots and loyalists during the Revolutionary War.

Smith and Livingston had received the important commission to edit a compendium of New York's laws from the previous sixty years. In an attempt to safeguard his claim to a particular land grant, Colden demanded that Smith omit a reference to it in the compendium and threatened to have the governor withhold Smith's pay if he didn't comply. "I resented the Meanness and Injustice of this attempt upon my Honor," Smith wrote in his diary years later, "and told him, that he and his money might go to the Devil, and rushed from the Room."[21]

In part to attack petty royal functionaries—greedy "placemen" like Colden—the Triumvirate had launched New York's first literary magazine, the *Independent Reflector,* an influential early expression of the ideals and rhetoric that culminated in the Revolution almost a quarter of a century later.[22] One of the journal's essays, all of which were penned by the Triumvirate, announced the writer's aim of "vindicating the civil and religious RIGHTS of my Fellow-Creatures: . . . exposing the peculiar Deformity of publick *Vice* and *Corruption*; and displaying the amiable charms of *Liberty,* with the detestable Nature of *Slavery* and *Oppression.*"[23] For Presbyterians, the stakes of the debate were high: The establishment of the Anglican Church and an American episcopacy, they feared, would extend the tyranny of the Crown over the spiritual as well as the political lives of the colonists.

When the *Reflector* folded under political pressure from its opponents, Smith began recording his observations of important events in a diary, which he called his *Historical Memoirs.* In 1757 his highly partisan *History of the Province of New-York* was published in London. In it he went out of his way to attack Colden and a parade of royal governors, while the representatives of the people in the Assembly and the Livingstonites came in for high praise.

Like the *Independent Reflector* before it, Smith's *History* warned that the booming wartime economy of the 1740s and 1750s—a result of King George's War and the Seven Years' War—had spawned a culture of materialism that weakened the moral fiber of New York's affluent citizenry, giving rise to an elaborate new etiquette, a shallow and pretentious concern for refined manners, which merely served to justify the orgy of conspicuous consumption.[24]

During the final years of the 1750s, Smith also enjoyed tremendous success as a lawyer, and the young idealist underwent a transformation, helping the colony's major landowners consolidate their wealth by fending off lawsuits filed by the Crown.* Smith and Cadwallader Colden clashed again in

---

*In the process, Smith helped the Livingstons and their allies hold on to land they had stolen from the Native Americans using fraudulent surveys.

1760, when James De Lancey died suddenly and Colden ascended from the Council to become lieutenant governor. The zealous defender of the Crown's interests despised New York's politically connected lawyers, who helped landowners avoid payment of rents to the royal government that were stipulated in their land grants. Smith, on the other hand, saw himself as the defender of basic British rights—liberty and property—against encroachment by the Crown. Though not born into the New York establishment, by 1763 Smith had truly arrived: He was the highest-paid lawyer in the province and had moved his family into the mansion at No. 5 Broadway that had belonged to the late James De Lancey.[25]

As the Stamp Act crisis came to a head over the next two years, Smith found himself pulled in two directions.[26] Since he was a likely candidate for a judgeship, and even for chief justice of the colony, he looked forward to a large salary on the bench that would only be secure if the Crown collected enough revenue. On the other hand, the Sugar and Currency Acts of 1764 and the rumor of a stamp act had disturbing implications for American rights. If the colonial legislatures shared their power over taxation with Parliament, they would be surrendering their only bulwark against arbitrary rule.

At first, Smith decided to play an active role in protesting the new taxes. He urged New York's assemblymen to pressure Colden, who agreed to call the legislature into session. Smith then drafted the Assembly's petition to the House of Commons. When American petitions were ignored and the Stamp Act became law the following year, Smith continued to oppose it. New Yorkers even started referring to the shrewd, articulate lawyer as "Patriotic Billy."

However, the Stamp Act riot raised the specter of mob rule and civil war for Smith and his circle, and they started to look for ways to avoid such an outcome. Smith envisioned the creation of an American Parliament as a peaceful solution to the conflict with the mother country and a means of preserving the empire. Modeled on the British Constitution, this new body was to have a lower house with delegates from the legislature of each colony. The upper house was to consist of ten councillors chosen by the king for life. A governor general was to preside as its executive. The colonies would have been able to tax themselves, and the existing British Parliament would have retained its supremacy in all other areas. Smith sent the plan to London, where, predictably, it was ignored.

In a more practical vein, Smith helped local officials negotiate with Colden in the days immediately following the violence of November 1, 1765, and the lieutenant governor agreed to transfer the stamps from the fort to City Hall. Thousands of New Yorkers watched peacefully as wagons carted

William Smith Jr.

the boxes of paper up Broadway and over to Wall and Broad Streets, where they were turned over to the mayor. Colden pledged not to enforce the tax, and the long-awaited arrival of the new governor also helped diffuse the crisis. Sir Henry Moore saw no reason to use force with the city's residents. He believed that if the colonists refused to conduct any business that required stamps, it would quickly immobilize the city's economy, at which point they would cave in and accept the tax.

By the end of November, it was clear that such a strategy of passive resistance on the part of the colonists was not affecting all of them equally. Merchants who shut down their businesses lost profits, but they had a cushion of wealth to sustain them if necessary. However, the seamen, dockhands, porters, and other day laborers who handled their cargoes were one step from the almshouse.[27]

At a town meeting on November 26, 1765, a third political force emerged in New York to represent these workers and to question the wisdom of the aristocratic De Lancey and Livingston factions. The Sons of Liberty, or Liberty Boys, was initially a secretive organization, and the exact date of its inception is unknown, but it was probably formed sometime in October in response to the Stamp Act. Similar groups of the same name sprang up in other colonies at that time.

The name was derived from a celebrated exchange between two members on the floor of Parliament in February 1765. Colonel Isaac Barré demolished the assertion by Charles Townshend that the ungrateful colonists who opposed Prime Minister Grenville's taxes were biting the hand that had carefully planted and nurtured them in the New World. Barré reminded Townshend that the colonies were settled by people fleeing religious persecution in England. "They planted by your care?" Barré thundered. "No! your Oppressions planted em in America." He went on to describe the colonists as "Sons of Liberty."[28]

The leaders of the Liberty Boys in New York included Isaac Sears, Alexander McDougall, John Lamb, and Marinus Willett. Operating outside of the Assembly and the legal framework of government, they drew support not only from middle-class artisans but also from those poorer white males who were denied the vote. The fact that the day laborers, sailors, apprentices, and servants who marched to the fort on the night of November 1 did not loot the city indiscriminately was attributable in part to the orchestration of the event by Sears, McDougall, and Lamb. The mobs got out of control but ultimately confined their actions to specific, symbolic government targets.[29]

At the mass meeting on November 26, the Sons of Liberty proposed a radical solution to the Stamp Act crisis and the plight of the unemployed: New York should boldly defy the new law and resume business as usual without stamps. Because Sears, McDougall, and Lamb were not from the elite families of New York, they were eminently qualified to lead the city's workers. They had started at the bottom and done well for themselves. Sears, for example, the city's most militant and influential agitator, was a merchant who had made a small fortune as a privateer plundering enemy ships during the Seven Years' War. He also earned a reputation for bravery when he challenged and nearly captured a ship armed with almost twice as many guns as his own. Adored by the sailors and artisans on the waterfront, he was dubbed "King Sears" by aristocrats who feared his power to mobilize people in the streets.

William Smith and his partners in the Triumvirate, William Livingston and John Morin Scott, also attended the town meeting in November. New Yorkers soon realized that these three men, who a dozen years earlier had been New York's most eloquent defenders of liberal values, were unwilling to take a firm stand in the stamp crisis. Despite challenges from the Liberty Boys, the political lawyers dominated the meeting and took charge of drafting instructions to the Assembly on behalf of the city's residents—resolutions that stopped short of demanding a full resumption of business in defiance of the law. This display of conservatism by men who had once been crusading reformers cast them as "betrayers of the people" and left them politically isolated.[30]

At the beginning of 1766, just a few months after the Stamp Act riot in the city, the new governor, Sir Henry Moore, silenced a tenant uprising on the estates of the Livingstons and other proprietors in the Hudson Valley by sending in British troops. The rebellious farmers had hoped for lower rents and stable leases but fared much worse than their urban counterparts had in November: Moore assembled a panel of lawyers, judges, and councillors to put the malefactors on trial. Married to a Livingston, Smith could hardly be an impartial judge, but he ultimately agreed to serve, and led the tribunal in meting out harsh sentences, at which point the governor was satisfied; he stepped in with a pardon and spared the life of the ringleader.[31] Smith and John Morin Scott, the other Whig Triumvirate member who passed judgment on the insurgents, had demonstrated once again that in the hour of crisis, they could be expected to waffle and then close ranks with the established authorities.

CHAPTER 2

The Monster Tyranny Begins to Pant

～

Six months after the Stamp Act riot, all the city's bells rang in unison again, but this time in joy not protest. The nonimportation agreements that American merchants signed in response to the Stamp Act had hurt their British trading partners enough that they too clamored for relief from Parliament. When news confirming the repeal of the Stamp Act reached New York at three in the afternoon on May 20, 1766, "a sudden joy was immediately diffused thro' all ranks of people in the whole city," the *New York Post-Boy* reported. "Neighbours ran to congratulate each other, and all the bells in town were set a ringing, which continued till late at night, and began again early next morning."[1]

In the rush of good feelings, the Assembly commissioned statues of the king and of William Pitt, the former prime minister who was an ardent defender of American rights and had argued for the repeal of the Stamp Act on the floor of Parliament. When news of the Stamp Act's demise first arrived in New York, the Liberty Boys celebrated by taking an old ship's mast and erecting a flagstaff, later called the "Liberty Pole" or "Tree of Liberty," on the Common. Attached to the pole was a board with the inscription "George III, Pitt and Liberty," and a dozen barrels were suspended by ropes from the top.[2] The maypole of English folk celebrations, a traditional springtime fertility symbol, was fused in the public's mind with the ancient Roman liberty pole or pike held by the figure of Libertas in the Temple of Liberty—an image familiar to Americans from English pamphlets and engravings during the Seven Years' War.³ The towering pine mast planted in the ground took on a political meaning and soon became a rallying point for mass meetings and an emblem of the American cause.

It also became the site of a long, violent contest between residents and British troops. Two regiments arrived in the city in June and were quartered in the Upper Barracks on the northern end of the Common near the pole. Residents, who resented paying taxes to support the soldiers, were angered further when the latter supplemented their meager pay by moonlighting, and took jobs away from the poor by accepting even lower wages. The soldiers, incensed by the disrespectful and ungrateful populace they were assigned to protect, cut down the pole on August 10. People took it as an "Insult to the town," and "it gave great Uneasiness," according to the *Post-Boy*.⁴

While no one was killed in the riot that broke out the following day, August 11, 1766, several people were wounded, and it was the first time American colonists clashed openly with British regulars. "A considerable mob assembled on the Common consisting of 2 or 3000 chiefly Sons of Liberty, headed by Sears in order to come to an Explanation with the Officers and Soldiers for Cutting down a pine post where they daily exercised, called by them the Tree of Liberty," Captain Montresor, the British engineer, wrote in his journal. "These Sons of Liberty used the most scurrilous and abusive language against the officers and soldiers present who never seemed to resent it, till a volley of Brick Bats ensued and wounded some, upon which they defended themselves with their Bayonets."⁵

The *Post-Boy* reported the event quite differently. "It appears from many Affidavits, that the Soldiers were intirely the Aggressors: And the people are in general very uneasy that such a Number of arm'd Men, without any visible Occasion for them, are station'd among us, and suffer'd to patrol the Streets, as in a Military or conquer'd Town."⁶

After the encounter, a second Liberty Pole lasted only a month. When a third one was cut down in March 1767, its replacement was "cased below with iron to prevent such another action."⁷ The British soldiers tried cutting it down, digging it up, and blowing it up without success. The *New York Journal* considered these attacks in themselves "trivial, and only considered as of importance by the citizens, as it showed an intention to offend and insult them."⁸ A far greater threat had taken shape in London.

When Parliament repealed the Stamp Act, it also passed the Declaratory Act, affirming its right to tax the colonies in the future "in all cases whatsoever."

Accordingly, in June and July of 1767, the Townshend Acts became law.* Aside from duties on lead, glass, paint, paper, and tea shipped to America, the new legislation included the Mutiny Act, which punished New York's Assembly for failing to obey the Quartering Act (passed in 1765): It had refused to appropriate funds to house and feed British troops on New York's territory. The governor was ordered to veto all legislation until the Assembly obeyed.

While this standoff continued, William Smith strengthened his relationship with Governor Moore, who appointed him to a seat on the De Lancey–dominated Council in November 1767, from which he struggled vainly to help the Livingston faction maintain its sizable majority in the Assembly, as it was battered from both the right and the left.[9] Governor Moore soon dissolved the Assembly as punishment for its protest against the Townshend duties, and during a new election in 1768, the Liberty Boys threw their support behind the De Lancey party because they felt the Livingstonites hadn't protested loudly enough, not only against the Townshend duties but against the Stamp Act and the Mutiny Act as well. Though still in the minority, the De Lanceyites gained seats in the Assembly and declared themselves the true defenders of American liberty.

At the end of 1768, New York's merchants plunged ahead, apart from the Assembly, and joined the nonimportation movement initiated by Massachusetts to protest the Townshend program. New York's Assembly still had not formally responded to the Massachusetts Circular Letter that called for the unified boycott. Had it done so, Moore, under instructions from London, would have dissolved the Assembly again. However, the De Lancey faction realized that taking the initiative to defy the ministry and bring about a dissolution would attract votes from middle- and working-class New Yorkers, and it continued to exploit the Livingstonites' vulnerable middle-of-the-road position by proposing that the Assembly draft a positive reply to Massachusetts. When the much-reduced Livingston majority, coached by William Smith, scrambled to counter its rivals by drafting letters and creating committees of correspondence, Moore dissolved the Assembly for the second time. A new election in 1769, again influenced by the Sons of Liberty, swept away the laggard Livingston majority completely and turned over control of the Assembly to the De Lanceyites for the first time in nearly a decade.[10]

New York's internecine family politics had visibly become a cynical game in which broader ideals were espoused merely for political gain and abandoned

*Charles Townshend, who debated Colonel Isaac Barré in 1765, had since become Chancellor of the Exchequer and proposed the new acts.

just as easily. The merchant princes, however, were playing with issues that soon leaped beyond the narrow confines of New York's rivalries and engulfed them completely.[11] The colony's political system still favored the oligarchic rule of the established families and their seasoned leaders, but the increasing enfranchisement of artisans through freemanship and the growing power of the Sons of Liberty had begun to impact the old order. Procedural changes were also harbingers of greater transformations to come: In 1769, amid an outcry for reform—including the use of a secret ballot—the Assembly opened its sessions to the public for the first time.[12]

In September 1769, Governor Moore died unexpectedly after a short illness, and Cadwallader Colden, still biding his time on the Council at the age of eighty-one, became acting governor. Since he had been passed over twice when the governorship seemed within his grasp, Colden was determined to impress the ministry and finally win the office with all of its prestige and emoluments. He formed an alliance of convenience with the De Lanceys by promising to reward their party with government patronage and to sign a bill allowing the colony to issue more paper money. In exchange, the De Lancey–led Assembly caved in to the Mutiny Act on November 22, 1769, by appropriating 2,000 pounds for the support of the British army in New York.

New Yorkers loudly denounced the capitulation with broadsides against the assemblymen and a demonstration on the Common. The broadside of December 16 that called for the rally was addressed "To the betrayed inhabitants of the city and colony of New York" by an anonymous writer who signed it, "A Son of Liberty." He declared that the Assembly was providing funds to support "troops kept here, not to protect but to enslave us,"[13] and he attacked the De Lanceys for their naked political ambition. The Assembly struck back against this "false, seditious and infamous libel"[14] with a reward of 100 pounds for the name of the author.

With Colden in power and the De Lanceys in control of the Assembly as well as the Council, William Smith set out to win the support of the Sons of Liberty and align them with the Livingstons. He dissented loudly on the Council, calling for the removal of British troops not only from Boston, where they had been sent to crush resistance to the Townshend program, but from New York as well. He condemned the New York Assembly's military appropriation in the strongest terms. Smith's most extreme statements—a call for the use of secret ballots, and condemnations of the elitist Council on which he served—were published anonymously in letters and broadsides.[15]

The Liberty Pole.

In January 1770, the Liberty Boys expressed similar ideas at large rallies in front of the Liberty Pole, where their best orators—including John Lamb—railed against the De Lanceys' corrupt bargain. The struggle over the pole itself was renewed one night when British soldiers sawed through the iron braces, drilled a hole, and filled it with gunpowder. Before they could detonate the charge, the troops were caught in the act by patrons at Montagne's Tavern, across Broadway from the Common, which had become the headquarters of the Liberty Boys. According to an American broadside, the soldiers came over to Montagne's and "broke seventy-six squares of his windows, entered his house, and stopped him in the passage with swords, and threatened if he stirred to take his life," which scared the customers into leaving precipitously through the windows.[16] Several days later the soldiers "availed themselves of the dead hour of night," according to the *Post-Boy*, and "sawed and split the pole in pieces, and carried them to Mr. Montagne's door, where they threw them down."[17]

Isaac Sears

The rhetoric escalated when an American broadside complained of having to pay not only for quartering the troops and supporting of the poor whose jobs they stole, but also "a poor tax to maintain many of their whores and bastards in the work-house."[18] The soldiers printed up a broadside of their own deploring the ingratitude of the citizens toward them, and ridiculing the Sons of Liberty, who defended their Liberty Pole as if "their freedom depended on a piece of wood, and who may well be compared to Esau, who sold his birth-right for a mess of pottage."[19]

On January 19, the attacks on the Liberty Pole and the simmering war of words erupted in a bloody melee called "the battle of Golden Hill." The incident began when Isaac Sears took it upon himself to prevent half a dozen soldiers from posting their broadside at an outdoor market near the East River wharves.[20] "Mr. Sears seized the Soldier that was fixing the Paper, by the Collar, and asked him what Business he had to put up Libels against the Inhabitants? and that he would carry him before the Mayor. Mr. Quackenbos [who accompanied Sears] took hold of one that had the Papers on his arm: A soldier standing to the Right of Mr. Sears, drew his Bayonet; upon which the latter [Sears] took a Ram's Horn, and threw it at the former, which struck him in the Head, and then the Soldiers, except the two that were seized, made off and alarmed others in the Barracks."

Sears and Quackenbos hauled the soldiers to the mayor's house, where a crowd soon gathered in the street. While the mayor considered how to judge the case, a band of twenty redcoats "with Cutlasses and Bayonets" arrived to spring their two comrades. The leaders of this group appeared to be drunk, while the two soldiers inside didn't want to be rescued but preferred to lay their case before the city officials. The mayor ordered the soldiers to sheathe their weapons and return to the barracks.

The onlookers followed them through the streets, brandishing every kind of wooden club they could find, including the "Rungs" pulled out of "some Sleighs that were near." At the summit of Golden Hill,* more soldiers appeared, and this emboldened the redcoats, "which was soon manifested by their facing about, and one in silk stockings and neat Buck-skin Breeches (who is suspected to have been an Officer in Disguise) giving the Word of Command, 'Soldiers, draw your bayonets and cut your Way through them:' The former was immediately obeyed and they called out, 'Where are your Sons of Liberty now?' and fell on the Citizens with great Violence, cutting and slashing."

When one man lost his stick, several soldiers reportedly chased him "down to the main street, cut a Tea-Water man driving his Cart, and a Fisherman's finger; in short, they madly attacked every Person they could reach: And their Companions on Golden-Hill were more inhuman; for besides cutting a Sailor's head and Finger, that was defending himself against them, they stabbed another with a Bayonet, going about his Business, so badly, that his Life was thought in Danger." The soldiers were finally driven off when the residents menaced them with two halberds—long poles armed with both an ax blade and a steel spike at one end. The New York papers all confirmed that no one was killed,[21] but there were many cuts and bruises and some serious wounds.†

The soldiers' broadside had sneered at the Americans for their attachment to a wooden mast, but Sears and the other radical leaders had clearly found in the Liberty Pole a powerful and tangible symbol that could stir the emotions of the people and keep them politically engaged. As Colden put it, the "ill humour" had been "artfully worked up between the Towns people and the soldiers."[22]

Sears bought a small lot near the Common for the fifth pole, which went up on February 6, 1770. The large pitch pine mast "was drawn through the streets from the ship-yards, by six horses, decorated with ribb[ons], three

---

*A former wheat field bounded by today's William, John, Fulton, and Cliff Streets.
†This clash has been singled out as the "first blood-shed of the Revolution." The "Boston Massacre," which commonly bears that title as well, and in which there were fatalities, was fueled in part by news of the events at Golden Hill and at Nassau Street, where a riot took place the following day. The tragedy in Boston occurred only six weeks later.

flags flying, with the words Liberty and Property and attended by several thousands of the inhabitants." This time the pole was protected by iron bars attached with flat rivets and by iron hoops. While French horns played "God Save the King," it was planted in a hole twelve feet deep and "secured in the ground by timber, great stones and earth."[23] It stood forty-six feet above the ground, had a twenty-two-foot topmast with a gilt weathervane that spelled the word *Liberty,* and would last for more than six years.

The day after the grand installation, an informer testified that James Parker, printer of the *Post-Boy,* had produced in his shop the libelous broadside of December 16, 1769. When Parker and all of his apprentices were arrested and questioned, they revealed that the writer was thirty-eight-year-old Alexander McDougall, a leader of the Sons of Liberty.[24] He was charged with libel against the government and put in jail.

McDougall's hostility toward the De Lanceys and the British government ran deep. The son of Scottish immigrants, he was exposed to the writings of the Whig Triumvirate through the Presbyterian Church and went on to read widely in the literature of political and religious dissent.[25] McDougall had economic reasons to oppose the Crown's policies as well. Like Sears, he had made a fortune as a privateer in the last war and then prospered as a merchant in the West Indian trade. McDougall also owned a tavern on the waterfront and a great deal of land in Albany County. Combined with his wife's considerable wealth, these assets left no doubt that he could afford bail.[26]

McDougall chose to stay in jail, however, to highlight the similarities between himself and John Wilkes, the famous English radical who was jailed for libel against the king in 1763 and again in 1768. Wilkes had published a pamphlet called the *North Briton,* and number 45 was the issue the government deemed libelous. By coincidence—or providence, as the highly aroused populace believed—the forty-fifth page of the *Votes and Proceedings* of New York's Assembly contained McDougall's broadside and the decision to arrest him.[27] The Liberty Boys dubbed McDougall "the Wilkes of America" and made him famous throughout the colonies.

The decision of the British government to prosecute Wilkes and repeatedly bar him from taking his seat in Parliament had inflamed his constituents, and the massive riots that gripped London brought the country to the brink of revolution.[28] That the Liberty Boys invoked his name in New York in 1770 was a sign of how extreme the radicals' position had become in the space of a decade and how far the Anglo-American relationship had deteriorated. After

Alexander McDougall

years of economic stagnation, aggravated by continual encroachments on the colonists' fundamental rights, the local drama unfolding in New York's jailhouse was bound to reverberate in a larger arena.

Hundreds of visitors flocked to McDougall's cell and played on the number 45 to equate his struggle for freedom of speech with that of Wilkes. A week after his arrest, on the forty-fifth day of the year, forty-five of McDougall's friends had dinner with him in his cell, consumed "forty-five pounds of beef steaks, cut from a bullock of forty-five months old," and ended the meal with forty-five toasts. Since McDougall was Scottish, the number also had a more somber connotation: It evoked the abortive Second Jacobite Rebellion of 1745, dubbed "the 45." The Scottish Highlanders who supported the Young Pretender, Bonnie Prince Charlie, in his attempt to overthrow King George I were slaughtered at Culloden Moor the following year.[29]

Because no one wanted the unpopular task of prosecuting McDougall, his confinement and the attendant theatrics lasted for three months. When William Smith was cornered by his adversaries in the Council and asked for his professional opinion of the case, he grudgingly provided them with ammunition. From a strictly legal point of view, "if they chose to prosecute," he believed that the broadside was libelous and they had grounds to proceed.[30] However, Smith declined to take on the task himself, and the prosecution faltered.

Eventually, the De Lanceys and Colden managed to indict McDougall by convening a grand jury packed with their cronies. John Morin Scott, in an effort worthy of his membership in the Triumvirate, pointed to the landmark case of the printer John Peter Zenger in 1735 as a precedent and asserted that truth was a sufficient defense against the charge of libel.[31] The jury ignored Scott's arguments, but McDougall made only one appearance in court before the case was dismissed; the death of James Parker, the printer, left the prosecution without its main witness.

During the McDougall case, in April 1770, the colonists won another round in the battle against parliamentary taxation. The boycott of British goods begun in November 1768 to protest the Townshend Acts resulted in the repeal of all the duties except the one on tea. Like the Declaratory Act, which followed the repeal of the Stamp Act, the duty on tea was a face-saving measure. By retaining it, the new prime minister, Frederick Lord North, proclaimed Parliament's supremacy and British sovereignty in the colonies. The conflict had not been resolved, only postponed.

As the British ministry perhaps intended, the partial repeal of duties sowed division among the colonists. New York's merchants wanted to resume importation of all British goods except tea. The Sons of Liberty strenuously opposed the action: At a public meeting Sears issued a death threat to anyone breaking the nonimportation agreement before other colonies agreed to do so.[32]

To make the case for resuming trade, the merchants avoided the use of mass meetings, where the Liberty Boys would have carried the day by acclamation. Instead, the merchants polled the city's residents individually by going from house to house, knowing that most people would be intimidated by the presence of gentlemen on their doorstep and would provide the desired response.[33] The Liberty Boys tried to disrupt the survey, and the issue ultimately led to a large riot. On July 7, supporters of the Liberty Boys and their new allies, the Livingstons, clashed with the foot soldiers of the De Lanceyite merchants in "the battle of Wall Street."[34]

The merchants' henchmen were the clear winners in the brawl, and the nonimportation movement collapsed a week later. When New York resumed trade with Britain, other cities were appalled and charged New Yorkers with abandoning the cause. Philadelphians sent a letter asking for New York's Liberty Pole since they clearly had no more use for it.[35] However, a return to some semblance of economic normalcy was badly needed to alleviate widespread hardship in all of the colonies, and despite petitions and other efforts by the Liberty Boys to keep nonimportation alive, eventually trade resumed, except for tea.

On the surface, relations with Britain grew warmer: In August 1770 the city unveiled on Bowling Green the equestrian statue of King George that had been ordered after the repeal of the Stamp Act. Colden reported to London that government officials, clergymen, and other prominent guests marched in a procession around the gilt figures of horse and rider and toasted the king "under a discharge of 32 pieces of cannon and band of musick playing at the same time from the ramparts of the fort."[36] This monument and another dedicated on Wall Street in September to honor William Pitt were the first statues ever erected in New York City.[37]

Despite Colden's fawning loyalty, in October the ministry passed over him for a third time and sent a Scottish nobleman, John Murray, the earl of Dunmore, to succeed the late Sir Henry Moore as governor of New York. The venal, boorish Dunmore made Colden look like a genius and a saint. William Smith tried to insinuate himself into the new governor's confidence and offer him advice, but threw up his hands in despair after a few months. "Was there ever such a Blockhead," Smith vented in his diary.[38] The ministry reassigned Dunmore to Virginia less than a year later. The demotion provoked him to spend his last night in New York stumbling through the streets in a drunken rage.

The long-suffering Colden faced disappointment once more in July 1771, when William Tryon became the governor of New York. While he was known as "the Butcher" in North Carolina for his handling of a rebellion there,[39] Tryon initially managed to be quite popular in New York. Heeding the advice of William Smith, he plotted a middle course and tried to stay clear of New York's divisive politics. He resolved "not [to] steer by the popular voice nor be a dupe to the Assembly or Council."[40] It was a strategy that Smith had adopted for himself in response to the demise of the Livingston majority in the Assembly: He disengaged himself from party loyalties and focused on exerting his influence over the governor.[41]

With the resumption of trade, economic conditions in New York improved for a couple of years, and political protest subsided. However, in June 1772, the collapse of the British credit system ruined numerous New York businesses and swelled the ranks of the unemployed. Because the effect was similar in Scotland, Ireland, and England, a wave of angry emigrants, evicted from their homes and farms, landed in New York, hoping for a fresh start, and finding little opportunity.[42]

During the next few years of growing resentment and apparent political calm in Anglo-American relations, George Washington visited New York on the peaceful mission of enrolling his stepson at King's College.[43] Martha Custis had been a widow at the time she married Washington, and in addition to a son, she brought to the marriage a sizable fortune which, combined with Washington's inheritance, made him one of the richest men in America.

As well as money and property, Washington possessed more military experience than almost any other American. As a result of his missions against French outposts in the northwest during the Seven Years' War, Washington had risen from the rank of lieutenant colonel to become commander of the Virginia militia by the age of twenty-three. With only 700 men under his command, he struggled to defend a 350-mile stretch of frontier. He also took part in the British expeditions against Fort Duquesne in 1755 and 1758. Washington's exploits gained him a certain amount of fame, which he enjoyed, but the tendency of British commanders to ignore his rank and disregard his sound advice had been a great frustration. Having married Martha in January 1759, he resigned his commission at the end of the year and returned to Mount Vernon.

At the time of his visit to New York in late May 1773, Washington was forty-one years old and had been a successful planter in Virginia and a member of that state's House of Burgesses for a dozen years. Since 1770, when Virginia's legislature was dissolved, he had also been a conspicuous participant in the colony's nonimportation movement. Washington espoused the radical position that Americans should not plead for their natural rights with petitions to the king and Parliament. His career in the House of Burgesses had been rather undistinguished, but the clarity of his vision in the Anglo-American conflict quickly set him apart from contemporaries, whose subtle, legalistic perspective left them trapped by indecision. Early on, he accepted that his political stance was likely to lead to war with England.

Nonetheless, on the trip to New York, Washington was perfectly willing to indulge the aristocratic pretensions of his amiable host, William Alexander, and to address him as Lord Stirling.[44] When a jury in Edinburgh decided in favor of Alexander's claim to a lapsed Scottish earldom, but the British House of Lords did not, he blamed the latter for playing politics, returned to America, and took the title anyway. Friends addressed him as "my lord," his wife as Lady Stirling, and the couple's daughter as Lady Kitty, even if they found the titles a bit ridiculous.

Stirling, one of the old Whig Club's lesser lights in his youth, had assumed the mantle of his late father, James Alexander, a prominent lawyer in the New York establishment who, along with William Smith Sr., defended John Peter

Zenger in 1735.* Stirling became one of the first governors on the board of King's College and served on the royal Council. He also improved both his financial and social status by marrying into the powerful Livingston family: His wife, Sara, was the sister of William Livingston, the Whig Triumvirate's dominant member.

Despite his aggressive efforts, Stirling did not, however, receive even a fraction of the ten million acres in the New World that King James I had granted to the first earl of Stirling. On paper, they included Nova Scotia, much of Canada, and an Indian island called Matowac—better known as Long Island. The couple instead pooled their sizable inheritances and purchased a large estate in Basking Ridge, New Jersey, where their extravagant mansion remained perpetually under construction.

After meeting up with Washington at the Jockey Club in Philadelphia, Stirling brought him to the mansion for a pleasant two-day visit. Washington proceeded to New York, where the De Lanceys and Bayards hosted him at dinner during his stay. Washington also attended a party for General Thomas Gage, the commander in chief of British forces in the colonies, at Hull's Tavern on Broadway. One newspaper described the "cheerfulness and harmony which presided at every table," as a testament to Gage's "affable and benevolent deportment during his ten years' residence in this province."[45]

This cordial atmosphere in New York—the British military headquarters in North America—did not last much longer. On May 5, 1773, the British ministry had invited fresh confrontation with the colonies by passing an act giving the British East India Company a monopoly on the tea trade to America. To rescue the ailing company, the government cut the price of tea in half by removing the heavy tariff it once carried. But the Townshend duty of three pence per pound was kept in place. The British hoped to lure Americans with a price even lower than that for smuggled Dutch tea: By purchasing the British tea, they would have effectively agreed to parliamentary taxation.

However, the Americans saw the trap and resisted violently.[46] When the first tea ships arrived in Boston that winter, the colonists refused to land their cargo. On December 16, 1773, men disguised as Mohawks boarded one of the tea ships in Boston Harbor and emptied the crates into the har-

*After Smith and Alexander were disbarred by Chief Justice James De Lancey, Andrew Hamilton of Philadelphia successfully defended Zenger.

New Yorkers throwing tea off the British ship *London.*

bor. A few days later, while New Yorkers awaited the tea ship *Nancy* and debated how to handle the cargo, an express rider named Paul Revere arrived with news of the Boston Tea Party. Revere was a silversmith and political cartoonist who led Boston's radical artisans. His report stiffened New Yorkers' resolve not to accept the tea when it arrived. Governor Tryon had hoped to avoid a "tea party" in New York, but when the *Nancy* finally arrived at Sandy Hook in April 1774 the governor was away on a trip to England. The *Nancy* had been battered by storms, which damaged its masts and snapped its anchor chain. However, the *New York Journal* thought the elements had been kind, considering it had "on board something worse than a Jonah."[47]

On April 22, while the *Nancy* was still down at the Hook, a second ship, the *London*, sailed past it and arrived at the wharves in New York, where a vigilant crowd confronted the captain. He was the same man who had brought the stamps in 1765, and in Tryon's absence, Cadwallader Colden, now eighty-six, again found himself in charge. Once more he was not to have his way. Not waiting for darkness or disguises, the men on the docks boarded the *London*, found eighteen chests of tea, and threw them into the river. New York's tea party convinced the *Nancy*'s captain to turn around and head back to England without ever approaching the wharf.

Two weeks later the shocking news arrived in New York that Parliament had passed the Boston Port Bill. As punishment for the Boston Tea Party, the city's port was closed until the owners of the tea were compensated, and General Gage took most of his troops to Boston to enforce the sanctions, called the Coercive Acts. The Americans quickly dubbed them the Intolerable Acts, along with the Quebec Act, passed that same month.

This last measure, designed to secure the loyalty of the French population in British Canada, extended the border of the Province of Quebec to the Ohio and Mississippi Rivers and threatened American land claims in the area. The law also bolstered the Roman Catholic Church in the province, restored French civil law (which lacked trial by jury), and established a provincial government that had no representative assembly and would be dominated by the Crown. The British had planned to reorganize the provincial government since they acquired Canada from France in 1763 at the end of the Seven Years' War, but the timing of the Quebec Act in 1774 convinced Americans that it was a direct attack on their rights and institutions.[48]

"A general consternation and disgust works among the people," William Smith wrote in his diary on May 18. "I fear we shall lose all that attachmt. we once had to so great a degree for the parent country."[49] Instead of submitting to the Coercive Acts, the Bostonians' Committee of Correspondence sent letters to the other colonies calling for unity and resistance.

Sears and McDougall wrote back on behalf of New York's Committee of Correspondence agreeing to nonexportation and nonimportation of goods to and from Britain, with the stipulation that it be "under such Regulations as may be agreed upon by Committees from the Principal Towns on the Continent, to meet in a general Congress to be held here for that Purpose"—the first call for a continental congress made by any public body in the colonies.[50] While Samuel Adams, Benjamin Franklin, and John Hancock had each suggested the idea in letters and speeches during the previous year, they did so as private individuals, not in any official capacity.

New York's Committee of Correspondence was the first to go beyond a theoretical discussion to a specific proposal.[51]

The letter was signed on May 15, 1774. The following day both the Sons of Liberty and the city's merchants met at the Exchange to nominate a new and larger committee "to correspond with the neighboring Colonies on the present important crisis."[52] The radicals were surprised to find the wealthiest merchants in attendance. "The De Lanceys urged their friends to attend and pushed them in, to mix with the Liberty Boys," William Smith noted. Whereas before they had remained aloof, they realized they had to join the revolutionary movement in order to control what they considered the excesses of the mob and its demagogic leaders. "Many People of Property dread the Violences of the lower Sort," Smith wrote.[53] They didn't want a repeat of the Stamp Act rioting. The Sons of Liberty had created the Committee of Correspondence during the Stamp Act crisis, and the conservatives now wanted it to reflect their views as well. A compromise was reached by creating a committee of fifty that included all but two of the radicals' twenty-five nominees and twenty-seven others. One extra member was added to make this the Committee of Fifty-One.[54]

With the closing of Boston's port set to take effect on June 1, Massachusetts appealed to the other colonies for economic aid. Funds and barrels of grain flowed in, and political solidarity followed: Through the committees of correspondence, New York's call for a general congress spread and was soon embraced by all of the colonies.

The conservatives on the Committee of Fifty-One did manage to make the Revolutionary movement in New York more moderate than in other colonies, but they were also carried along by events and many chose to resist the British ministry when it passed further repressive measures against Massachusetts. If they had not, the radicals would have taken control.[55]

This became clear during the summer when it was time to name representatives to the first Continental Congress, which was created, indirectly, by New York's original call for such a body. It was to meet in Philadelphia, the largest city in the colonies, on September 5. The Committee of Fifty-One had to be goaded into action by a threat from the Liberty Boys that they would name their own slate of delegates.[56] After a protracted contest with the radicals, the committee managed to have its own list of five moderates approved by voters, but only after these men pledged publicly that they would work for a general boycott when they reached Philadelphia. New York was moving down the road to revolution: The city's most prominent citizens, the pillars of the community, had now joined the illegal committees and congresses that would soon replace the colonial government.

John Jay, Isaac Low, James Duane, John Alsop, and Philip Livingston were New York's delegates to the first Continental Congress. When they left New York for Philadelphia on September 1, 1774, cheering crowds saw them off, "with Colours flying, Music playing, and loud Huzzas at the End of each Street."[57]

Four days later the Continental Congress set to work. It protested Parliament's recent acts and formed a "Continental Association" of all Americans to stop importing goods from Britain after February 1 of the following year. The delegates also agreed to convene a second congress on May 10, 1775, "unless the redress of grievances . . . be obtained before that time."[58] Congress further resolved that if the king and Parliament continued to ignore its petitions, exports too would be cut off after September 15. New York represented a sizable portion of this economic threat. Every year, the British relied on raw materials such as iron and timber from the city and its hinterlands, worth roughly 130,000 pounds sterling, and New Yorkers imported British textiles, home furnishings, and other goods valued at about half a million pounds sterling, the latter figure constituting one quarter of Britain's annual revenues from exports to the American colonies.[59]

"May God prosper the Americans in their resolutions, that there may be one asylum at least on the earth for men, who prefer their natural rights to the fantastical prerogative of a foolish perverted head because it wears a crown." Charles Lee, a disgruntled British army officer who arrived in America at the end of 1773 during the height of the tea crisis, had written these words in a letter to a friend almost a decade earlier when Americans were resisting the Stamp Act.[60] A disheveled, foulmouthed, temperamental man, who went nowhere without his beloved dogs, Lee was not one to restrain his biting verbal style. Not surprisingly, he had alienated key political allies and failed to win promotion in the military. During the 1760s he traveled widely as a soldier of fortune, and the misery he witnessed under German and Turkish rulers had made him vigilant about the potential for tyranny at home in England.

When Lee landed in New York in 1773, he immediately joined forces with the radicals and added his own voice to the chorus of protest against the British tea tax. Bearing a letter of introduction from Benjamin Franklin, Lee moved on to Philadelphia, where he befriended other prominent patriots and impressed them with his knowledge of European affairs, his erudition, and, most important, with the breadth of his military experience. His habit of carrying around a copy of Thucydides in the original Greek enhanced his image.[61]

Lee also traveled to Virginia, where he met Richard Henry Lee (no relation) and worked with Thomas Jefferson to organize protests. He returned to Philadelphia in the spring of 1774 and urged residents through a published address to abandon moderate measures and forge ahead with strict boycotts. In July this address was distributed as a broadside in New York, where Alexander McDougall entrusted Lee with a letter for Samuel Adams in Boston. Lee began a lifelong friendship with Adams, who introduced him to Joseph Warren, John Hancock, and other leading figures in the resistance movement. With war becoming a distinct possibility, the idea of having Lee command troops against the British began to germinate.

Ezra Stiles, later the president of Yale College, met Lee in Newport, Rhode Island, when he passed through, and was one of a small minority who had doubts about the Englishman at that time, feeling his denunciations of the king and his ministers might have been motivated by bitterness rather than conviction. Because Lee had failed to win promotion in the British army, Stiles noted in his diary, "he is chagrinned and disappointed—he published a bold sensible well written address to the citizens of New York. Whether he is a pimp for the ministry or a sincere friend to public liberty, is to me uncertain."[62]

Nonetheless, when Lee returned to Philadelphia in late August, he gained the confidence of the congressional delegates by the sheer force of his personality. He was witty, self-confident, and spoke in lofty terms about liberty as a universal ideal. He attended private dinners with the most influential delegates—John Adams, George Washington, Patrick Henry—as if he himself were a member of Congress. By October, Lee had made no secret of his willingness to accept a command in an American army, and he drew up a plan for organizing such a force, which he presented to John Adams.

Because of his increasing stature among the colonists, a year after his arrival in America, Lee was uniquely positioned to discredit a Tory pamphlet, titled *Friendly Address to All Reasonable Americans*, written anonymously by an Anglican clergyman, the Reverend Dr. Myles Cooper, president of King's College. James Rivington, a loyalist New York printer, published the essay in November 1774. The pamphlet disheartened many opponents of British taxation by belittling their objections and then arguing that resistance was futile anyway because of the British army's obvious superiority.

Lee's rebuttal, *Strictures upon A "Friendly Address to All Reasonable Americans,"* was soon reprinted in every major American city. Lee's experience in the Seven Years' War and his European exploits allowed him to hold forth as a leading military authority in America, and he was able to reassure Americans that the mighty British war machine was far from invincible. Lee praised the performance of American troops in the Seven Years' War and pointed out that the redcoats' ability to march in neat columns would do them little good against the irregular tactics of the Americans, who were at home on wilderness terrain. The British also lacked great generals, Lee argued; the mold had been broken with the death of James Wolfe in the last war. Lee concluded with a flight of rhetoric and a call to arms: "The monster Tyranny already begins to pant; press her now with ardor, and she is down."[63]

The author of the anonymous pamphlet had to be an "ecclesiastick," Lee announced, because "he has that want of candour and truth, the apparent spirit of persecution, the unforgivingness, the deadly hatred to dissenters, and the zeal for arbitrary power which has distinguished churchmen in all ages, the more particularly the *high* part of the Church of England."[64] Lee's blistering attack strongly implied that Myles Cooper was lobbying to be appointed bishop in America, and revealed that religion, always a key ingredient of the city's rancorous politics, had become a combustible element in the imperial crisis.*

Once Congress had taken a strong position on nonimportation, Americans throughout the colonies were forced to choose sides. In November 1774, New York's moderate Committee of Fifty-One gave way to a more radical Committee of Sixty, which prepared to enforce the February 1, 1775, deadline set forth in the Continental Association by appointing a subcommittee—known as the Committee of Inspection—to inspect ships coming into the harbor. Backed up by the mobs, this subcommittee planned to turn away ships from England before they could unload their cargo.

The Association agreement also attacked the enemy within: the habits of refinement and luxury cultivated by years of consuming Britain's exports and imitating its pastimes. The agreement exhorted Americans to "discountenance and discourage every species of extravagance and dissipation, especially all horse-racing, and all kinds of gaming, cock-fighting, exhibition of shews, plays, and other expensive diversions and entertainments." The call for fru-

---

*Thomas Paine's *Common Sense*, which appeared two years after Lee's essay, was unquestionably the most influential and famous pamphlet of the American Revolution. However, Lee's *Strictures*, which suffered the same obscurity as its author after the war, played an important role in advancing the American cause at a critical moment when many remained undecided about resistance. Lee's essay was "probably one of the most influential pieces of propaganda in the Revolutionary period," according to his modern biographer (Alden, *General Charles Lee*, p. 62).

gality was familiar from the writings of the Whig Triumvirate and set a moral tone compatible with the deprivation the city's residents expected to face because of the boycott on imports. The sacrifices required of them would be in the name of republican austerity and virtue.[65]

When the *James*, a ship loaded with coal and dry goods, docked at Murray's wharf at the foot of Wall Street shortly after the Association deadline of February 1, 1775, protesters turned out and intimidated the captain. New York's tea party less than a year earlier had occurred at the same wharf, which was owned by Robert Murray, a wealthy Quaker merchant. The *James* sailed back out into the Upper Bay to avoid the hostile crowd, but returned to the waterfront on February 9, escorted by a British warship, the *Kingfisher*. When the captain came ashore, however, the navy could not protect him from the mob, which marched him through the main streets of the city while residents jeered. The *James* soon left the city without unloading its cargo.

Less than a week later, however, a second ship arrived from England, this one owned by Robert Murray and named after his second daughter, Beulah. The Committee of Inspection used its patrol boat to prevent the *Beulah* from docking at the waterfront, but Murray was determined to land the two-ton cargo, which included bolts of fabric and bales of pepper. He argued that the goods had been ordered before the Association was announced and should therefore be exempt from the boycott. The committee rejected his claim and sent its patrol boat to follow the *Beulah* and make sure it left New York.

Robert Murray flouted the Association's authority not out of loyalty to Britain but rather because he was anxious about the bottom line in several commercial enterprises he had struggled to build over the course of twenty years. By 1775 Murray owned not only a wharf but also several ships and a stunning mansion outside of town.* There he entertained the city's more established merchants and their wives as equals. In mid-February, his desire to hold on to all he had worked for evidently got the better of him. The *Beulah* spent the next two weeks at the Narrows, apparently waiting out a spell of foul weather before returning to England. On the night of March 5, however, just as the *Beulah* appeared ready to sail through the channel at Sandy Hook and out into the Atlantic, the captain managed to shake off the committee's patrol boat and rendezvous with a vessel off Staten Island that Murray had dispatched from New Jersey to help unload his goods.

Murray's men transferred the cargo to his store in Elizabeth, but Isaac Sears, who led New York's Committee of Inspection, soon tracked down the contra-

---

*Where Thirty-seventh Street now intersects Park Avenue in the Murray Hill neighborhood.

band. The nonimportation committee in Elizabeth interrogated Murray's associates and eventually broke down their silence. Murray's promise to reship the merchandise, a formal apology, and a large cash contribution for repairs to a local hospital satisfied the Elizabeth committee. However, New York's inspectors, including Alexander McDougall, wanted to make an example of Murray and threatened to banish him from the city. Because of his wealth and prominence, Murray's actions had damaged the committee's reputation among the other colonies and threatened the unity on which the Continental Association depended.

William Smith appealed to McDougall for leniency on behalf of the Murrays, but it was Mary Murray, Robert's wife, whose voice was decisive in protecting him. She wrote to McDougall and Sears, the committee's most influential members, and pleaded with them not to exile her husband and his brother John, who was a partner in the family business. She asked for the inspectors' intercession "to prevent an Evil, which if brought upon them, must involve their innocent Wives and helpless children in Unspeakable Distress."[66] Her appeal to their humanity, and her reputation as an ardent patriot, won them over.

The committee relented in the matter of punishment, but its vigilance in the cases of the *James* and of the *Beulah* had kept the Association's cordon intact against British imports. "The success which the violent party have had in preventing their vessels from landing their cargoes has given them great spirits," Lieutenant Governor Colden complained in a letter to Lord Dartmouth. "Your Lordships will believe it has chagrined me a good deal."[67]

CHAPTER 3

A General Insurrection of the Populace

~⌇

I n December 1774, as positions hardened on both sides of the Atlantic, Benjamin Franklin, then sixty-eight years old and a colonial agent in London, found himself playing chess and chatting about the Anglo-American conflict with a vivacious fifty-three-year-old widow named Caroline Howe.[1] She was a prominent and active socialite with broad interests, including politics. These friendly contests and conversations took place over several weeks, during which time Franklin was also approached by agents representing the prime minister, Frederick Lord North, and the colonial secretary, William Legge, earl of Dartmouth.* Anxious to prevent the conflict from becoming a war, the two moderate ministers conducted secret talks with Franklin through their emissaries.† The analogy between chess and diplomacy was not lost on Franklin, who always traveled with a portable set. "Several very valuable qualities of mind," he wrote in *Morals of Chess*, "are to be acquired or strengthened" by playing the game.[2]

---

*North had become prime minister in 1770 and proceeded to antagonize the colonists by keeping the duty on tea and introducing the Boston Port Bill in 1774. He did not believe these measures were wise or just, but acted under pressure from King George III to serve him loyally and fend off the opposition in Parliament. North's secret diplomatic efforts reflected his own policy preferences (Boatner, *Encyclopedia*, pp. 811–12).

†Thomas Villiers, Baron Hyde represented North and also enlisted the help of two prominent Quakers, David Barclay and Dr. John Fothergill, but their talks with Franklin quickly reached an impasse (Gruber, *Howe Brothers*, p. 53).

Caroline Howe checkmating Benjamin Franklin.

For his part, North acknowledged freely that he lacked the qualities of mind to conduct a war. He was not the "one great director," who could mobilize and coordinate all the branches of government as William Pitt had done so brilliantly in the Seven Years' War. "Upon military matters I speak ignorantly, and therefore without effect," North confessed. He also lacked the command bearing of a war leader: He was nearsighted and moved awkwardly, his bulging eyes, thick lips, and round cheeks giving him "an air of a blind trumpeter," according to one observer.[3]

On the other hand, the genial, cherubic prime minister was a master of the political maneuvering and horse trading required of the majority leader in the House of Commons. Considered lazy and weak by many contemporaries, he was also a pragmatic politician, willing to compromise with the Americans in order to avoid using sanctions and military force, which, he reasoned, would never regain the loyalty of the colonies. Ravaged and crushed into submission, they would be useless to the mother country even if they were kept in the empire. However, Franklin insisted on a plan for reconciliation that even North and Dartmouth found unacceptable: The colonists had to be allowed to tax themselves and manage their own domestic affairs.[4]

Determined to find a negotiated solution, the ministers turned to Caroline's brother, Richard Lord Howe, the head of their powerful aristocratic family and Britain's most celebrated admiral.* A moderate like North and Dartmouth, he was also highly ambitious: He relished the prospect of even greater fame and glory as the architect of reconciliation—the savior of the empire.[5] Caroline introduced him to Franklin on Christmas Day, 1774.

Navy men reverently called Howe "Black Dick," because of his dark skin and the fearlessness he had displayed under fire when chasing down French ships during the Seven Years' War. During a thirty-year career that began when he was eighteen, Howe had advanced rapidly, winning both the admiration and obedience of officers and sailors without resorting to imperious commands or harsh discipline. Instead he adopted an approach that he proposed to use with the rebellious colonies: Take an interest in their problems, listen to their grievances, and watch their list of demands dwindle as a result.

This technique did not detract from Howe's authority in the navy, and likewise he believed Parliament should remain the supreme legislative authority throughout the empire. However, he hoped to defuse the present crisis by laying aside British hard-liners' demands for explicit American acknowledgment of parliamentary supremacy, and by exploring ways to raise revenue—possibly by voluntary contributions—that would not constitute a tax and at the same time would not undermine Parliament's authority.[6]

Howe's attitude toward the American colonies, while clearly paternalistic, was also infused with genuine affection. His older brother George, like Richard himself, was a tremendously popular commander who had led both British and American troops during the Seven Years' War; when he was killed at Ticonderoga in 1758, the Massachusetts authorities allocated funds for a monument to him in Westminster Abbey, a moving tribute for which Admiral Howe remained grateful. As a member of Parliament, Howe conscientiously attended the House of Commons, where he spoke out against the Stamp Act and the prosecution of John Wilkes.

Howe's independence as a politician was particularly striking because of his close personal relationship to King George III. The fact that Howe's mother was probably an illegitimate daughter of George I was an open secret in London society. Howe, his mother, and his siblings were favorites at court, treated like family, and bestowed with pensions and gifts that seemed to con-

---

*Caroline's late husband, coincidentally, was also named Howe.

Admiral Richard Howe

firm the rumor as fact.[7] Howe was a commanding presence—even if his heavy eyebrows, big nose, and full lips made him less than handsome—and his demeanor reminded some acquaintances of George I, the man who was almost certainly his grandfather. Howe was also a regular adviser to George III on questions concerning the navy. The admiral's public attacks on the colonial policies of his supremely powerful patron and friend might have caused a rift, but the king just chided him gently.[8]

At North's suggestion, Howe began to meet secretly with Franklin, who rebuffed the admiral's flattery and his hints that financial rewards from the ministry lay in store for help in brokering a peace. The talks continued but by mid-January 1775 had produced only a lukewarm endorsement from Franklin for Dartmouth's cherished idea of a British peace commission that would travel to America and consider its grievances. A second peace plan drawn up by Franklin essentially repeated the basic position of the Continental Congress— that the colonies would not tolerate parliamentary taxation and interference in their internal affairs—and Howe rejected it.[9]

For the next six weeks, while other emissaries kept talks with Franklin afloat, Howe focused on convincing the ministry to approve a peace commission and send him to America as its leader. Given that the king, most of the ministers, and a majority in Parliament all favored a hard line against the colonies, Howe's effort seemed likely to fail. The ministry had just rejected Dartmouth's proposal for a peace commission, and even if Howe, armed with Franklin's endorsement, succeeded where Dartmouth had failed, it appeared the ministry was likely to make meaningful negotiations impossible by insisting that the colonists first acknowledge Parliament's supremacy.[10]

Howe told the ministers that such a precondition for discussing grievances and concessions would doom any effort toward reconciliation. He argued instead that the restraints on New England's trade should be removed in order to foster a dialogue, and that the peace commissioner should be empowered to reopen Boston's port as soon as the bill for its tea party was paid. By the spring of 1775, he had made little progress. Franklin, for his part, had agreed to serve on a peace commission, but only if the ministry agreed to *his* preconditions, already spelled out in his two peace plans. Howe began to doubt that the commission would ever materialize.[11]

While negotiations proceeded in England, New York's Assembly failed to follow the legislatures of all the other colonies in approving and adopting the proceedings of the Continental Congress. The conservative Assembly elected in 1769 was still in place, and Colden had called it into session in January; the measure in favor of adopting a ban on imports from Britain, along with the other proclamations of Congress, lost by a slim margin. In February the assemblymen refused to appoint delegates to the second Continental Congress scheduled to convene in May. Dominated by the De Lanceyite mercantile faction, the Assembly had become reactionary and increasingly irrelevant.[12] Most New Yorkers considered the Committee of Sixty to be their "true Representatives," the assemblymen having "long since forfeited the esteem of their constituents."[13]

The loyalism of its Assembly threatened New York's reputation among American patriots in the rest of the colonies, though many outside the province understood the unique conditions in New York that made its path to rebellion slower, more tortuous, and more difficult. The committee of Charleston, South Carolina, wrote to the New York committee: "We are not ignorant of that crowd of placemen, of contractors, of officers, and needy dependents upon the Crown, who are constantly employed to frustrate your Measures. We know the dangerous tendency of being made the headquarters of America for many years." They were confident, nonetheless, that New York's "love to Constitutional Liberty, to justice, and your posterity, however depressed for a little while, will at last surmount all obstacles, and do honour to New York."[14]

Keeping New York in step with the Revolutionary movement and forging its place in what the Charleston committee called "the great chain of

American union"[15] required sidestepping the Assembly. On March 1 the Committee of Sixty suggested that a provincial convention be called for the purpose of electing representatives to the second Continental Congress. Three days later, in a mass meeting, voters approved the idea and authorized the committee to name delegates to the convention. On April 20 the Provincial Convention met at the Exchange and named twelve delegates to Congress. By drawing its authority directly from the people, the Provincial Convention had usurped the role of the moribund Assembly, which was too weak to protest.

As the old political institutions were threatened and New Yorkers split into opposing camps, violence against Tories increased. One particularly outspoken loyalist, a recent immigrant named William Cunningham who made his living in New York breaking horses and giving riding lessons, was brought to the Liberty Pole by "a mob of above two hundred men," forced to his knees, and ordered to damn King George. When he blessed the king instead, "they dragged him through the green, tore the cloaths off his back, and robbed him of his watch."[16] Cunningham fled to Boston in March, where General Gage made him provost marshal (chief of military police). In the succeeding weeks other loyalists in New York were tarred and feathered, paraded through the streets, and forced by the mobs to make similar patriotic statements and oaths.

On Sunday morning, April 23, 1775, a messenger from Boston galloped down the Bowery Lane to the Common blasting a trumpet and calling New Yorkers to gather at the Liberty Pole.[17] After he announced that American lives had been lost at Lexington and Concord on April 19, and that the Americans who answered the call to arms had pursued the British back to Boston and besieged the city, New Yorkers were "in a state of alarm; every face appeared animated with resentment," one resident recalled.[18] People leaving church soon filled the streets. "At all corners People inquisitive for News. Tales of all kinds invented believed, denied, discredited," William Smith wrote in his diary.[19]

There was a "general insurrection of the populace," wrote Marinus Willett, one of the radical leaders who took over the city as loyalists either joined the rebellion, pretended to, or fled. People seized and emptied two ships loaded with bread, flour, and supplies for British troops in Boston. When they couldn't get a key to the Arsenal in City Hall (at Wall and Broad Streets), they broke in and took 600 muskets with bayonets and cartridge boxes for each. One hundred people stayed to guard the rest of the arms, while another 100 watched over the city's gunpowder depot next to the Fresh Water Pond. Having seized all the other public stores, the armed citizens then formed a voluntary corps to govern the city.[20] Isaac Sears's large brick house on Queen Street became the de facto seat of government as well as militia headquarters.[21]

Because William Tryon was still away in England, it was Colden, the acting governor, who tried to preserve the legal government. The next day he summoned the Council and other city officials to ask their advice. Thomas Jones, a loyalist judge, recalled that he "boldly proposed that the militia should be called out, the riot act read, and if the mob did not thereupon disperse, to apprehend and imprison the ring leaders." The plan was absurd, because the militia consisted almost entirely of Liberty Boys.[22] "This proposal was immediately opposed by William Smith, one of his Majesty's Council," Jones observed, "who openly declared 'that the ferment which then raged in the city was general and not confined to a few; that it was owing to a design in the British Ministry to enslave the Colonies, and to carry such design into execution by dint of a military force; that the battle of Lexington was looked upon as a prelude to such intention, and that the spirit then prevailing in the town (which he represented as universal) would subside as soon as the grievances of the people were redressed, and advised to let the populace act as they pleased.'"[23]

Smith embodied the dilemma of choosing between king and country, and his views were anathema to the judge and to most of the others present. Nonetheless, the loyalists at the Council meeting did not challenge Smith's advice. Jones later recalled that "Nobody replied, the times were critical, a declaration of one's sentiments might be dangerous, the Council broke up, and nothing was done."[24] Colden soon retreated to his Long Island estate.

Lamb and Sears demanded the keys of the Customs House from the collector, Andrew Elliot, dismissed all of the officials, and locked its doors. They sent word to Philadelphia and other cities that New York's port was closed. "The merchants are amazed and yet so humbled as only to sigh or complain in whispers," William Smith wrote in his diary. "They now dread Sears's train of armed men," which he conducted "with the pride of a dictator."[25] In the succeeding days business stagnated while armed citizens paraded constantly around the city without a definite purpose, and the British soldiers never left their barracks. "Troops were enlisted for the service of rebellion, the Loyalists threatened with the gallows, and the property of the Crown plundered and seized upon wherever it could be found," Jones reported.[26]

The potential for chaos in the city soon led to calls for a regular government.[27] In a mass meeting at the Merchants' Coffee House on April 29, residents signed a "General Association," a document aimed at "preventing the anarchy and confusion on which attend the dissolution of the powers of government." They agreed to obey the Continental Congress, New York's Provincial Convention, and the Committee of Sixty "until a reconciliation between Great Britain and America, on constitutional principles (which we most ardently desire) can be obtained."[28] Yet even as the document spoke of reconciliation, New Yorkers were about to expand the powers of the Revolutionary bodies that governed the city and the province. A few days later, voters unanimously agreed to replace the Committee of Sixty with a more diverse and more representative Committee of One Hundred. The Provincial Convention, which had completed its task of naming a delegation to the second Continental Congress, dissolved itself, and twenty-one representatives from the city were named to the Provincial Congress, a body that would soon eclipse the colonial Assembly and eventually become the state legislature. Alexander McDougall and John Morin Scott were the most radical of the twenty-one, but most were moderates and conservatives.

From May 6 to 8, New York showed its enthusiasm for the American cause when it hosted the Massachusetts and Connecticut delegates to the second Continental Congress, who stopped on their way to Philadelphia. As they approached the City, "the roads were lined with greater numbers of people than were ever known on any occasion before. Their arrival was announced by the ringing of bells and other demonstrations of joy."[29]

As the Congress convened in Philadelphia, a New York mob began to chase down prominent and outspoken royalists. On the night of May 10, Myles Cooper, president of King's College, was awakened by a former student, Alexander Hamilton, who warned him that "a throng of several hundred men" was approaching. (Hamilton was never a loyalist, but he detested mob rule.) Cooper barely escaped "only half dressed, over the College fence; reached the shore of the river, when he found shelter in the house of Mr. Stuyvesant."[30] The following night he left the island for the safety of a British ship. Cooper, along with Colden, John Watts, Henry White, and Oliver De Lancey, had been accused in print two weeks earlier of encouraging British aggression in Massachusetts with assurances of New York's "defection and submission."[31] In addition to men like Cooper and De Lancey, a population of less prominent loyalists was thought to be concentrated in Queens County on Long Island, a region of farms that could provision an invading British force.

The possibility that New York's Tories were scheming to hand the city over to the British was particularly alarming because rumors of a coordinated

British strategy for subduing the colonies had begun to emerge, and the capture of New York was critical to the plan. It was said that General Sir Guy Carleton, the governor of British Canada, would bring a force of Frenchmen, Indians, and redcoats up the St. Lawrence and Richelieu Rivers, down Lake Champlain and Lake George, and through the Hudson River Valley, and that control of the Hudson and the city at its mouth would divide the colonies in half and doom the rebellion.[32]

While mobs took action in the city, to the north, the Green Mountain Boys, led by Ethan Allen and Benedict Arnold, reacted to the threat from Canada. They captured Fort Ticonderoga on May 10 and went on to take the fort at Crown Point two days later, strongholds at the northern border of New York's territory that would soon help the colonies launch an offensive into Canada.

On May 23, delegates from New York's various counties arrived in the city, and the Provincial Congress met for the first time at the Exchange. Three days later the British man-of-war *Asia*—equipped with sixty-four guns—arrived in the harbor from Boston under the command of Captain George Vandeput. Colden was relieved to have some protection but complained bitterly that it had not arrived sooner—before the legal government lost control of the city. However, the ship still posed an enormous threat, forcing the Revolutionary government to prepare for war while in constant fear of bombardment. The Provincial Congress began to stockpile arms and ammunition and to raise five regiments of militia while doing everything necessary to appease the British. It worked out a tenuous truce with Vandeput by authorizing local merchants to provision the British ships. The conservative delegates still hoped for reconciliation; the rest wanted to prevent war from breaking out before the city was ready.

New Yorkers continued to perform military drills while the British garrison looked on, and despite a shortage of weapons, the committee of One Hundred rejected the idea of seizing the barracks. The idea of compromise, Marinus Willett lamented, "pervaded our councils and checked the adoption of spirited measures."[33] Instead of imprisoning the five companies of redcoats, the committee allowed them to board the *Asia*. However, having heard that the British were taking carts with chests full of arms in addition to the single muskets allowed for in the compromise with the Committee, Willett intercepted them on their way to the waterfront. He could see the column of troops coming down Broad Street with the carts, lightly guarded, up front. Alone, Willett grasped the bridle of the first horse, stopping the whole line. As Willett spoke with the commanding officer, the Tory mayor, Whitehead

Marinus Willett

Hicks, appeared. However, by then Willett's men had summoned a crowd, which silenced Hicks and began to commandeer the carts.

At this point, two prominent New York patriots, John Morin Scott and Gouverneur Morris, also arrived. The outbreak of hostilities with Britain had inspired Scott to return to his youthful convictions and side with the radicals; he never wavered again. While Scott defended the wisdom of seizing the arms, the aristocratic and conservative Morris called for law and order, for restraint instead of provocation on the part of the colonists. In the tussle over the wagons on Broad Street, New York's ambivalence during its final year as a colony—both its daring and its caution—was on display.

The crowd finally pulled the carts out of the line, and the remaining 100 soldiers marched to the harbor and "embarked under the hisses of the citizens."[34] The Provincial Congress stepped in to demand the return of the guns, but to no avail. They were eventually used by the first troops raised in New York by order of the Continental Congress.

In Philadelphia, John Adams made a motion in early June for Congress to adopt the American forces around Boston as its own Continental Army and name George Washington as its commander in chief. "Mr. Washington, who happened to sit near the door, as soon as he heard me allude to him, from his usual modesty, darted into the library-room," Adams later recalled.[35] John Hancock, then president of Congress, looked pleased when Adams began to speak, expecting his own name to be submitted, but grew ashen when

Washington was nominated instead, according to Adams. Hancock was certainly a greater political figure than Washington at the time, but his military experience was negligible. He did not expect to become the commander in chief, but believed he should have had the honor of declining the appointment. Charles Lee might have been a serious contender for the position, but his English birth counted against him, despite his liberal views.

Nonetheless, Washington was not confirmed immediately. The delegates were divided, and a period of intense lobbying ensued. Some hesitated to put a southerner in charge of forces from New England, but ultimately came to agree with Adams that this would "have a great effect in cementing and securing the union of these colonies."[36] This basic political calculation elevated Washington above the field of remaining candidates, and on June 16 a unanimous Continental Congress asked him to accept the appointment.

Washington's modest reply seems to have been calculated to ward off the charge of hubris from his contemporaries and perhaps from whatever deities might influence his fate as he embarked on a venture that, given the power of the British military, was likely to end in failure. He accepted the "momentous duty" and promised to "exert every power [he] possess[ed] . . . in support of the glorious cause." However, he added, "Lest some unlucky event should happen, unfavourable to my reputation, I beg it be remembered, by every gentleman in this room, that I, this day, declare with the utmost sincerity, I do not think myself equal to the command I am honored with."[37] He concluded by declining any compensation beyond his expenses.

A few days later, Washington received his orders from Congress. They included a clause that enjoined him to use "your best circumspection (and advising with your council of war)" when making decisions. Interpreting the clause literally, Washington dutifully planned not only to consult his generals at critical moments but to abide by their majority vote.[38]

Washington believed in the subordination of the military to civilian authority as a democratic safeguard, and indeed, Congress reserved to itself the power to appoint and promote the army's officers. Artemas Ward, then in charge of the army around Boston, was named second-in-command and Charles Lee third. Philip Schuyler and Israel Putnam were also chosen as major generals, along with eight brigadier generals. Horatio Gates, an Englishman who had settled in Virginia and was a longtime friend of Washington, became his adjutant general. The commander in chief selected his own aide-de-camp, Thomas Mifflin, and private secretary, Joseph Reed. On June 23 Washington and his entourage were given a ceremonial send-off complete with a military parade through the streets of Philadelphia as they left for Boston.

George Washington

. . .

"They had not proceeded twenty miles from Philadelphia," Adams wrote, "before they met a courier with the news of the battle of Bunker's Hill," which had taken place on June 17.[39] The Americans had held their ground in a trench and mowed down wave after wave of British troops; eventually they ran out of ammunition and retreated, allowing the British to claim victory. The cost, however, was exorbitant: The frontal assault left more than 1,000 British soldiers dead or wounded that day. One British officer observed that "a few such Victories would Ruin the Army."[40]

During the battle, General Thomas Gage, the commander in chief of British forces in America, was assisted by three major generals who had recently arrived together from England: Henry Clinton, John Burgoyne, and William Howe, the admiral's younger brother. General Howe agreed with his older brother that a destructive civil war was not the way to keep the colonies loyal and preserve the empire; he too cherished the bond of friendship sealed by the monument to their slain brother. When running for a seat in Parliament the year before, he had courted disgruntled voters by publicly criticizing the government's belligerent colonial policy. He went so far as to say that there weren't enough men in the entire British army to enforce the repressive measures in the vast territory of the American colonies, and that he would vote for their repeal. The general also promised never to serve against the colonists.

In 1775, while continuing to make that claim in public, Howe privately informed North and Dartmouth that he would be willing to go to Boston as second-in-command. Howe knew the ministry was unhappy with Gage and hoped to replace him before long. Howe envisioned that as commander in chief he would play a key role in determining British policy and in moving both sides toward a peaceful, negotiated solution.

Howe's impressive military record convinced the hard-liners in the ministry to overlook his blatantly conciliatory stance and send him to America. Lord George Germain, a warmongering zealot who advised the ministry and later conducted the war as secretary of state for the American colonies, turned out to be Howe's biggest supporter. He believed that Howe's service in America during the Seven Years' War would enable him to teach European soldiers how to fight in the wilderness. As a battalion commander during the Seven Years' War, Howe had gained fame both for his bravery and for the strict discipline that made his troops the "best trained . . . in all America."[41] He was instrumental in General James Wolfe's capture of Quebec, where he led an advance party that climbed the forbidding Heights of Abraham.

Soon after arriving back in America in 1775, Howe proposed the tactics at Bunker Hill and personally led his men into the withering fire from the Americans. Every man on Howe's personal staff was either killed or wounded, and the experience made a lasting impression on him. The tenacity and effectiveness of the Americans also caused the ministry to toughen its stance toward the rebellion.

The *Cerberus*, which had brought Howe, Clinton, and Burgoyne to Boston, arrived back in England with the alarming news of Bunker Hill on July 25, and by August 2 the ministry had adopted nearly all of the measures advocated by Germain since June. Howe replaced Gage as commander in chief, 2,000 reinforcements were sent to Boston immediately, and an army of 20,000 men—British troops from bases around the globe and foreign mercenaries— was scheduled to arrive in America by the spring of 1776. Germain argued that Native Americans should be enlisted if necessary to augment these forces. He also lobbied successfully to make a "decisive blow" against New York the new focus of British strategy.[42]

General William Howe

Since Boston occupied a peninsula with a very narrow neck and the surrounding countryside of farms, forests, and stone walls provided ideal cover for the Americans even if the British managed to break out of the siege, New York City appeared to be a far better base of operations for subduing the colonies. Located in the middle of the Atlantic seaboard and at the mouth of the Hudson River, New York's harbor promised to shelter Britain's powerful navy and enable it to penetrate the continent to support the army.

The British grand strategy was to put armies at both ends of the Hudson River and have them meet in Albany, halfway between Fort Ticonderoga and New York City. In the absence of roads through the wilderness, the northern army was to descend from Canada via Lake Champlain and Lake George, a water route much used by both the French and the English in previous wars. Control of the Hudson would sever the mid-Atlantic and southern colonies from New England. Massachusetts and Virginia, whose representative assemblies had shown the most radical opposition, would be isolated and silenced and the rebellion brought to an end. In New York City, unlike these two cockpits of the Revolution to the north and south, the British expected military intelligence and assistance from the governor and from numerous grateful loyalists, particularly in Queens County on Long Island.

The Americans had also focused on New York; on "the vast Importance of that City, Province, and the North River which is in it . . ." John Adams later wrote to Washington, "as it is the Nexus of the Northern and Southern

Colonies, as a kind of Key to the whole Continent, as it is a Passage to Canada to the Great Lakes, and to all the Indian Nations. No Effort to Secure it ought to be omitted."*43 Given the use of the Lake Champlain–Lake George–Hudson River axis during the Seven Years' War for invasions in both directions, the Americans could assume that British plans would target both ends of this route. George Washington echoed Adams's remark when he called New York City "a post of infinite importance."44

New York's advantages for the British had occurred to Major General Henry Clinton, and he had put them on paper even before setting sail to Boston on the *Cerberus* in the spring.45 Clinton was practically a New Yorker, having grown up on Long Island when his father, George, was the governor of the province in the 1740s, and having served as an officer in the New York militia. Clinton also owned some parcels of land in New York and Connecticut that he inherited from his father.

A gifted strategist, Clinton had the ability to look at a map and quickly grasp the relationships between geography, land forces, and sea power. However, he lacked the temperament and diplomatic skills to muster support for his plans, and his superiors often rejected them.46 Before Bunker Hill, Clinton proposed, in addition to a frontal assault, to trap and destroy the rebels by landing troops in their rear and sealing off the neck of the Charlestown Peninsula. Howe chose instead to attempt a flanking maneuver, which failed. Instead of capturing the Americans, he merely drove them out and retook the ground.

When Howe's promotion took effect in late September 1775 and Clinton became his second-in-command, distrust between them soon developed as Clinton criticized his chief's plans and indelicately proposed ideas of his own that Howe ignored. The problem was partly a conflict of personalities and styles: Clinton had good ideas but careened between extreme shyness and tactless aggression, whereas Howe preferred not to consult talented subordinates because he felt threatened by them. Their personal tension was exacerbated by the command structure. Howe was keenly aware that if he took Clinton's suggestions and failed, he would ultimately be held responsible and Clinton would succeed him (just as Howe had succeeded Gage). As the siege of Boston continued, Howe dispatched Clinton to the outpost on the

*The Hudson was also called the North River.

Charlestown Peninsula, the first of several assignments that would put distance between them.[47]

On his way to Boston, Washington arrived in Newark on June 25. Just as the New York Provincial Congress sent a delegation to escort him across the Hudson and into the city, news arrived that Governor Tryon was at Sandy Hook, having returned from England. Once again the Provincial Congress tried to please both sides. They instructed the commander of the local militia "to send one company of militia to Powle's Hook* to meet the Generals. That he have another company at this side of the ferry for the same purpose; that he have the residue of his battalion ready to receive either the Generals or Governor Tryon, which ever shall first arrive, and to wait on both as well as circumstances will allow."[48]

Washington arrived at four P.M., and Tryon avoided a conflict by waiting until eight to come up to the city; so each received a stirring welcome. However, Tryon clearly sensed that New York had changed during his absence. "I had no Time to say anything to the Govr.," William Smith later recalled, "but barely that there was a great and strange Reverse since he left us in the State of our Public Affairs, which he answered with a sigh."[49]

Smith noted that the people in the streets would have insulted any other royal governor but cheered Tryon because they liked him personally. Nonetheless, before he left the next day, Washington gave the following order to General Philip Schuyler, who was about to take command of continental forces in the province of New York: "Keep a watchful eye upon Governor Tryon, and, if you find him attempting, directly or indirectly, any measures inimical to the common cause, use every means in your power to frustrate his designs."[50]

Washington reached Boston on July 2, 1775, and took command of the forces that Congress would formally adopt as the Continental Army by a vote on the twenty-fifth. The grand title aside, transforming a chaotic encampment of nearly 17,000 undisciplined and poorly armed civilians from different colonies into a professional, national army remained a Herculean task. When the numerous local groups were consolidated into divisions, brigades, and regiments, officers resented their loss of rank, while many privates insisted they would only serve in a unit with others from their particular

*Jersey City (also spelled Paulus Hook).

colony, county, or township. Unable to supply uniforms, Washington introduced a system of cloth markings—cockades, ribbons, and shoulder knots—to indicate rank and distinguish the officers from the privates. More difficult was eradicating the New Englanders' egalitarianism and getting the men to obey their superiors. The Pennsylvania, Maryland, and Virginia riflemen who arrived in July and August also had a fierce independent streak that had to be tamed. Worst of all, the Connecticut troops had enlisted only until December 10 and the rest until January 1.[51]

While Washington continued the siege, Congress pressed on with its own busy agenda: organizing a supply system for the army, issuing the first Continental money, establishing a postal system, and proposing a plan for the confederation of the colonies.[52]

At the same time John Dickinson divided the Congress by sponsoring a final effort to compromise with Britain. The "Olive Branch" Petition to the king was signed by all the members on July 8, even though some considered it far too conciliatory. It fell on deaf ears anyway, as the king and the ministry would not recognize Congress, only individual colonies. A letter to Philadelphia from a sympathetic Londoner, also written on July 8, warned that the time for making concessions had passed. "If you submit, sixty of you are to be hanged in Philadelphia, and the same number in New York; five hundred pounds is offered for Captain Sears's head in particular—a secret order."[53]

As peaceful gestures were accompanied by preparations for war in both Britain and America, the Continental Congress, among its other ambitious enterprises, had authorized an American invasion of Canada.[54] Having failed to incite rebellion in Canada through verbal appeals, Congress hoped to acquire a fourteenth colony by force while depriving the British of a northern front from which to attack New York. In early August detachments from Manhattan began sailing up the Hudson to meet Major General Philip Schuyler, the commander of the Northern Department,* at Ticonderoga, where troops from New England also joined the expedition. Washington hoped to defeat the royal governor, General Sir Guy Carleton, and capture Canada by making simultaneous attacks on two cities: While Schuyler gathered his forces to seize Montreal, Benedict Arnold took 1,000 men from Boston along a water route through the Maine wilderness to reach the city of Quebec.†

---

*Schuyler ranked just below Washington, Ward, and Lee. His department included New England and the province of New York and would soon extend into Canada.
†Quebec and Montreal were both cities in the Province of Quebec, as they are today.

. . .

As the summer of 1775 wore on, the New York Provincial Congress abandoned some of its caution and ordered the militia to remove the royal guns mounted on the Battery, the curving stone rampart extending from river to river at the southern tip of Manhattan, right below Fort George.[55] At midnight on August 23, John Lamb's artillery company led the raid, using ropes to drag the heavy cannons up Broadway to the Common. Like Sears, Lamb was a self-made man in his forties and a member of the Sons of Liberty. Adept at public speaking, and fluent in Dutch, French, and German, he served as the organization's liaison to the city's major ethnic groups. Alexander Hamilton, who had left King's College to join the New York artillery, and his college roommate, Hercules Mulligan, a burly Irish-American tailor, helped haul the naval guns, which weighed more than a ton each and were mounted on carriages with small wheels not intended for long distances.

Having removed eleven of the twenty-one guns, the Americans were spotted by British sailors in a sloop dispatched by Captain Vandeput, who had received intelligence from Governor Tryon about the rebel operation. The British sailors at the Battery fired a musket as a signal to the *Asia*, 1,000 yards away in the East River off Murray's wharf at the foot of Wall Street. Thinking they were under attack, the colonists fired at the sloop and killed one man. The *Asia* responded with some cannonballs and grapeshot, a warning round to the thieves at the Battery. All over the city people panicked and prepared to flee, imagining that a British invasion was in progress.

After a pause, the militia resumed its task with fresh urgency, so Vandeput raised the stakes: At three in the morning, a full thirty-two-gun broadside from the *Asia* rocked the city and lit up the sky. The guns, loaded with solid shot, not firebombs, were aimed at the Battery, where they destroyed some small buildings and did little damage to the rest of the city. The next day Tryon brokered a compromise: The cannons arranged in front of the Liberty Pole would stay where they were; the rebels would keep their hands off the king's stores; the *Asia* would hold its fire; and local merchants would continue to provision the warship.

Despite the truce, a loyalist pastor, Ewald Shewkirk of the Moravian Church, wrote in his diary less than a week later: "The Moving out of Town continues, and the City looks in some Streets as if the Plague had been in it, so many Houses being shut up."[56] People feared British cannon-ades on one hand and arrest by patriot committees on the other. One loy-alist merchant was determined to avoid "the punishment of being sent to the mines of Simsbury [Connecticut] which are punishments daily inflicted on those poor culprits who are found or even supposed to be inimical."[57] By early September, at least a third of New York's population of almost 25,000 had fled.[58]

In London Admiral Howe had learned a lesson from his younger brother in his attempt to get appointed as commander in chief of the North American naval forces.[59] Since the ministry clearly had no interest in a peace commission, Howe planned to get over to the colonies as a com-mander and then use his position to open negotiations. For six months, between March and September, he had spoken in favor of coercive mea-sures in Parliament and carefully cultivated closer relationships with the ministers whose opinions he found repugnant. Howe courted Germain in particular, because he had become increasingly influential as an adviser to the ministry.

In October North finally won approval for a peace commission from the ministry and Parliament; masking his intentions, he had silenced his oppo-nents by simultaneously introducing new military initiatives, including an expedition to establish a presence and support the loyalists in the southern colonies.[60] Most of the ships and men—eight regiments under Commodore Sir Peter Parker and Charles Lord Cornwallis—were to sail from Ireland to North Carolina, where a smaller fleet from Boston was to meet them on the Cape Fear River. Their assignment from the ministry was to make a show of force that would bring out the silent majority of loyalists the government believed existed in Virginia and the Carolinas. Not until the summer, after establishing a strong outpost for the loyalists, was the fleet to sail north to take part in the invasion of New York City. In London, the moderates still faced the task of ensuring that the peace commission had real authority to negotiate with the colonists, and its prospects dimmed when a reshuffling of the cabinet a few weeks later made Germain colonial secretary in place of the moderate Dartmouth, who could no longer bear the thought of waging war against the Americans.

However, North persevered and managed to expand the commission's powers, once again by attaching the proposed changes to new measures aimed at punishing and subduing the colonies. Whereas the Boston Port Bill had closed Boston Harbor in 1774, and two additional restraining bills at the beginning of 1775 required that Americans trade only with Great Britain and the British West Indies, the Prohibitory Act, passed on December 22, 1775, superseded those laws by imposing a total embargo on all American trade. With its new powers, the peace commission could not only accept surrender and grant pardons but also remove the new trade sanctions and discuss the colonists' grievances with them. At the same time, Dartmouth and other moderates convinced North that Admiral Howe should be the sole commissioner and also the commander in chief of the North American naval squadron, though the appointments still had to be approved by the rest of the ministry.

The Continental Congress spurred the crackdown on loyalists in October 1775 by officially advising provincial committees to arrest anyone "whose going at large may . . . endanger the safety of the colony, or the liberties of America."[61] Governor Tryon, who remained loyal to the Crown and had begun to fear the mobs in New York, moved to the *Dutchess of Gordon*, a British merchant ship anchored in the East River under the protection of the *Asia*. On this floating City Hall, Tryon waited for permission to return to England while he kept the colonial government functioning and preserved its legal legitimacy by continuing to hold meetings of the Council. By statute, failure to hold regular sessions would have led to dissolution of the Council. Though Tryon's activities rallied the city's loyalists, the Provincial Congress made no move to stop him.[62]

Isaac Sears, the street-brawling Son of Liberty—or "Spawn of Liberty and Inquisition,"[63] as the engineer John Montresor derisively called him and his posse of vigilantes—by this time had lost patience with the "trimming" and truces of the Provincial Congress and had moved his base of operations to Connecticut. In November Sears raided Westchester County with 100 men on horseback, seizing three prominent loyalists—a judge, a clergyman, and a mayor—and sending them to New Haven "under a strong guard." The horsemen also set fire to a sloop used for provisioning the *Asia*. The following day, November 23, they rode into New York at high noon "with bayonets fixed" and shut down James Rivington's loyalist *Gazetteer* by taking all of the type from his office at the foot of Wall Street. The city was half deserted, but a large crowd gathered outside the Merchants' Coffee House to cheer the raiders as they "marched out of town to the tune of *Yankee Doodle*."[64]

Miffed that rebels from Connecticut had interfered in New York's affairs, the Provincial Congress wrote to Connecticut's governor, Jonathan Trumbull,* requesting the release of the three prisoners and the return of Rivington's type—not that they had any sympathy for Rivington. "We are fully sensible of his demerits; but we earnestly wish that the glory of the present contest for liberty may not be sullied by an attempt to restrain the freedom of the Press."[65] Rivington never got his type back, but Trumbull did free the prisoners.

"Such a dirty, mercenary spirit pervades the whole, that I should not be surprised at any disaster that may happen," Washington wrote to his secretary, Joseph Reed, regarding the Continental Army and the soldiers who demanded bounties and failed to reenlist at the end of 1775.[66] In mid-November, Congress had issued enlistment papers throughout the colonies to recruit an army of some 30,000 men to serve until December 31, 1776. However, only 3,500 of the troops around Boston agreed to stay. When the rest left for home, unmoved by Washington's exhortations or Charles Lee's curses, the commander in chief had to ask Massachusetts and New Hampshire to send thousands of militia as temporary replacements. By January 1, 1776, the day "giving commencement to the new army, which, in every point of View, is Continental," as Washington told the troops,[67] the combined force of veterans, raw recruits, and short-term militia he had cobbled together was growing slowly but amounted only to some 10,000 men.

While Washington predicted a British attack out of Boston if General Howe learned how few men and how little ammunition he actually possessed, Isaac Sears warned of impending disaster in New York City. Thoroughly disgusted with the local authorities, Sears had gone to Cambridge, where he reported to the Continental Army headquarters on the dangerous situation in New York: a concentration of armed loyalists in Queens County poised to assist a British invasion; royal military stores left behind in the empty barracks and never seized by the Provincial Congress; and the provisioning of enemy warships by the city's merchants. Sears's warnings and guerrilla tactics soon got the full attention and support of the Continental Army's second ranking offi-

---

*Unlike Tryon, Trumbull was an ardent American patriot and had been since the Stamp Act crisis. He was elected governor of Connecticut in 1769.

cer, Major General Charles Lee, who had moved up when Artemas Ward resigned.[68]

Lee had just returned to Cambridge from a successful mission in Rhode Island, where he had intimidated Newport's prominent Tories and fortified the city in defiance of the *Rose*, a British man-of-war stationed in the harbor. Unlike the *Asia* in New York, the *Rose* never opened fire, and Lee was emboldened to continue his efforts in other cities. When he heard Sears's report, Lee seized the opportunity. He wrote a dramatic letter to Washington saying he could barely sleep at night as he worried about "the consequences of the enemy's possessing themselves of New York."[69] Lee proposed to occupy the city and fortify it with gun batteries, trenches, and earthworks while suppressing the Tories both on Manhattan and Long Island.

At the same time, Washington received intelligence reports about a squadron of British ships preparing to head south from Boston: two men-of-war, five transports, two bomb vessels, and 300 marines. The addition of several flat-bottomed boats pointed to an amphibious landing, and New York's archipelago was a possible target. Lee's letter warned in closing that "the delay of a single day may be fatal," and the alarmist tone seemed justified.[70]

Washington did not realize that the British squadron, led by General Clinton, was only planning a brief stopover in New York City on its way to reinforce the expedition North had dispatched from England to the Carolinas. Howe had finally gotten his difficult subordinate out of the way, at least temporarily. Washington had concerns about his own temperamental deputy but valued Lee's "good sense and spirit," and seems not to have worried that Lee might be eager for the separate command in New York in order to outshine and replace him.[71]

"He is the first officer in military knowledge and experience we have in the whole army," Washington confided to his brother. "He is zealously attached to the cause, honest and well-meaning but rather fickle and violent I fear in his temper."[72] The Mohawk Indians had formed a similar impression twenty years earlier when Lee married a chief's daughter and had twins with her. Abrasive and hot-tempered, he was named "Boiling Water."[73]

Despite his misgivings, Washington issued marching orders on January 8, 1776, authorizing Lee to raise volunteers from Connecticut and request Continental troops from the commander in New Jersey. With this force he was to put New York "in the best posture of defence, that the season and circumstances will admit"; disarm the Tories, particularly on Long Island; inspect the forts in the Hudson Highlands forty miles north of the city; and finally, capture the supplies left in the royal barracks.[74] Lee set off for New York immediately, accompanied by his newly appointed adjutant, Lieutenant Colonel Isaac Sears.

CHAPTER 4

From Bouweries to Barricades

~⌒

The man who promised to fortify New York against the British had to be carried into the city on a stretcher. Charles Lee was afflicted with gout, and his feet were painfully swollen. He had intended to make a triumphal entry in late January of 1776, leading 1,500 Connecticut volunteers he had raised with the help of Sears and Governor Trumbull, but complications arose as he prepared to cross the Connecticut border into New York. Worse than the attack of gout and a heavy snowstorm was an urgent letter from the Committee of Safety of the New York Provincial Congress, an eight-member group dominated by Alexander McDougall and John Morin Scott.* The committee asked Lee to clarify the purpose of his mission and insisted that he proceed no farther if he was at the head of an army.[1] The inhabitants were already panicked by the news of Lee's approach, fearing he would provoke the British into bombarding the city again. It had been bad enough when Vandeput opened fire in August; a similar exodus in January, the committee wrote, would send terrified women and children fleeing into the countryside in the dead of winter.[2]

A contemporary described Lee as "tall and extremely thin; his face ugly, with an aquiline nose of enormous proportion."[3] His height was an illusion, however, created by the big head and beaklike nose up top and the tiny hands and feet at the ends of

---

*The Committee of Safety met daily to conduct public business when the Provincial Congress was not in session.

Major General Charles Lee

his attenuated limbs.[4] "I remember him well," an American soldier wrote in his pension application decades after the war, "he was a small man, and the soldiers used to laugh about his great nose."[5]

Along with laughter, Lee inspired devotion and a measure of awe in the troops he led. His experience, along with his eccentricities and affectations, gave him a worldly, exotic quality that lent his military pronouncements an aura of infallibility. Lee's insistence on having his dogs at his side, for example, may have reminded more sophisticated observers of Prussia's Frederick the Great, who always had a similar pack of hounds in attendance. American officers and their men were likely to know that Lee had been a lieutenant colonel in the British army, a demanding position that was not merely a sinecure to be bought and sold as were certain higher ranks. During the Seven Years' War he had fought in America and made an astonishing recovery from stomach wounds that might have killed him. In 1762 he distinguished himself in Portugal by leading 300 grenadiers and cavalrymen in a daring midnight raid that routed a much larger Spanish force and destroyed its ammunition depot. He survived an earthquake in Constantinople during the Russo-Turkish War and cheated death again when he barely escaped a winter storm in the Balkans.

All of this was true, but if the delegates to Congress had scrutinized Lee's credentials, they would have seen that his broad travels boiled down to relatively little accomplishment in the field. In Turkey, for example, he had been an observer and not a participant in the hostilities. His title of major general in the Polish army was merely ceremonial, an honor bestowed by his friend, King Stanislaus. Similarly, the full colonelcy in the Portuguese army was a decoration for his brief service there—his one true hour of glory. Nonetheless, Lee's advice about how and where to dig trenches had proved useful during the siege of Boston, and Washington was impressed.[6]

Washington's hesitation about sending Lee to fortify New York City stemmed mostly from unresolved questions about his own newly created position at the head of the Continental forces. The impasse at the Connecticut border revealed that the powers of the Continental Congress, the army, and the commander in chief—their jurisdictional authority—had yet to be tested and defined. When Washington had inquired about the extent of his own authority, John Adams had assured him, in a letter of January 6, that he could send Lee to New York. However, New York's delegates to the Continental Congress agreed with McDougall that such an expedition had to be invited by the local authorities, and insisted that Congress deputize a special committee to meet Lee in New York and mediate between him and the Committee of Safety to settle the dispute.[7]

Accordingly, Thomas Lynch, Benjamin Harrison, and Andrew Allen arrived in New York on January 30, where they presided over a shouting match between McDougall and Scott on one side, and the commander of Lee's advance units, Colonel David Waterbury, on the other. The Committee of Safety demanded Lee's assurance that he would submit to its authority once he entered the city; Waterbury refused to be bound by any higher authority. In the end, the Continental Congress asserted itself in a national role and forged a compromise: Lee and his troops would be answerable to Congress. Both sides were pleased, and the general, borne on a litter, entered the city on February 4, escorted by a procession of the local cavalry.*[8]

The following day, just before he went to a meeting with Lee, congressional mediator Andrew Allen dashed off a letter to his wife, describing the events of the past twenty-four hours. "This Town has been in the greatest Confusion and Distress ever since we arrived; the People had taken it into their heads that we had come with positive orders from the Congress to Gen'l Lee to attack the men of war lying here which would have introduced the Destruction

---

*Allen and his colleague Thomas Lynch were also on a secret mission to meet with James Drummond, a Scot who claimed to be vested with authority from the ministry to negotiate with the colonies. Drummond also met with William Smith and with Henry Clinton in New York. For accounts of Drummond's peace efforts see Willcox, *Portrait,* pp. 71–76, and Fleming, *1776,* pp. 132, 140–149.

of the Town." Residents started to put their belongings on wagons and flee the city, Allen wrote, but "with difficulty we quieted their apprehensions with assurances that the purport of our Journey was directly the Reverse."

No sooner had the people been calmed than their "Fears were revived" with even greater cause, by the arrival of Gen'l Clinton, who was sighted off Sandy Hook on the very day that Lee arrived in the city. "I fully expected that Hostilities would immediately have commenced," Allen told his wife, "and the scene which then would have ensued was sufficient even in Idea to shock my Humanity." He envisioned women and children driven out in the cold "without the necessaries of life," and without shelter to cover their "wretched heads." Pregnant women, the elderly, and the sick would amount to a large number of people in a city as big as New York, Allen concluded, and many were bound to die in a sudden evacuation.[9]

At the request of the Committee of Safety, the Tory mayor of New York, David Matthews, was rowed out to speak with Clinton on board the *Mercury* and learned that he would not set foot in the city but had merely stopped off to greet his old friend, William Tryon, on the *Dutchess of Gordon*, anchored in the East River at the northern end of the city's commercial waterfront, a succession of wharves that extended from the Battery to the shipyards.* Clinton had arrived without any men-of-war, only a single frigate, a supply ship, and two transports.[10]

Despite his social connections and disclaimers, however, Clinton was in New York for more than a friendly visit. He exchanged military intelligence with Governor Tryon, and they discussed the best way to capture the city, either by seizing the northern tip of Manhattan at Kingsbridge, or by taking Brooklyn Heights and threatening the city with artillery aimed across the East River. Oddly, while he obscured his intentions about New York, Clinton publicly revealed to New Yorkers, and thus to Lee, that his real destination was the Carolinas.[11]

Compounding the fear that gripped the city's residents and the local authorities was the devastating news from Canada: The American expedition had failed to seize Quebec. General Schuyler had become seriously ill early in the campaign, and his second-in-command, General Richard Montgomery, had led the troops on to victory at Montreal. Montgomery was New York's own hero, an able commander who was also extremely handsome and universally admired. When Montgomery and Benedict Arnold converged on Quebec in late December 1775, their forces were weakened by the long jour-

---

*The shipyards were at the site where the Brooklyn Bridge stands today.

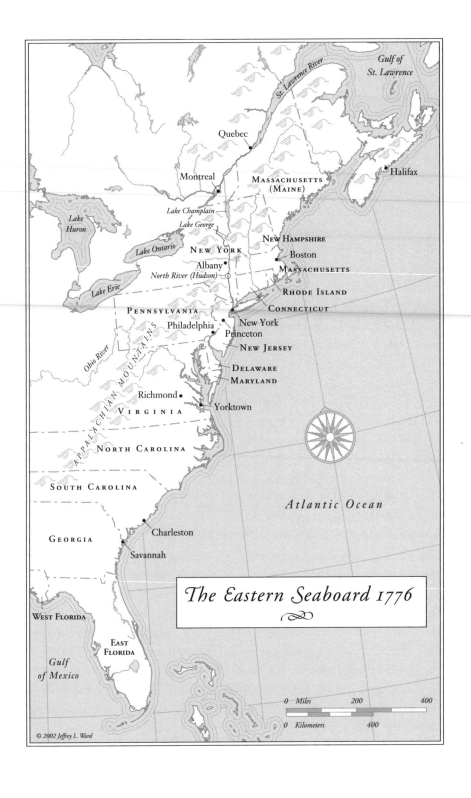

Gulf of
St. Lawrence

St. Lawrence River

Quebec

Montreal   MASSACHUSETTS   Halifax
                            (MAINE)

Lake Champlain
Lake George

Lake
Huron

Lake Ontario   NEW YORK   NEW HAMPSHIRE
                Albany   Boston
North River (Hudson)   MASSACHUSETTS

Lake Erie   RHODE ISLAND
          PENNSYLVANIA   CONNECTICUT

          Philadelphia   New York
                 Princeton
                   NEW JERSEY

Ohio River   DELAWARE
                            MARYLAND

          Richmond
          VIRGINIA   Yorktown

          NORTH CAROLINA

SOUTH CAROLINA   Atlantic Ocean

GEORGIA   Charleston

               Savannah

WEST FLORIDA   *The Eastern Seaboard 1776*

     EAST
     FLORIDA

Gulf
of Mexico

0   Miles   200   400

0   Kilometers   400

© 2002 Jeffrey L. Ward

ney and the onset of winter. However, the terms of enlistment for many of the troops were about to expire, so Montgomery launched an attack anyway. General Carleton was ready for them, and the assault was a disaster for the Americans. Montgomery was killed, and the First New York Regiment was decimated; one of Alexander McDougall's sons was killed and the other taken prisoner. (McDougall had raised the regiment, but he did not go with it to Canada.) Arnold was seriously wounded but remained outside the walls of Quebec, struggling to resume the siege.[12]

While the fear of bombardment in New York was unwarranted and hostilities did not begin, the panicked exodus from the city took place nonetheless. One New Yorker wrote to a friend in England that the arrival of both Lee and Clinton "threw the whole city into such a tumult as it never knew before, moving away their effects. All that day and all night were their carts going, and boats loading, and women and children crying, and distressed voices heard in the roads in the dead of night."[13]

By February 1776, the Provincial Congress had become increasingly bold: It had raised a militia and four Continental regiments; endorsed a Tory hunt in Queens County; and, more recently, allowed Lee's contingent to enter the city and take over the royal barracks. Not the least of these provocative steps was a refusal to provision Clinton's squadron.

At the same time, the Revolutionary government kept supplying the *Dutchess* and the *Asia* under the terms of the truce brokered by Tryon in August after the theft of the guns from the Battery. A second warship, the *Phoenix,* had arrived in December 1775 and was also part of the arrangement. The delegates were satisfied that their own piecemeal preparations for war would continue to go unpunished by cannonades, but they knew that the men-of-war could disrupt the harbor trade with Long Island and New Jersey that was annually the city's lifeline until a spring thaw reopened the flow of food and other goods along the Hudson from the north.[14]

Lee, whose mission was to prepare for war, could not abide any traffic with the ships, and friction between Washington's second-in-command and the local authorities continued. Lee was less concerned about food going aboard the ships than he was about the governor receiving his Council, the mayor, and other Tories on the *Dutchess* every day. Lee placed sentries at the wharves to prevent Tryon from keeping the royal government of the province afloat, in both a legal and physical sense.

The need to take action against the loyalists had recently become more urgent because Captain Richard Hewlett of Hempstead, Long Island, had begun leading his partisans on raids to steal muskets from their patriot neighbors. Hewlett also distributed powder, flints, and musket balls delivered to him at Rockaway by a boat from the *Asia*. In mid-January, New York's Provincial Congress, which had failed in its own efforts to intimidate Hewlett and his allies, was happy to have the Continental Congress send Colonel Nathaniel Heard of New Jersey with 1,200 militia to suppress the Tories. Using a voter list, Heard scoured Queens County for two weeks and administered a test oath to 800 loyalists. He also confiscated 1,000 muskets and arrested nineteen of the twenty-six most active Tory leaders.[15]

Lee was ready to round up the entire Tory population in Kings and Queens Counties and imprison them in Connecticut. While he had Washington's blessing, the Continental Congress would not allow such drastic measures. Even more so, the Provincial Congress was determined to pursue a moderate course with the British; when Lee clamped down on Tryon's visitors in February, the Committee of Safety responded by releasing the nineteen Tories Heard had arrested the previous month.

A week after his arrival, on February 12, Lee struck back against the committee and the British by completing John Lamb's interrupted cannon heist at the Battery, this time in broad daylight on a Sunday morning. (The Sons of Liberty, led by Lamb and Sears, were eager to carry out Lee's agenda, even as the Committee of Safety, under McDougall and Scott, made the preservation of the city, and therefore the postponement of a battle, their top priority.) A throng of men and boys gathered to help the soldiers drag the ten remaining guns up Broadway. They made "an astonishing Uproar," a startled William Smith noted in his diary, "and the Work continued all Day long with an almost intire neglect of public Worship."[16]

The guns joined the eleven others in front of the Liberty Pole, where British ships were unable to get at them. In response to Lee's provocation, the captain of the *Phoenix* sent a boat to inspect the situation at the Battery, but when it reported back to him, rather than responding, the ships weighed anchor and left the East River. The *Mercury*, with Clinton aboard, sailed down to Sandy Hook, joined its transports, and left for the South that evening. The *Asia*, with the *Dutchess* in its shadow, took up a position in the harbor. The *Phoenix* dropped down below the Narrows to Gravesend Bay.[17]

Despite the movement of the ships, the New York authorities continued to allow trade with the British vessels. Lee warned Washington in a letter that if aggressive steps were not taken, "the Provincial Congress and the inhabitants will relapse into their former hysterics; the men-of-war and Mr. Tryon will return to their old stations at the wharves, and the first regiments who arrive from England will take quiet possession of the town and Long Island."[18]

The day after he arrived in New York, Lee sent his engineer to reconnoiter the ground at Horn's Hook on Manhattan's northeastern shore* and on Long Island. Then Lee met with the ad hoc committee from the Continental Congress and New York's Committee of Safety to hammer out a plan for the area's defenses. For the next month, the general moved about gingerly on his swollen feet, while his engineer surveyed and marked out the sites of the fortifications.[19] Lee summed up his view of the task when he wrote to Washington on February 19 that the city, "so encircled with deep navigable water,"[20] would ultimately be impossible to defend against the British navy. Instead, he could only hope to turn New York into "an advantageous field of battle,"[21] he told New York's Committee of Safety—to make a British invasion as difficult and costly as possible.

Lee's assessment ignored the fact that all of the "deep navigable water" around New York City could only be accessed by two very narrow and treacherous passageways. Most obvious was the shallow channel between Sandy Hook and the sandbar that extended to the north up to Coney Island. This channel, and several smaller ones that cut through the sandbar, connected the Lower Bay with the Atlantic. North of the harbor, ships could come through Long Island Sound and the aptly named Hell Gate, where colliding currents created riptides and whirlpools in a rocky strait defined by Horn's Hook, Montresor's Island† and the shore of Queens County. Strangely, he never proposed fortifying Sandy Hook and bombarding the British fleet where it would have been most vulnerable: The sandbar concealed in the shallow water forced ships to wait for high tide and cooperative winds before passing one at a time through the channel.

Lee also disregarded a congressional resolution that advised New York's Committee of Safety to see about fortifying the Staten Island and Long Island shores facing each other at the Narrows or "obstructing or lessening the depth of water" there.[22] The printer John Holt, in a letter to congressional delegate Samuel Adams, outlined a strategy for keeping the British fleet out of New York's waters altogether (and prompting the two men-of-war present to leave) "by our immediately erecting one or more strong Forts at & near

*Now Carl Schurz Park at the foot of East Eighty-ninth Street.
†Today called Randalls Island.

Hell Gate and others on each Side below at the Narrows, with some Floats near them to obstruct the quick passing of ships. Some floating Batteries would also be of the utmost importance."[23]

Instead of heeding these voices, Lee's plans, which Washington approved, focused on keeping the British off of Brooklyn Heights and out of the East River.[24] Lee reasoned that if the British could be limited to an attack on Manhattan from the south, west, or north, the Americans could then contest every hill and inflict heavy casualties. Lee envisioned fighting for the city, street by street and house to house, using barricades and redoubts.*

In the east, British gun batteries placed on Brooklyn Heights would dominate the city and its wharves, while providing cover for British warships operating in the East River after they entered from Long Island Sound through Hell Gate, or from New York Harbor past Governors Island. Long Island was also the food supplier for any army that wished to hold lower Manhattan, and the market boats came across at Brooklyn Ferry right under any guns that might be mounted on the Heights.

To seal off access to the East River from the Sound, Lee's plan (nearly all of which would be executed by his successors) called for a fort at Horn's Hook and another across from it on the Queens shore or on Montresor's island. To close the lower end of the river, gun batteries facing Long Island were to be installed in the city itself, at the foot of Catherine Street (at the intersection of Cherry) where the East River was narrowest; on a rise just north of it called Rutgers's "first hill;" and at Coenties Slip, just west of Water Street, a block north of Broad.

These batteries would be complemented by guns in a citadel on Brooklyn Heights. A chain of three redoubts connected by trenches for 3,000 to 4,000 men were to protect the main fort. With the cannons of the Brooklyn Heights installations aimed at the East River, Lee neglected to defend against a possible British attack by land from the interior of Long Island.

Kings County—the future borough of Brooklyn—remained a bucolic landscape in 1776. The county was carved into six townships—Brooklyn, Bushwick, Flatbush, Flatlands, Gravesend, and New Utrecht—each with its own town center of the same name, Brooklyn being the area farthest to the northwest, which included Brooklyn Heights.

The soldier or traveler who crossed over from Manhattan was greeted by the sight of Columbia Heights, the part of Brooklyn Heights facing the East River, which "caught the eye . . . as 'a noble bluff,' crowned with fields and

---

*Small, simple, usually circular forts with dirt walls.

woods, and meeting the water at its base with a shining beach."[25] A mile and a half beyond the settlement at Fulton Ferry, on the King's Highway, the village of Brooklyn itself consisted of a few houses close to the Dutch church, which stood in the middle of the road. Farther east on the highway, still in the township of Brooklyn, stood the village of Bedford, after which the thoroughfare continued all the way out to Jamaica and beyond to the eastern end of Long Island.[26]

Lee assumed he had the east covered and that the British would have to attack Manhattan from the south, west, or north. He knew they could have easily sailed right up to the Battery at the southern tip of the island and stormed its low wall with a landing party before seizing Fort George and using it to dominate the city—as they had tried to do before the Stamp Act riot. Lee therefore had the two bastions* and the wall on the north side of the fort torn down, and he installed cannons at a barricade on Broadway that were aimed at the fort's interior so the British would not have been able to seize it without being attacked from the city.

On the west, all the streets leading to the Hudson River were to be barricaded. To the north, Lee envisioned three forts that would dominate the roads leading down to the city. The Bowery Lane was to be secured by the guns of two star-shaped redoubts, one on Bayard's Hill, at the center of the island, and the other on Jones's Hill (ironically, the property of Thomas Jones, the loyalist judge). A British advance along the Greenwich Road, to the west, was to be stopped by a third fort on Lispenard's Hill. To complete this string of forts across the island along the line of Grand Street, Lee also planned to add circular batteries between the high points.†

Lee predicted that the British might seize the two bridges over the Harlem River (King's Bridge and the Freebridge) to cut Manhattan's only links to the mainland before moving down the island to capture the city. Accordingly, his plan called for redoubts on various hills all the way to the northern end of Manhattan.[27] He also pinpointed where roadblocks could hamper the movement of enemy artillery on the major arteries north of the city, of which there were only two, both emanating from the Bowery Lane

---

*Towers or other projecting elements at the corners of a fort that support the curtain wall between them and enable the defenders to catch enemy troops in a cross fire as they approach the wall.

†Bayard's Hill stood a few blocks west of the Bowery at Grand and Mulberry Streets; Jones's Hill was just north of today's Broome and Pitt Streets on Corlear's Hook; and the circular batteries occupied the intersections where Norfolk and Eldridge Streets now cross Grand (Johnston, *Campaign*, pt. 1:88).

where it split just north of the city limits.*[28] The right fork continued north as the Post Road to Albany and Boston, while the left fork became the Bloomingdale Road.

A former Indian trail that became a road in 1703, the Bloomingdale Road ended abruptly on the farm of Adrian Hoaglandt.† East of Hoaglandt's was Benjamin Vandewater's farm, and they were the northernmost residents in the Bloomingdale division whose small village stood a half-mile to the south.[29] The Dutch named the district after a town near Haarlem in Holland called Bloemendael (blooming dale), a reference to its "vale of flowers," and it remained a bucolic landscape of hills, trees, and streams.[30]

Roughly a mile north of their split, a cross road connected the Post Road with the Bloomingdale Road. After this intersection, the Post Road continued on its northeasterly course for almost a mile until it turned to the northwest, cutting diagonally across the upper east side of the island, and intersecting with a second cross road a half mile farther, and a third a mile beyond that. The Post Road continued northwest through McGowan's Pass and across Harlem Plains, before turning sharply to the north and skirting the base of Harlem Heights, a long plateau running from north to south.‡

The Post Road continued all the way to King's Bridge, a small wooden bridge that crossed the Harlem River where it narrowed and became Spuyten Duyvil Creek. Built by Frederick Philipse in 1693, the span generated toll revenues for the already wealthy landowner. In the mid–eighteenth century, local farmers built the Freebridge to avoid the toll.§ Kingsbridge (one word) was the name given to the adjacent areas both north and south of that

---

*At the intersection, today, of Twenty-third Street and Fifth Avenue.

†The Bloomingdale Road followed the course of today's Broadway; Hoaglandt's farm was at today's West 108th Street.

‡The first cross road lay roughly along the line of today's 42nd Street on a slight diagonal between Seventh and Lexington Avenues. The second one ran along today's 70th Street, while the third crossed present-day Central Park at about 95th Street. Harlem Plains today is the area from 110th to 125th Street between Fifth and Morningside Avenues. Above 125th Street, the western edge of this plain is marked by St. Nicholas Avenue. Harlem Heights consists of the areas known today as Manhattanville and Hamilton Heights.

§Today's Marble Hill neighborhood in the Bronx was originally the northern end of Manhattan Island, and its northern boundary was marked by Spuyten Duyvil Creek; King's Bridge stood near present-day West 230th Street. In the early 1900s the curving creek bed was filled in and a ship canal was built to the south, connecting the Harlem River with the Hudson. Now a plaque marks the site of the old King's Bridge, and a substantial modern structure carries Broadway across the Harlem River. The Freebridge ran roughly east-west where a new bridge connects University Heights in the Bronx with Inwood in Manhattan (at 207th Street).

bridge.* North of the bridge the Post Road split into two roads, one east to New England (the Boston Post Road) and one north to Albany. Because it connected New York City with these areas at the northern end of Manhattan, the Post Road was also called the Kingsbridge Road.

Lee sketched out his plan with his engineer, but the actual construction of these works had to wait until more troops arrived in the city. The brief, emergency enlistments of Lee's 1,500 Connecticut volunteers were due to expire on March 25, and an infusion of minutemen from Westchester and Dutchess Counties brought in only 500 men. With individual companies from other sources, Lee still had an inadequate workforce. The minutemen began to arrive on February 15 and broke ground on the fort at Horn's Hook. Ten days later, replacement volunteers came down from Connecticut and began work on the Brooklyn Heights defenses.[31]

Lee also sent his engineer forty miles up the Hudson to inspect work that had been started earlier on forts in the Highlands, where he also marked out a site for a new fort to be named after New York's fallen hero in the Canadian campaign, Richard Montgomery. Depending on which side held them, the Highland forts had the potential to play a critical role in either foiling or facilitating the British grand strategy, since they commanded both the Hudson River and the overland routes between New York City and Albany, where the British forces on both ends of the river were supposed to meet.

The day after Lee arrived to prepare New York for battle, Admiral Howe and his allies won the first half of their power struggle in London.[32] On February 5, Howe kissed the king's hand in confirmation of his appointment as commander in chief of the North American naval squadron. Germain, the newly appointed secretary of state for the American colonies, and other doubting ministers had ended up joining forces with North and Dartmouth—as they had previously for General Howe—because they felt the benefit of Admiral Howe's extraordinary professional ability outweighed the risk posed by his political views.

Yet Howe still hadn't achieved his original goal of becoming a peace commissioner, and most of the ministry would have preferred to abolish the commission altogether. Since that would have been politically difficult, Germain set out instead to neutralize the commission by insisting that a second commis-

---

*Today, the areas in the Bronx north of the bridge are called Marble Hill, Kingsbridge, and Kingsbridge Heights. Inwood is the neighborhood south of the bridge, in Manhattan.

sioner be appointed to serve with Howe—one who would oppose concessions. After the admiral threatened to quit as commander in chief, a compromise was reached in mid-February: Admiral Howe's brother, William—whom Germain considered more reliable than Richard—was named the second commissioner.

Germain, however, went a step farther and demanded that the Howe brothers' written instructions for the peace commission clearly state that the colonists had to formally acknowledge Parliament's supremacy before any negotiations could begin, peace be declared, or sanctions be removed. North and Dartmouth, seeing that Germain intended to mobilize a vast army and preferred to crush the rebels rather than look for a negotiated settlement, both announced that they were ready to resign. Germain threatened to do the same, and the king ordered the prime minister and the colonial secretary to work out their differences. The compromise they agreed to was, in reality, a triumph for Germain and his faction. The wording of the commission's instructions was reformulated, but Germain's requirements effectively remained in place.

By March, Howe had lost yet another round with Germain and was undoubtedly frustrated by the debate over preconditions for negotiation with the rebels. Nonetheless, he remained in London trying to expand his authority by demanding changes in other aspects of the written instructions—even as the delays threatened to render his mission to America moot.

CHAPTER 5

We Expect a Bloody Summer
at New York

~

e want you at N. York—we want you at Cambridge—we want you in Virginia—but Canada seems of more importance," John Adams gushed to Charles Lee. Ideally, Congress wanted him everywhere at once. "A luckier, a happier expedition than yours to N. York was never projected. The whole whig world is blessing you for it, and none of them more than Your Friend and Servt."[1] Lee's work in New York remained unfinished, but Congress, thoroughly pleased with his organizational, tactical, and engineering skills, moved him to the next trouble spot. Despite the desperate need to shore up the Canadian campaign, Congress was even more concerned about General Clinton's expedition to the Carolinas and dispatched Lee from New York on March 7 to fortify the major cities in the South.

The implementation of Lee's plan for New York was entrusted to newly commissioned Brigadier General Lord Stirling, whose promotion was clinched when an armed British transport full of coal and provisions ran aground off Sandy Hook and Stirling led a small band of volunteers to capture it. Once the conservative fifth wheel of the Triumvirate's old Whig Club, Stirling had seemed the least likely to become an ardent patriot. By the start of the Seven Years' War he had become a merchant, filling government contracts, and had then gone to England to settle some disputed bills and pursue his Scottish peerage.[2]

When Stirling built his mansion in New Jersey soon after he

William Alexander, Lord Stirling

returned to America, he served on His Majesty's Council in that province and befriended the royal governor, William Franklin, Benjamin's son out of wedlock. Stirling remained silent in the conflict over taxation, appearing to accept British assertions about the supremacy of Parliament. He assumed the lavish lifestyle he had enjoyed among his aristocratic British friends; between his spendthrift habits and poor returns on various investments, he ran through a fortune of almost 100,000 pounds, and just before the Revolution, creditors seized the contents of his mansion and disposed of it piecemeal at public auctions.[3]

Despite his fondness for inherited wealth and titles, however, when fighting broke out near Boston in 1775, Stirling quickly and steadfastly sided with the Americans. His detractors, like the loyalist Judge Jones, claimed that Stirling saw the rebellion as an opportunity to throw off his financial problems, an accusation that is not borne out by any evidence.[4] His true motivation, as he wrote to William Franklin, stemmed from "the rejection [by the king of America's] most humble, dutiful, and respectful, petitions to the Throne . . . the battles of Lexington and Bunker's Hill . . . the wanton and cruel destruction of Charlestown, and . . . the design of the Ministry to bring indiscriminate ruin on the Colonies of this Continent."[5]

Stirling and Charles Lee became good friends during the fortification of New York, and the two men sang each other's praises. When Stirling took over in March 1776, he accepted Lee's conclusion that the British would try to attack the city itself, and he moved quickly to complete the barricades and roadblocks that Lee had prescribed. Soon he was able to write to Washington that the city's defenses were progressing rapidly.

Stirling reported: "[All of my men] excepting the necessary guards are employed . . . on this and Long Island in executing the fortifications agreed upon by General Lee and myself. In these works we are assisted every day by about 1000 of the inhabitants of the City who have turned out on this occasion with great alacrity, the inhabitants and the Negroes taking their tour of duty regularly and I have the satisfaction to see that according to the numbers, the work goes on amazingly well."[6] By paying a stiff fine to hire substitutes, New York's gentlemen could have exempted themselves from service, but most chose not to. The work crews, mustered every morning with fife and drum, included residents of every social class. The wealthiest, with their soft hands, "worked so long, to set an example, that the blood rushed out of their fingers."[7]

Stirling's forces completed most of Lee's plans in the city and started on the works in Brooklyn. Instead of the string of three redoubts on the crest of Brooklyn Heights, however, a single large fort was constructed there which bore Stirling's name. On the plateau of Brooklyn Heights another fort, an enormous hexagonal citadel covering five acres, named the Congress, was also started, mostly with the labor of Kings County slaves. Like Lee, Stirling did not provide for a possible attack in the rear from the interior of the island. On March 17 he did express concern in a letter to John Hancock, the president of Congress, that the British might land on the Long Island shore at the Narrows, but with his crews fully occupied completing Lee's plans, Stirling decided to "defer doing anything there until the other works are complete, and more troops arrive."[8]

As the work progressed, Stirling wrote to Washington that he thought they had "little to fear from General Howe, should he attempt anything in this quarter." In closing, he said, "I could wish General Howe would come here in preference to any other spot in America as I believe it would now be of least detriment to the American cause; besides, then I should have the honour of serving under your immediate command."[9]

Two weeks after Lee's departure, Washington wrote Stirling a triumphant letter announcing that the ten-month siege of Boston had produced a victory: On St. Patrick's Day, Howe had withdrawn all of his troops onto the warships and transports in Boston Harbor without destroying the city, and the Americans were in "full possession." Howe had decided to evacuate soon after the Americans mounted a substantial number of cannon on Dorchester

Heights, which commanded the city—guns captured at Fort Ticonderoga on Lake Champlain and dragged to Boston on sledges during the winter.

Flush from this turn of events, Washington was optimistic about the campaign he anticipated in New York, despite the obstacles. If all went well, he wrote Stirling, "we shall have the opportunity of securing and putting the continent in a tolerable posture of Defence; and that the Operations of the Summer's Campaign will not be so terrible as we were taught to expect from the Accounts and Denunciations which the Ministry have held forth to the Public."[10]

Washington could not be sure, at first, whether Howe's departure was a feint, and he proceeded with caution, protecting both Boston and New York by sending the army south in discreet stages.[11] The British fleet lingered at the mouth of the harbor for ten days and then headed out to sea, leaving Washington to assume it was bound for New York—when its true destination was Halifax, Nova Scotia. Howe intended to attack New York, but first he needed a port where his men could recover their strength, he could receive reinforcements, and the nearly 1,000 Boston loyalists on board could be resettled.

Expecting an attack on New York within days, Washington sped his best units to the city first. Brigadier General William Thompson arrived on March 20 and took over from Stirling. Next came Colonel Edward Hand with a regiment of Pennsylvania riflemen, who went over to Long Island and reconnoitered the ground in Kings County. Two Maryland rifle companies and one from Virginia were stationed on Staten Island. At the same time, Stirling was able to extend the system of fortifications from New York City across to the New Jersey shore, where he supervised the construction of defensive works at Paulus Hook, Amboy, and Elizabeth. To keep the British off Staten Island—which might have served as a staging area to invade New Jersey—Stirling marked out the sites for forts there, but they remained unfinished. With its coastal areas reasonably secure, New Jersey's Committee of Safety sent 2,000 militia over to help defend New York.[12]

Washington had sent urgent pleas to Congress, to Stirling, and to Governor Trumbull, that they immediately send reinforcements from New Jersey and Connecticut to defend the city while the main body of the army was still in transit. His message to Trumbull was particularly emphatic: "You are sensible, Sir, of the great importance of a strenuous exertion at this critical period, a period which may in its consequences determine the fate of America." The lengthy siege of Boston proved how difficult it was to dislodge the British from a city, so Washington was determined to get his army to New York ahead of Howe's fleet. New York was "a post of infinite importance both to them and us," Washington wrote, "and much depends on priority of possession."[13]

Washington had ample cause to be concerned about delays.[14] With the thaw of spring the unpaved roads between Boston and New York were muddy and sometimes impassable, magnifying the logistical problem of getting enough teams of horses to pull wagons of equipment and supplies for an army of 10,000 men. The troops themselves had to walk most of the way. Washington hired a fleet of small merchant vessels at Norwich and New London, Connecticut, to transport the men on the last leg of the trip, thereby saving a few days and ensuring that the soldiers were not too exhausted to dig trenches and fight the British when they got to New York; but the journey still took about ten days. Brigadier General William Heath sailed into the East River with his brigade on March 30, ready to take over from General Thompson, followed soon after by Major General Israel Putnam, who assumed overall command until Washington arrived.

Stirling and Washington may have felt logistically and mentally prepared for an invasion, but most New Yorkers were terrified by the prospect of armies clashing on their doorstep. Joseph Reed and congressional delegate Robert Morris, among others, believed that the majority of patriots and loyalists alike still hoped for some type of reconciliation with the king and Parliament instead of all-out war and independence. They waited anxiously for each new development. However, packet boats were the fastest link with England; under ideal conditions it took them a month to deliver mail and at least six weeks more to bring back a reply. As the weather and winds were rarely ideal, the return trip from England to America could take three months.[15]

By the spring of 1776, New Yorkers had known for several months that Parliament had approved a peace commission, but what terms the commissioners would offer once they arrived in America became a matter of intense speculation and debate.[16] Trying to move a wavering populace toward independence, Whig newspapers warned readers that the envoys were not coming to engage in meaningful negotiation, but merely to offer pardons and regain the submission of rebellious colonists. Their real motive, the papers asserted, was to show the Crown's European rivals, France and Spain, that everything was under control. An editorial on March 20 exhorted Americans to "Remember the Stamp Act!" along with a list of other British treacheries in the last dozen years.[17]

Isaac Sears, Marinus Willett, and the other Liberty Boys made sure New

Yorkers remembered the Stamp Act by reviving the practice of burning effigies, which had been popular a decade earlier. (Sears, who had become Stirling's adjutant when Lee left New York, was bumped from that position when the Continental Army arrived with its own staffing system.)[18] On March 22, 1776, their target was Governor Tryon; when he issued an appeal to the city to return to the royal fold, his effigy was paraded through the streets and hung from a gallows. Labels attached to the figure proclaimed: "Behold the bloody tool of the sanguinary Despot, who is using his utmost efforts to enslave you!" and "Tories take Care!!!"[19]

The rhetoric of the mobs and of patriots in general displayed an idealism that was not without its ironies and contradictions. The New York papers were unself-consciously filled with ads offering rewards for runaway African-American slaves printed alongside fervent denunciations of England's tyranny and enslavement of the colonies.[20] And the radicals who orchestrated crowds to burn effigies were themselves guilty of censorship and destruction of property in the name of defending freedom for Americans. Sears had already shut printer James Rivington down a few months earlier. At the end of March, Samuel Loudon, a printer who attempted to publish a rebuttal to Thomas Paine's revolutionist pamphlet, *Common Sense,* was interrogated by the radicals and had all of his copies burned by a mob. The irony was especially sharp in New York, the city that championed freedom of the press with the acquittal of John Peter Zenger in 1735. By 1776, however, the radicals argued that the time for a polite exchange of ideas had passed; war was approaching, and the printed word had become an essential weapon in the struggle.

Washington, like the editorialists in New York, regarded the British announcement of a peace commission as part of this propaganda war, as a divide-and-conquer stratagem: If Americans could be set to arguing the merits of reconciliation versus independence, they would fail to prepare for a vigorous defense of New York. By delaying the arrival of the commissioners, the British would gain time to build up their forces. Washington predicted that the commissioners would never offer agreeable terms. Americans, he wrote, should rely solely on "the Protection of a kind Providence and unanimity among ourselves."[21]

Among those who continued to debate the fine points of the imperial crisis was William Smith, who attended Tryon's Council meetings on the floating capitol. However, his tone with the governor had become less flattering. During a heated discussion after dinner one night, Smith offended Tryon by accusing the

British government of mishandling the crisis and driving the colonies toward independence, which had not been one of their original demands.

The atmosphere grew more tense both onshore and off: A broadside appeared, calling for the assassination of anyone who showed himself to be a traitor by visiting Tryon's "nest of sycophants" aboard the *Dutchess of Gordon*. Smith decided, for his own safety and that of his family—including a baby girl who was born under the threat of bombardment from the *Asia*—to move up to his newly completed country house at Haverstraw in the Hudson Highlands. Smith instructed two black servants to look after the empty house in town and forward his mail. The Smiths left with most of their furniture and other belongings on March 29, 1776, and did not return for almost two and a half years—part of the growing exodus from the city.[22]

"We all live here like nuns shut up in a nunnery," one resident of Manhattan wrote to a friend. "No society with the town for there is none there to visit; neither can we go in or out after a certain hour without the countersign."[23] By the first week in April New Yorkers were experiencing martial law for the first time, complete with curfews, passwords, and sentry posts, courtesy of Major General Israel Putnam, also known as "Old Put."

Putnam's nickname was not used to his face, but it was nonetheless a term of affection.[24] At fifty-eight, he was a hero of both the Seven Years' War and the Battle of Bunker Hill, and his adventures were legendary. Even before he entered the military, Putnam was revered in his Connecticut town because he tracked down a wolf that had been preying on his neighbors' livestock. When the wolf holed up in its den, Putnam crawled, headfirst, into the dark cave and shot it. Later he was captured by Indians and rescued just as they were about to burn him alive. He also survived a hurricane that shipwrecked him off the coast of Cuba.

Putnam also had a compassionate side: When the British cracked down on Massachusetts in the wake of the Boston Tea Party, he drove 130 sheep from his farm in Connecticut to Boston, where he donated the flock to the city's poor. Not long after his return, word reached Putnam in Connecticut that the British were heading for Lexington. He reportedly left his mule in its harness in the middle of a half-plowed field and raced to the scene without even stopping to change his clothes.

Putnam wasted no time in New York either. With far more troops at his disposal than Charles Lee had had, Putnam was able to send scouting parties

Major General Israel Putnam

to prevent the British warships from taking on freshwater at a landing known as the Watering Place on the northeastern shore of Staten Island.* After his troops skirmished with a landing party there, Putnam also took steps to cut off the enemy's food supply by cracking down more aggressively than Lee was able to on trade with the British ships in the Upper Bay and the East River. Putnam declared in a letter to John Hancock, the president of the Continental Congress, that hostilities had begun in the province of New York.

Again reflecting the compromise that had put Congress in charge of the army's operations in New York—and the delegates' tendency during the campaign to involve themselves in the military's strategic decisions—Putnam also reported to Hancock that he wanted to "take possession of Governor's Island," which he considered "a very important post." In his eyes, control of the little island that divides the mouth of the East River had the potential to keep the British navy out of that waterway and thus to protect Manhattan's entire east side as well as Brooklyn Heights. "Should the enemy arrive here, and get post there [on Governors Island]," Putnam declared, "it will not be possible to save the city, nor could we dislodge them without great loss."[25] Putnam did not wait for a response. On the night of April 8, he seized the island with 1,000 men and had them entrenched before dawn.†

*Today the neighborhood of Tompkinsville.
†Until its Coast Guard station was closed in 1997, Governors Island was the oldest continuously operated military post in the United States, having been manned since 1799.

Putnam also established a gun battery on Red Hook, the knob of land—at that time an island at high tide—projecting from the Brooklyn Peninsula directly across the narrow channel from Governors Island. These cannon, along with guns in the batteries on Brooklyn Heights, Governors Island, and the southern tip of Manhattan, were all trained on the mouth of the East River, where obstructions had been sunk to keep British ships out, or at least slow them down and make them easier targets.

"Oh the houses in New York, if you could but see the insides of them! . . . Kennedy's new house, Mallet's and the one next to it, had 600 men in them! . . . If the owners ever get possession again," a genteel New Yorker lamented, "I am sure they must be years in cleaning them, unless they get new floors and new plaster the walls."[26] Not only was the fortification effort scarring the face of the city—with earthworks and ditches and felled trees everywhere—but the crews of mud-smeared diggers were wrecking the interiors of elegant mansions that had been designated as barracks. The once prosperous and beautiful city rapidly became an armed camp as a committee appointed by the Provincial Congress lodged the arriving troops in abandoned houses.

Most of the houses were filled with soldiers but devoid of the furnishings residents had taken with them, so the men slept in pairs on the hard floors in order to share blankets, spreading one under them and covering themselves with the other.[27] They stored and cooked their own rations, and were liable to eat food that was both spoiled and undercooked. The city water supply was overburdened and contaminated, which also contributed to the spread of disease.[28] "Our Company are now about one half of them very low with the Camp Disorder, or Bloody Flux, which is very prevalent through out the whole Army," Lieutenant Isaac Bangs, an army surgeon, wrote in his journal as the weather grew warmer, "& though it Emaciates them very much yet it is not very mortal, as not more than one in our Reg't has died with this disorder."[29]

Bangs was describing the dysentery that resulted from overcrowded and unsanitary conditions. Smallpox—a far more lethal disease than the intestinal disorders the men suffered—took a heavy toll, but was contained by isolating the infected men on Montresor's Island and by prohibiting the then-risky practice of inoculation.[30]

When Washington and his staff reached New York in mid-April, ten days behind Putnam, the city officially became the headquarters of the Continental

Army, which, on paper at least, consisted of roughly 10,000 troops. To complete New York's defenses, Washington organized them into four brigades, under Heath, Joseph Spencer, Nathanael Greene, and Stirling. As the only major general in the city, Putnam became Washington's second-in-command, while Horatio Gates remained adjutant general. Three of the brigades remained on Manhattan, while Nathanael Greene's crossed over to Long Island.

In early May, the Manhattan brigades moved out of their barracks into three camps on a line north of the city, from which they could be efficiently deployed to work on the fortifications that remained incomplete. The works that Lee and Stirling had started required additional labor with picks and shovels before they could be fitted with artillery. Between the cannons from Boston and those lying on the Common in front of the liberty pole, the Americans had almost 100 guns. A foundry in the city also contributed some brass field pieces to the total. Nonetheless, this number fell short of what was needed for all the forts, and most of the guns were, in any event, too small to be effective against ships from the shore. The army was also desperately short of muskets and had to canvass from house to house in the surrounding counties to see if residents would sell their spare firearms.[31]

Washington also focused intently on suppressing the Tories, who wanted to hand the city over to the British without a fight. He cracked down on the flow of goods and intelligence between New York and the British ships that continued despite Lee's and Putnam's efforts at enforcement. Washington denounced the merchants who profited by supplying the British warships, as those "sundry base and wicked persons preferring their own present private emolument to their country's weal."[32] He also had the Provincial Congress appoint a Committee of Seven—a special court that could issue summonses to suspected Tories, put them on trial, and imprison them. Those who ignored the summonses were to be arrested by the Continental troops.

Complying with a congressional order from Philadelphia in April, Washington also sent reinforcements to bolster the expedition in Canada, where Benedict Arnold's siege of Quebec continued. Brigadier Generals William Thompson and John Sullivan sailed up the Hudson toward Albany and the Great Lakes with ten regiments. A feisty, combative New Hampshire lawyer, Sullivan had been elected to both the first and second Continental Congresses—despite the fact that he had antagonized many of his constituents with lawsuits for unpaid debts. Sullivan's impetuousness and hot temper raised doubts in Washington's mind, but he also considered this son of Irish immigrants who arrived in America as indentured servants to be "active, spirited," and "enterprizing."[33]

After the transfer of so many troops to Canada in April, Washington's small army urgently needed reinforcements, and at the end of May Congress called him to Philadelphia for consultations about the imminent campaign in New York. The delegates affirmed their desire to defend the city and drew up a plan to raise an additional 23,800 troops, to be called up from the militias of seven colonies for short-term service in the Continental Army and referred to as "New Levies." Ten thousand of them were to occupy the defenses in New Jersey to shield the capital city of Philadelphia, leaving Washington almost 14,000 more men in New York. However welcome the new troops were, of the roughly 23,000 men in and around the city, only 19,000 were present and fit for duty, and of these, most were entirely without training or military discipline and unlikely to stand their ground under enemy fire. Adding to Washington's troubles, he lost his trusted adjutant, Horatio Gates, when Congress made him a major general on May 16 and assigned him to the Northern Department as Schuyler's second-in-command.[34]

At the beginning of May an item from a London paper reprinted in New York infuriated many readers with evidence that Lord North's vaunted peace commission might indeed be a ruse after all. To remedy their own shortage of troops, the British had hired "1000 men called Jagers," the article explained, "[Germans] brought up to the use of the rifle barrel guns in boar-hunting. They are amazingly expert. . . . These men are intended to take part in the next campaign in America and our ministry plume themselves much in the thought of their being a compleat match for the American rifle-men."[35] American responses to the article expressed shock and a deep sense of betrayal: Apparently, the king had not found enough English volunteers to sail across the Atlantic and fight their own countrymen, so he had hired foreign mercenaries to hunt down his wayward American subjects.

George III had initially approached Catherine the Great of Russia, because she owed him a favor in return for his support during the recent Russo-Turkish War. However, her promise of 20,000 troops suddenly evaporated after France and Prussia sent secret agents to change the empress's mind. In the end, Britain's third Hanoverian king turned to his many royal relatives in the German principalities, and they were far more obliging—for a price. Their mercenaries were not like today's soldiers of fortune, but rather like slaves, because their rulers collected the fee for each man's service. The landgrave of Hesse-Cassel provided two-thirds of the nearly 18,000 Germans who first joined the British forces in America. The count of Hanau, the duke of Brunswick, and the prince of Waldeck supplied the rest. A reputation for both skill and savagery preceded these mercenaries. In tones of mixed derision and terror, they were all called Hessians.[36]

Parliament had finally ratified the treaties for the Hessians' services in February, after much haggling with the German princes. The army of 20,000 men the ministry had called for in August 1775 was slowly taking shape and would be even larger than hoped. General Howe had retreated to Halifax with 7,000 soldiers and 4,000 sailors. Reinforcements from bases around the world—Scotland, Ireland, Gibraltar, and Majorca—joined him there to regroup for the descent on New York. Admiral Howe was expected to assume command of the gathering fleet at Halifax, but in the middle of May he still had not arrived. The transports full of Hessians, convoyed from Europe by British warships—and Henry Clinton's southern expedition—were to meet the Howes in New York Harbor, where the offensive would begin.[37]

Just when American distrust of British motives and plans had increased sharply, Admiral Howe finally received the ministry's complete written orders for the peace commission. When the months of sparring with Germain ended, the papers had slowly worked their way through the ossified bureaucracy of the Admiralty, where they were at last approved and then laboriously copied by clerks in the moldering basement rooms at Whitehall.[38] At dawn on May 11, 1776, Admiral Howe at last set sail from St. Helens on the Isle of Wight, traveling on his flagship, the *Eagle*, without any convoy of other warships or troop transports. Having left behind the delays of officialdom on land, however, Howe soon encountered obstacles of another sort. Ten days out, a severe storm flooded the hold and nearly sank his ship. Adverse winds continued after the storm as the *Eagle* made its way through fields of icebergs far taller than its masts.[39]

"We expect a very bloody summer at New York and Canada," Washington wrote to his brother on May 31, "as it is there, I presume, the grand efforts of the enemy will be aimed, and I am sorry to say that we are not, either in men or arms, prepared for it." Washington expected General Howe's fleet at any hour, and the American siege of Quebec had finally ended in yet another disaster. Before Sullivan and Thompson could arrive with reinforcements, General John Burgoyne had come to Sir Guy Carleton's rescue. The appearance of Burgoyne with a fleet in the St. Lawrence River on May 6 enabled Carleton to emerge from the walled city with his army, scatter the dwindling, diseased American forces, and drive them southward toward Montreal in a chaotic retreat.

The optimism that Washington shared with Lord Stirling in the middle of March had largely melted away, and the commander in chief placed his faith in a higher power: "However, it is to be hoped that if our cause is just, as I do most religiously believe it to be, the same Providence which has in many instances appeared for us, will still go on to afford us aid."[40]

CHAPTER 6

A Mighty Fleet of Ships
Our Enemies Have Got

〜

Smoke signals and semaphores were still the most sophisticated forms of high-speed telecommunications in 1776. Lookouts on the "Heights and Head Lands at the entrance of the Harbour" were to use flags and fires to alert Washington's headquarters at No. 1 Broadway about the approach of an enemy fleet, "in case anything formidable should appear."[1] In early June several British ships finally arrived off Sandy Hook, and their behavior was a clue that more were on the way: They repeatedly stretched away into the Atlantic and came back, revealing that they were expecting a fleet from the north. Trying to defend both ends of the Hudson at once, Washington hurried to replace the troops that had been drained away by the campaign in Canada. From Connecticut he asked that they be sent "as fast as they can possibly be raised; without waiting to make up the whole complement to be furnished for this Place, before any of them march."[2]

Aside from the movements of the waiting battleships, the discovery of a Tory conspiracy on June 20 was a sure sign that the British were coordinating an imminent attack.[3] The Conspiracy Committee of the Provincial Congress traced the plot to Governor Tryon, who allegedly planned to arm as many as 500 Tories to join the British offensive against the city. Rumors spread that they planned to blow up the Americans' powder magazines, set fire to the city, spike the cannons, cut down the wooden King's Bridge connecting northern Manhattan to the mainland, and finally to capture or assassinate the American generals. Washington was to be stabbed or else poisoned with a dish of his favorite Long Island peas, some said, but was saved by a warning from his house-keeper, the daughter of Sam Fraunces, owner of the famous tavern.* In another embellishment of the story, the peas were thrown out in a chicken coop, where all of the birds then died.

The arrests began with a raid at one A.M. on June 22: Continental troops seized the mayor, David Matthews, at his home in Flatbush, as he was accused of carrying money from Tryon to a gunsmith on Broadway to pro-cure arms for the city's loyalists. Some twenty suspects were apprehended, including the gunsmith and two soldiers, Thomas Hickey and Michael Lynch, who were members of Washington's Life Guard, the corps that pro-tected his headquarters. The mayor and the gunsmith, along with eleven other alleged plotters, were transferred to jails in Connecticut for safekeeping during the war; only Hickey was tried and formally convicted. Three accom-plices testified against him, apparently in exchange for clemency. On June 28, in the first military execution of the American Revolution, Hickey was hanged in front of a crowd of 20,000 troops and spectators gathered on the Common, a grisly sight that Washington hoped would be "a warning to every soldier in the Army."[4]

On the day that the plot was discovered, Oliver De Lancey evaded the summons he had recently received from New York's Revolutionary govern-ment. That night he sneaked out of his house in the village of Bloomingdale and with Charles Apthorp and William Bayard paddled down the Hudson in a canoe to the *Asia*. The following day they joined Tryon on the *Dutchess*. New York's leading Tories had slipped through the lines.[5]

Not long after De Lancey's flight, William Smith received a summons at his country house in Haverstraw, where he had taken refuge with his family in March. The Committee of Safety in New York demanded his presence to determine if he was a friend of the American cause, and if he was among "those who are ready to risque their Lives & Fortunes in Defence of the Rights and Liberties of America."[6] Smith had spent the past few months in the country refining the legalistic argument he had begun to expound in his recent dispute with Governor Tryon on board the

---

*Today an early-twentieth-century reconstruction of the original tavern is open to the public at Broad and Pearl Streets. It houses a museum and a restaurant.

Dutchess. Britain was to blame, Smith felt, for ignoring American petitions, particularly in August 1775, and for starting the war. However, both sides were morally and politically obligated, Smith wrote, to consider the good of the whole—of the united empire—and to work toward a compromise that would preserve it.

Smith dodged the summons by staying put and writing a letter to his friend Gouverneur Morris, in which he professed his friendship for America and recalled his record of patriotism at the time of the Stamp Act. Smith also set forth his view of the present crisis: that the move toward independence constituted a breach of contract on the part of the colonies. Morris wrote back that the moment of truth had arrived, and Smith's lofty objectivity would not do. Smith's prominence, and his talents, Morris wrote, entitled his country-men to call for his help. The fate of "every Gentleman in the Country," Morris warned, "depends upon the Decision of his present Conduct."[7] Despite his friend's reply, on the eve of the battle for New York, Smith continued to defer the difficult choice that he knew would indeed put his life and fortune at risk, no matter which side he chose.

The catharsis of Hickey's execution was brief, because the same day brought more frightening news. Two American privateers sent word to the city that the British fleet—consisting of 130 ships—had sailed from Halifax on June 9 and could be expected at Sandy Hook any day. General William Howe himself had already arrived on June 25 with a dozen ships, including his own man-of-war, the *Greyhound*, and anchored in the Lower Bay, making no attempt to come ashore while he waited for the rest of his fleet. The news of the twenty-eighth was even more alarming, however, since no fleet even approaching that size had ever been seen in North America.

Another piece of news shocked New Yorkers, in a different way: General Howe had brought with him a young married couple he had met in Boston—Elizabeth Loring and her husband, Joshua—and had taken Elizabeth as his mistress.[8] Joshua Loring was a merchant in Boston and had sold wine and liquor to the British both there and in Halifax. Howe had apparently secured the favors of his wife with the promise of greater profits to come, and fulfilled this indecent proposal soon after he arrived in New York by appointing Loring as his commissary of prisoners, a position that came with a high salary tradi-tionally supplemented by significant graft.

Howe's weakness for Betsey Loring, and the pair's addiction to gambling, which was said to be her influence, had first become apparent in Boston, according to Judge Thomas Jones. There, in the fall of 1775, Jones wrote, "nothing seemed to engross his attention but the faro table, the play house, the dancing assembly, and Mrs. Loring."[9]

"It will be in vain for us to exspet to Keep the Shiping out of the North River unless we can fortify at the narrows where I intend to view as soon as the wether is good," Colonel William Douglas wrote home to his wife in Connecticut. "The Fenoex* now lays there in order to guard that place, but will not fire on us."[10] Douglas had only just arrived in New York—marching from New Haven on June 20, leading a regiment raised at his own expense—but already he grasped what Charles Lee had not: The best defense for the city and the Hudson was to keep the British out of the Upper Bay altogether.

An ardent patriot—and a devoted family man—Douglas closed a subsequent letter with instructions to his wife for running their farm, which was in jeopardy because all the hired help had gone to war; Douglas assured her that the ruin of the farm was inconsequential and the salvation of America would be "a most Noble Reward."[11] In a third letter to his wife at about this time, Douglas urged her to keep their four children in school at all costs, so they would eventually be able to write to him. Clearly, he suspected it might be a very long war. "My most Tender Love to our Little ones," he wrote. "it is for their Happiness I hope we are now Ingaged."[12]

A veteran of the Seven Years' War, the thirty-four-year old Douglas had been a teenager when he served under Israel Putnam at the surrender of Quebec in 1759. Like Sears and McDougall in New York, Douglas later made his fortune as the captain of a merchant ship sailing out of New Haven to the West Indies. When fighting broke out in 1775, he raised a company of troops, received a captain's commission, and took his men to Canada with supplies for General Montgomery. There he commanded a small fleet on Lake Champlain and helped capture St. Johns. After his return to New Haven, he raised the regiment that he brought to New York, and Governor Trumbull made him a colonel.[13]

Despite the insight and initiative of a few men like Douglas, the creation of choke points at Sandy Hook and the Narrows was neglected too long. The

*The British warship *Phoenix*.

Colonel William Douglas

Provincial Congress had taken only one modest step to disrupt the British fleet at its point of entry into New York's waters: It gave orders to disable the lighthouse at Sandy Hook, and the glass in its lantern accordingly was smashed and the oil pumped out of its cisterns.

True to the reports, the main body of the fleet did start to arrive on June 29, and by the next day, the whole fleet from Halifax had sailed past Sandy Hook into the Lower Bay. From their rooftops New Yorkers looked on with a mixture of fear and fascination at the threatening forest of masts and billowing sails. One astonished observer reported: "I was upstairs in an outhouse and spied as I peeped out the Bay something resembling a wood of pine trees trimmed. I declare at my noticing this, that I could not believe my eyes, but keeping my eyes fixed at the very spot, judge you my surprise when in about ten minutes, the whole Bay was full of shipping as ever it could be. I declare that I thought all London was afloat."[14]

Admiral Howe had not reached Halifax until June 23, almost six weeks after his departure from England.[15] Finding that his brother had already left for New York, he sailed south immediately, expecting to reach the city, with any luck, in about six days. Once again, however, the elements held him back, in the form of headwinds that left him idling under a fierce summer sun. Then his navigator got lost and mistook the island of Nantucket for Long Island.

Faced with mounting delays, Howe decided to get a modest but immediate start on his peace mission by demonstrating his goodwill toward American ships. When the *Eagle* crossed paths with a Nantucket whaler—a type of vessel exempt from the British blockade established by the Prohibitory Act—Howe not only released it but gave the Americans brandy as proof of English generosity and his friendly intentions. The next day he set another vessel free even though it was subject to the ban on American trade.

Howe also worked with his secretary, Ambrose Serle, to draw up a declaration explaining the powers of the peace commission, and tried to find an American vessel that would take it ashore in New England. The document announced that Admiral Howe and his brother were authorized to pardon anyone who pledged allegiance to the Crown. Any colony, county, or town would be declared at peace and have trade sanctions lifted as soon as it restored royal government.

Howe was already receiving a substantial second salary as a peace commissioner, and he undoubtedly expected even greater rewards, both political and financial, if he managed to save the empire. His proclamation hinted at similar incentives for individuals in the colonies who would help to advance the peace process, stating that "due Consideration shall be had to the meritorious Services of all Persons, who shall aid and assist in restoring the public Tranquility in the said Colonies, or in any Part or Parts thereof."[16] Howe also prepared letters to the colonial governors, asking for their help in spreading the word about the commission, and wrote to Benjamin Franklin, who had become a friend during the secret negotiations in London almost two years earlier. Unable to find a willing messenger among the American vessels he encountered, Howe was forced to delay the release of his peaceful overtures until the *Eagle* finally managed to reach New York.

Unaware of Admiral Howe's location, the British fleet already gathered in Lower New York Bay prepared to land General Howe and his army on Staten Island. At ten A.M. on July 2, just as the tide was turning against them, the ships weighed anchor and sailed up toward the Narrows. Had the Americans fortified the shores on both sides of this strait, the British convoy would have been an easy target. By eleven o'clock, the tide had turned completely, and the favorable light breeze had become a headwind. The transport ships "fell into great confusion, all dropping upon one another . . . which obliged us to come to an anchor," one British officer recorded in his diary. "Some of the ships within 7 or 800 yards of Long Island. We observed a good many of the Rebels in motion on shore. They fired musquetry at the nearest ships without effect. About 12 [noon] the ships nearest were ordered to drop down with the tide. Lucky for us the Rebels had no cannon here or we must have suffered a good deal."[17]

General Howe's flagship, the *Greyhound*, and two other men-of-war made it past the Narrows and signaled for the transports to join them when the tide turned again. By nine P.M. a heavy rain pelted the British, but they had landed—otherwise unopposed—on Staten Island. The inhabitants welcomed the occupying army, while the entire local militia deserted to join its ranks.[18] Well counseled by Oliver De Lancey, Howe had found the perfect staging area from which to launch an invasion of the city.

With British might gathered in New York, the results of Henry Clinton's expedition against Charleston still unknown, and the Canadian effort in tatters, Congress was anxious to formalize the foreign alliances it had been seeking, particularly with France. The French had been carefully monitoring the growing split between England and the American colonies since the Stamp Act crisis and in December 1775 agreed in principle to start sending arms and money to the rebels covertly. To obtain a formal, open alliance and a commercial treaty with France, the united American colonies first had to prove worthy of support by becoming a distinct nation and demonstrating that they intended to separate from England permanently. Otherwise, the French feared, their overt attacks on the British might rekindle American affection for the mother country and thrust them into a war with a reunited British empire—the kind of war they had just lost in 1763.[19]

On the day that General Howe's army disembarked on Staten Island, delegates approved the Declaration of Independence, and two days later, on July 4, Congress publicly proclaimed the independence of the thirteen former colonies.* Admiral Howe had not even arrived, but his peace proposals had become obsolete before he could offer them, as he was not authorized to negotiate with the colonies as independent states.

Only New York abstained from what would have been a unanimous vote by the thirteen delegations in Philadelphia.[20] Four of New York's five delegates

*Most of the fifty-six delegates signed the document on August 2, but at least six delegates added their names at a later date. Signing was an act of treason, and the names were kept secret to prevent targeted retribution, which occurred nonetheless. In January 1777, Congress made the signatures public by formally sending a copy of the document to each state (Boatner, pp. 539–40, 1007).

personally favored independence, but a resolution passed in the New York Provincial Congress on April 21, 1775, bound them to seek a reconciliation with England, and these instructions had yet to be amended. The Provincial Congress felt constrained as well: On May 31, 1776, the Continental Congress had recommended to all of the colonies that they form new governments and establish themselves as states, but the New York authorities believed they had no mandate to take such a step, much less to vote for independence.

On June 17 they called an election in which voters vested a new provincial congress with this power. On the twenty-fourth the names of the new representatives were announced, and their first session was scheduled for July 9. New York's cautious path to independence was determined by moderates and conservatives in the Provincial Congress, but also by the menacing guns of the British ships in the harbor. While independence was being declared in Philadelphia, New York's Provincial Congress was moving out of the city and up to the courthouse in White Plains, hauling with it all its documents and stores of gunpowder.

The newly elected fourth Provincial Congress met in White Plains on July 9, declared that New York had been a state since April 20, 1775 (the day after Lexington and Concord), and changed its name to the Convention of the Representatives of the State of New York. It approved the Declaration of Independence and wrote directly to John Hancock in Philadelphia to inform him of the vote, while 500 handbills with the Declaration and the Convention's own resolutions began rolling off the presses for distribution to the public.

At six P.M. that evening, the Declaration of Independence was read to Washington's troops at their various parade grounds, and on the Common, where it was greeted with cheers. A mob of soldiers and civilians then marched down Broadway to Bowling Green, where they toppled the equestrian statue of King George III. "In it were 4,000 pounds of lead, & a Man undertook to take of[f] 10 0z of Gold from the Superficies, as both Man & Horse were covered with Gold Leaf," Lieutenant Isaac Bangs wrote in his journal. "The Lead, we hear, is to be run up into Musquet Balls for the use of the Yankies, when it is hoped that the Emanations of the Leaden George will make as deep impressions in the Bodies of some of his red Coated and Torie Subjects, & that they will do the same execution in poisoning and destroying them, as the superabundant Emanations of the Folly & pretended Goodness of the real George have made upon their Minds."[21]

The mob cut off the statue's nose and the crown of laurels that were part of the depiction of the king as the Roman emperor Marcus Aurelius. The

The Declaration of Independence being read to
Washington's troops, July 9, 1776.

mutilated head was then put on a spike outside a tavern. The British engineer John Montresor eventually retrieved it and had it sent to England so the ministry might see the zeal of the rebels firsthand.[22]

In his orders the following day, Washington chided the troops for joining the mob, but his chief concern was for gathering intelligence about General Howe's plans. Four British prisoners, snatched from Staten Island, informed Washington that Howe had 10,000 soldiers with him and before making any moves was waiting for 150 more ships carrying another 15,000 troops, as well as for his brother, who was on his way from England.

Washington expected the British to attack New York City and New Jersey simultaneously, and took advantage of their delays to keep working on the fortifications and to get reinforcements from the neighboring states. He also had cattle and other livestock removed from the expected path of the British invasion, hoping to deprive them of much-needed food in the approaching campaign.

As the British forces accumulated, Washington's expectations for withstanding their offensive dwindled, to the point where he simply wished to make the enemy pay a terrible price to take and hold New York. On July 10, in a letter to John Hancock, Washington wrote that if the British captured the city he hoped they would have to "wade thro' much blood and slaughter," and "at best be in possession of a Melancholly and Mournfull victory."[23]

Two days later, starting at three in the afternoon on July 12, New Yorkers experienced a terrifying prelude to the battles ahead. With a steady wind blowing from the south, the British decided to test the American defenses by sending two ships up the Hudson. The *Phoenix* with forty guns and the *Rose* with twenty fired on the city as they sailed virtually unharmed past the thundering batteries on Manhattan and at Paulus Hook. With the wind and tide in their favor, the ships proved that they were too fast, and that the river was too wide at its mouth, for the American artillery to stop them.

The incident was also a shocking display of the American troops' inadequate training and discipline. "The Cannon of the City did but very little execution, as not more than half the Number of Men belonging to them were present," Lieutenant Isaac Bangs wrote in his journal. "The others were at their Cups & at their usual place of abode, Viz., on the Holy Ground." Some of these intoxicated men apparently reported to their stations, when they would have done better to stay away. Bangs recorded that "by the carelessness of our own Artilery Men, Six Men were killed with our own cannon, & several others very badly wounded. It is said that several of the Company out of which they were killed were drunk, & neglected to Spunge, Worm, & stop the Vent, and the Cartridges took fire while they were raming them down."[24] The sponge would have extinguished sparks from the previous charge of powder and prevented them from igniting the new cartridge prematurely, which caused the cannon to explode.

The British salvos from the *Phoenix* and *Rose* also took their toll. "When they came this side of Trinity Church, they began to fire smartly," Pastor Shewkirk of the Moravian Church wrote in his diary that Friday. "The balls and bullets went through several houses between here and Greenwich. Six men were killed, either some or all by ill-managing the cannons, though it is said that a couple were killed by the ships' firing; one man's leg was broke, etc. The six were put this evening into one grave on the Bowling Green. The smoke of the firing drew over our street like a cloud and the air was filled with the smell of the powder."[25]

As the cannonballs from the warships put holes in several rooftops, pan-

The *Phoenix* and the *Rose* sail up the
Hudson River, July 12, 1776.

icked New Yorkers continued to abandon the city, now by the hundreds. "Women, and children, and some with their bundles came from the lower parts, and walked to the Bowery, which was lined with people," Shewkirk noted.[26] Amid the tumult, one resident tried to look on the bright side, exclaiming that while his cow had been killed in the attack, it would still make "good market beef."[27]

The captain of the *Rose* and his staff celebrated with a bowl of punch and a bottle of claret on the quarterdeck as the ships made their way past the riflemen on Jeffrey's Hook* and the guns of a half-built fort on Mount Washington in northern Manhattan, en route to Tarrytown thirty miles

---

*A spit of land extending into the Hudson from the Manhattan shore at the base of Mount Washington.

upriver. There had been relatively minor damage to their sails and rigging, and the most serious casualty was a sailor on the *Phoenix* whose leg was later amputated.[28] Washington assumed correctly that the *Phoenix* and *Rose* were sent to interrupt American supply lines between New York and Albany, and possibly to establish a link between Howe and the British northern army under Sir Guy Carleton on its way south from Canada. Washington suspected the ships might also distribute arms to the Tories along the Hudson and destroy several American frigates that were under construction just north of the forts in the Highlands. So far the Americans were unable to stop them.

At six o'clock that evening, after nine weeks at sea, Admiral Howe's solitary ship, the *Eagle*, at last sailed through the Narrows. "Nothing could exceed the Joy, that appeared throughout the Fleet and Army upon our Arrival," Admiral Howe's secretary, Ambrose Serle, wrote breathlessly in his journal. "We were saluted by all the Ships of War in the Harbour, by the Cheers of the Sailors all along the Ships, and by those of the Soldiers on the Shore. A finer Scene could not be exhibited, both of Country, Ships and men, all heightened by one of the brightest Days that can be imagined." Serle noted that the firing of the ships' guns was not only to welcome Admiral Howe but also to celebrate the passage of the *Phoenix* and *Rose* up the Hudson "in Defiance of all their vaunted Batteries."

Soon the *Eagle* was safely anchored, "in full View of New York, and of the Rebels' Head Quarters under Washington, who is now made their Generalissimo with full Powers," Serle wrote with apparent disdain. General Howe came aboard with several officers, including Admiral Molyneux Shuldham, who was about to cede his command to Admiral Howe. Serle was shocked to learn from them "that the Congress had now announced the Colonies to be INDEPENDENT STATES, with several other Articles of intelligence that proclaim the villainy and the madness of these deluded people."[29]

General Howe, who conducted the briefing, did not take the rebel threat lightly, however. The Declaration of Independence indicated a determination to fight rather than negotiate, he told his brother, and the rebels were heavily entrenched on Manhattan and Long Island with as many as 35,000 men and more than 100 pieces of artillery. Certainly, the arrival of several hundred deserters and loyalists in the British camp was gratifying, but it was hardly an indication that the rebellion was about to collapse. Announcing the arrival of the peace commission would have little impact, the general predicted.

Ignoring his brother's advice, Admiral Howe waited only until the following day to send out the proclamation and the letters to the colonial governors that he and Serle had written during their Atlantic crossing.[30] A lieutenant carried them across to Perth Amboy, New Jersey, where he distributed them to American couriers. Since Admiral Howe assumed the Americans would treat the correspondence as intelligence and route it directly to Congress instead of its intended recipients, he deliberately left the letters unsealed to ensure that every messenger who handled them would read about his peace initiative and spread the word throughout the mid-Atlantic region and the South. He also sent a frigate to Rhode Island with copies of the proclamation and letters to the New England governors.

Admiral Howe then wrote a letter to Washington, proposing that they meet and begin direct negotiations. On July 14 the admiral sent a naval officer to Manhattan by rowboat with a flag of truce and the letter, addressed to "George Washington, Esq." Despite the Declaration of Independence, Admiral Howe was not prepared to acknowledge Washington's status as the military leader of a sovereign country.

Washington dispatched two of his most trusted aides to meet the British envoy: Colonel Joseph Reed, originally Washington's military secretary and now his adjutant general, and Colonel Henry Knox, the army's artillery expert. In a letter to his wife, Knox described the interception of Lord Howe's emissary by three American boats, and the formal, almost surreal exchange that followed.

> They came within about four miles of the city and were met by some of Colonel [Benjamin] Tupper's people, who detained them until his Excellency's pleasure should be known. Accordingly, Colonel Reed and myself went down on the barge to receive the message. When we came to them, the officer, who was, I believe, captain of the *Eagle* man-of-war, rose up and bowed, keeping his hat off: "I have a letter, sir, from Lord Howe to Mr. Washington."
>
> "Sir," says Colonel Reed, "we have no person in our army with that address."
>
> "Sir," says the officer, "will you look at the address?" He took out of his pocket a letter which was thus addressed: "George Washington, Esq., New York" "Howe."

"No sir," says Colonel Reed, "I cannot receive that letter."

"I am very sorry," says the officer, "and so will be Lord Howe, that any error in the superscription should prevent the letter being received by *General Washington*."

"Why, sir," says Colonel Reed, "I must obey orders."

"Oh yes, sir, you must obey orders, to be sure."

Then, after giving him a letter from Colonel Campbell to General Howe, and some other letters from prisoners to their friends, we stood off, having saluted and bowed to each other. After we had got a little way, the officer put about his barge and stood for us and asked by what particular title he chose to be addressed.

Colonel Reed said, "You are sensible, sir, of the rank of General Washington in our army?"

"Yes, sir, we are. I am sure Lord Howe will lament exceedingly this affair, as the letter is quite of a civil nature, and not a military one. He laments exceedingly that he was not here a little sooner"; which we suppose to allude to the Declaration of Independence; upon which we bowed and parted in the most genteel terms imaginable.[31]

Washington and most of his staff believed the peace commission had nothing to offer, and they continued to reject Admiral Howe's improperly addressed letters, as the admiral continued to deny Washington's rank, at least in writing. On July 15 the British received a letter from Washington protesting the mistreatment of American prisoners in Canada. Admiral Howe's reply, sent under another flag of truce the following evening, was addressed to "George Washington, Esq. and etc. etc." as if to imply his rank without stating it. Again Knox and Reed refused the letter. On the seventeenth a third messenger under a white flag was escorted by American boats to the waters off Governors Island, this time to ask if "His Excellency General Washington" would receive the adjutant general of the British army. Washington immediately accepted and set a meeting for noon on the twentieth.[32]

Knox wrote to his wife that General Howe's adjutant, Lieutenant Colonel James Paterson, was very polished and gracious. "In the course of his talk every other word was, 'May it please your Excellency,' 'If your Excellency so pleases'; in short, no person could pay more respect than the said adjutant-general."[33] However, when he produced the letter again, another standoff about protocol ensued. Washington finally insisted that if the Howes had come simply to grant pardons, the Americans did not need to be pardoned for defending their natural rights. And if the Howes wanted to negotiate, he told Paterson, they should address themselves to Congress.

Knox observed that Washington's commanding presence seemed to overpower the Englishman, and the devoted American colonel's description of the scene suggests that Washington's innate qualities, and the poise he had consciously labored to acquire as a young man, had already made him an iconic figure. "General Washington was very handsomely dressed and made a most elegant appearance. Colonel Paterson appeared awe-struck, as if he was before something supernatural. Indeed I don't wonder at it. He was before a very great man indeed."[34] Paterson politely declined refreshments and left, pleading that he was expected for dinner with the Howes on board the *Eagle*.

A majority of delegates in Congress—staunch advocates of independence—were delighted that Washington had rejected Admiral Howe's letters. At the same time they needed to appear reasonable to the many Americans who thought peace talks should be given a chance; to demonstrate without entering into negotiations that Admiral Howe was trying to exploit their desire for peace and restore royal government without offering any meaningful concessions.[35]

When Howe's declaration and his letters to the governors found their way to Congress, as he predicted they would, the solution became obvious: The delegates immediately had all of the material published so that Americans could see for themselves how "the insidious court of Britain has endeavoured to amuse and disarm them."[36] Since Admiral Howe's declaration offered to reward anyone who promoted a peaceful settlement, Congress was also eager to demonstrate that its members were immune to bribery.

Even Admiral Howe's private letter to Benjamin Franklin was published, so that his response, dated July 20, could be printed next to it. Franklin's letter was a scathing piece of propaganda, condemning Britain's "abounding pride and deficient wisdom." Yet it also contained striking references to the long friendship between the two men.

> Long did I endeavor, with unfeigned and unwearied zeal, to preserve from breaking that fine and noble china vase, the British empire; for I knew that, being once broken, the separate parts could not retain even their share of the strength or value that existed in the whole, and that a perfect reunion of those parts could scarce ever be hoped for. Your Lordship may possibly

remember the tears of joy that wet my cheek, when, at your good sister's in London, you once gave me expectations that a reconciliation might soon take place.

Those expectations had been bitterly disappointed, Franklin continued, but the personal bond remained.

The well-founded esteem and, permit me to say, affection, which I shall always have for your lordship, makes it painful to me to see you engaged in conducting a war, the great ground of which, as expressed in your letter, is "the necessity of preventing the American trade from passing into foreign channels." To me it seems that neither the obtaining or retaining of any trade, how valuable soever, is an object for which men may justly spill each other's blood; that the true and sure means of extending and securing commerce is the goodness and cheapness of commodities; and that the profit of no trade can ever be equal to the expense of compelling it, and of holding it, by fleets and armies.

Franklin stated that a peace treaty would only be possible if Britain recognized the United States as a separate nation—and acted quickly before they entered into foreign alliances. Concluding that Admiral Howe's "hope of being instrumental in a reconciliation" would be "impossible on any terms given you to propose," Franklin urged him to resign his command and enter private life.[37]

Admiral Howe had no intention of relinquishing his dual appointment, which had cost him so much time and effort, and in which he apparently still had a great deal of faith. In the aftermath of the response to his letters he hosted various other Americans on the *Eagle* and treated them with great respect, even going so far as to apologize for the insulting titles he had felt constrained to use in addressing the letters to Washington.[38]

Despite these shipboard visits, the diplomatic option had clearly run its course for the moment, and the admiral decided to see if military action would bring the Americans to the negotiating table. His brother, however, still wasn't ready to attack. General Howe's grim assessment of the American defenses convinced him to wait for reinforcements, and a letter from Lord Germain on July 27 supported his decision.[39]

Even without the reinforcements, the British armada was a formidable sight. On the same day that Howe received the letter from Germain, Gold

Selleck Silliman, an American officer, wrote to his son. "You would be surprised if You was here to see what a Mighty Fleet of Ships our Enemies have got; they lie down against Staten Island, more than a Mile in Length from East to West, and so thick & close together for the greatest part of the Way, that You cant see through where they are no more than if it was a thick Swamp; and the Regulars expect as many more soon and then we expect bloody Work of it."[40]

CHAPTER 7

The British Juggernaut
Reaches Full Strength

⁓

On August 1, a battered British fleet with "shattered masts and pierced hulls" sailed in past Sandy Hook to join the Howes in New York. Sir Peter Parker's nine warships and thirty-five transports, carrying 3,000 men under the command of General Henry Clinton and his subordinate, Charles Lord Cornwallis, had survived the British defeat at the end of June in South Carolina.[1] Clinton, by abandoning his own plan and accepting Parker's vague proposal for capturing Charleston, had failed miserably in his first independent command—which Howe had given him after their disagreement in Boston. Charles Lee, to whom Clinton had carelessly revealed his itinerary when he stopped in New York in February, had reached Charleston first and directed the fortification and defense of the city.[2]

Congress thanked Lee profusely for saving the vital southern capital. However, Lee's achievement at Charleston, like his efforts in New York and his military record in Europe, did not hold up well to careful scrutiny. General William Moultrie acknowledged Lee's contributions, but he justly received most of the credit for holding Charleston, because he stayed to defend a crucial fort on Sullivan's Island during a heavy British bombardment when Lee thought the post should be abandoned.[3]

A few days after Parker and Clinton arrived in New York, twenty-two more ships arrived from England and Scotland. At this point, General Howe had enough men to launch the invasion, but he decided to wait for more camp equipment, including the kettles and canteens his troops would need in the field, particularly in the heat of summer.[4] Finally, on August 12, after being lost on stormy seas for three and a half months, Commodore William Hotham arrived with the additional equipment. His convoy of more than 100 ships included 85 transports carrying 1,000 British Guards and the first contingent of Hessians: some 7,800 soldiers commanded by General Philip von Heister.[5]

The commander of the *Rainbow,* one of the escort ships, got an introduction to the treacherous sandbars hidden beneath the waters around Sandy Hook. "We are at length arrived at this place [New York] with most of the convoy," Admiral Sir George Collier wrote in his journal on the twelfth, "but in coming in an unskilful pilot run my ship aground upon one of the sands; there was luckily a very light breeze of wind and no swell so we got off without damage, and anchord with all the convoy below the narrows."[6] Britain's most competent naval officers, of whom Collier was one, were entirely dependent on the goodwill and the abilities of local pilots to enter the port of New York.

Staten Island presented an idyllic landscape to the new arrivals. It was "a hilly country, covered with beautiful forests composed mostly of a kind of fir-tree, the odor of which can be inhaled at a distance of two miles from land," a Hessian lieutenant wrote. "Peaches, chestnuts, apples, pears, grapes, and various kinds of nuts grow here in wild profusion, mingled with roses and blackberry bushes. The climate and soil are, without exception, the loveliest, healthiest, and most agreeable on the face of the globe."[7] A chaplain was even more emphatic: "I am inexpressibly glad to set foot on Staten Island. Scarcely can I restrain myself from kissing God's earth. Is she not our mother?"[8]

Also swelling the British ranks were fugitive black slaves, including 100 men from Virginia who had been promised freedom if they joined Lord Dunmore's "Ethiopian Regiment" and fought for the king. After Dunmore ended his brief tenure as governor of New York in 1771 with an ugly drinking binge, he had become the royal governor of Virginia. In November 1775 he proclaimed all the slaves and indentured servants belonging to the colony's "Rebels" to be free, if they were "able and willing to bear Arms," as "his Majesty's Troops." Alarm spread up the eastern seaboard, as white Americans, including Washington, envisioned a general uprising of the slave population. However, military defeats and smallpox soon decimated Dunmore's forces, and the men who arrived with him on Staten Island on August 13, 1776, were merely a remnant of his scattered corps. Fugitives from other states replenished their numbers, however, and Washington received worrisome reports that the British had organized a new regiment of some 800 black troops for their offensive in New York.[9]

In terms of numbers, the British force had reached full strength. It consisted of 24,000 soldiers who could be deployed quickly, using a portion of the nearly 400 transport ships, as well as smaller landing craft the British built on Staten Island. Thirty warships protected the transports and stood ready to support an invasion. Ten thousand sailors ensured that all of the fleet's intricate moving parts—the sails, rigging, cannon, and oars—could operate simultaneously. To the inexperienced American troops peering over the improvised dirt walls in front of their trenches, and even to their more seasoned officers, this massive display of British military might across the harbor was awesome and daunting.[10]

"I shall rite Soon. You will excuse my Shortness. there is seventeen more sail in the offing," William Douglas wrote to his wife on August 13, the day after von Heister arrived with his Hessians. The heightened sense that mortal combat was imminent came through in the staccato pace of his letter—and in his increasing emphasis on an afterlife. "I hope God will support us in the hour of Tryal and give us harts to play the man for our Cuntry and grant us victory to take to himself the glory," Douglas wrote. "I wish you and our Little ones Prosparious & Happy in this and the other world."

Douglas also expressed to his wife the particular sense of betrayal and outrage Americans felt at seeing German mercenaries arrive in New York to assist the British—who only recently had been their countrymen. "If the Hesien troops are Lucky as to fall into our hands," Douglas wrote, "I am in hopes they will meat with Such Treatment as Properly belongs to their Bloody Crime, for we have had no Dispute with them, but [they] have Turned themselves out as murderours of the Inosent."[11]

The powerful British warships were vulnerable in one respect, however. On the night of August 16, a band of daredevil patriots tried to set the *Rose* and *Phoenix* on fire by riding out into the Hudson north of the city aboard flaming vessels and latching on to the warships. In a letter to one of his brothers, a young captain from Connecticut named Nathan Hale described the attack, which was carried out by men from his company and regiment.

> Last Friday Night, two of our fire-vessels—a Sloop and Schooner—
> made an attempt upon the Shiping up the River. The night was too
> dark, the wind too Slack for the attempt. The Schooner, which was

intended for one of the Ships had got by before She discovered them; but as Providence would have it, she run athwart a bomb-catch* which she quickly burnt. The Sloop, by the light of the former discovered the *Phoenix*—but rather too late,—however she made Shift to grapple her, but the wind not proving sufficient to bring her close along side, or drive the flames immediately on board, the *Phoenix* after much difficulty got her clear by cutting her own rigging.

The incendiaries escaped into small whaleboats through an opening cut in the stern of each fire vessel,[12] and their work was valued highly, according to Hale: "The Gen. has been pleased to reward their bravery with Forty Dollars each except the Last man that quitted the Fire Sloop who had Fifty. Those on board the Schooner receive the Same."[13] While the physical damage was minimal, the struggle in the darkness gave the *Rose* and *Phoenix* an effective scare. By the eighteenth the British warships had sailed back down the Hudson from Tarrytown to rejoin the fleet.

"I must own that the present situation of the numerous fleet is extremely critical," Sir George Collier wrote in his journal, "as the rebels have six fire ships now in sight lying close under the cannon of the town; the first dark night when the wind blows strong down the river, they probably will send them in flames, to burn us, and I foresee if they attempt it the loss of half our transports and merchant ships—who from terror will cut their cables, fall aboard one another, and if not burnt will be wrecked on the shore."

Collier's fears were never fulfilled, but the threat to the fleet cost the British a great deal of sleep. "The Admiral has favored me with the post of honor, of lying advanced above all the shipping and nearest to the enemy; Collier wrote, "I therefore never go to bed during the night, nor do my officers, or men; as our safety (as well as the fleet's) depends on our vigilance."[14]

Despite their superiority in manpower, the Howes had greater concerns than fire ships. Admiral Howe's fleet was barely adequate to accomplish the ministry's objectives. With a total of seventy-three warships at his disposal in the North American squadron, the admiral was expected to support the army's operations in Quebec, Halifax, New York, and St. Augustine while blockad-

---

*A bomb ketch was a sailing vessel designed as a platform for one or two heavy mortars that pitched explosive shells in a high arc at targets on land.

ing all of American trade from Nova Scotia to Florida. Similarly, General Howe realized that he would need far more men than he had in order to conquer and hold the enormous expanses of territory in the American colonies. As he had told his constituents in England, the entire British army wasn't large enough for the task. Lord Germain was also aware of the problem and believed it would be solved when the vast, silent majority—the loyalists, whose numbers he consistently overestimated—were encouraged to rise up and throw off the tyranny of Congress. Until that time, General Howe had concluded that the best way to avoid a long and costly war was to capture Washington's army or destroy it in a single decisive battle.[15]

However, in the middle of August, when he was finally ready to launch his offensive, General Howe suddenly changed his strategy.[16] Instead of keeping to his stated goal of trapping the Americans, he decided to expel them from New York City and take control of the entire area. The commander in chief ignored Henry Clinton and William Tryon, who both urged him to land at Kingsbridge or Spuyten Duyvil—or any other point on Manhattan above the rebels—in order to cut them off from the mainland. Howe had set his sights on Long Island.

The flat, fertile island with its orchards, wheat, corn, and cattle would, Howe reasoned, make the army less dependent on its precarious supply lines, which stretched across the Atlantic. Long Island was also loyalist terrain, where inhabitants were likely to assist the British offensive. Heard's and Lee's efforts to neutralize the Tories had been ineffectual, and during the summer, General Nathanael Greene had been too busy building fortifications to hunt for "inimicals." New York City itself was Howe's main objective, but he recognized that seizing it first would put the British at the mercy of the American batteries on Brooklyn Heights, a repeat of what had caused the British to retreat from Boston. By invading Long Island, driving the rebels out of their fortifications, and then threatening New York City with artillery from Brooklyn Heights, Howe intended to accomplish his new objectives with a minimum of casualties.

In refusing to trap the rebels, Howe also began to rely less on ending the war with one battle and more on the hope that the rebellion would gradually disintegrate in the face of the British juggernaut. He planned to establish outposts on the borders of any newly conquered territory to defend it throughout the winter, because he believed the war would require at least one more campaign, starting in the spring.

This shift to a focus on territorial objectives—seizing high ground, water routes, and cities—was an embrace of traditional principles of military science as they were practiced in Europe and constituted a significant reversal for General Howe. He had been chosen to put down the American rebellion because of his experience with the unconventional tactics demanded by the New World. While contemporary documents are inconclusive about General Howe's precise motives, his brother's agenda as a peace commissioner may have been a major influence during the month since his arrival. Moreover, the bloodbath at Bunker Hill, the pounding the British had taken from American batteries at Charleston, and General Howe's overestimate of Washington's troop strength in New York probably all contributed to his adoption of a cautious, conservative approach. Hoping to protect his troops, he refused to divide them among Kingsbridge, Staten Island, and Long Island. These soldiers would soon be adept at fighting in the terrain of the colonies, and Howe regarded them, as he told Germain in a letter of August 6, as "the stock upon which the national force in America must in future be grafted."

While the Howes spent the summer waiting for reinforcements and adjusting their strategy, Washington's men completed and extended Charles Lee's original plans for the American defenses. In June Washington had decided to fortify the northern end of Manhattan in order to control King's Bridge and the Freebridge.[17]

The main northern citadel, soon named Fort Washington, was built on Manhattan's highest point, 230 feet above the Hudson River.* Designed by Colonel Rufus Putnam, the army's chief engineer and the general's cousin, the five-sided earthwork was enormous, but it was crudely constructed and lacked many essential features of an effective fortress, among them a barracks for the men and a well to provide water during a siege. Nonetheless, Putnam and the commander of its garrison, Colonel Robert Magaw, had every confidence in the fort. In the worst-case scenario, they believed, the garrison could be evacuated across the Hudson.

Below the fort, Jeffrey's Hook protruded into the Hudson, making this the narrowest point in the river for miles in either direction. After the incident of July 12, when the *Phoenix* and *Rose* sailed undeterred past a battery on the promontory and the guns of the fort-in-progress above it, the Americans had sent their own squadron of armed sloops under Colonel Benjamin Tupper up to Tarrytown, where they attacked the British ships

---

*The summit of this hill, known today as Washington Heights, is now occupied by Bennett Park. Markers in the ground indicate the site where part of the fort once stood.

with little effect. In the meantime, the Americans hastily sank obstructions, trying to close the gap between Jeffrey's Hook and the New Jersey shore behind the British warships. When the fire ships prompted the British to sail back down to the fleet, the warships managed to work their way around the obstructions without difficulty.

As a result, Washington also ordered the construction of Fort Constitution, later called Fort Lee, directly across the Hudson from Fort Washington in order to aim guns from both shores at the line of obstructions in the river. Fort Independence was added on Fordham Heights in Westchester to support Fort Washington and protect King's Bridge from the north.

On Long Island, Rufus Putnam had augmented Lee's plan in order to protect Brooklyn Heights and the forts Stirling had built there from a possible attack not only from the East River but also from the rear, finally recognizing the potential threat from the interior of Kings County. Farther inland and southeast of Brooklyn Heights, newly promoted Major General Nathanael Greene had put his 4,000 troops to work on a new chain of forts, redoubts, and connecting trenches a mile and a half long that lay like a beaded choker across the neck of the peninsula.[18]

Unlike the much larger Fort Washington, these five redoubts were carefully finished.[19] Each was surrounded by a wide ditch, as were the breastworks that linked them. The sides of the forts bristled with sharpened stakes to deter the British from storming the walls. The surrounding woods had been cut down to expose the enemy fully to the forts' cannons, and the felled trees stacked as an additional barrier along most of the perimeter. At both ends of the line— Wallabout Bay in the north and the Gowanus Marsh in the south—the trenches continued from the last fort to the water's edge, thus sealing off the peninsula.* On his right flank, Greene built a pair of V-shaped batteries pointing at a milldam across Gowanus Creek. To the left of the milldam, he left a gap in the defensive line because the creek itself provided a natural barrier.

At the center of the line, the Jamaica Road (connecting the Brooklyn Ferry with the farms of eastern Long Island) ran through the defenses. Rufus Putnam had designed the forts so that the line dipped inward here: He

---

*"Brooklyn" is the anglicized spelling and pronunciation of *breukelen,* a Dutch word meaning "marshland." Soft and spongy because it was the bed of a valley, the ground received the runoff from the surrounding hills. Gowanus Creek was a snaking tidal inlet that penetrated the peninsula from Gowanus Cove and was surrounded by an extensive marsh. Local farmers supplemented their diet and incomes by harvesting oysters from the creek, and the motion of the tides worked the mills that were built along its course (Johnston, *Campaign,* pt. 1:45 note and pt. 1:47; Parry, *Life at the Old Stone House,* pp. 1, 17).

Cobble Hill Fort

expected the British to approach on the Jamaica Road, and hoped to draw them into this pocket, where they would be caught in a cross fire. Three more forts stood on the peninsula inside this principal line. On Red Hook, the four guns of Fort Defiance guarded the channel between Governors Island and Brooklyn to discourage a British landing on the western tip of the peninsula. If the British landed behind the fort or crossed Gowanus Creek to get around the main line of fortifications, they would be met with fire from the four guns of the Cobble Hill Fort located at the center of the peninsula. Fort Stirling stood at the Brooklyn shore.

Washington had been immediately impressed by Nathanael Greene during the siege of Boston, when the thirty-three-year-old arrived from Rhode Island at the head of a meticulously organized and fully equipped contingent of 1,500 men that put the ragtag Continental Army to shame.[20] Greene managed his troops the way he had helped run his father's thriving foundry, one of the largest in Rhode Island. A Quaker, Greene had renounced the Friends' philosophy of nonviolence and was expelled from his congregation in 1773, when he first joined the militia in order to resist British policies. But he had trouble rising through the ranks because other officers said he didn't have the look of a commander: Greene was overweight, walked with a limp, and had one eye that was clouded by a bout with smallpox. However, his calm demeanor inspired confidence, and politics soon offered a better path: He was elected to the Rhode Island legislature and then appointed brigadier general of the state's "Army of Observation," which he led to Boston.

General Nathanael Greene

Beyond his basic training in the militia, everything Greene knew about strategy and warfare he had taught himself from books. Since he had grown up in the foundry hammering iron ship anchors and chains, while receiving some tutoring in Latin and math at home, he had far less formal education than some of his genteel counterparts in the Continental Army. Nonetheless, Greene's performance in Boston quickly earned him Washington's trust and a reputation as his best general. Charles Lee was technically the army's second ranking officer, but Greene was the favorite to replace the commander in chief in the event of his death or capture.

The excavation and construction of the Brooklyn defenses required an enormous amount of labor, and when a soldier took his shift with pick and shovel, he was said to be "on fatigue duty." When the exhausted men shed their filthy clothes and sought relief from the summer heat, they quickly got into trouble with the locals. "Complaints have been made by the inhabitants situated near the Mill Pond," Greene announced in his general orders, "that some of the soldiers come there to go swimming in the open view of the women and that they come out of the water and run to the houses naked with a design to insult and wound the modesty of female decency." He warned that such "beastly conduct" would be punished "with the utmost severity."[21]

Ultimately, the soldiers' habit of relieving themselves in the ditches around the forts proved to have the most serious consequences. By August, a new and invisible enemy had breached the walls: Fecal contamination caused the spread of typhoid fever, while many of those who lived in tents at the fortifications were struck down with typhus, carried by infected lice. Not considered distinct diseases, together they were called "putrid fever," and the symptoms—diarrhea, high fever, and prostration—lasted for weeks.[22] Compounding the situation, the water from public pumps was no longer safe. "The air of the whole city seems infected," wrote Solomon Drowne, an American doctor. "In almost every street there is a horrid smell."[23]

Fully a quarter of Washington's army was out of commission, as thousands of men found themselves in makeshift hospitals. Along with King's College, the mansions of wealthy loyalists outside the city in Bloomingdale, Greenwich, and Kips Bay were taken over, while nurses were sought through ads in the newspapers. Still, the men overflowed outside. "In almost every barn, stable, shed, and even under the fences and bushes, were the sick to be seen."[24]

In Brooklyn General Greene fell ill with a high fever on August 15 and was ferried back to Manhattan. At a crucial moment, Washington was suddenly and indefinitely deprived of the trusted commander who was most familiar with the essential Brooklyn Heights defenses—and, more important, with the intricacies of the surrounding terrain.

To fill Greene's command until he recovered, Washington made a choice on August 20 that was frowned on by some of his staff. General John Sullivan had recently returned from the fighting in Canada, and not in triumph.[25] When he and General William Thompson had arrived in Canada with their ten regiments in early June, Sullivan tried to resurrect the crumbling Canadian expedition, but at Montreal Benedict Arnold convinced him it was time to cut their losses and head south to Crown Point on Lake Champlain. Smallpox was ravaging the troops, as were malaria and dysentery, and Sullivan found he had arrived just in time to preside over a retreating, demoralized army. The Canadian expedition, which had begun with high hopes ten months earlier under Richard Montgomery, had finally collapsed. All that remained was to take defensive action against the imminent British invasion of northern New York: Arnold set his men to work building a fleet of gunboats to confront Carleton's forces on Lake Champlain, forcing Carleton to waste the precious summer months building a fleet of his own.

Soon after the retreat, Sullivan's pride had been hurt further when he learned that, as a last-ditch effort, Congress had promoted Horatio Gates over

General John Sullivan

him to lead the troops in Canada as General Schuyler's second-in-command in the Northern Department. Infuriated, Sullivan requested a leave of absence and stormed down to Philadelphia to submit his resignation. Calmed down by his friends, he resolved his differences with Congress and was sent to New York and soon promoted to the rank of major general.[26]

Sullivan was unaware that Washington's assessment of him was largely responsible for his being superseded by Gates. In an evaluation he sent to Congress in June, Washington wrote that despite Sullivan's strengths, he also had "wants" and "foibles." The "latter are manifested in a little tincture of vanity, and in an over desire of being popular, which now and then leads him into some embarrassments." However, Washington softened his critique when it came to Sullivan's relative lack of military experience, frankly expressing doubts about his own ability to manage the impending campaign in New York. "His wants are common to us all; the want of experience to move upon a large Scale; for the limited, and contracted knowledge which any of us have in Military Matters stands in very little Stead; and is greatly over balanced by sound judgement, and some knowledge of Men and Books; especially when accompanied by an enterprizing genius, which I must do Genl. Sullivan the justice to say, I think he possesses . . ."[27] In appointing him to command the Brooklyn lines, Washington clearly hoped Sullivan's initiative and energy would compensate for his shortcomings.

As it happened, Sullivan made the final and ultimately the most important addition to Charles Lee's scheme of defense: He decided to take advantage of the natural barrier provided by Gowanus Heights, a densely wooded ridge running parallel to the chain of redoubts two miles to the south.[28] Part of the terminal moraine—a ridge that runs the length of Long Island and was formed when the last glacier of the ice age deposited the rocks and soil in its path and then retreated—the hills run roughly east-west and, at that time, overlooked the patchwork of Dutch towns and farms that spread southward across the glacier's sandy but fertile outwash plain, where the nutrients from the soil in the terminal moraine had washed down from its outer slope.[29]*

To attack the American fortifications at the base of the peninsula, it was clear the British would have to go through one of the four passes where roads crossed the ridge through its natural depressions—from west to east, the Martense Lane, Flatbush, Bedford, and Jamaica Passes. At the three western-most passes Sullivan set his troops to work cutting down trees for roadblocks and throwing up breastworks where guns could be mounted. He planned to station some 800 men at each pass, where they could attack the advancing British forces and then drop back to the American fortifications. However, in part because it was farther away, Sullivan made no such preparations at the fourth ravine through Gowanus Heights, on the American left wing—a "deep winding cut," four miles from the Brooklyn Heights fortifications: the Jamaica Pass.[30]

The Howe brothers had begun embarking their invasion force on Sunday, August 18, the same day that the *Phoenix* and *Rose* returned from their trip up the Hudson. Because of stormy weather, it took several days to get 15,000 men on the transports. Colonel Edward Hand, whose riflemen had been patrolling the Long Island shore, reported late in the afternoon of the twenty-first that "at least fourteen sail of transports, some of them crowded with men, now under sail; and more, from the noise, are hoisting anchor."[31]

Early that evening, a courier came to Manhattan from New Jersey with further details. The previous night, Brigadier General William Livingston, former head of the Whig Triumvirate and currently the commander of the New Jersey militia, had sent the courier to Staten Island, where he had made contact with a resident agent, probably a member of the Mersereau family, which spied for Washington throughout the war.[32] According to the courier, the agent claimed to have infiltrated the British camp and eavesdropped on a discussion in which orders for a three-pronged night attack were given to the generals. Some 20,000 men—already embarked on transport ships—

---

*Today, the names of Queens and Brooklyn neighborhoods reflect the primordial topography: Jamaica Hills, Crown Heights, and Bay Ridge overlook Flatbush and Flatlands (Burrows and Wallace, *Gotham,* p. 4).

were to land on Long Island and up the Hudson, while another 15,000, still being held in reserve on Staten Island, would later cross over to New Jersey for attacks on Bergen Point, Elizabeth, and Amboy.[33]

With his army already spread out in a precarious line that stretched all the way from New Jersey to Brooklyn via Kingsbridge, New York City, and Governors Island, Washington had anticipated an attack in all of these locations. However, his forces straddled two rivers, and it was clear that if British ships took control of the Hudson or the East River, the American army would be divided into several parts that could easily be trapped. The American troops were put on alert for the possible night attack.

Instead came an ominous, destructive event that felt, at least to one witness, even more unsettling than a clash of arms.[34] Major Abner Benedict looked toward the city from the ramparts on Brooklyn Heights that evening at about seven. "In the west slowly rose a thunder-cloud . . . which seemed solid as marble," Benedict later told a friend; it blocked out the sun "like a total eclipse, and sudden darkness fell on sea and land." The cloud, "surcharged with electricity," rose higher and higher, and "the deep reverberations that rolled along the heavens without intermission" sounded like waves crashing on the shore.

Soon it began to rain.

> All before had been the skirmishing that precedes the battle, but now like some huge monster that cloud suddenly gaped and shot forth flame. Then followed a crash louder than a thousand cannon discharged at once. It was appalling. The soldiers involuntarily cowered before it. In a few moments the entire heavens became black as ink, and from horizon to horizon the whole empyrean was ablaze with lightning, while the thunder that followed did not come in successive peals, but in one long and continuous crash, as if the very frame work of the skies was falling to pieces, accompanied with a confused sound, as though the fragments were tumbling into a profound abyss. The lightning fell in masses and sheets of fire to the earth, and seemed to be striking incessantly and on every side. . . . The fort was as silent as the grave, for the strongest heart bent before this exhibition of God's terrible majesty. It did not pass away like an ordinary shower, for the cloud appeared to stand still, and swing round and round like a horizontal wheel over the devoted city. It clung to it with a tenacity that was frightful.

Benedict theorized that "the vast amount of arms collected in and about the city held it by attraction and drew from it such a fearful amount of electricity."

The storm finally ended three hours later, and reports came in the following morning "of the devastation and death the storm had spread around." Benedict reported that "the excitement could hardly have been greater, and the returns caused more surprise, if there had been a night attack on the camp." Casualties included a soldier who had no visible injury but "was struck deaf, dumb, and blind," according to Benedict.

> A captain and two lieutenants belonging to McDougall's regiment were killed by one thunderbolt; the points of their swords melted off, and the coin melted in their pockets. Their bodies appeared as if they had been roasted, so black and crisped was the skin. Ten men camped outside the fort near the river . . . were killed in a single flash. . . .
>
> In battle we hear the roar of the guns, and after the smoke and tumult have passed away, we expect to see bleeding and mangled forms scattered around. But there seems a hidden meaning, some secret purpose, when the bolt is launched, by an invisible arm, and from the mysterious depths of space.

CHAPTER 8

The Invasion of Long Island

~◡

A t nine A.M. Admiral Howe fired a signal gun from the deck of his flagship, raised a blue-and-white ensign, and watched 1,000 oars dip in unison below the calm surface of Gravesend Bay. The morning of Thursday, August 22, had broken clear and bright following the thunderstorm, and the lush farmland of Long Island glistened after the rain. The advance corps of 4,000 troops under Clinton and Cornwallis had just waded ashore, as a second wave of landing craft broke away from the line of transports in the bay and rowed briskly toward the beach. The empty troop-ships were then displaced by another set of transports, which in turn filled the next contingent of flatboats.[1]

To escort the seventy-five flatboats, the British had built eleven bateaux and two galleys over the summer, smaller craft with shallow drafts that moved in over the shoals close to the Gravesend beach while firing from guns mounted in their bows. The frigates *Phoenix*, *Rose*, and *Greyhound*—their sails spread out to dry in the hot sun and their broadsides aimed at the shore—protected the entire landing operation. Two bomb vessels—*Carcass* and *Thunder*—also stood by, equipped with mortars that could pitch explosive shells in a high arc over the flotilla and onto the shore.[2]

Just to the north, at the Narrows, Sir George Collier aimed the *Rainbow*'s guns at Denyse's Ferry, a stone building from which General Greene had harassed the arriving fleet with some

British landing craft approaching Brooklyn, August 22, 1776.

light artillery in July.* Collier's position also commanded the Gowanus Road, the route the Americans would have used to send reinforcements to the landing site; it ran along the shore and linked Denyse's with the Brooklyn Ferry.[3]

However, the Americans made no move to contest the landing, and it proceeded smoothly. The surface of the bay teemed with more than 400 vessels, moving forward and dropping away in orderly procession. Admiral Howe's secretary, Ambrose Serle, was delirious: "In a Word, the Disembarkation of about 15,000 Troops upon a fine Beach, their forming upon the adjacent Plain . . . exhibited one of the finest & most picturesque Scenes that the Imagination can fancy or the Eye behold."[4]

The beauty of the landing for the British was also in its efficiency. The British grenadiers and light infantry, the Scottish Highlanders, and the Hessians had all embarked before dawn, but once the boats were towed into position at Gravesend Bay, it took a mere three hours—from nine until noon—to row them ashore. The landing craft they had built on Staten Island—with hinged flat bows that became ramps—also facilitated the arrival

---

*Today the Verrazano Narrows Bridge meets the Brooklyn shore where Denyse's Ferry once stood, and the Belt Parkway passes under the bridge next to a promenade at the water's edge. Above the parkway sits Fort Hamilton, an army base. To the south, where the British landed, lies Dyker Beach Park.

of forty pieces of artillery on Long Island. The fleet continued to bring over the army's baggage, supplies, wagons, and horses, while General Howe dispatched his troops to occupy southern Kings County, in a line roughly parallel to the American positions on Gowanus Heights to the north. The Gowanus Road curved to the east just below Denyse's Ferry and continued through the townships of New Utrecht, Gravesend, and Flatlands. Howe's army encamped along an eight-mile arc between Denyse's Ferry on the west and the marshes of Jamaica Bay on the east.[5]

Howe immediately sent General Cornwallis north with a substantial detachment of men and six fieldpieces to seize the village of Flatbush and probe the American defenses at the Flatbush Pass. Colonel Edward Hand, whose regiment of Pennsylvania riflemen had been patrolling Kings County since April, had gathered 300 of them near the beach where the British landed, but decided an attack would have been futile and withdrew to the wooded heights above Flatbush.* As they pulled back, Hand's riflemen harassed Conwallis's left flank and set fire to the grain and forage the British needed for their horses. Hand's scorched-earth campaign was made easier by a last-minute decree from the Provincial Congress forcing local farmers to stack their hay and wheat in the fields so that it was ready to burn. The battle had not begun, but already eyewitnesses in Manhattan saw columns of smoke rising from Long Island.[6]

"Crack! Crack! An alarm from Red-Hook. Crack! Crack! Crack! The alarm repeated from Cobble-Hill," an American chaplain on Long Island wrote in his journal on the morning of August 22. "Orders are given for the drums to beat *to arms.* The enemy have been landing for some time down at the Narrows, and, it is said, have now ashore several thousand."[7] Washington was at his headquarters in Manhattan when the guns at the Brooklyn forts alerted him to the British invasion. Detailed verbal reports brought to the Brooklyn lines by messengers from Colonel Hand's rifle regiment were then ferried across to Manhattan, though at this stage they were extremely inaccurate: They informed Washington that about 8,000 British troops had landed on Long Island, probably based on the assumption that Cornwallis's detachment was the entire invasion force.[8]

Since the agent's report from Staten Island the night before asserted that 20,000 British troops had been embarked for an attack "on Long Island and

---

*Now the hills in Prospect Park.

up the North River,"[9] Washington assumed the landing of the 8,000 on Long Island was a feint, and that the remaining 12,000 troops were still on the transports, ready to land at Kingsbridge for a descent on New York City. Washington believed they were trying "to draw our Force to that Quarter, when their real design may perhaps be on this."[10]

Underestimating the size of the invasion, Washington sent only six regiments* to reinforce General Sullivan on Long Island, who braced for an all-out attack. That night, Sullivan ordered all officers and men at the Brooklyn lines and on Gowanus Heights who were not on guard duty to sleep in their clothes with their muskets in their arms.

Despite the sleepless night in all of the American camps, Colonel William Douglas wrote to his wife from Manhattan the next day, Friday, August 23: "our troops are Rally in high Sperits & it is a General voice Let them come on as soon as they Can or Dare."[11] Still the attack did not come, and the day was spent in small skirmishes.

That morning, American troops with artillery support emerged from the woods at Flatbush Pass and attacked the Hessian guards posted just north of Cornwallis's camp in Flatbush village, an engagement in which Hand's Pennsylvania riflemen saw their vaunted Hessian counterparts face-to-face for the first time. The Americans drove the Hessian sentries back toward the village, burned several houses where they had established outposts, and dragged at least one corpse back to the hills as evidence of their contact with this fearsome enemy.[12] "The Idea which we at first conceived of the Hessian riflemen was truly ridiculous," an American officer wrote shortly after the attack, "but sad experience convinces our people that they are an Enemy not to be despised."[13]

In the afternoon the Highlanders brought up two cannons from the village and mounted them on a breastwork across the Flatbush Road, and an exchange of artillery fire lasted for the rest of the day. At the same time, Admiral Howe's ships traded cannon fire with the battery at Red Hook as they tried to work their way up through the channel between Governors

---

*Continental Army regiments were supposed to consist of a little more than 700 men (eight companies of 76 soldiers plus officers). In reality, however, a regiment might have as few as 100 men, and a brigade, composed of several regiments, often had only 200 or 300 men. Eventually, in practice, any combination of units commanded by a brigadier general was considered a brigade, while a colonel commanded each regiment. A battalion was a smaller unit under a lieutenant colonel that served independently or as part of a regiment. British regiments officially consisted of ten companies of 38 soldiers plus officers, but they also varied in size from 300 to 1,000 men (Symonds, *A Battlefield Atlas*, p. 1; Manders, *The Battle of Long Island*, p. 4).

Island and the Brooklyn shore, in order to enter the East River and bombard the Brooklyn Heights forts, but the wind was against them.

Also on the twenty-third, Washington began taking daily trips to Long Island in order to assess the British threat. He still suspected the Gravesend landing might be a diversion, but the arrival of new militia units from Connecticut allowed him to send four more regiments to Sullivan on Long Island with the understanding that they would return immediately if Admiral Howe's fleet moved against the city. The reinforcements enabled General Sullivan to keep larger contingents at each of the three main approaches to the Brooklyn plateau: the Martense Lane, Flatbush, and Bedford Passes. Washington also had General Heath dispatch 1,000 men under General Thomas Mifflin from Kingsbridge down to Bloomingdale, overlooking the Hudson River, where the agent had indicated the British fleet might land more troops. From here, Mifflin could observe the Hudson and also be ready to move forward to Brooklyn or back to Kingsbridge.[14]

After his visit to Long Island on Saturday, August 24, Washington wrote to Putnam that he was concerned about "a scattering, unmeaning, & wasteful fire, from our people at the enemy," and ordered a stop to the undisciplined skirmishing of the past two days. Not only did the American riflemen's frontier tactics of shooting whenever they pleased serve to discourage deserters from crossing over to the American camp, Washington wrote, but "as we know not the hour of the enemy's approach to our lines but have every reason to apprehend that it will be sudden & violent, whenever attempted; we shall have our men so scattered & (more than probable) without ammunition, that the consequences must prove fatal to us."[15] Straining to anticipate the British offensive, Washington wanted no distractions or false alarms.

By Sunday the best evidence of British intentions had started to come from Staten Island, where they were striking their tents and once again sending ships down through the Narrows to Gravesend Bay. Belatedly, Washington concluded that "they mean to land the Main Body of their Army on Long Island, and make their grand push there," and he sent over six more regiments from Manhattan.[16] To make up for the fact that these thousands of men had no common uniform, Sullivan's orders stated that "All troops in this department are desired to wear a green bough or branch of a tree in their hats, till further orders."[17] The brigades were placed under the command of Brigadier Generals Heard, Stirling, John Nixon, and Samuel Parsons.

Parsons was a Harvard-trained lawyer who settled in Lyme, Connecticut, entered politics, and became active in the resistance movement against Britain. He had served eighteen consecutive terms in the state's assembly, where he advocated colonial unity and is credited with originating the plan for the first colonial congress—the Stamp Act Congress, which met in New York City in 1765. Parsons started as a major in the state's militia, became a colonel in April 1775, and in May joined the Continental Army. After helping to plan the capture of Ticonderoga and participating in the siege of Boston, Parsons came to New York, where he had just been promoted to brigadier general on August 9.[18]

Because so many reinforcements had been concentrated on Long Island, Israel Putnam—one of the original five major generals appointed by Congress, and Washington's highest-ranking subordinate in New York—was entitled to assume command there, and when he requested the assignment, Washington agreed to it. For the second time that summer, Sullivan was superseded. Yet even as Washington did so, he adopted Sullivan's significant modification of Lee's and Greene's plans for defending the peninsula and embraced it as his main strategy for the coming battle: Washington ordered Putnam to put his best troops at the passes and prevent the British from ever reaching the man-made fortifications. These men should defend the natural barrier, Washington wrote, and "at all hazards prevent the Enemy's passing the Wood and approaching your Works."[19]

While Washington brought over reinforcements, General Howe used political means to bolster his own position on Long Island. He issued a proclamation, which was distributed as a handbill and promised those "forced into Rebellion, that on delivering themselves up at the Head Quarters of the army, they will be received as faithful Subjects; have Permits to return peaceably to their respective Dwellings, and meet with full Protection for their Persons and Property." Anyone "willing to take up Arms for the Restoration of Order and Good Government within this Island," the proclamation continued, "shall be disposed of in the best Manner, and have every Encouragement that can be expected."[20] Howe's army had already absorbed the militia of the four townships in southern Kings County, and the proclamation drew little additional response. However, quality proved to be more important than quantity in this case, and Howe gained what he needed: a few knowledgeable Tory guides and spies.[21]

Howe also brought over additional troops and field artillery. On Sunday, the twenty-fifth, the ships that the Americans had seen heading through the Narrows to Gravesend Bay landed some 4,300 Hessians under

General von Heister, bringing Howe's forces on Long Island to almost 20,000. He left between 3,000 and 4,000 men on Staten Island and apparently tried to reinforce Washington's misconception, which had not been kept secret, that only 8,000 British troops were on Long Island. Howe used his cavalry to prevent American scouts from penetrating southern Kings County, where they might have spied on the British encampments, and he seems to have disseminated this estimate of 8,000 with Americans he detained and released, as well as with his own troops, some of whom deserted bearing this disinformation.[22]

"I have but a moment of time to rite as the boat is waiting," Colonel William Douglas told his wife before crossing over to Long Island with part of his regiment on Monday, the twenty-sixth. "The two armies are Intrenched on Long Island and very near to each other. . . . both lines are constantly Reinforcing, and by all appearance a Generall Action Cant be far off." In the postscript he offered a prayer for his children: "I hope God will be their God and Father."[23] By the evening, when Washington completed his daily inspection of the Brooklyn lines, it was the Americans who had 8,000 to 9,000 troops on Long Island.[24] Washington had gradually become convinced that the main attack would take place there, and he brought over as many troops as possible without leaving New York undefended.

Despite the reinforcements, given that most American regiments were reduced by camp fever to some three-quarters of their full strength, the Americans were actually outnumbered by more than two to one by Howe's forces. Since most of the American troops remained within the fortifications, the 3,000 who were stationed outside the lines, on Gowanus Heights, were outnumbered by almost seven to one.[25]

On the eve of the battle, General Parsons was in overall command of the Gowanus Heights deployments.[26] Stirling commanded the American right wing (the Gowanus Road and Martense Lane Pass) with Sullivan on the left and center, which included the Bedford and Flatbush Passes. Under orders from Putnam, who directed the entire Long Island operation from his headquarters inside the American lines on Brooklyn Heights, there were about 800 men at each of the three western passes and 300 more in the woods just north of Gowanus Creek, protecting the gap between Red Hook and the western end of the American lines. On the American left flank, in the east, Colonel Samuel Miles's two battalions of riflemen were stationed on the ridge between the Bedford and Jamaica Passes. According to Parsons, Miles

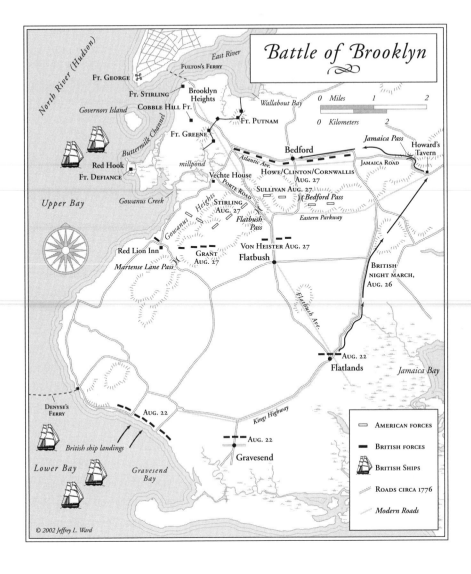

Battle of Brooklyn

was "to watch the motion of the enemy on that part, with orders to keep a party constantly reconnoitering to and across the Jamaica Road." Along this six-mile perimeter from one end of the Heights to the other, "sentinels were so placed as to keep a constant communication between the three guards on the three roads," Parsons wrote to John Adams.[27]

Miles had also discovered, through the persistence of his scouts, that the British were concealing a substantial number of troops to the south, in particular a contingent at Flatlands (the easternmost village on the crescent of British encampments) that was well positioned to come through the Jamaica Pass. Miles also noticed that Cornwallis had moved all of his troops out of Flatbush to Flatlands village and replaced them with Hessians, a clear indication that the main thrust would not be at the center, as expected, but farther east.[28]

"On the landing of the British army on Long Island, I was ordered over with my rifle regiment to watch their motions," Miles wrote.

> I marched near to the village of Flatbush, where the Highlanders then lay, but they moved the next day to Gen'l Howe's camp, and their place was supplied by the Hessians. I lay here within cannon shot of the Hessian camp for four days without receiving a single order from Gen'l Sullivan. . . . The day before the action he came to the camp, and I then told him the situation of the British army; that Gen'l Howe, with the main body, lay on my left, about a mile and a half or two miles, and I was convinced when the army moved that Gen'l Howe would fall into the Jamaica road, and I hoped there were troops there to watch them. Notwithstanding this information, which indeed he might have obtained from his own observation, if he had attended to his duty as a general ought to have done, no steps were taken, but there was a small redoubt in front of the village which seemed to take up the whole of his attention.[29]

For his part, Sullivan lamented a lack of troops. "I was very uneasy about a road through which I had often foretold the enemy would come, but could not persuade others to be of my opinion. . . . I had paid horsemen fifty dollars [of his own money] for patrolling by night, while I had the command, as I had no foot for the purpose."[30] He barely had cavalry either: The patrol that he stationed in the Jamaica Pass consisted of just five officers on horseback.

Washington had earlier declined the services of a cavalry unit from Connecticut because he didn't want the burden of feeding their 400 mounts, and the men had refused to serve as infantry. The local cavalry from Kings County was busy helping Brigadier General Nathaniel Woodhull, the commander of the Queens and Suffolk County militias, drive all the remaining horses, cattle, and sheep on western Long Island east to Hempstead Plains, where they could be guarded and kept away from the British army.[31]*

---

*Woodhull's belated and halfhearted herding efforts angered Washington, who had information that the British were short of provisions and had warned the New York Provincial Congress earlier in the summer not to let the livestock fall into their hands. The Provincial Congress, of which Woodhull was president, had declined to take action until the last minute (Field, *The Battle of Long Island*, pt. 1: 289–90).

So Sullivan settled for what he had and ordered his scouts to gallop back and notify Miles if the British arrived at the Jamaica Pass, so his riflemen could shift from the ridge, facing south, to the Jamaica Road, where they could stall the enemy advance from the east until they received reinforcements.

One of Miles's subordinates, Lieutenant Colonel Daniel Brodhead, also complained that the American high command failed to put enough men on the left flank on the eve of the battle. "Gen'ls Putnam and Sullivan and others came to our camp which was to the left of all the other posts and proceeded to reconnoiter the enemie's lines to the right, when from the movements of the enemy they might plainly discover they were advancing towards Jamaica, and extending their lines to the left so as to march round us."[32]

Brodhead refrained from naming the commander in chief, though Washington was among the "others" with Putnam and Sullivan studying the enemy positions through their spyglasses from the Flatbush Pass. Whether or not Washington fully inspected and approved the disposition of the troops on Gowanus Heights before he returned to Manhattan on the evening of the twenty-sixth is not known. In either case, Washington's "want of experience to move upon a large Scale," which he had confessed to in his letter to Congress regarding Sullivan in June, clearly affected his judgment. The reshuffling of British troops at Flatbush, a clear signal of intent, merely led him to "apprehend they would in a little time make a general attack."[33]

Washington's tactics may have been muddled, but his words to the troops that night were unambiguous. While he gave orders that any man who attempted "to skulk, lay down, or retreat without Orders" would be "instantly shot down as an example," he sought to inspire his men with patriotism as well as fear. "The Enemy have now landed on Long Island, and the hour is fast approaching on which the Honor and Success of this army and the safety of our bleeding Country depend," he told the soldiers. He reminded them of the American victories at Boston and Charleston, which showed "what a few brave men contending in their own land, and in the best of causes can do, against base hirelings and mercenaries."[34]

The troop movement detected by Miles and Brodhead was a sign that General Howe had grudgingly accepted Henry Clinton's daring plan for seizing the Jamaica Pass. Only a day earlier, on the twenty-fifth, the proposal had been ridiculed and rejected at headquarters—not surprisingly, since Howe and his second-in-command had not been on speaking terms since the landing on Long Island. Clinton's advice about striking at Kingsbridge had been ignored, and he disapproved of almost every other aspect of Howe's handling of the New York campaign. Howe in turn resented Clinton's presumption in deluging him with advice. "My zeal," Clinton admitted later, "may perhaps on these occasions have carried me so far as to be at times thought troublesome."[35]

Motivated by a desire to crush the rebellion, Clinton wrote, "I could not be satisfied with being a mere passive machine that was only to act as directed." He added, disingenuously: "I thought it my duty likewise, though a subordinate officer, to sometimes exercise my own eyes and understanding in examining the face of the country and the positions and strength of the enemy, and to take the liberty of humbly submitting to the Commander in Chief, when he permitted me, such measures for that purpose as my observations suggested."[36]

Clinton, whose knowledge of Long Island dated back to his youth in New York as the governor's son, had reconnoitered the area on the twenty-fourth. He came up with a plan to encircle the Americans on Gowanus Heights by sneaking around their left wing at the Jamaica Pass, an ambitious adaptation of a classic maneuver known as "turning the enemy's flank." After submitting it to Howe through an intermediary the next day, Clinton then had to wait a day, during which he knew only that his proposal "did not seem to be much relished."[37]

"The position which the rebels occupy in our front may be turned by a gorge [the Jamaica Pass] about six miles from us, through a country in which cavalry may make the *avant garde*," Clinton had written in his plan.

> That, once possessed, gives us the island; and in a mile or two further we shall be on the communications with their works at Brooklyn. The corps which attempts to turn this flank must be in very great force, for reasons too obvious to require detailing. The attack should begin on the enemy's right by signal; and a share taken in it even by the fleet, which (as the tide will then suit) may get under way and make every demonstration of forcing the enemy's batteries in the East River, without, however, committing themselves. The efforts to be made by the army will be along the *dos d'ane** at the points of Flatbush, New Utrecht, etc. These the principal; many other small ones to cooperate. They should all be vigorous but not too obstinately persisted in, except that which is

*The donkey's back, the ridge of Gowanus Heights.

designed to turn the left of the rebels, which should be pushed as far as it will go. The moment the corps gets possession of the pass above Howard's House* the rebels must quit directly or be ruined.[38]

Clearly, there was nothing humble about Clinton's condescending tone, and his brash assertion of the plan's inevitable success smoothed over the fact that a substantial British column would have to traverse six miles of unknown territory at night, inviting an ambush at every bridge and ravine and from the woods that lined the route. At headquarters, Major General James Grant favored the simpler approach of smashing directly through the nearby passes. He had fought on the American frontier during the Seven Years' War and had recently boasted in Parliament that with 5,000 men he could march the entire length of the continent and the rebels would be helpless to stop him. He also felt superior to Clinton, who had received his training in Europe, in the "German school," during that war. Howe and his staff took turns condemning the plan as a piece of "German jargon," with the commander in chief reportedly adding the inane remark that "as the rebels knew nothing of turning a flank, such a movement would have *no* effect."[39]

Then on August 26, after Oliver De Lancey assured Howe that with the help of local guides the terrain would be easy to cross even in the dark, he changed his mind.[40] Clinton had proposed that the expedition "begin to move at nightfall, so that everything may be at its ground by daybreak; and that light infantry and chasseurs may cover its left flank in such strength as to effectually prevent the enemy's patrols from forcing them and thereby making a discovery of our intentions."[41] Howe summoned Clinton to headquarters and instructed him to put his plan into action that evening.

Cornwallis marched his units down from Flatbush to join Clinton, and at eight P.M. on the twenty-sixth, according to plan, the advance corps of about 4,000 troops with fourteen pieces of field artillery moved out from Flatlands in a long, narrow, and tightly formed column. This advance formation alone outnumbered the American troops stationed on Gowanus Heights. Clinton made every effort to conceal his movement by leaving campfires burning and positioning an entire regiment to make ordinary campground sounds, "for the purpose of drowning the noise of our cannons over the stones, masking our march, and preventing the enemy's patrols from discovering it."[42] Any inhabitants in the path of the column or its flanking guards were immediately captured to prevent an alarm from spreading by word of mouth.

---

*The Jamaica Pass, near an inn on the Jamaica Road.

Oliver De Lancey and his son, Oliver Jr., a cavalry officer, marched in the column, as did three loyalist guides, who chose an indirect route to the Jamaica Pass in order to keep their distance from Miles and his riflemen on the American left. Moving slowly along the edge of the woods and marshes around Jamaica Bay and toward the village of New Lots, the entire column came to a halt at a bridge over a saltwater creek, where the jittery British commanders sent out skirmishing parties to detect an ambush in the darkness. To their amazement and relief, the Americans had completely neglected a potentially devastating choke point.[43]

Nonetheless, the British remained on edge. "Between eleven and twelve o'clock, being in a lane, we heard much firing in the rear of the column," Clinton later recalled, "which made me hasten to get into the open fields which cross the country to the Jamaica road. It, however, turned out nothing, and we continued our march unmolested."[44] The firing probably came from the sentry posts above Flatbush village, where Colonel Thomas Knowlton's Rangers were attempting to capture a Hessian guard and were mistakenly fired on by American militiamen who hadn't been informed of the mission. Had General Nathaniel Woodhull remained in the "open fields" where he and his militia had been driving cattle only hours earlier, Clinton's secret night march would almost certainly have been discovered and an alarm sounded. Less than two miles to the east, however, along the county line, Woodhull remained unaware of Clinton's progress.[45]

At about two A.M., according to Clinton, "my guides informed me we were within a quarter of a mile of Howard's House, which was only a few hundred yards from the gorge I wished to lay hold of. Upon this I immediately sent forward a patrol to examine if it was occupied, which, falling in with another belonging to the enemy composed of five officers, had fortunately the address to take them all without noise."[46] General Sullivan's mounted guards had positioned themselves in front of the pass since they expected the British to advance along the Jamaica Road. By leaving the roads and cutting across the fields, Clinton's patrol had seized them from behind.[47]

Unaware of what a critical blow had just been struck—that these five officers were the only Americans guarding the Jamaica approach to the Brooklyn forts—Clinton interrogated the prisoners to find out if the pass was manned. "Finding by their report that the gorge was not occupied, I immediately posted a detachment there; and, ordering parties to be distributed along the Bedford and Newtown roads, which pass through it, I waited for daylight to take possession in force," Clinton wrote.[48]

To secure all the buildings in the area, Clinton struck when the lights in the tavern went out and the last of the farm wagons had left for the dawn ferry at Brooklyn. While soldiers with bayonets prevented anyone from flee-ing their homes, the British broke into the tavern and woke up the owner, William Howard, his wife, and their son. In the barroom Howard was ordered, on pain of death, to guide the British across the ridge by a footpath that would allow them to inspect the Jamaica Pass without going through it.* Then, with Howard and his son leading the way, a British patrol took the Rockaway Path around the pass to the Jamaica Road, enabling Clinton's whole force to take control of the pass at dawn.[49]

Two hours after seizing the pass, Clinton was joined by General Howe, who had left Flatlands at midnight, at the head of the main flanking army, an additional 6,000 men in a column that stretched for two miles, moving slowly forward by moonlight, hauling supplies and fourteen more cannon. Howe's orders for the march had been ominous and secretive, indicating a major operation without revealing its destination. "The Army will strike their tents and load their Baggage at 0 o'clock this Night and form at the Head of their respective Encampments, and there wait for further Orders[;] the Men to carry their Canteens, Camp Kettles, Provisions and Necessaries; No more than two Waggons will be allowed to each Regiment for the Tents and Baggage."[50] Howe evidently tried to strike a balance between traveling light and seeing that the men had the essential supplies he had waited for during much of the summer. Anticipating the stress of battle, Howe also ordered that all surplus rum not already in the men's canteens be loaded onto the wagons. "The greatest Silence and Attention to be observed by the Troops," Howe's orders concluded.

The grueling march covered only a mile every hour; the British even used saws instead of axes to quietly remove young trees from their path. Captain Sir James Murray later wrote: "[The march was] as disagreeable a one as I remember to have passed in the course of my campaigning. . . . We dragged on at the most tedious pace from sunset till three o'clock in the morning, halting every minute just long enough to drop asleep and to be dis-turbed again in order to proceed twenty yards in the same manner. The night was colder too than I remember to have felt it, so that by daybreak my stock of patience had begun to run very low."[51] After Howe's and Clinton's columns

---

*The Rockaway Path was a bridle path that had been an Indian trail and marked the border of the settlement called Bedford, as it was defined in the purchase of land from the local tribes (Stiles, *History of Brooklyn*, p. 1:267, footnote 1). The footpath ran through what is now the Cemetery of the Evergreens, where signs amid the graves indicate its route (Johnston, *Campaign*, pt. 1: 179–80; Gallagher, walking tour).

were joined in the fields on the other side of the Jamaica Pass, the soldiers had to make do with a brief rest and a cold breakfast before the final leg of the march, along the Jamaica Road to Bedford.

The British had yet to execute their flanking maneuver and spring their trap for the rebels, but already the people of Long Island were caught in a maelstrom between the two armies—their houses, fields, and gardens burned or pillaged by one side or the other. As the Provincial Congress finally took drastic action to starve Howe's forces, the local farmers had been allowed to keep only a bare minimum of food, while the rest of their crops were destroyed. The herding of livestock east to Hempstead Plains left every neighborhood of three or four families with only one cow and one horse.[52] Many of these Dutch inhabitants loaded their households onto farm wagons, buried their valuables or hid them under the hearthstone, and fled behind the American lines on the peninsula or out to eastern Long Island.[53] Others, like Nicholas Vechte, who owned a stone farmhouse near Gowanus Creek, chose to stay.[54] Adding to the inhabitants' anxiety and indecision were rumors that the Scottish troops under Howe had been lured to America under false pretenses, "that the Highlanders expected America was already conquered, and that they were only to come over to settle our lands, for which reason they had brought their churns, ploughs, &c."[55]

In Manhattan a confident mood prevailed, nonetheless, as Washington's forces stood by to reinforce those in Brooklyn or defend the city. "All the troops are in high spirits, and have been under arms most of the day, as the [British] fleet have been in motion, and are now, as is generally thought, only waiting for the tide to change," one Manhattan resident wrote shortly after the invasion of Long Island. "Forty-eight hours or less, I believe, will determine it as to New-York, one way or the other."[56]

CHAPTER 9

The Battle of Brooklyn

∽

The largest battle of the American Revolution was set in motion by an unexpected encounter in a watermelon patch. During the night, following Clinton's written plan, General Grant had been moving into position on the British left wing to distract the Americans from the activity of the British right wing on its way to the Jamaica Pass. From Denyse's Ferry, Grant had marched quietly up the Gowanus Road toward the Martense Lane Pass, leading a column of 5,000 that included 2,000 Royal Marines and two companies of Long Island Tories. At eleven P.M. two of his scouts were attracted by watermelons—an American delicacy—growing near the Red Lion Inn at the junction of the Gowanus Road and the Martense Lane Pass.* The melon patch at the inn had been planted as a further enticement for tourists who came to see what local lore claimed was the devil's hoofprint in a nearby rock.[1] Edward Hand's riflemen fired on the melon poachers, and they retreated.

Grant had his troops observe the American position at the inn for the next three hours. As they waited, Hand's seasoned riflemen were relieved just after midnight, having been on duty for four days straight, and units of new levies—untested militia—took their place. Then, at about two A.M., as Clinton's advance corps arrived near Howard's House, Grant sent almost 300 men into the pass with guns blazing, and the terrified American guards

---

*Near today's Fifth Avenue and Thirty-sixth Street in Brooklyn, at the southwest corner of Green-Wood Cemetery.

fled up the Gowanus Road. Their commander, Major James Burd, was captured along with a few of his men, but not before he sent messengers to alert General Putnam in Brooklyn Heights that the British had attacked his position on the American right wing.[2]

Putnam roused all of the encampments and sent the men to their posts along the entire length of the American fortifications. Using signal lights on Brooklyn Heights, he alerted Washington to come over from Manhattan. Following Washington's orders that he should hold Gowanus Heights at all costs with his most reliable men, Putnam then rode down from the forts to put Lord Stirling into action, reaching his camp next to Nicholas Vechte's farmhouse south of Gowanus Creek at about three A.M.* Stirling immediately gathered close to 2,000 men to confront Grant, including troops from Delaware and Pennsylvania along with Colonel William Smallwood's elite First Maryland Regiment, which was well-trained and -equipped and highly motivated.[3] However, it was General Parsons who reached the American right wing first.

"On the day of the surprise I was on duty," Parsons wrote in a letter to John Adams,

> and at the first dawn of day the guards from the west road near the Narrows came to my quarters and informed me the enemy were advancing in great numbers by that road. I soon found it true and that the whole guard had fled without firing a gun; these (by way of retaliation I must tell you) were all New Yorkers and Pennsylvanians; I found by fair daylight the enemy were through the woods and descending the hill on the north side, on which with 20 of my fugitive guard, being all I could collect, I took post on a height in their front at about half a mile's distance—which halted their column and gave time for Lord Sterling with his forces to come up.[4]

Grant appeared to be marching straight for the inner lines on the neck of the peninsula, and Stirling set out to stop him. Later he recalled: "I accordingly marched and was on the Road to the Narrows just as the day

---

*Today the Vechte farmhouse is a visitors' center called the Old Stone House Historic Interpretive Center, near Fifth Avenue and Third Street in Park Slope. Moved and reconstructed about a block from its original location, the house stands in the middle of a playground across the street from the William Alexander Middle School, named for Lord Stirling, who defended this crucial patch of ground.

light began to appear. We proceeded to within about half a Mile of the Red Lyon, and there met Col: Atlee, with his Regiment, who Informed me, the Enemy was in Sight, indeed I then Saw their front between us and the Red Lyon."[5] With the British advancing along the Gowanus Road, Stirling quickly sized up the terrain, leaving the detachment under Colonel Samuel Atlee to the left side of the road where it narrowed, and forming a line with the bulk of his men on a piece of high ground that would give them an advantage over the invaders. The forward detachment took the brunt of Grant's fire and lost one man before it retreated to a wooded hill on the left, taking a position between Parsons and the Delaware Continentals, led by Colonel John Haslet. By about seven A.M., an American artillery company had joined them and trained its two guns on the road in front of Grant.[6]

The British had also drawn themselves up in several lines to attack the Americans. The chance meeting at the watermelon patch had become a major confrontation that stretched for a quarter of a mile and helped convince the Americans that the main British attack would be along the Gowanus Road. With the two sides confronting each other in regular battle formation, it was the first time during the Revolution that the Americans had faced the British in the open field. Unlike Lexington and Concord and Bunker Hill, there were no fortifications or even stone walls to hide behind, only hedges and trees. In this sense, the Battle of Brooklyn was the first pitched battle of the war.[7]

Unlike the Howes, General Grant and many other British officers had a fierce disdain for the rebelling colonists and wanted to crush them into submission. They ridiculed the Americans' fortifications and their attempts to confront the British war machine without much artillery or experience using it, and with a motley collection of antiquated firearms.

Muskets, fowling pieces, blunderbusses—any kind of gun that would fire bullets or buckshot was pressed into service. The rebels had "brown Bess" muskets from when they had fought alongside the British in the Seven Years' War almost two decades earlier. Older still were thirty- and sixty-year-old muskets from King George's War (1744–45) and Queen Anne's War (1702–13) that were found in the supplies of New England towns.[8]

There was also a limited number of American-made muskets both new and old. In the thirty years preceding the Revolution, firearms manufacturing had become a major colonial industry, producing an estimated 100,000 mus-

The "Brown Bess"

kets annually by 1774. However, demand was so great that guns and accessories were also one of the colonies' main imports. The British cut off arms exports to the colonies a year before the fighting broke out, but the Americans neglected to establish armories and stockpile weapons. As a result, the army faced a shortage of guns and struggled to keep the men supplied with ammunition that would fit the variety of arms they did have.[9]

The one superior weapon some American soldiers had, which the British lacked, was the rifle.[10] Produced mainly by German and Swiss gunsmiths in Pennsylvania, it had four or five times the range of a musket and was far more accurate.* The spiral groove inside the barrel of a rifle caused the bullet to rotate and fly a straighter course. While this technology originated in central Europe around 1500, and some of the Hessians carried short, large-bore rifled guns, the longer barrel and smaller caliber of the American rifle made it much more precise.

However, the rifle was only effective as a sniper's weapon and for fighting in the woods. Because it lacked a bayonet and took much longer to load, it would have made a poor substitute for the musket as standard issue for regular infantry, even if it had been produced in great quantities. A rifle took several minutes to load because the powder had to be measured from a horn (instead of being premeasured in a paper cartridge) and the ball, wrapped in a cloth patch, had to be forced down the slender barrel, which became clogged with the powder's residue and had to be cleaned after five or six shots. The musket was also more useful in the open battlefield or from a trench, because its larger bullet could help repel an enemy charge. The heavier lead ball was only effective up to about 100 yards, but it would stop a man

*The rifle's maximum range was 300 to 400 yards, versus 80 to 100 yards for a musket (Peterson, *Continental Soldier,* pp. 27, 41).

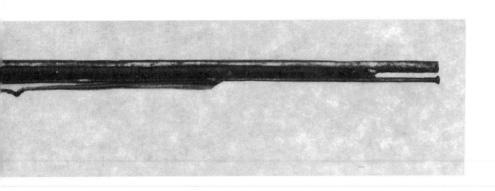

in his tracks. Unlike the smaller rifle bullet, which tended to pass through the body, the musket ball usually stayed inside, tearing at flesh and organs until its momentum was spent.[11]

While priming and loading the musket involved a four-step process, well-drilled troops, following their officers' commands, could load and fire every fifteen seconds. The chain reaction of flint, spark, and powder often failed to ignite the charge in the barrel, and because the barrel usually wasn't perfectly straight, when the gun did go off it was inaccurate. However, these defects could be minimized by training soldiers to simply point the musket in the general direction of the enemy without taking aim, to rely on the collective firepower of the line to assault the mass of the enemy.[12]

Grant's disdain aside, given all of the musket's deficiencies and the rifle's advantages, the British did not have better weapons than the Americans, only many more of them, and each one had a bayonet. Only a few American units—from Maryland and Delaware—had bayonets. Twenty-one inches long, with a three-sided blade, the bayonet made gaping wounds that could not be sutured. They healed slowly if at all, and men who survived an attack were prone to die of infection. The bayonet thus made a far more efficient weapon than the cumbersome and imprecise flintlock musket to which it was attached.[13]

Basic field tactics were adapted to this fact. Soldiers entered the field in columns that shifted into lines two ranks deep and packed shoulder to shoulder. A third line of men filled in the gaps when soldiers in the two lines ahead of them fell under enemy fire. Finally, when they arrived within fifty or even thirty yards of the enemy, the soldiers would fire one or two volleys before ending the attack with a bayonet charge. While each defender in a trench aimed his gun at the attacker directly in front of him, the British took advan-

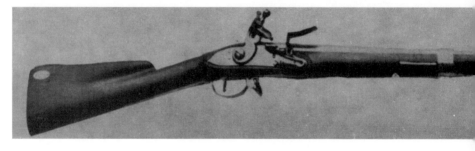

An American rifle

tage of the exposed areas below the left arm, which was raised and extended to support the gun barrel. Each British soldier was trained to shift at the last instant and, in a coordinated, surprise movement, plunge his bayonet into the heart or stomach of the enemy to his left.[14]

Grant initially sent a body of men forward against Stirling's right, but when the Americans not only held their ground but opened fire with their two cannons, he pulled the troops back, switching to a steady artillery barrage that still failed to dislodge the Americans. "The enemy," one American soldier wrote, "advanced towards us, upon which Lord Stirling, who commanded, drew up in a line and offered them battle in true English taste. The British then advanced within two hundred yards of us, and began a heavy fire from their cannon and mortars, for both the Balls and Shells flew very fast, now and then taking off a head. Our men stood it amazingly well."[15] The Americans, unaware of the British strategy of envelopment, believed they were holding back the enemy's main thrust. Legend holds that Stirling recalled for his men the boast General Grant made in Parliament the previous year, and exhorted them to show the Englishman he couldn't even get as far as the millponds behind them with the 5,000 men presently at his disposal.

When Grant sent a detachment eastward to link up with the Hessians he was expecting from von Heister in the center, Stirling detected the attempt to encircle him and ordered Parsons and Atlee to seize the high ground on his left flank.* Here they fought off three charges from the enemy and inflicted the highest losses on them that were incurred at any point during the whole day of fighting.[16] Parsons's men killed a Colonel Grant and, finding his name in his hat, rejoiced because they mistakenly believed they had dispatched the obnoxious General Grant himself. As the morning developed, the Americans

*Now known as Battle Hill in Green-Wood Cemetery.

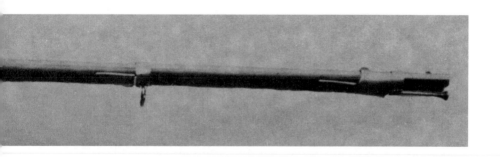

had lost only a handful of men and seemed to be holding back the British left wing. To the east, however, the battle had taken a very different turn.

By 8:30 A.M. Clinton and Howe had moved their 10,000 troops through the Jamaica Pass along the turnpike itself and had reached the village of Bedford.* The British troops were exhausted, having marched all night, but they had gained a tremendous advantage: They were behind the Americans' left and center. At nine A.M., precisely as planned, Howe fired two cannons, announcing his arrival to Grant and von Heister on the south side of the ridge.

Colonel Samuel Miles, who had been guarding the American forward position to the east of Bedford Pass, learned from his scouts of the British advance along the Jamaica Road, and at about seven A.M. he had marched east toward the pass with 500 of his men.[17] However, because he was in the woods and the British were on the road, he passed the front of their column without seeing it and encountered the rear instead. "I arrived within sight of the Jamaica Road," Miles later recalled, "and to my mortification I saw the main body of the enemy in full march between me and our lines, and the baggage guard just coming into the road."[18]

Miles sent word back to Putnam about Howe's column, but it reached him just as the British arrived at Bedford. Miles then tried to retreat, but the British discovered him in the woods and he was soon captured with half of his men; the other half fled back to the forts on Brooklyn Heights. The American guards at the Bedford Road saw Miles's scattered, fleeing men, and they too ran to safety within the fortified lines, setting off a chain reaction as the British advanced.[19]

From the crossroads at Bedford village, Cornwallis dispatched his units

*The village is now the intersection of Nostrand Avenue and Fulton Street in Bedford-Stuyvesant.

to cut off the American retreat to the Brooklyn forts. Before they reached the Bedford Pass, the Continentals stationed there had pulled back. They heard von Heister's artillery in front of them and the sounds of Howe's arrival and Americans retreating in the rear and decided not to wait for the vise to close. As they sprinted to safety, they merged with the disintegrating American center: General Sullivan and his men retreating from the Flatbush Pass.[20]

Hundreds of rebel troops raced through the woods and fields and across Gowanus Creek to reach the forts on the peninsula, with Cornwallis's grenadiers chasing them right up to the walls. Most of the Americans survived the terrifying sprint, though some were captured by the British, while others were bayoneted by the Hessians, who refused their surrender.

As one particularly bloodthirsty British officer wrote, "The Hessians and our brave Highlanders gave no quarters; and it was a fine sight to see with what alacrity they dispatched the rebels with their bayonets, after we had surrounded them so they could not resist. We took care to tell the Hessians that the rebels had resolved to give no quarter—to them in particular—which made them fight desperately, and put to death all that came into their hands."[21] Yet Sullivan, who had stayed behind to bring up the rear of his escaping column, was proof that such lurid tales were exaggerated: He was captured unharmed in a cornfield by three Hessian grenadiers before he could reach the forts.[22]

The battle in the center was over by about eleven A.M.; all that remained was to finish off Lord Stirling's forces on the Gowanus Road. At this moment, had General Howe assaulted the forts, he probably would have won a devastating victory. Instead, he pulled his troops back with repeated orders not to storm the American defenses.

"Had they been permitted to go on it is my opinion they would have carried the redoubt," Howe recalled in his official account of the battle, "but as it was apparent that the lines must have been ours at a very cheap rate by regular approaches, I would not risk the loss that might have been sustained in the assault and ordered them back to a hollow way in the front of the works out of the reach of the musketry."[23] Howe was so confident of trapping the rebel army that he preferred to dig trenches and proceed with a formal siege when the dust of the battle had settled. Politically, and perhaps personally, he couldn't bear a repeat of Bunker Hill, where, a year earlier, the Americans had held a fortified position and killed or wounded more than 1,000 British troops in a single day. It may also have occurred to Howe that his troops were exhausted; they had been marching all night and fighting half the morning.

Clinton, not surprisingly, condemned Howe's decision and had even disobeyed his orders:

> General Vaughan, who led the grenadiers, having pressed after the enemy up the hill beyond a road which Sir William Howe was unwilling we should pass, was called back by his orders. I must confess that (notwithstanding I knew the Commander in Chief's wishes) I had permitted this move, and I had at the moment but little inclination to check the ardor of our troops when I saw the enemy flying in such panic before them. I was also not without hopes that His Excellency, who was on a neighboring hill and, of course, saw their confusion, might be tempted to order us to march directly forward down the [Jamaica] road to the [Brooklyn] ferry, by which, if we succeeded, everything on the island must have been ours.[24]

Clinton concluded that if Howe had given such an order, "the completest success would most likely have been the consequence. For there is no saying to what extent the effect resulting from the entire loss of that army might have been carried in that early stage of the rebellion, or where it would have stopped."[25] Clinton's modern biographer put it more bluntly and succinctly, arguing that "Howe lost as good a chance as Britain ever had of winning the war at a stroke."[26]

Major General John Vaughan "stormed with rage" at the lost opportunity, but by then his grenadiers were under fire from Fort Putnam and its semicircular "lunette" battery, and they were ordered to pull back.[27]

From seven to eleven A.M., Lord Stirling's men had remained strongly positioned in the woods near the Gowanus Road on the American far right, trading artillery fire with Grant. As the three British columns—Grant in front of them, von Heister to their left, and Cornwallis in their rear—converged on their position, Stirling and the entire American right wing were in danger of being wiped out.

Stirling managed to disengage from Grant, and the rising ground he had staked out concealed his withdrawal at least temporarily. However, his men soon ran into Cornwallis's forces stationed around the Vechte farmhouse and blocking the Porte Road.* With Grant closing in on what was now his rear,

*Today, First Street in Park Slope.

Stirling ordered his troops to plunge into the marsh on their left and make their way as best they could by wading and swimming across Gowanus Creek. The incoming tide created a swift current, and the creek was about eighty yards wide along this stretch.[28]

To protect this retreat from Cornwallis, Stirling took about 250 of his best-trained troops, the Marylanders, on what appeared to be a suicide mission: a preemptive strike against Cornwallis's position in and around the Vechte farmhouse and its orchard. They formed ranks, charged Cornwallis's position, and fell back into the surrounding woods several times.[29] Major Mordechai Gist recalled that Stirling "encouraged and animated our young soldiers with almost invincible resolution."[30] One of the soldiers said that Stirling "fought like a wolf."[31] A biographer of Stirling has noted that "neither he nor anyone else could have predicted that this overweight, rheumatic, vain, pompous, gluttonous inebriate would be so ardent in battle."[32] This sacrificial rearguard action gave hundreds of men—the bulk of the American right wing—a chance to escape across the marshes along Gowanus Creek.

As the battle raged in Brooklyn, on Manhattan a fifteen-year-old private named Joseph Plumb Martin was walking up Broadway toward the Common as part of a work detail when an officer from his regiment caught up with him and announced that they had all been ordered to reinforce their colonel, William Douglas, on Long Island. "Although this was not unexpected to me, yet it gave me rather a disagreeable feeling, as I was pretty well assured I should have to snuff a little gunpowder," Martin recalled years later in his memoirs.

> However, I kept my cogitations to myself, went to my quarters, packed up my clothes, and got myself in readiness for the expedition as soon as possible. I then went to the top of the house where I had a full view of that part of the Island; I distinctly saw the smoke of the field artillery, but the distance and the unfavorableness of the wind prevented my hearing their report, at least but faintly. The horrors of battle then presented themselves to me in all their hideousness; I must come to it now, thought I. Well I will endeavor to do my duty as well as I am able and leave the event with Providence.[33]

Martin's regiment was marched to the ferry at the foot of Maiden Lane, where the boats set out amid the cheers of "numerous spectators who

Americans retreating across Gowanus Creek, August 27, 1776.

thronged the wharves," and soon crossed the East River. When Martin and his regiment climbed the hill from the ferry to the plateau of Brooklyn Heights, they began to meet the wounded men—"another sight I was unacquainted with, some with broken arms, some with broken legs, and some with broken heads. The sight of these a little daunted me, and made me think of home, but the sight and the thought vanished together."[34]

Martin was confronted next by the shockingly uneven quality of the officer corps. As the battle raged within sight of his regiment, he saw a lieutenant making a spectacle of himself. Looking back on the event, Martin was not sure if the man was drunk or terrified by the prospect of combat and death. "I thought it fear at the time, for he ran around among the men of his company, sniveling and blubbering, praying each one if he had aught against him, or if *he* had injured anyone that they would forgive him, declaring at the same time that he, from his heart, forgave them if they had offended him, and I gave him full credit for his assertion; for had he been at the gallows with a halter around his neck, he could not have shown more fear or penitence. A fine soldier you are, I thought, a fine officer, an exemplary man for young soldiers!"[35]

On the other hand, Martin's immediate superiors prepared for battle in quieter ways, which he respected. In the absence of uniforms, which the army couldn't afford, the officers of the new levies wore red, white, or green cockades in their hats to indicate their rank and distinguish them from the standing militia and Continentals. When asked why they were removing the bright ornaments, "the lieutenant colonel replied that he was willing to risk his life for his country, but unwilling to stand a particular mark for the enemy to fire at," Martin wrote. "He was a fine officer and a brave soldier."[36]

Martin's regiment soon arrived at Gowanus Creek, on the north side opposite Lord Stirling and the Marylanders, in time to witness the American right fleeing across the marsh as Stirling attacked Cornwallis. In the marsh, a gun crew struggled to bring up a cannon that was badly needed to cover the American retreat.

> We overtook a small party of the artillery here, dragging a heavy twelve-pounder upon a field carriage, sinking half-way to the naves in the sandy soil. They plead hard for some of us to assist them to get on their piece; our officers, however, paid no attention to their entreaties, but pressed forward towards a creek, where a large party of Americans and British were engaged. By the time we arrived, the enemy had driven our men into the creek, or rather millpond, (the tide being up), where such as could swim got across; those that could not swim, and could not procure anything to buoy them up, sunk.[37]

Washington and his generals were able to see the action from the Cobble Hill Fort, which was perched on a small hill inside the American fortified lines.* Washington had waited until midmorning to come over, because Admiral Howe had sent his ships up toward the mouth of the East River in an apparent attempt to launch a simultaneous attack on New York City, though the wind, blowing from the north, kept them out. Finally convinced that Long Island was the center of the day's action, Washington had crossed over.[38]

---

*The hill has been leveled and is now the site of the Independence Savings Bank at Court Street and Atlantic Avenue.

Legend holds that at the Cobble Hill Fort, Washington cried out in dismay when he witnessed the selfless determination of Stirling and the Marylanders: "What brave fellows I must lose this day!"[39] Cornwallis's superior numbers and the hail of bullets and artillery fire finally overwhelmed them, and Gist and Stirling ordered the men to disperse and save themselves. Gist made it across the creek with eight men, but almost all the others were captured.[40] Unable to escape, Stirling found a way to at least deny the boastful General Grant the satisfaction of capturing him—by surrendering himself to General von Heister.[41]

Parsons and Atlee—who had been holding the hill on Stirling's left flank before he retreated—turned to see that the line they were defending was gone. With Grant pressing them, they too tried to escape but found Cornwallis blocking the road. Unable even to get to the creek, their men dispersed into the woods and with Atlee most became prisoners. Parsons managed to hide in a swamp with seven of his men and sneaked back to camp at dawn the next day.[42]

The day's fighting had been a stunning success for the British. Howe reported only 61 killed, 267 wounded, and 31 taken prisoner or missing. Even with the Hessian losses—2 killed and 26 wounded—which were never included in the British figures, all of Howe's forces, by their own accounting, suffered fewer than 400 casualties.[43]

On the American side the casualty estimates varied widely. For propaganda purposes, the British grossly exaggerated the number of Americans killed or captured at 3,300 up to 4,000—figures that simply make no sense given the number of Americans who eventually left Long Island after the battle. Shortly after it ended, Washington put his losses at "seven hundred to a thousand killed and taken,"[44] and later settled on the figure of 800 casualties, "more than three fourths of which were taken prisoners."[45] Modern authorities agree that Washington was not far off the mark: American losses, they conclude, were close to 900 prisoners taken (including three generals—Sullivan, Stirling, and Woodhull—and some 90 other officers) and about 200 men killed or wounded.[46] Woodhull would soon be counted among the dead: He was captured near the county line by British dragoons who inflicted sword wounds that became infected.

The Battle of Brooklyn—the largest engagement of the war in terms of soldiers on the battlefield—was not the scene of large-scale slaughter that has often been portrayed by nineteenth- and twentieth-century historians in both Britain and the United States. And whereas the Americans lost an enormous number of men as prisoners, the British appear to have suffered a greater loss of men killed and wounded.

Howe had won the day, but he might have won much more. Had he and his army continued along the Jamaica Road instead of stopping at Bedford and firing his signal guns, Howe probably would have surrounded the American outer lines and cut off every escape route back to Brooklyn Heights.[47] Had he been willing to storm the Brooklyn fortifications when the Americans had initially been routed, he might well have overrun Washington's army. As it was, the bulk of the American forces remained intact inside the Brooklyn Heights defenses.

Still, the battle was a terrible defeat for the Americans, and there were those who thought it might have been averted by properly securing the Jamaica Pass. "I think the hills might have been well maintained with 5000 men," Brigadier General John Morin Scott wrote to John Jay. "I fear their natural strength was our bane by lulling us into a state of security and enabling the enemy to steal a march upon us."[48]

General Parsons was more pointed in his analysis, contributing to the flurry of mutual recriminations between the general officers and their subordinates that was both a symptom and a cause of the burgeoning morale crisis in Washington's army. "I still am of the opinion," Parsons wrote, "if our guards on the West road and Col. Miles on the East End of the hills had done their duty, the enemy would not have passed those important heights, without such very great loss as would have obliged them to abandon any further enterprise on the Island."[49] Even the commander in chief was denounced by those in the lower ranks after the disastrous battle: "Would to Heaven General Lee were here, is the language of officers and men," wrote Delaware's Colonel John Haslet.[50]

On the evening of August 27, however, Washington had no time to analyze what had gone wrong that day. Expecting the British to launch a full-scale attack on the fortified lines, he strode back and forth across the neck of the peninsula, alternately encouraging his men and threatening them not to abandon their posts. Stationed at regular intervals along the lines were 120 American grenadiers with slow matches burning and half a dozen grenades each in their bags. The attack never came, however, and the Americans saw the British pitch their white tents a mile and a half away on the plateau in front of them and settle down for the night.[51]

CHAPTER 10

A Wise and Most Fortunate Retreat

⌒)

T his was the first time in my life that I had witnessed the awful scene of a battle, when man was engaged to destroy his fellow-man," a young lieutenant named Benjamin Tallmadge wrote about the Battle of Brooklyn. "I well remember my sensations on the occasion, for they were solemn beyond description, and very hardly could I bring my mind to be willing to attempt the life of a fellow-creature."[1]

When the war broke out Tallmadge, like his friend Nathan Hale, was a schoolteacher in Connecticut, both having graduated from Yale in 1773. Tutored in Greek and Latin by his father, a minister, the eager, precocious Tallmadge was qualified to enter Yale at the age of twelve. He enrolled at fifteen, an age his father considered more proper, and went on to become the class valedictorian. Tallmadge was contemplating a career in law in 1775, and joining the military was the farthest thing from his mind. After Bunker Hill, however, his friend John Chester, who had fought there, became a colonel and offered Tallmadge a lieutenant's commission in his regiment. Tallmadge later recalled in his memoirs: "The whole country seemed to be electrified. Among others, I caught the flame which was thus spreading from breast to breast."[2]

As Chester's adjutant, Tallmadge found himself in the Bedford Pass during the Battle of Brooklyn.

> Before such an overwhelming force of disciplined troops, our small band could not maintain their

ground, and the main body retired within their lines at Brooklyn, while a body of Long Island Militia under Gen. Woodhull, took their stand at Jamaica. Here Gen. Woodhull was taken prisoner and inhumanly killed. The main body of our army, under Major-Gen. Sullivan and Lord Stirling, fought in detached bodies, and on the retreat, both of those officers were made prisoners. I also lost a brother the same day, who fell into their hands, and was afterwards literally starved to death in one of their prisons; nor would the enemy suffer relief from his friends to be afforded to him.[3]

Tallmadge was twenty-two at the time; his brother, William, was twenty-four.

"Our intrenchment was so weak, that it is most wonderful the British General did not attempt to storm it soon after the battle," Tallmadge remembered.[4] On the morning of Wednesday, August 28, Washington brought over reinforcements from Manhattan to bolster the beleaguered Long Island troops, a decision that put the better part of the Continental Army—about 9,500 men—at grave risk in Brooklyn.* As Tallmadge wrote, they were "exposed every moment to an attack from a vastly superior force in front, and to be cut off from the possibility of retreat to New York by the fleet, which might enter the East River."[5] For the moment, a steady wind from the northeast kept the warships out.

Brigadier General Thomas Mifflin and his brigade of Pennsylvania Continentals and New York levies were among those crossing over to Brooklyn. Like Nathanael Greene, Mifflin was a paradox: a fighting Quaker. Despite his pacifist upbringing in Philadelphia, Mifflin left Pennsylvania's Assembly to become a radical member of the Continental Congress in 1774, actively recruiting and training troops when he returned to state politics after the war broke out. He had been an aide-de-camp to Washington, quartermaster general, and a colonel in the Continental Army before his promotion to brigadier general in May 1776.[6]

Two regiments of Continentals from Essex County, Massachusetts, which also arrived that morning, soon proved to be indispensable. Led by

---

*After the battle Washington had 9,500 men in Brooklyn (Ward, *The War of the Revolution*, 1:235; Manders, p. 47). He had a total of about 18,000 men present and fit for duty in New Jersey, Manhattan, and Long Island combined.

Colonels John Glover and Israel Hutchinson, they comprised mostly fish-ermen and other expert mariners from the towns of Marblehead, Salem, Lynn, and Danvers. These "amphibious units"—dressed in white caps, short blue coats, and canvas breeches waterproofed with tar—looked ready for action, be it combat or a fishing expedition to the Grand Banks. Dangerous conditions and strict discipline were already routine for them on shipboard, where the safety of the vessel and its crew depended on split-second obedience to the captain's orders. The air of competence and confi-dence they exuded inspired the young battle-shocked troops in Brooklyn.[7] "The faces that had been saddened by the disasters of yesterday, assumed a gleam of animation on our approach," Captain Alexander Graydon later recalled, "accompanied with a murmur of approbation in the spectators occasionally greeting each other with the remark that *'these were the lads that might do something.'*"[8]*

Glover, like Washington, was born in 1732, acquired some military experience in the militia before the Revolution, and played an active role in the colonial resistance movement in his state, serving on the Marblehead Committee of Correspondence. Unlike the commander in chief, however, Glover's rise to local prominence more closely resembled that of McDougall and Sears, men of humbler origins: He started as a shoemaker and barkeeper before prospering as a merchant, shipowner, and captain in the West Indian trade. After his militia regiment was incorporated into the Continental Army, Glover and his men participated in the siege of Boston, where Washington authorized them to assemble a small fleet of armed vessels and capture British supply ships entering Massachusetts Bay.[9] In Brooklyn, Washington immedi-ately assigned the Marblehead mariners to the critical left wing of the defenses, between Fort Putnam and Wallabout Bay, where the British were likely to focus their attack.

As the new arrivals took up their positions that day, a storm blew in from the northeast, preventing the British ships from sailing into the East River from the harbor. The Americans were safe, for the moment, but mis-erable nonetheless. It began to rain heavily, and they had no shelter. The few tents they had were useless, since the men had to be outside, constantly scan-ning the plateau for a British attack. They struggled to keep their weapons and ammunition dry and to stay awake at their posts along the perimeter of the forts.[10] "You may judge of our situation," Brigadier General John Morin

---

*Graydon's unit was one of two Pennsylvania regiments that arrived with Glover's men, for a total of about 1,300 reinforcements.

Scott wrote to John Jay, "subject to almost incessant rains, without baggage or tents and almost without victuals or drink, and in some part of the lines the men were standing up to their middles in water."[11]

Down at Gowanus Creek, across the water from the ground Stirling had fought so hard to hold, Colonel William Douglas's regiment still occupied the same position it had taken during the battle. However, hunger pangs drove some of the men to venture across the creek to the fields on the far side, Joseph Martin remembered.

> The next day, in the afternoon, we had a considerable tight scratch with about an equal number of the British, which began rather unexpectedly, and a little whimsically. A few of our men . . . went over the creek upon business that usually employed us, that is, in searching for something to eat. There was a field of Indian corn at a short distance from the creek, with several cocks of hay about half way from the creek to the cornfield; the men purposed to get some of the corn, or anything else that was eatable. When they got up with the haycocks, they were fired upon by about an equal number of British, from the cornfield. [A full-scale skirmish ensued.] I do not recollect that we had anyone killed outright, but we had several severely wounded, and some, I believe, mortally.[12]

On Wednesday evening, General Howe's engineers staked out the high ground opposite Fort Putnam on the American left, and British sappers began digging a system of trenches that would shield the army as it approached and besieged the American position. They worked all night with picks and shovels, and by the morning of Thursday, August 29, the British had dug a 300-yard trench parallel to the American lines and a mere 600 yards away. A second trench, projecting at an angle from one end of the first, was in progress, suggesting the zigzagging path they intended to dig toward Fort Putnam's lunette battery, the most exposed and commanding piece of the American line because it was built out in front of the rest on elevated ground, at the end of its own connecting trench. At the rate they were digging, the British would have been within musket shot of the Americans in less than twenty-four hours, and it would have been nearly impossible to dislodge them from their advancing trench.[13]

While the sound of their picks and shovels rang out in the steady rain that continued through Thursday, Washington secretly prepared to leave the British empty-handed. General Mifflin—after inspecting the lines the previous night—had joined Joseph Reed in urging Washington to make a full retreat to Manhattan. The decision had been hard enough; carrying it out was a monumental challenge. The East River was fully a mile wide, with a strong tidal current, and Washington had only ten flatboats at the ferry, which he needed to transport the army's horses, cannon, gunpowder, and shot in addition to barrels of flour and salt pork.[14] For the 9,500 soldiers Washington hoped to evacuate in a single night—with all of their baggage, tents, and equipment—he had General Mifflin requisition "every flat bottomed boat and other craft . . . fit for transporting troops" from General Heath at Kingsbridge.[15]

To maintain security, the order made it sound as if the boats were needed to bring more reinforcements over from New Jersey and to bring back the sick and others who were to be relieved. After the intelligence failures that had led to disaster two days earlier, Washington had begun to sharpen his skills at covert operations. He knew the soldiers might have made a mad rush to the ferry if they knew the truth, while a single defector or spy could also mean ruin. Reed, who had urged the retreat, and the other aides in Washington's official "family" were informed, but aside from Mifflin, who had seconded Reed, even the generals were kept in the dark.[16]

Nonetheless, General Heath read between the lines of Mifflin's order and was quick to comply.[17] An order also went out to Assistant Quartermaster Hugh Hughes in New York City "to impress every kind of water craft from Hell Gate on the Sound to Spuyten Duyvil Creek that could be kept afloat and that had either sails or oars, and have them all in the east harbor of the city by dark."[18] The orders went out a little before noon, leaving only eight hours to gather the boats.[19]

Late in the day on the twenty-ninth, Washington convened a war council at his headquarters in a mansion on Brooklyn Heights, "a spacious and costly house, having large chimneys, from which it was known as 'the Four Chimneys.'"[20] Present were Major Generals Putnam and Joseph Spencer, and Brigadier

The war council, August 29, 1776 (left to right: Washington, Parsons, Spencer, Mifflin, Scott, McDougall, Putnam, Wadsworth, and Fellows).

Generals Mifflin, McDougall, Parsons, Scott, James Wadsworth, and John Fellows. General Mifflin agreed to propose the retreat to the assembled generals as long as he could have an opportunity to redeem his honor by demonstrating his boldness in the field. If the group agreed to a retreat, he wanted to bring up the rear, and if they decided instead on some type of offensive action, he wanted to lead it.[21]

At first, Scott, who had been one of the Whig Triumvirate in his youth and more recently a member of the New York Provincial Congress, was appalled when the retreat was suddenly proposed. "I as suddenly objected to it from an aversion to giving the enemy a single inch of ground," he explained in his letter to John Jay. "But [I] was soon convinced by the unanswerable reasons for it. . . . The resolution therefore to retreat was unanimous and tho formed late in the day, was executed the following night."[22]

Washington had also just received intelligence from General Heath that British warships had come through Long Island Sound to Flushing Bay. They were apparently poised to cover a possible crossing by Howe's army at the northern end of the East River, and an advance against Kingsbridge, which would have cut off the Americans' link to the mainland, even if they did escape to Manhattan. The news provided yet another reason to leave Long Island immediately.[23]

. . .

While the generals met, the rank and file waited in limbo, trying to ignore their hunger while keeping themselves and their gunpowder dry. Colonel William Douglas's regiment remained in its advanced, isolated position beyond Gowanus Creek. The British may have suspected that the unit was bait for an ambush, and did not attack them again. "Our regiment was alone," Joseph Martin wrote,

> no other troops being near where we were lying. We were upon a rising ground, covered with a young growth of trees; we felled a fence of trees around us to prevent the approach of the enemies' horse. We lay there a day longer. In the latter part of the afternoon there fell a very heavy shower of rain which wet us all to the skin and much damaged our ammunition. . . . Just at dusk, I, with one or two others of our company, went off to a barn, about half a mile distant, with the intent to get some straw to lodge upon, the ground and leaves being drenched in water, and we as wet as they.[24]

Martin did not find any straw in the barn, so he settled for two sheaves of wheat and quickly returned to his regiment.

"When I arrived," Martin continued, "the men were all paraded to march off the ground; I left my wheat, seized my musket and fell into the ranks." Douglas's regiment had been ordered back to the forts, where, at about ten P.M., when darkness had set in, the regiments began marching down to the ferry. "We were strictly enjoined not to speak, or even cough, while on the march," according to Martin. "All orders were given from officer to officer, and communicated to the men in whispers. What such secrecy could mean we could not divine. We marched off in the same way that we had come onto the island, forming various conjectures among ourselves as to our destination."[25]

Glover's and Hutchinson's Massachusetts mariners were down at the ferry landing by seven P.M., ready to man the arriving boats. However, the Pennsylvanians remained in the front lines on the left as part of General Mifflin's rear guard. The skirmishing on the left had been fierce, and these units were instructed to prepare for an assault on the British that night. Graydon, however, was not fooled: "But when I considered the extreme rashness of such an attempt, it suddenly flashed upon my mind, that a retreat was the object; and that the order for assailing the enemy, was but a cover to the real design. . . . There was a deep murmur in the camp which indicated some movement; and the direction of the decaying sounds, was evidently towards the river."[26]

Standing on the stairs of the ferry landing in the darkness, without a single lantern burning, General McDougall conducted the embarkation.* He was an experienced mariner from his days as a ship captain and merchant in the West Indian trade, and his warning that even the largest British warships would be able to navigate the channels around Governors Island and sever Washington's link to Manhattan had weighed heavily in favor of the retreat. Washington personally oversaw the whole operation, moving back and forth between the landing and the fortifications on horseback.

The embarkation began at eight P.M. and went smoothly at first. An hour later, however, the outgoing tide ebbed and reversed direction, flowing southward toward the mouth of the river; at the same time the steady wind from the northeast began to blow furiously, increasing the strength and speed of the tide.[27] The wind that had so far kept the British ships out of the river gradually threatened to sweep the American sailboats right into their grasp. While the slower rowboats—their oars wrapped in cloth to muffle the sound—could still be used, the likelihood that half the army would be stranded on Long Island at daybreak spurred McDougall to send an aide with a message to Washington urging him to call off the retreat, but he was unable to find him, and the grueling transfer of troops continued, one mariner later recalling that he made eleven round-trips that night.[28]

"Providentially," as a number of Americans believed, the gale from the northeast stopped by around eleven P.M., and the wind began to blow from the southwest, enabling the mariners to use the sailboats.[29] Admiral Howe's fleet, however, did not take advantage of the shift in the wind to enter the mouth of the East River, where the retreat was partly screened by Governors Island and armed American row-galleys.[30]

For the next few hours, the night was "remarkably still, the water smooth as glass," according to one soldier, and the boats were safely loaded down with men and baggage, until their gunwales were only three inches from the water.[31] The mariners rowed and sailed the two-mile round-trip, making up for lost time.

Then, at about two A.M., the firing of a cannon shredded the silence. In

*The ferry landing still exists today next to the elegant River Café at the base of the Brooklyn Bridge.

General Washington guiding the retreat, August 29, 1776.

the front lines, Graydon could not tell if the sound came from the British or the American camp. "The effect was at once alarming and sublime," he later recalled. "If the explosion was within our lines, the gun was probably discharged in the act of spiking it; and it could have been no less a matter of speculation to the enemy, than to ourselves."[32] When the silence resumed as mysteriously as it had been broken, the evacuation continued with added urgency as twilight was expected within a few hours.[33]

Throughout the night, as the small boats went back and forth behind them, the army's best-trained troops, including Benjamin Tallmadge, remained at their posts along the line of forts, their campfires burning, until the last possible moment in order to conceal the retreat—much as Clinton had masked his movements three nights earlier. "The troops began to retire from the lines in such a manner that no chasm was made," Tallmadge later recalled. "As one regiment left their station on guard, the remaining troops moved to the right and left, and filled up the vacancies."[34]

One thousand men under the direction of General Mifflin shared the burden and the honor of bringing up the rear, with orders to drop back to the Brooklyn Church in the middle of the ferry road if the British stormed the lines—and to fend off a cavalry charge by having a row of men kneel in front of the church with long spears.[35] "It was one of the most anxious, busy nights that I ever recollect," Tallmadge wrote, "and being the third in which hardly any of us had closed our eyes to sleep, we were all greatly fatigued."[36]

Between two and three A.M., when the evacuation was at its peak and thousands of men still remained in Brooklyn, a misdirected order almost gave the operation away. Washington sent an aide-de-camp, Alexander Scammell, to hurry the soldiers marching for the ferry, and the latter rushed along the battlements delivering the order to every commander, including General Mifflin, who argued that he must be mistaken. When Scammell insisted, Mifflin put his troops in motion.

They had gotten halfway to the river, Alexander Graydon later recalled, "when it was announced that the British light horse were at our heels." The troops were "halted and formed, the front rank kneeling with presented pikes, which we had with us, to receive the charge of the supposed assailants," Graydon wrote. "None, however, appeared." The false alarm, he guessed, sprang "from the fear of those who gave it, magnifying the noise of a few of our horsemen into that of squadrons of the enemy."[37]

His battalion had not gone much farther, according to Graydon, when it was halted again, this time without an immediate explanation. At the head of the column, Colonel Hand reported, Washington himself arrived on his big gray horse and said: "Good God! General Mifflin, I am afraid you have ruined us by so unseasonably withdrawing the troops from the lines."[38] The ferry landing was still crowded with men, and the arrival of more would have caused chaos. After a heated exchange they identified the erroneous order, and Mifflin's men returned to their posts for several more hours, believing that the enemy had not noticed their absence.

In fact, the British did become suspicious in the early morning hours. At about four A.M., after noticing that there were no longer any American pickets outside the lines, Captain John Montresor, the British chief engineer, led a patrol over the barrier of felled trees to the breastworks and found them empty. Why no action was taken in response to his report remains a mystery.[39] The retreat also attracted the attention of a Tory woman, the wife of John Rapalje, scion of an old Dutch family, who sent her black slave to alert the British, but he was captured and delayed for several hours by Hessian guards who did not speak English and could not understand his Dutch.[40]

Just before dawn, the situation at the landing was tumultuous enough, even without the premature arrival of Mifflin's men. The orderly embarkation broke down as the crowd surged forward from the beach to the landing, and the men, climbing over each other, jammed themselves into the small boats. To stem the mad rush, one of Washington's aides later recalled, the commander in chief approached an overcrowded boat, where he held a large stone up in the air with both hands and threatened to "sink it to hell" unless the men got out immediately.[41]

"As the dawn of the next day approached," Tallmadge wrote,

> those of us who remained in the trenches became anxious for our own safety, and when the dawn appeared, there were several regiments still on duty. At this time a very dense fog began to rise, and it seemed to settle in a peculiar manner over both encampments. I recollect this peculiar providential occurrence perfectly well; and so very dense was the atmosphere that I could scarcely discern a man at six yards' distance.
>
> [Even after the sun rose], the fog remained as thick as ever. Finally the second order arrived for the regiment to retire, and we very joyfully bid those trenches a long adieu. When we reached Brooklyn ferry, the boats had not returned from their last trip, but they very soon appeared and took the whole regiment over to New York; and I think I saw Gen. Washington on the ferry stairs when I stepped into one of the last boats that received the troops. I left my horse tied to a post at the ferry.
>
> The troops having now all safely reached New York, and the fog continuing as thick as ever, I began to think of my favorite horse, and requested leave to return and bring him off. Having obtained permission, I called for a crew of volunteers to go with me, and guiding the boat myself, I obtained my horse and got off some distance into the river before the enemy appeared in Brooklyn. As soon as they reached the ferry we were saluted merrily from their musketry, and finally by their field pieces; but we returned in safety.[42]

By about seven A.M., when the fog began to clear off and the last Americans left Governors Island, the British could be seen on Brooklyn Heights, occupying the forts.[43]

The fighting in Brooklyn had ended as it began, with the strenuous pulling of oars across New York's waters. First it was the dazzling spectacle in bright sunlight of the confident British flotilla landing at Gravesend. In the end it was the muffled oars of the Marblehead mariners moving through darkness and then through the fog to safety on Manhattan. Except for a few heavy cannon, which sank into the mud, and some cattle that proved intractable, Washington managed to bring over his artillery and supplies, horses and wagons, and even the barrels of provisions for his men.[44] Amazingly, only three stragglers were captured and four men wounded (by the British firing from the shore) during the entire evacuation.[45]

"In the history of warfare I do not recollect a more fortunate retreat," Tallmadge reflected. "Gen. Washington has never received the credit which was due to him for this wise and most fortunate measure."[46] Indeed, given its impact, Washington's flawless evacuation of Brooklyn is one of the greatest moments in the annals of warfare. And yet, even allowing for the weather, how he pulled it off has been a source of debate ever since.

"General Howe is either our friend or no general," declared General Putnam, whose own abilities as a commander were in question after the defeat on Long Island. "He had our whole army in his power . . . and yet suffered us to escape without the least interruption. . . . Had he instantly followed up his victory, the consequence to the cause of liberty must have been dreadful."[47]

A British officer named Charles Stedman, who later wrote a history of the war, favored the theory that it was the Howe brothers' friendship with the Americans—whom they regarded as fellow countrymen—and not the general's incompetence that resulted in their escape after the Battle of Brooklyn. Stedman wrote:

> It cannot be denied but that the American army lay almost entirely at the will of the English. That they were therefore suffered to retire in safety has by some been attributed to the reluctance of the commander in chief to shed the blood of a people so nearly allied to that source from whence he derived all his authority and power. We are rather inclined to adopt this idea. . . . He might possibly have conceived that the late victory would produce a revolution in [American] sentiment capable of terminating the war without the extremity [of action] which it appeared to be, beyond all possibility of doubt, in his power to enforce.[48]

For the record, Howe explained that he fully intended to capture Washington's army in Brooklyn with a formal siege to minimize British casualties, but his precise motives at this pivotal juncture in history remain a conundrum today.

Perhaps the most prescient observation about the retreat and its impact on the course of the war as a whole came from Admiral Collier, the commander of the *Rainbow*, who wrote in his diary: "To my inexpressible astonishment and concern the rebel army have all escapd across the [East] River to New York! how this has happened is surprizing, for had our troops followd them close up, they must have thrown down their arms and surrenderd; or had our ships attackd the batteries, which we have been in constant expectation of being orderd to do, not a man could have escapd from Long Island. Now, I foresee they will give us trouble enough, and protract the war, Heaven knows how long."[49]

CHAPTER II

The First Submarine, a Peace Conference, and a Second Retreat

~

I n the morning, unexpectedly and to the surprise of the city, it was found that all that could come back was come back; and that they had abandoned Long Island," Pastor Shewkirk wrote in his diary when Washington's forlorn troops suddenly appeared after the retreat. The battle on Long Island had shattered their morale; gone were the confident predictions of success against the king's army, Shewkirk observed. "The language was now otherwise; it was a surprising change, the merry tones on drums and fifes had ceased, and they were hardly heard for a couple of days. It seemed a general damp had spread; and the sight of the scattered people up and down the streets was indeed moving. Many looked sickly, emaciated, cast down. . . . Many, as it is reported for certain, went away to their respective homes."[1] General Howe had failed to destroy Washington's army, but disillusionment and desertion threatened to do the job for him.

"Our situation is truly distressing," Washington immediately wrote to Congress. His steadily declining assessment of the Continental Army's prospects in the New York campaign had reached a new low. "Till of late I had no doubt in my own mind of defending this place, nor should I have yet If the Men would do their duty, but this I despair of."[2]

The troops' assessment of their generals had followed a similar trajectory. "Upon the whole, less Generalship never was shown in any Army since the Art of War was understood," Lieutenant

Colonel Daniel Brodhead declared about the battle, "except in the retreat from Long Island, which was well conducted."[3]

Brodhead's letter of September 5 to the Pennsylvania Convention reflected the growing rift between the high command and the lower ranks of the Continental Army, and also the corrosive sectional rivalry that was evident from the army's inception—when fear of its divisive effects prompted Washington's appointment as commander in chief in an attempt to balance competing regional interests. Brodhead defended the conduct of the "Southern" troops—from Pennsylvania, Maryland, Delaware, and Virginia—who had been disparaged by New England partisans like Generals Parsons and Sullivan.

"No troops could have behaved better than the Southern," Brodhead wrote,

> for though they seldom engaged less than five to one, they frequently repulsed the Enemy with great slaughter, and I am confident that the number of killed and wounded on their side, is greater than ours, notwithstanding we had to fight them front & rear under every disadvantage. I understand that Gen. Sullivan has taken the Liberty to charge our brave and good Col. Miles, with the ill success of the Day,* but give me leave to say, that if Gen. Sullivan & the rest of the Gen'ls on Long Island, had been as Vigilant & prudent as him, we might, & in all probability would have cut off Clinton's Brigade.

In a bitterly sarcastic postscript Brodhead added, "The Great Gen'l Putnam could not, tho' requested, send out one Reg't to cover our retreat."[4]

Angry about the failure of leadership on Long Island, and traumatized by the carnage, the soldiers deserted in droves. The militia, who were raised for short-term enlistment and had the least training and discipline, posed the biggest problem. "Great numbers of them have gone off; in some Instances, almost by whole Regiments, by half Ones & by Companies at a time," Washington told Congress, as he reiterated his belief that America needed a standing army in order to relieve the chronic shortage of troops.[5] Congress

---

*Sullivan's British captors treated him well, letting him send letters that gave his version of the battle.

had authorized the creation of the Continental Army in June 1775, but the 20,372 troops had never been fully raised. Instead, Congress adopted as the core of its army the farmers, artisans, merchants, lawyers, politicians, and others who had grabbed their guns and turned out voluntarily to besiege the British in Boston. These men, and other recruits, had been asked to enlist for a full year, from January to December 1776. Faced with a shrinking army right after the battle, Washington urged Congress to offer grants of land to soldiers in addition to their pay to get them to stay in the service for longer periods.[6]*

The problems of enlistment and desertion aside, Washington had to face the immediate danger posed by the British, who occupied the American forts in Brooklyn and threatened the city itself. "I exspect we soon have a Cannonade from our own Battery on Long Island, which I have the Mortification to think I helped build it myself," Colonel William Douglas wrote to his wife on August 30.[7]

Washington's position in Manhattan was untenable for another reason: If the British chose to land in Westchester or seize King's Bridge, there would have been no way to get off the island other than by boat to New Jersey, an option precluded by Admiral Howe's ships, which now controlled the harbor and both rivers. With the successful retreat on the twenty-ninth, Washington faced the possibility that he had escaped one trap only to fall into another.[8]

"I Don't like the Chance we run in being beet in our Communications with the Cuntry, and I fear this Island of NYork will Cost Amarica too much," Douglas wrote to his wife. "If we were once on the Main[land] they could not support their Land forces with their Shiping, but at this Place they may Guard three Sides of us without a single Centinal on the Land."[9]

Nathanael Greene, still recovering from his fever, urged Washington to abandon the city while burning it to the ground, it being largely Tory property anyway. "Remember the King of France," wrote the general who had never been to school but had assembled his own library of more than 200 books. "When Charles the Fifth, Emperor of Germany, invaded his Kingdom, he laid whole Provinces waste: and by that policy he starved and ruined Charles's army, and defeated him without fighting a battle."[10]

Brigadier General John Morin Scott, who stood to lose all of his assets, including a large estate on Manhattan, nonetheless agreed that the army

---

*Land bounties were eventually adopted with some success. However, the new system also resulted in widespread fraud, as "bounty jumpers" enlisted, deserted, and reenlisted in several locations to collect multiple premiums.

should pull out of New York. Congress, however, in response to Washington's request for guidance, stated emphatically that the city was not to be harmed even if the American army had to withdraw and leave it in the hands of the enemy.[11] On September 7, Washington's war council interpreted that message to mean that they should continue to defend New York. The generals decided to leave 5,000 men in the city itself under General Putnam and deploy the rest of the army to fend off a possible British landing to the north.

Washington had already reconfigured the army into three divisions, and he spread his inadequate force thinly along the fourteen and a half miles of Manhattan's eastern shore, from the Battery to Kingsbridge. While Putnam's five brigades guarded the city and its immediate environs, six brigades under General Spencer covered the area up to Horn's Hook and Harlem, and General Heath's two brigades protected Kingsbridge and the Westchester shore.[12] Not being certain where the British might land, Washington urged his generals to be ruthless in gathering information about the Howes' intentions.

"As everything in a manner depends upon obtaining intelligence of the enemy's motions, I do most earnestly entreat you . . . to exert yourselves to accomplish this most desirable end," Washington wrote.

> Leave no stone unturned, nor do not stick at expense to bring this to pass, as I never was more uneasy than on account of my want of knowledge on this score. Keep, besides this precaution, constant lookouts (with good [spy]glasses) on some commanding heights that look well on to the other shore (and especially into the bays, where boats can be concealed), that they may observe, more particularly in the evening, if there be any uncommon movements. Much will depend upon early intelligence, and meeting the enemy before they can intrench. I should much approve of small harassing parties, stealing, as it were, over in the night, as they might keep the enemy alarmed, and more than probably bring off a prisoner, from whom some valuable intelligence may be obtained.[13]

Washington's aggressive tactics also included deployment of the world's first combat submarine. Its designer was a mechanical genius from Saybrook, Connecticut, named David Bushnell, by chance the captain of the company that included Joseph Martin. Governor Trumbull recommended the inventor to Washington, and although the commander in chief had his doubts about the project, he was so impressed with Bushnell's ingenuity that he provided funds and other support for developing and testing the machine.[14]

"The external shape of the Submarine Vessel bore some resemblance to two upper tortoise shells of equal size, joined together," according to Bushnell, and his creation came to be known as the *Turtle*.[15] Composed of several large pieces of oak, scooped out and fitted together, it was bound with iron bands, the seams corked, and the whole vessel smeared with tar to keep water out. There was just enough room inside for one man to sit or stand and operate the controls. The top was made of a metal and opened on hinges, forming the entrance to the machine. Six small pieces of thick glass in the top were the only source of light: It was said that "in a clear day and clear seawater . . . [the operator] could see to read at the depth of three fathoms [eighteen feet]."[16]

To keep the craft upright and properly balanced, 700 pounds of lead were fastened to the bottom, "two hundred pounds of which were so contrived as to be discharged at any moment," to increase buoyancy.[17] Releasing the lead ballast was intended as a last resort, however, as the machine had a valve for bringing water into a chamber below the pilot and two pumps for pushing it out, "to enable the navigator, when under water, to rise or sink at pleasure."[18] A glass tube attached to the outside of the submarine enclosed a piece of cork, which rose as the machine descended, and fell with its ascent at a rate of about one inch for every six feet. Phosphorus on the cork made it glow in the dark, so the pilot could calculate his position underneath an enemy ship. A small pocket compass, with two pieces of shining wood to light it, was attached inside, providing the only means of nighttime navigation.

With one hand on the tiller, attached to a rudder, the pilot turned a crank to operate the external propeller that, with a great deal of human effort, moved the submarine forward at about three miles per hour in calm water. A second propeller in the top speeded the pilot's ascent and descent. The submarine contained enough air for a thirty-minute dive.[19]

The *Turtle*'s torpedo was a wooden powder magazine shaped like an egg, containing 130 pounds of gunpowder, a clock, and a gun lock and flint. It rode on the back of the submarine just above the rudder, where it was attached by a screw, one end of which, extending into the magazine, controlled the movements of the clock, while the other end penetrated the

The *Turtle*

submarine. A cord on the outside of the bomb secured it to a second, larger wood-screw that projected from the top of the submarine. When the pilot reached a position beneath a target, his first task was to drive the large screw into the hull of the enemy ship and disengage it from his own vessel. With the cord and the bomb attached to the target, he would then detach the bomb from the submarine by withdrawing its wood-screw, an action that set the clock in motion and left the pilot a fixed amount of time to flee the area.[20]

In August, Bushnell had asked General Parsons for a few volunteers "to learn the ways & mystery of this new machine."[21] A sergeant named Ezra Lee and two other men who had previously volunteered for the fire ships enlisted and took the machine to Long Island Sound for trials. While there, the British capture of Long Island prevented a return by water. On September 5, Parsons wrote to Heath asking for his help, and the submarine was conveyed by land from New Rochelle to the Hudson River and then back to the city.[22]

The submarine's prime target was Admiral Howe's flagship, the *Eagle*, lying north of Staten Island in the Upper Bay. The "first serene night was fixed upon for the execution of this perilous enterprise, and sergeant Lee was to be the engineer." On that night in early September, at eleven P.M., "a party embarked in two or three whale boats, with Bushnell's machine in tow. They rowed down as near the fleet as they dared, when sergeant Lee entered the machine, was cast off, and the boats returned."[23]

Lee initially drifted past his target, and had to crank against the tide for a few hours in his cramped quarters, to maneuver under the *Eagle*, by which time dawn was beginning to break. "He now applied the screw, and did all in his power to make it enter, but owing probably in part to the ship's copper, and the want of an adequate pressure, to enable the screw to get a hold upon the bottom, his attempts all failed."[24] Lee resurfaced and descended again for a second attempt on another part of the ship, but then decided he had better escape quickly before the British found him in their midst in broad daylight.

According to Bushnell, it was not the copper armor on the ship's hull that thwarted the mission. Copper is a relatively soft metal that the screw could have penetrated. Instead it was an iron plate, connected to the ship's rudder hinge by an iron bar, that Lee kept hitting. Bushnell's brother was better trained than anyone in the use of the submarine, but he had fallen ill right before the attack. A slightly more skillful pilot, the inventor believed, would have repositioned the submarine, attached the bomb, and blown Lord Howe and his ship sky-high.[25] Instead, Lee had to make his escape with the powder magazine still in tow.

On the way back, Lee's compass failed, and he had to surface "to ascertain his course, and at best made a very irregular zig-zag track." Several British soldiers on Governors Island rowed out toward the submarine, and Lee released the torpedo, "expecting that they would seize that likewise, and thus all would be blown to atoms together." The soldiers, however, saw the torpedo and "began to suspect a yankee trick, took alarm and returned to the island."[26]

The Americans soon escorted Lee back to Manhattan, while the torpedo drifted past Governors Island into the East River, "where it exploded with tremendous violence, throwing large columns of water and pieces of wood that composed it high into the air. Gen. Putnam, with many other officers, stood on the shore [as] spectators of this explosion."[27] According to Lee, "When the explosion took place, General Putnam was vastly pleased, and cried out in his piculiar way—'God curse 'em, that'll do it for 'em.'"[28]

During the first week of September, General Howe spread his numerous troops along the shore opposite Manhattan—from Red Hook all the way to Hell Gate—to keep the Americans guessing where he would attack, but day after day he made no attempt to cross the East River and pursue them. Admiral

Collier seethed sarcastically in his journal that Washington should have thanked General Howe for being such a

> generous, merciful, forbearing enemy who would take no unfair advantages. . . . For many succeeding days did our brave veterans, consisting of twenty-two thousand men, stand on the banks of the East River, like Moses on Mount Pisgah, looking at their promised land, little more than half a mile distant. The rebels' standards waved insolently in the air, from many different quarters of New York. The British troops could scarcely contain their indignation at the sight and at their own inactivity; the officers were displeased and amazed, not being able to account for the strange delay.[29]

Unbeknownst to the officers, Admiral Howe had resumed his peace efforts and presumably asked General Howe to await their outcome before launching another offensive. Since his letters to Washington had proved futile back in July, this time Admiral Howe used General Sullivan—a prisoner of war whom he released on parole—as an emissary to Congress in Philadelphia. As an officer, Sullivan had been treated well and had dined and conversed with Admiral Howe, who persuaded him to help arrange a face-to-face meeting with members of Congress. Sullivan's embassy infuriated John Adams. He called Sullivan "a decoy duck whom Lord Howe has sent among us to seduce us into a renunciation of our independence," and during Sullivan's presentation, he leaned over and muttered under his breath to Benjamin Rush that he wished the first shot fired by the British in the Battle of Brooklyn had gone through Sullivan's head.[30]

However, opinion was divided, and on September 6 Congress appointed a committee of three to meet with Admiral Howe on Staten Island. Five days later, Adams, Benjamin Franklin, and Edward Rutledge arrived at the Billopp House, a seventeenth-century stone manor at the southern tip of the island, where the Arthur Kill empties into Raritan Bay.*

"We walked up to the house between lines of guards of grenadiers, looking as fierce as the ten Furies," Adams later recalled.[31] He had shrewdly and courageously returned the officer Howe had sent as a hostage for their security, gaining instead the admiral's word of honor to protect the delegation, and enabling Adams to ignore, as he put it: "[the Hessians'] grimaces

---

*Today the Conference House is still standing and is open to the public.

The peace conference on Staten Island, September 11, 1776.

and gestures, and the motions of their muskets, with bayonets fixed, which, I suppose, military etiquette requires, but which we neither understood nor regarded."*

Howe explained that not only did he remain grateful to Massachusetts for the marble monument to his older brother in Westminster Abbey, but "he esteemed that honor to his family above all things in this world. That such was his gratitude and affection to this country, on that account, that he felt for America as for a brother, and, if America should fall, he should feel and lament it like the loss of a brother," Adams wrote. "Dr. Franklin, with an easy air and a collected countenance, a bow, a smile and all that naivete which sometimes appeared in his conversation and is often observed in his writings, replied, 'My Lord, we will do our utmost endeavors to save your lordship that mortification.'"

Adams could see that Howe looked hurt, but the admiral merely replied, "I suppose you will endeavor to give us employment in Europe," which

*Adams did take note of Howe's hospitality: "The house had been the habitation of military guards and was as dirty as a stable; but his lordship had prepared a large handsome room by spreading a carpet of moss and green sprigs from bushes and shrubs in the neighborhood, till he made it not only wholesome, but romantically elegant; and he entertained us with good claret, good bread, cold hams, tongues and mutton" (quoted in Commager and Morris, eds., *The Spirit of 'Seventy-six*, p. 455).

Adams took as a reference to an American alliance with France that would keep the British navy busy on both sides of the Atlantic. "To this observation," Adams noted, "not a word, nor a look, from which he could draw any inference, escaped any of the committee."

In fact, France had followed through on its agreement to supply the Americans with secret shipments of arms and ammunition while continuing to assess their prospects. Emboldened in part by this evolving alliance, Adams, Franklin, and Rutledge refused to negotiate. When it became apparent that Howe was not empowered to grant peace unless the Americans withdrew the Declaration of Independence, the talks quickly broke down. Franklin's optimism may well have been bolstered by his long experience with the game of chess as well as by the help from France. "We learn by chess," Franklin wrote in *Morals of Chess*, "the habit of not being discouraged by present appearances in the state of our affairs, the habit of hoping for a favorable change, and that of persevering in the search for resources."[32]

The day after the conference, Washington and his generals belatedly revised their strategy and voted to evacuate New York City completely.[33] Fearing a trap, they took advantage of the open-ended instructions from Congress and immediately began to move the whole army up to Harlem Heights. During the hot September days from the twelfth to the fourteenth, the Continental Army's evacuation of New York City continued without significant interference from the British. The horses and wagons, loaded with sick and wounded soldiers, supplies, and artillery, traveled north on Manhattan's two main roads to the plateau of Harlem Heights, where the rocky slopes would provide a strong defensive position for Washington's dwindling army.

During the ten days between Washington's retreat from Brooklyn and the peace conference on Staten Island, General Howe had also been busy— positioning his army to invade Manhattan and capture New York City.[34] After he seized Brooklyn Heights and Governors Island, Howe's artillery dominated the mouth of the East River, enabling him to harass the American batteries in lower Manhattan and start sending ships, troop transports, and landing craft upriver, using Governors Island and the cover of night to shield them. Between September 2 and 9, Howe gradually occupied Blackwell's, Buchanan's, and Montresor's Islands,* stationed frigates behind them, and

*Today they are Roosevelt, Wards, and Randalls Islands, respectively.

concealed his invasion flotilla in Newtown Creek,* an inlet between Queens and Kings Counties on the Long Island shore. After his brother's failed peace conference on the eleventh, General Howe stepped up the pace of his preparations, hoping to attack on the thirteenth.

Washington's retreat to Harlem Heights, meanwhile, was still about two days short of completion, and a shortage of wagons hobbled the operation: Between 3,000 and 4,000 American troops remained in the city, while others were in motion across the length of the island, protected only by the thin line of defenders along the East River shore.

*Newtown Creek is now part of the border between the boroughs of Brooklyn and Queens. The mouth of the creek is approximately opposite Thirty-second Street.

CHAPTER 12

The Invasion of Manhattan

~ ~

O n this day [September 13], General Howe wished to land upon the island of New York," Major Carl Leopold Baumeister of the Hessian forces wrote in his journal, "because 18 years ago on this day General Wulff* had conquered at Quebec, but also lost his life. The watchword for this end was 'Quebec' and the countersign 'Wulff,' but the frigates were too late for this attack as they only sailed out of the fleet at 5 o'clock on the evening of the 14th."[1] Howe also waited until the fourteenth to inform his officers where the invasion of Manhattan would take place. Unfavorable winds had delayed the last frigates, and at the same time, Generals Howe and Clinton had engaged in their ongoing dispute over strategy. Clinton had urged the commander in chief since July to seize Kingsbridge and trap the Americans once and for all.

When Washington successfully retreated from Brooklyn, Clinton wrote,

> I took the liberty, on being asked, upon this to advise that we should march as soon as possible to Hell Gate (as our raising batteries at that place would be the most likely to give jealousy), make every appearance of intending to force a landing on

*The British major general James Wolfe.

General Henry Clinton

York Island,* and when everything was prepared at Montresor's Island (which I would have laid hold of for the purpose) throw the troops on shore from thence at Morrisania,† and move forward directly to mask Kings Bridge by occupying the heights of Fordham. Had this been done without loss of time, while the rebel army lay broken in separate corps between New York and that place, it must have suddenly crossed the North River or each part of it fallen into our power one after the other.[2]

Once again, Clinton was overruled. Howe was determined to land on Manhattan and planned for a division led by Clinton to come ashore at Horn's Hook and another that he would lead himself at Kips Bay. However, after pilots expressed concern about the dangerous waters at Hell Gate, and after considering the strength of the rebel fort at Horn's Hook, Howe decided to concentrate his attack at Kips Bay. During the night of the fourteenth, the four warships that had sailed up the river earlier that day in an attempt to knock out the Horn's Hook battery sailed back down to support the landing. The seventy-five flatboats used during the Long Island invasion had already been concealed in the inlet off the river.

Clinton had numerous objections to landing so far south—most important, that it would take much longer and give the rebel army time to entrench

*Manhattan.
†The Bronx.

at Harlem Heights and Kingsbridge, from which they would have to be pried loose. Yet Howe believed he had gained an element of surprise by the change in tactics. "The Rebels had troops in their works round Kepp's Bay," Howe reported to Lord Germain, "but their attention being engaged in expectation of the King's troops landing at Stuyvesant's Cove, Horen's Hook, and at Harlem, which they had reason to conclude, Kepp's Bay became only a secondary object of their care."[3]

In the evening on the fourteenth, with 3,500 American troops still in the city, Washington transferred his headquarters from the Mortimer House near the city up to the summer home of Colonel Roger Morris, a loyalist who had fled to England.* High on a hill, the location allowed Washington to see for miles in every direction. In the immediate vicinity, the house overlooked the Harlem River and the small Dutch settlement of Nieuw Haarlem, which was then more than 100 years old.† Because of the ongoing British attempts to destroy the American battery at Horn's Hook, Washington expected the British landing in Harlem and had placed a screen of his best units between the village and the battery to protect his retreating army.

Washington might have guessed that Kips Bay‡ was another likely place for the invasion: It was deep enough for ships to sail in close to the shore, and a large meadow provided an excellent landing area. However, he had virtually neglected the cove. When the British ships descended on Kips Bay during the night of the fourteenth, only raw recruits—half of Colonel William Douglas's new levies and three militia regiments—were sent to defend its shores.[4]

Joseph Martin was one of the new levies on hand. The fifteen-year-old private, who had enlisted with unbounded faith that the Americans were invincible, had quickly grown cynical about his superiors' abilities and their concern for the safety and well-being of their men. According to Martin:

> [Half of our regiment] was sent off under the command of our major to man something that were called "lines," although they

*Located at 161st Street, and now the oldest house on Manhattan, it is known as the Morris-Jumel mansion and is open to the public.
†It stood in present-day First Avenue between 124th and 125th Streets (Bliven, *Battle for Manhattan,* p. 26).
‡This cove, had it not been filled in, would now extend from East Thirty-second Street up to East Thirty-eighth Street, and almost as far in as Second Avenue (Martin, *Private Yankee Doodle,* p. 32, footnote 15). The cove is gone, but the neighborhood has taken its name.

were nothing more than a ditch dug along the bank of the river with the dirt thrown out towards the water. . . . We arrived at the lines about dark and were ordered to leave our packs in a copse wood under a guard and go into the lines without them. What was the cause of this piece of *wise* policy I never knew, but I knew the effect of it, which was that I never saw my knapsack from that day to this, nor did any of our party unless they came across them by accident in our retreat. . . . We had a chain of sentinels quite up the river, for four or five miles in length. At an interval of every half-hour, they passed the watchword to each other, "All is well." I heard the British on board their shipping answer, "We will alter your tune before tomorrow night." And they were as good as their word for once.[5]

By dawn on the fifteenth, the four ships had positioned themselves end to end within 100 yards of the shore, the springs on their anchor cables allowing them to maintain broadside positions, with a combined total of more than eighty cannons pointed at the Connecticut regiments. When the ships arrived slightly to the north of his position, Colonel Douglas moved his men up to face them and then waited. The ships were within range, but Douglas decided that peppering them with musket fire would have been futile.[6] Martin's sarcasm makes clear that he saw an opportunity lost: "They appeared to be very busy on shipboard, but we lay still and showed our good breeding by not interfering with them, as they were strangers, and we knew not that they were bashful withal."[7]

At about seven A.M., Admiral Howe sent a man-of-war and two frigates up the Hudson in order to create a distraction and draw American forces away from the intended landing site at Kips Bay. In a reprise of July 12, the guns at Paulus Hook, New Jersey, thundered without effect at the passing ships, which "in sailing by fired whole broadsides on the shore of the city of New York," according to Major Baumeister.[8] Along with the British attack, the cross fire of the guns from New Jersey and New York "caused a cannonading which made the houses shake," Pastor Shewkirk wrote in his journal.[9]

By ten A.M. on the shore opposite Kips Bay, in Newtown Creek, the British had loaded the invasion force into the seventy-five flatboats and the accompanying galleys and bateaux. Together, the flotilla of eighty-four vessels carried about 4,000 men at a time. Packed in, shoulder to shoulder, the invading soldiers felt vulnerable, even if en masse they appeared to have the overwhelming advantage. "The Hessians, who were not used to this water business, and who conceived that it must be exceedingly uncomfortable to be shot at whilst they were quite defenceless and jammed so close together, began to sing hymns immediately," Francis Lord Rawdon, a British officer, later recalled. "Our men expressed their feelings as strongly, though in a different manner, by damning themselves and the enemy indiscriminately with wonderful fervency."[10]

As the British maneuvered the flatboats into a compact line in the middle of the East River, their red uniforms looked to Martin "like a large clover field in full bloom." The Americans were tensed for action, but the flatboats waited at "the edge of the tide" for the changing current to ease their approach to the Manhattan shore. Douglas apparently remained unsure exactly where the British intended to land, and did not call for reinforcements from other units posted at intervals along the shoreline to the south. Martin found the enemy "a little dilatory in their operations," and despite the gathering menace, the teenager grew restless, wandering away from the lines to explore an abandoned house. Then, a little before eleven, as the landing craft drew near, "all of a sudden there came such a peal of thunder from the British shipping that I thought my head would go with the sound," Martin recalled. "I made a frog's leap for the ditch and lay as still as I possibly could and began to consider which part of my carcass was to go first." The deafening bombardment created a blanket of white smoke that shielded the landing barges moving in under it; the British and the Hessians started coming ashore unopposed. "We kept the lines until they were almost leveled upon us," Martin wrote, "when our officers, seeing we could make no resistance and no orders coming from any superior officer and that we must soon be entirely exposed to the rake of their guns, gave the order to leave the lines."[11]

While Martin strongly implied that the men stayed in the lines until the last possible moment, and that there was a failure of leadership at the top levels of the army, Washington and his generals saw the situation differently. From their perspective, the British bombardment was primarily a tool of intimidation; the cannons could not be angled downward far enough, and the balls arced harmlessly over the American lines. The generals felt that the militia at the northern end of the lines, where the firing was heaviest, had immediately panicked and fled inland toward the Post Road. Their fear infected others, and—along with a false rumor that a retreat had been ordered—it soon spread along the entire shore to areas where the shelling had been lighter, or where the men had merely witnessed the bombardment. The steadiest officers, like Douglas, eventually had no choice but to leave as well.[12] The mutual recriminations and morale problems that began in the aftermath of the Battle of Brooklyn came to a head on September 15.

When the bombardment began, Washington heard it four miles away at the Morris House in Harlem and headed toward the sound on horseback with his aides. General Putnam also heard it down in the city; he ordered General Fellows to take his entire brigade from the fort at Corlear's Hook and three additional regiments from General Parsons (whose brigade manned the lines near the fort) to reinforce the troops wherever the bombardment might be. As a result, the American forces were in complete disarray, some marching toward the action and others running from it; they passed each other coming and going on the Post Road.[13]

Despite the confusion among the Americans, the British soldiers continued to feel vulnerable, as they had during the crossing. The first wave of British and Hessian troops under General Clinton had formed ranks in the meadow adjacent to the beach and waited anxiously for reinforcements—an additional 9,000 men—to be shuttled across the river. "We pressed to the shore, landed, and formed without losing a single man," Lord Rawdon later recalled. "As we were without artillery, upon an island where the enemy might attack us with five times our number, and as many cannon as he thought proper, it was necessary to attain some post where we might maintain ourselves till we were reinforced, which we knew could not be done quickly."[14]

Clinton, unlike his subordinates, was less concerned with a possible ambush than that the Americans might escape to Harlem Heights and Kingsbridge before he could deploy his men across the width of Manhattan to trap them.

> As soon as the troops were all on shore, in obedience to my orders, I laid hold of the height of Inclenberg* and sent forward Colonel [Carl] Donop with four battalions of Hessian Grenadiers, with a view to intercepting the retreat of the different parties of rebels who appeared before us in motion from all quarters. . . . It happened unfortunately, too, that much time was lost before the second embarkation landed . . . as by our stretching immediately across the island great numbers of the enemy must have been taken prisoners. But, my orders being to secure the Inclenberg, I

*Murray Hill.

did not think myself at liberty to attempt it before Sir William Howe joined us; and indeed I do not know but, had we made such a move, even then we should have cut off many of them who had not yet got over the [Hudson] river or Kings Bridge.[15]

Galloping south on the Post Road, Washington arrived just north of Inclenberg shortly before Clinton's troops seized it. At the crossroad that connected the Bloomingdale and Post Roads,* Washington encountered the fleeing militia. He also saw the American brigade from Corlear's Hook, which had just arrived and marched onto a large cornfield below the crossroad. The three additional regiments appeared a few minutes later, followed by General Parsons on horse-back.[16] At this point Washington himself entered the fray, trying to establish some order. He was furious at the sight of officers running away and troops following their example. Major General Heath explained their flight in his memoirs: "The wounds received on Long-Island were still bleeding; and the officers, if not the men, knew that the city was not to be defended."[17]

According to testimony Parsons later gave to a court of inquiry, Washington shouted: "Take the walls!" and "Take the cornfield!" Parsons rode into the field and tried to get his men organized to defend these positions.[18] Washington and his aides also rode among the troops, trying to get them in a line along the Post Road to confront the Hessians and British light infantry who had marched up from Kips Bay, accompanied by a steady drumbeat. But even the commander in chief's orders had little effect. The panic that seized the Connecticut militia had now spread to the troops from Corlear's Hook, who threw down their guns and ran away.

The arrival of the Hessians, who bayoneted and shot some Americans as they tried to surrender, heightened the terror. "I used every means in my power to rally and get them in some order," Washington later wrote to Congress, "but my attempts were fruitless and ineffectual; and on the appearance of a small party of the enemy, not more than sixty or seventy, their disorder increased, and they ran away in the greatest confusion, without firing a single shot."[19]

Washington's life was suddenly in grave danger. General Greene reported that the departing brigades "left his Excellency on the ground within eighty yards of the enemy, so vexed at the infamous conduct of the troops, that he sought death rather than life."[20] One legend asserts that "Washington threw

*At the site of today's New York Public Library at Fifth Avenue and Forty-second Street.

his hat on the ground, and exclaimed, 'Are these the men with which I am to defend America?' "[21]

"I have often read and heard of instances of cowardice," fumed Colonel Smallwood, "but hitherto have had but a faint idea of it till now. I never could have thought human nature subject to such baseness. I could wish the transactions of this day blotted out of the annals of America. Nothing appeared but fright, disgrace, and confusion." The fleeing men "were caned and whipped by the Generals Washington, Putnam, and Mifflin, but even this indignity had no weight, they could not be brought to stand one shot."[22]

Washington's aides finally had to lead him away to safety, according to James Thacher, an army doctor. "His Excellency, distressed and enraged, drew his sword and snapped his pistols, to check them; but they continued their flight . . . and the General, regardless of his own safety, was in so much hazard, that one of his attendants seized the reins, and gave his horse a different direction."[23]

Joseph Martin fled Kips Bay in the company of a neighbor from home. "We went into a house by the highway in which were two women and some small children, all crying most bitterly," Martin later recalled. "We asked the women if they had any spirits in the house. They placed a case bottle of rum upon the table and bid us help ourselves. We each of us drank a glass and bidding them good-by betook ourselves to the highway again."[24] After struggling to catch up with a body of men who were heading in the same direction, and discovering that they were Hessians, Martin and his friends quickly changed course and went north on the Post Road.

They reached the cornfield at the crossroad just as the Corlear's Hook regiments were fleeing. The scene forced Martin to concede: "The enemy's party was small, but our people were all militia, and the demons of fear and disorder seemed to take full possession of all and everything that day. When I came to the spot where the militia were fired upon, the ground was literally covered with arms, knapsacks, staves, coats, hats, and old oil flasks."[25]

Martin and his companion moved with the Americans streaming north through the woods and on the Post Road, encountering further scenes of panic and cowardice, and numerous obstacles, including enemy soldiers blocking the road. The two men were separated and reunited, and Martin refused to let his friend—who had become quite sick— give up. Martin too was feeling faint from the heat and from a total lack of sleep and food for more than twenty-four hours.

Eventually they reached a point in the road where American artillery officers had placed several fieldpieces and were preparing to make a stand against the British. The officers had stopped a few hundred Americans and ordered them to help defend the position. It had just rained, and everyone was soaked to the skin. Martin pleaded with one officer to let them pass since his friend would die if exposed all night to the damp, cold air. According to Martin, the officer responded that if his friend died "the country will be rid of one who can do it no good." Martin was outraged: "Pretty fellow! thought I, a very compassionate gentleman! When a man has got his bane in his country's cause, let him die like an old horse or a dog, because he can do no more!"[26]

When the officer got drunk sharing a canteen of liquor with a friend, Martin managed to slip past the roadblock with his sick neighbor and rejoin their regiment at Harlem Heights. In response to the charges of cowardice that were leveled against the militia during the Kips Bay affair, Martin wrote: "Every man that I saw was endeavoring by all sober means to escape from death or captivity, which at that period of the war was almost certain death. The men were confused, being without officers to command them. I do not recollect of seeing a commissioned officer from the time I left the lines on the banks of the East River in the morning until I met with the *gentlemanly* one in the evening. How could the men fight without officers?"[27]

In the panicked retreat, the officers ended up having to look to their own safety. William Douglas, the colonel of Martin's regiment, had recently mentioned in several letters to his wife that he needed a good horse; he had asked her to buy one and send it to him from Connecticut in the care of a neighbor, but the purchase had not been made yet. Fortunately for Douglas, he came upon another officer whose horse refused to jump over a fence. When the man dismounted and fled on foot, Douglas climbed over the fence, took the horse's reins, and coaxed it over after him. He was almost too exhausted to mount, but with the enemy closing in, he knew he would otherwise be killed or taken prisoner. Douglas pulled himself up into the saddle and rode off, just as the British arrived at the fence.[28]

In the face of the British landing and the pell-mell flight of the troops, General Putnam acted swiftly to control the damage by leading the remaining soldiers out of the city in an orderly fashion. Right after the rout in the cornfield, Putnam conferred with Washington on horseback* before charging down to the city to rescue the remaining 3,500 men under his command. They both realized the men had to be evacuated to Harlem immediately, before the British trapped them at the bottom of the island. The officers Putnam had left in charge in the city—Colonel Gold Silliman and Colonel Henry Knox—stood on the high ground occupied by the Bayard's Hill Fort,† and having witnessed the British invasion to the north, were determined to hold their position. When Putnam's aide, Major Aaron Burr, arrived with the order to retreat, he had to persuade them to follow him with assurances that he knew the terrain and could guide them up the west side of the island all the way to Harlem Heights.[29]

Putnam and his staff rode through the city ordering the troops to abandon the precious supplies, ammunition, and cannon that they had been in the process of moving out of the city. There was barely enough time to escape with their lives.

In the stifling heat the 3,500 men formed a column two miles long, which started to leave the city at four P.M. on a forced march that would cover twelve miles by nightfall. The column stayed close to the Hudson River, moving north on a country lane toward Greenwich, a district of farms and country houses.‡ When the front of the column reached the William Bayard and Oliver De Lancey estates,§ the last marchers were back at Chambers Street.[30] Flanking guards moved along a few hundred yards to the east watching for British troops. Above Greenwich, the column entered the woods to avoid the Bloomingdale Road, which lay to the east. Farther on, when it seemed unlikely that the Americans would encounter any British troops, the column got on the Bloomingdale Road and followed it up the West Side.[31]

Colonel David Humphrey later recalled the sight of Putnam in action, conducting the march. "I had frequent opportunities, that day, of beholding him . . . flying, on his horse, covered with foam, wherever his presence was most necessary. Without his extraordinary exertions, the guards must have been inevitably lost, and it is probable the entire corps would have been cut to pieces."[32]

---

*In the middle of today's Times Square, at Broadway and Forty-third Street.
†It stood at the intersection of today's Grand and Mulberry Streets.
‡Today's West Village and Chelsea.
§Near today's Twenty-third Street and Eighth Avenue.

Major Aaron Burr

.   .   .

While Putnam's column left the city at four P.M., General Howe looked out over Kips Bay from the top of Inclenberg as the second division of his troops finally completed its landing. Howe carefully followed the traditional principles of military science by consolidating his forces on high commanding ground, and bringing them to full strength before allowing forays in which they might otherwise be outnumbered and surrounded by the enemy.[33] Had Howe allowed Clinton to proceed directly to the Hudson shore, however, he might well have cut off thousands of Americans to the south. Given that the Americans had slipped from Howe's grasp on Brooklyn Heights, the delay at Inclenberg fueled more speculation about his motives among British officers and prominent loyalists.

Because Howe and his staff accepted refreshment at Robert Murray's home during that hot afternoon of September 15, a legend sprang up attributing Howe's delay at Inclenberg to the feminine wiles of three other women: Mary Murray and two of her daughters, Susannah and Beulah. Mrs. Murray opened the wine cellar at the mansion and served cakes and Madeira to the British generals and Governor Tryon, who teased her about her American sympathies: Two of her cousins had fought on the American side in Brooklyn two weeks earlier.[34]

The Murrays had a superb reputation as hosts, often entertaining distinguished international guests, and they were at the center of New York's sophisticated social life. Howe would have been drawn to them and their stunning house, built during the war-fueled economic boom of the 1750s and early 1760s, and considered one of the loveliest spots on the island.[35] There is little evidence, however, that Mary Murray's actions were either deliberate or actually delayed General Howe even in the unlikely case they were intended to. Like Howe, she was almost certainly unaware of Putnam's column and its whereabouts. Furthermore, Howe's decision to halt the army at Inclenberg until all of his troops had landed was written into Clinton's orders before the invasion.[36]

Nonetheless, Howe's predilection for women and entertainment made him an easy mark for critics, and the legend grew over the years that as Howe dallied at Inclenberg, the Americans slipped away yet again and escaped up the island's west side.

Only when Howe's forces had reached full strength late in the afternoon on September 15 did he venture out from the landing area. At five P.M. a Hessian brigade marched south on the Post Road securing the territory between the beachhead and the city, where residents had placed a white flag on the Bayard's Hill redoubt. At the same time, Admiral Howe dispatched 100 marines in small boats to occupy the city itself.[37]

Between the American departure and the British arrival, the city was looted. Pastor Shewkirk noted in his diary:

> There was a good deal of commotion in the town; the continental stores were broke open, and people carried off the provisions; the boats crossed to Powles' Hook backward and forward yet till toward evening; some people going away and others coming in; but then the ferry boats withdrew, and the passage was stopped. Some of the king's officers from the ships came on shore, and were joyfully received by some of the inhabitants. The king's flag was put up again in the fort, and the Rebels' taken down. And thus the city was now delivered from those Usurpers who had oppressed it so long.[38]

North of Kips Bay, Howe's main force headed up the Post Road in belated pursuit of Washington's fleeing army. "As soon as the second embarkation was landed," General Howe reported to Lord Germain, "the troops advanced towards a corps of the enemy upon a rising ground three miles from Inclenberg, towards King's Bridge, having McGowan's Pass in their rear, upon which they immediately retired to the main body of their army."[39] In fact, the Americans gave the British some stiff resistance before they fell back. Washington had assigned what remained of Colonel William Smallwood's elite Maryland regiment to delay the enemy by stationing themselves half a mile south of the pass,* giving the American forces at Horn's Hook and along the East River in the Harlem area more time to retreat. At McGowan's Pass the Post Road ran between two hills before descending steeply to Harlem Plains. This was the most advantageous spot for a small detachment to impede the progress of a much larger force. Smallwood posted his men behind rocks in the hilly terrain and planned to attack the British column as it approached along the road. If necessary, he resolved to give up ground slowly and retreat to the pass to make a stand.[40]

The British marched up the East Side unaware that Putnam's column was moving on a parallel path to the west. When the British encountered Smallwood's men, a brief exchange of musket fire convinced them that the Americans were ready to stand their ground. So the British headed west on a cross road that took them over to the Bloomingdale Road. Smallwood's action had covered the northern Manhattan retreat but inadvertently deflected the British toward Putnam's column.

Had the Americans been caught below the intersection and forced to fight off the British arriving on their right flank, the result would have been disastrous, according to Humphrey. "Our men, who had been fifteen hours under arms, harassed by marching and counter-marching, in consequence of incessant alarms, exhausted as they were by heat and thirst . . . if attacked, could have made but feeble resistance."[41] However, by the time Howe's troops reached the Bloomingdale Road, the last American regiment had almost passed the intersection. One colonel was killed in the ensuing skirmish, but the rest of the column escaped.

"With no other loss," Colonel Humphrey wrote, "we joined the army, after dark, on the heights of Harlaem.—Before our brigades came in, we were given up for lost by all our friends. So critical indeed was our situation, and so narrow the gap by which we escaped, that the instant we passed, the enemy closed it by extending their line from river to river."[42]

Smallwood's men pulled back and left McGowan's Pass to the British as planned. By the end of the day, the British left wing was stationed at Bloomingdale in the west and the right at Horn's Hook in the east. All of Manhattan below the line connecting these points was in British hands.

*At what is now Ninety-sixth Street and Fifth Avenue.

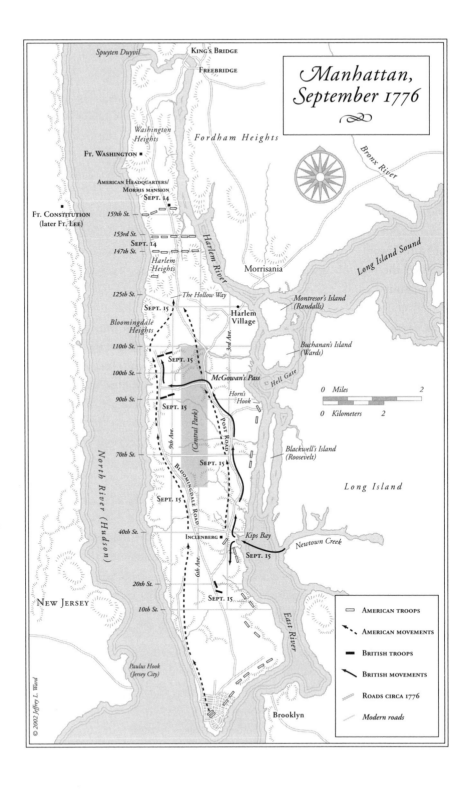

Manhattan,
September 1776

Spuyten Duyvil
KING'S BRIDGE
FREEBRIDGE

Washington
Heights
FT. WASHINGTON ■

Fordham Heights

Bronx River

AMERICAN HEADQUARTERS/
MORRIS MANSION
SEPT. 14

FT. CONSTITUTION
(later FT. LEE)

159th St. —

153rd St. —
SEPT. 14
147th St. —

Harlem
Heights

Harlem River

Morrisania

Long Island Sound

125th St. —
SEPT. 15

The Hollow Way

Bloomingdale
Heights

110th St. —

SEPT. 15
100th St. —

Harlem
Village

3rd Ave.

Montresor's Island
(Randalls)

Buchanan's Island
(Wards)

McGowan's Pass

90th St. —
SEPT. 15

Horn's
Hook

Hell Gate

0   Miles   2

0   Kilometers   2

70th St. —

9th Ave.

POST ROAD

(Central Park)

Blackwell's Island
(Roosevelt)

SEPT. 15

SEPT. 15

BLOOMINGDALE ROAD

Long Island

40th St. —

6th Ave.

INCLENBERG ■

Kips Bay

Newtown Creek

SEPT. 15

NEW JERSEY

20th St. —

SEPT. 15
10th St. —

East River

AMERICAN TROOPS
AMERICAN MOVEMENTS
BRITISH TROOPS
BRITISH MOVEMENTS
ROADS CIRCA 1776
Modern roads

North River (Hudson)

Paulus Hook
(Jersey City)

Brooklyn

© 2002 Jeffrey L. Ward

·   ·   ·

In the course of the invasion the British had lost only a handful of men. The Americans, however, had lost more than 350, including 17 officers, who were taken prisoner; only a few Americans were killed or wounded.[43] Again Howe's plan had unfolded with almost perfect precision, and he gained the strategic terrain he sought, but again he failed to entrap Washington's army, which slept in Harlem Heights about a mile and a half above the British forward line.

Perhaps Joseph Martin was correct, in the end, that the fleeing soldiers had followed the most sensible course. In effect they accelerated and completed the evacuation that the generals had already agreed was imperative. Benjamin Trumbull, a chaplain with the First Connecticut Regiment, wrote in his journal: "The men were blamed for retreating and even flying in these circumstances, but I imagine the fault was principally in the general officers in not disposing of things so as to give the men a rational prospect of defence and a safe retreat should they engage the enemy. And it is probable many lives were saved, and much [loss] to the army prevented, in their coming off as they did, tho' it was not honourable. It is admirable that so few men are lost."[44] American pride had been hurt, but the army remained intact to fight another day.

As with the narrow escape from Brooklyn, however, this one left the Americans in no mood for rejoicing at their good fortune. "That night," Colonel Humphrey recalled, "our soldiers, excessively fatigued by the sultry march of the day, their clothes wet by a severe shower of rain that succeeded towards the evening, their blood chilled by the cold wind that produced a sudden change in the temperature of the air, and their hearts sunk within them by the loss of baggage, artillery, and works in which they had been taught to put great confidence, lay upon their arms, covered only by the clouds of an uncomfortable sky."[45]

CHAPTER 13

The Battle of Harlem Heights

~⁀

own the Hudson from where Washington's troops shivered on Harlem Heights, the three British warships that had created a distraction during the Kips Bay invasion remained a menace off of Bloomingdale, anchoring the western end of the British cordon that extended from river to river.* Seven miles below the line, New York City had suddenly become occupied territory, or as loyalists like Pastor Shewkirk saw it, the city had been liberated. Shewkirk wrote gleefully in his diary on Monday, September 16:

> In the forenoon the first of the English troops came to town. They were drawn up in two lines in the Broad Way; Governor Tryon and others of the officers were present, and a great concourse of people. Joy and gladness seemed to appear in all countenances. . . . The first that was done was, that all the houses of those who have had a part and a share in the Rebellion were marked as forfeited. Many indeed were marked by persons who had no order to do so, and did it perhaps to one or the other from some personal resentment.[1]

The letters *GR* painted on these houses indicated that they had become the property of the king, George Rex.[2] In his delight

---

*The British line passed across the top of today's Central Park.

over New York's deliverance by the British, Shewkirk saw a marvelous portent in the Scriptures. "The word of this day was remarkable: 'Israel shall be saved in the Lord, with an everlasting salvation; ye shall not be confounded world without end,'" he quoted in his diary.[3]

However, loyalists who had fled, leaving property in the city, were far less joyous when they returned on the sixteenth. One resident, quoted in a London paper, reported: "[The city was] a most dirty, desolate and wretched Place. My House had been plundered by the Rebels of almost every thing I had left behind."[4] Reverend Charles Inglis wrote that the city displayed "a most melancholy appearance, being deserted and pillaged."[5]

In its desperate need for raw materials, the Continental Army had taken all of the city's brass door knockers and all of the church bells without regard to religious denomination. However, the British decision to seize dissident churches and turn them into overcrowded prisons full of American troops was a targeted act of retribution that accentuated the religious strife so evident in the origins of the war. Pastor Shewkirk noted that the prisoners were kept in the Dutch and Presbyterian churches.[6] The Churches of England, which rioters had broken into more than a decade earlier during the Stamp Act crisis, enjoyed the protection of an occupying army.

The British seized rebel property beyond the city as well. General Howe established his headquarters at Mount Pleasant, one of Manhattan's most splendid estates, which belonged to James Beekman and overlooked the East River an hour's ride from the city.* He may have chosen the Beekman mansion for its beauty, but its location also had military advantages: It placed Howe in the center of his command, midway between the city and the main body of the army to the north, and not far from the brigade he had left to secure Long Island.[7]

"The retreat was effected with but little or no loss of Men, though of a considerable part of our Baggage," Washington recounted in a letter to Congress started before dawn on September 16, attributing this to the "disgracefull and dastardly conduct" of the troops. "Most of our Heavy Cannon, and a part of our Stores and provisions which we were about removing were unavoidably left in the City. . . . We are now encamped with the Main body of the Army on the Heights of Harlem, where I should hope the Enemy would meet with a defeat in case of an Attack, If the Generality of our Troops

---

*The house stood near today's First Avenue and Fifty-first Street.

would behave with tolerable bravery, but experience to my extreme affliction has convinced me that this is rather to be wished for than expected." On an optimistic note, he added "However, I trust that there are many who will act like men, and shew themselves worthy of the blessings of Freedom."[8]

Washington needed detailed information about the position of the British left wing in order to determine if General Howe planned to dig in or quickly launch a major offensive. The commanding position of his headquarters, the Morris House, afforded a clear view of Harlem Plains, which would have given him an early warning if the British right wing advanced any farther from McGowan's Pass. However, if the British left wing moved up the West Side, along the Bloomingdale Road, its approach would have been masked by the thick woods that covered much of the area, then known as Bloomingdale Heights.*

Two interlocking pieces of property, the farms belonging to Adrian Hoaglandt on the west and Benjamin Vandewater on the east, covered the area and had only been partially cleared for cultivation. Their two houses and that of Nicholas Jones were the only buildings in the vicinity above Bloomingdale Village. General Greene's division was posted on the rocky southern slopes of Harlem Heights, but even his pickets out in front could not see the British encampment, which was across a valley called the Hollow Way that separated the two elevations, and concealed by the dense growth of trees. The Americans also built a redoubt on the Point of Rocks, a craggy projection at the southeastern corner of Harlem Heights, from which they could look out over Harlem Plains to the east and watch the ragged northern face of the Bloomingdale plateau to the west.[9]

"I have sent out some reconoitring parties to gain Intelligence If possible, of the disposition of the Enemy," Washington added in his letter to Congress before dawn on September 16.[10] Assigned to cross the Hollow Way into enemy territory and discover General Howe's arrangements, the reconnaissance party of 120 men was drawn from Lieutenant Colonel Thomas Knowlton's Rangers—the corps of volunteers from the New England regi-

---

*Today called Morningside Heights, the name for this area, extending from 110th to 125th Streets east of Riverside Drive, was inspired by the glow of the rising sun on the plateau's eastern slope, now covered by Morningside Park. Harlem Heights (known today as Manhattanville and Hamilton Heights) was the plateau above present-day 125th Street, with the Hudson on the west and St. Nicholas and Edgecombe Avenues on the east. The major thoroughfare of 125th Street, also called Martin Luther King Jr. Boulevard, was then no more than a country lane, less than a mile long, that connected the Post Road with a landing on the Hudson at about 132nd Street. The lane ran on a northwesterly course toward the river through the center of a valley called the Hollow Way (Dolkart, *Morningside Heights*, pp. 3–5; Johnston, *Harlem Heights*, pp. 46–48).

ments that Washington counted on without hesitation. Knowlton, thirty-seven, a farmer from Connecticut who fought under General Putnam in several campaigns during the Seven Years' War, had also emerged as a hero from the Battle of Bunker Hill. Knowlton was fearless and led his adoring troops by example; as one soldier put it, he never said, "Go on, boys!" but always "Come on, boys."[11]

Before dawn on September 16, the scouting party, which included Knowlton's brother, Daniel, and his sixteen-year-old son, Frederick, moved south across the Hollow Way and headed for the Bloomingdale Road, where the British were last seen the night before.[12] They passed Hoaglandt's house at the northern terminus of the road and penetrated about a mile below the American lines. As the sun came up, they encountered the most advanced British pickets at Nicholas Jones's stone farmhouse.* The British scouts fired their guns as a signal to the British light infantry and the Forty-second Highlanders camped a little farther south, while Knowlton's men fired a few shots and then retreated behind a stone wall. The British soon advanced in a column, and in the ensuing skirmish each side fired more than 1,000 rounds before Knowlton and his men retreated across the valley to the American lines.[13] There had been few casualties, but the Battle of Harlem Heights had begun.

While Knowlton's men were engaging the British, Washington was pulled from his headquarters by a report that the British had arrived, as he put it in a later letter: "in several large bodies upon the plains, about Two & a half miles from hence. I rode down to our advanced posts to put matters in proper situation if they should attempt to come on. When I arrived there, I heard a firing which I was informed, was between a party of our Rangers under the command of Lieutt Col Knolton, and an advanced party of the Enemy."[14] The report of the enemy on the plains to the east had proved incorrect, so Washington sent his adjutant, Joseph Reed, to look for Knowlton and to see if the British had moved their main force up to Bloomingdale Heights.

A little before nine A.M., Reed, who had found Knowlton and seen the British light infantry moving rapidly northward, reported back to Washington that the Rangers had just returned to the American lines. Word of the corps' brave showing spread quickly through the ranks, and Reed urged Washington to build on Knowlton's success by engaging the British on a

*The road ended at today's 115th Street. Jones's house stood near Broadway and 106th Street.

Lieutenant Colonel Thomas Knowlton

larger scale. Just then, "the enemy appeared in open view," Reed reported in a letter to his wife, "and in the most insulting manner sounded their bugle horns as is usual after a fox chase. I never felt such a sensation before. It seemed to crown our disgrace."[15]

Knowlton's men "came in & told me, that the body of the Enemy, who kept themselves concealed consisted of about three Hundred, as near they could guess," Washington wrote. "I immediately ordered three companies . . . under the command of Major [Andrew] Leitch, & Col. Knolton with his Rangers, composed of Volunteers from different New England Regiments, to try to get in their Rear, while a disposition was making as If to attack them in front, and thereby draw their whole attention that way."[16] The Americans quickly planned to lure the British infantry into the Hollow Way while sending a detachment to the east, across the valley, and up the bluffs to get behind them. The flanking party under Knowlton and Leitch consisted of 230 men. For the frontal feint, 150 volunteers from Brigadier General Nixon's brigade were ordered to make noise as they entered the Hollow Way and to remain there while making the British think they were ready to charge straight up the other side.

The British took the bait. John Chilton, a tobacco planter from Virginia, later described the action in a letter.

We discovered the enemy peeping from their heights over the fencings and rocks and running backwards and forwards. We did not alter our position. I believe they expected we should have ascended the hill to them, but finding us still, they imputed it to fear and came down skipping towards us in small parties. At a distance of about two hundred and fifty or three hundred yards they began their fire. Our orders were not to fire till they came near, but a young officer (of whom we have too many) on the right fired, and it was taken [up] from right to left. We made about four fires. I had fired twice and loaded again, determined to keep for a better chance, but Colonel [George] Weedon calling to keep up our fire (he meant for us to reserve it, but we misunderstood him), I fired once more. We then all wiped and loaded and sat down in our ranks and let the enemy fire on us near an hour. Our men observed the best order, not quitting their ranks, though exposed to a constant and warm fire. I can't say enough in their praise; they behaved like soldiers who fought from principle alone.[17]

Eventually the rest of Nixon's brigade was brought down into the valley, and the return fire from the Americans caused the British to retreat. They headed for cover behind a post-and-rail fence overgrown with bushes at the northern end of Hoaglandt's property,* while Nixon's men pushed forward up the slope, firing on the retreating British.[18]

Tragically for the Americans, this action was premature, putting the British to flight before the flanking party had time to get behind them. The force led by Knowlton and Leitch arrived at the fence at the same time as the British, and the assault planned for their rear, ended up on their side instead, allowing the British troops time to turn and face their attackers. Knowlton died from a musket ball in the small of his back, while Leitch was shot three times in the space of a few minutes and died of his wounds a day later. Reed wrote to his wife that he helped Knowlton off the field "and when gasping in the agonies of death all his inquiry was if we had drove the enemy."[19]

At this point, Washington sent in reinforcements, and General George Clinton (an American cousin of the British commander) had two fieldpieces brought up that helped dislodge the British from their position behind the fence. "Our regiment was now ordered into the field," Joseph Martin wrote, "and we arrived on the ground just as the retreating enemy were entering a thick wood, a circumstance as disagreeable to them as it was agreeable to us at that period of the war. We soon came to action with them. The troops engaged, being reinforced by our regiment, kept them still retreating."[20]

*The fence straddled today's Broadway between 123rd and 124th Streets.

By noon the British had fallen back to a buckwheat field,* where they made a stand. General Howe sent reinforcements, and Captain John Montresor had a pair of cannons hauled over from McGowan's Pass.[21] At least 1,800 Americans, representing all of the states, were engaged in the fighting, led by Generals Putnam, Greene, and Clinton, and the battle raged for two hours until the British ran low on ammunition and retreated again.

The Americans pursued them dangerously close to the British main camp, and to Admiral Howe's frigates anchored off Bloomingdale. As Martin later recalled, the American advance ended when the British "found shelter under the cannon of some of their shipping lying in the North River."[22] British reinforcements came up, ready for a full-scale clash between the armies, the type of general engagement that Washington had decided to avoid. He sent his aide-de-camp, Lieutenant Tench Tilghman, to pull the troops back. As if answering the morning's insulting bugle call, "they gave a hurra and left the field in good order," Tilghman wrote.[23] The Battle of Harlem Heights had ended by three P.M. precisely where it began with the skirmish at dawn, in front of Nicholas Jones's farmhouse.[24]

"How many of the enemy were killed and wounded could not be known, as the British were always as careful as Indians to conceal their losses," Martin wrote. "There were doubtless some killed, as I myself counted nineteen ball holes through a single rail of the fence at which the enemy were standing when the action began."[25] On this point the commander in chief and the private were in agreement. Sounding like a hunter tracking his prey, Washington wrote to Nicholas Cooke of the Rhode Island Assembly: "From some of their wounded Men which fell into our Hands, the appearance of blood in every place where they made their Stand and on the fences they passed, we have reason to believe they had a good many killed & wounded, tho they did not leave many on the Ground."[26]

The minute tallying of losses on both sides was clearly an important exercise, since these numbers—a potent form of propaganda—were reported to the governments in both London and Philadelphia. In his letter to Congress, begun on the sixteenth and finished on the eighteenth, Washington concluded: "[We] had about Forty wounded, the Number of Slain is not yet ascertained, but It is very inconsiderable. By a Serjeant, who deserted from the Enemy & came in this Morning, I find that their party was greater than I

---

*Today the site of Barnard College.

immagined." That his men had beaten a combined force of light infantry, Highlanders, and Hessian riflemen made Washington all the more proud. "The Deserter reports that their loss in Wounded & Missing was Eighty Nine, and Eight killed—In the latter, his Account is too small as Our people discovered and buried double that Number." The casualty figures also trickled down to the rank and file. "This Affair I am in hopes will be attended with many salutary consequences," Washington continued, "as It seems to have greatly inspired the whole of our Troops."[27]

Indeed, the relatively small battle, despite the loss of two exceptional officers, gave a tremendous boost to American morale. The same soldiers who had arrived on Manhattan two weeks earlier in a narrow escape from Brooklyn and had then fled the British invasion at Kips Bay saw for the first time that they could make the enemy's best troops turn and run. Washington praised "their great resolution and bravery," which put the enemy "to flight when in open Ground," and dislodged them "from posts they had Seized, Two or Three times."[28]

Colonel Humphrey wrote:

> An advantage so trivial in itself produced, in event, a surprising and almost incredible effect upon our whole army. Amongst the troops not engaged, who during the action, were throwing earth from the new trenches, with an alacrity that indicated a determination to defend them, every visage was seen to brighten, and to assume, instead of the gloom of despair, the glow of animation. This change, no less sudden than happy, left little room to doubt that the men, who ran the day before at the sight of an enemy, would now, to wipe away the stain of that disgrace, and to recover the confidence of their general, have conducted themselves in a very different manner.[29]

For the British, by contrast, the Battle of Harlem Heights added to the ongoing friction between Generals Howe and Clinton. Although he minimized this American victory in his account of the war, Clinton was clearly rankled by it.

> On my going the next morning [September 16] to take command of the foreposts, I found that the light infantry, having with rather too much impetuosity pursued some parties of rebels toward their works, had got themselves somewhat disadvantageously engaged

under a heavy fire of grape, upon which I directly advised the officer who led them to fall back a few yards to more favorable ground. This was effected with certain precautions but not without some loss, as the rebels were in considerable force—not less than 7000 men. It, however, since appears that we might have held this post, which would have probably been a better one than that we took afterward, as it might have saved us the dangerous passage of Hell Gate.

Clinton implied that if the British had moved up in force and seized Bloomingdale Heights, they would have been well positioned to cross the Harlem River into Morrisania and arrive behind the American lines at Kingsbridge as he had repeatedly suggested. "But the Commander in Chief had, without doubt, very sufficient reasons for ordering me to retreat," Clinton added, with thinly veiled opprobrium, "which we did at dusk without receiving a single shot from the enemy."[30]

"We remained on the battleground till nearly sunset, expecting the enemy to attack us again, but they showed no such inclination that day," Martin wrote. "The men were very much fatigued and faint, having had nothing to eat for forty-eight hours. . . . While standing on the field after the action had ceased, one of the men near the lieutenant colonel complained of being hungry. The colonel, putting his hand into his coat pocket, took out a piece of an ear of Indian corn burnt as black as coal. 'Here,' said he to the man complaining, 'eat this and learn to be a soldier.'"[31]

Fortunately for Martin, a substantial meal, of sorts, awaited him behind the American lines.

We now returned to camp, if camp it was: our tent held the whole regiment and might have held ten millions more. When we arrived on the ground we had occupied previous to going into action, we found that our invalids, consisting of the sick, the lame, and the lazy, had obtained some fresh beef. Where the commissaries found the beef or the men found the commissaries in this time of confusion I know not, nor did I stop to ask. They were broiling the beef on small sticks in Indian style round blazing fires made of dry chestnut rails. The meat when cooked was as black as coal on the outside and as raw on the inside as if it had not been near the fire. "I asked no questions for conscience's sake," but fell to and helped myself to a feast of this raw beef, without bread or salt.[32]

In the calm after the battle, with their basic survival attended to, the men had time to reflect on the death of fellow soldiers and to perform, at least in a cursory fashion, the rituals that helped them accept the day's losses. "When we came off the field we brought away a man who had been shot dead upon the spot, and after we had refreshed ourselves, we proceeded to bury him," Martin wrote.

> Just as we had laid him in the grave in as decent a posture as exist-ing circumstances would admit, there came from the house towards the grave two young ladies who appeared to be sisters. As they approached the grave, the soldiers immediately made way for them with those feelings of respect which beauty and modesty combined seldom fail to produce, more especially when as in this instance accompanied by piety. Upon arriving at the head of the grave, they stopped and with their arms around each other's neck stooped forward and looked into it, and with a sweet pensiveness of countenance which might have warmed the heart of a misog-anist, asked if we were going to put the earth upon his naked face. Being answered in the affirmative, one of them took a white gauze handkerchief from her neck and desired that it might be spread upon his face, tears at the same time flowing down their cheeks. After the grave was filled up, they retired to the house in the same manner as they came. Although the dead soldier had no acquaintance present (for there were none at the burial who knew him) yet he had mourners and females too. . . . Such a sight as those ladies afforded at that time and on that occasion was worthy and doubtless received the attention of angels.[33]

CHAPTER 14

The Great Fire and the Execution of Nathan Hale

~

On September 21 the aged Cadwallader Colden, the man who had single-handedly done so much to spark the resentment and inflame the passionate resistance of New Yorkers against the long arm of the Crown in the dozen years before the war broke out, died of natural causes at his estate in Flushing, on Long Island.[1] On that same day, the city itself caught fire.

Just after midnight, on the morning of September 21, an American prisoner named John Joseph Henry on the British frigate *Pearl* in New York harbor looked toward the city and saw "a most beautiful and luminous, but baleful sight." A fire that appeared from a distance "the size of the flame of a candle," was in fact "the burning of an old and noted tavern called the 'Fighting Cocks' . . . to the east of the battery and near the wharf." Henry then saw "another light at a great distance from the first, up the North River," which seemed to him a different fire. Boatloads of British sailors immediately rowed toward the city, Henry wrote, when he returned to Pennsylvania and became a judge after the war. "This circumstance repelled the idea that our enemies were the incendiaries, for indeed they went in aid of the inhabitants."[2]

Fanned by strong winds that drove the flames northward, the fire ultimately consumed most of the city's west side, charring a mile-long swath through the town and destroying almost 1,000 buildings, about a quarter of the city. Had the wind not shifted to the west, the flames would probably have spread up through the center and could well have consumed it all. The most notable structure to be lost was the city's tallest: Trinity Church, the most visible symbol of the Church of England in New York, had a wooden steeple that became a great flaming pyramid against the night sky.

The Americans' modest but timely victory at Harlem Heights five days earlier had done far more good for their morale that it did harm to General Howe's army. However, this next setback afflicted the British, and the refugees who sought their protection in the occupied city, for years to come. Maps showing the long, relatively narrow footprint of the damaged area suggest that the fire was not the result of a concerted attempt to destroy the whole city, but rather that it began accidentally at a single point and was shaped by the impersonal force of a shifting, driving wind, which eventually died out. The undeveloped grounds of King's College, the northern limit of the damaged area, also brought the blaze to a natural end by acting as a fire line.[3] Nonetheless, the debate over the origins of the conflagration simmered long after the ashes had cooled.

"My Lord: Between the 20th and the 21st instant, at midnight, a most horrid attempt was made by a number of wretches to burn the town of New-York, in which they succeeded too well, having set it on fire in several places with matches and combustibles that had been prepared with great art and ingenuity," General Howe wrote to Lord Germain on September 23. "Many were detected in the fact, and some killed upon the spot by the enraged troops in garrison; and had it not been for the exertions of Major-General [James] Robertson, the officers under his command in the town, and the brigade of Guards detached from the camp, the whole must infallibly have been consumed, as the night was extremely windy."[4]

Howe predictably cast himself and his army in the best light when writing to the secretary of state for the American colonies, who controlled the funds, supplies, provisions, and reinforcements for the war. Governor William Tryon, however, in his letter to Germain on the twenty-fourth, suggested that, while the soldiers did a good job of demolishing structures that would have allowed the fire to spread, chance and the elements played an even greater role in sparing the city. "The town was thought to be saved more by a sudden change in the wind (which blew strong) and pulling down intermediate houses, than by water," Tryon wrote.[5] Howe's letter was misleading in another respect as well. Whereas his brother was quick to send marines from the fleet into the city, the general's ingrained caution apparently held him back once again. "No assistance could be sent from the Army 'till after daybreak, as the General was apprehensive the Rebels had some design of attacking the Army," a British officer named Frederick Mackenzie wrote in his diary.[6]

In his letter to Germain, Tryon attempted to implicate Washington in the disaster—while pointedly ignoring his proper title: "Many circumstances lead to conjecture that Mr. Washington was privy to this villainous act, as he sent all the bells of the churches out of town, under pretence of casting them into cannon; whereas it is much more probable to prevent the alarm being given by ringing of the bells before the fire should get ahead beyond the reach of the engines and buckets; besides, some officers of his army were found concealed in the city, supposed for this devilish purpose."[7]

Because the destruction fell disproportionately on property owned by Trinity Church, to which large grants of land on the city's west side had been deeded, Tryon, like Mackenzie, suspected that the Church of England had been targeted by rebel arsonists. The governor pointed out to Germain that "excepting a few houses and St. Paul's Church . . . almost all the houses on the church estate, with Trinity Church, are totally consumed. It really seems the conflagration was directed against the interest of the church. The ship-docks, warehouses, and the commercial part of the city is as yet safe."[8]

To this day, however, neither the accusations of arson nor of a plot actively or tacitly approved by Washington have ever been substantiated with more than circumstantial evidence. The strongest indication of arson—that the fire appeared to break out in several places at once, in buildings that were not adjacent to each other—is easily explained by the fact that New York's rooftops consisted primarily of cedar shingles. Even Mackenzie points out in his diary that "there is no doubt . . . that the flames were communicated to several houses by means of the burning flakes of the Shingles, which being light, were carried by the wind to some distance."[9] While the British rounded up and interrogated more than 200 suspects, no one was convicted, and all of them were eventually released.[10]

Nonetheless, some Americans, like Colonel Silliman, remained convinced, as he wrote to his wife on the twenty-fifth, that "it was not the regulars, but some of our own people in the city that set it on fire, for they executed several of our friends there for it the next day."[11] John Joseph Henry, the prisoner on the *Pearl*, agreed. When the officer and the crew of the boat from the *Pearl* returned from the city later that morning, Henry wrote, they asserted that "the burning of New York was the act of some mad-cap

Americans." They claimed to have seen one American "hanging by the heels dead, having a bayonet wound through his breast," because "he was caught in the act of firing the houses." They saw another "who was taken in the act tossed into the fire, and that several who were stealing, and suspected as incendiaries were bayonetted."[12]

Other Americans went farther, however, and accused the British troops of having set the fire deliberately in order to plunder the city. Whether or not the looting was premeditated, it apparently did occur. The sailors from the fleet, who were the first to arrive in the city and did most of the fire fighting, were also the first to profit from the blaze, according to Major Baumeister, "taking care to pay themselves well by plundering other houses near by that were not on fire."[13] In a letter from Harlem Heights on the twenty-fifth, an American officer wrote: "The Hessians are continually plundering and are countenanced by their General; and General Howe dares not punish them for fear of producing a general mutiny."[14]

The day after the fire, on September 22, Washington described the blaze in a letter to John Hancock as an "Accident" and denied any knowledge of its origins.[15] Washington's extraordinary deference to civilian authority through-out his military career strongly suggests that he would not have disobeyed his instructions from Philadelphia to spare the city even if it was lost—or have lied to the president of Congress in a piece of official correspondence. A let-ter to Washington's cousin, Lund Washington III, two weeks after the blaze, in which the commander in chief privately vented his criticisms of Congress, also supports the conclusion that he followed the delegates' wishes—even as he vehemently disagreed with them.

"Had I been left to the dictates of my own judgement, New York should have been laid in Ashes before I quitted it," Washington wrote to Lund,

> —to this end I applied to Congress, but was absolutely forbid—that they will have cause to repent the Order, I have not a moments doubt of, nor never had, as it was obvious to me (cov-ered as it may be by their Ships) that it will be next to impossible for us to dispossess them of it again as all their Supplies come by Water, whilst ours were derived by Land; besides this, by leaving it standing, the Enemy are furnished with warm and comfortable Barracks, in which their whole Force may be concentred—the

place secured by a small garrison (if they chuse it) having their Ships round it, & only a narrow Neck of Land to defend—and their principal force left at large to act against us, or to move to any other place for the purpose of harrassing us. This in my judgement may be set down am[on]g one of the capitol errors of Congress.

"In speaking of New York," Washington continued, after a digression, "I had forgot to mention that Providence—or some good honest Fellow, has done more for us than we were disposed to do for ourselves, as near One fourth of the City is supposed consumed," adding with regret "[h]owever enough of it remains to answer their purposes."[16]

Whatever its origins, the impact of the fire on the city was devastating. "It is almost impossible to conceive a Scene of more horror and distress," Mackenzie wrote in his diary about the fire.

> The Sick, The Aged, Women, and Children, half naked were seen going they knew not where, and taking refuge in houses which were at a distance from the fire, but from whence they were in several instances driven a second and even a third time by the devouring element, and at last in a state of despair laying themselves down on the Common. The terror was encreased by the horrid noise of the burning and falling houses, the pulling down of such wooden buildings as served to conduct the fire . . . the seeing the fire break out unexpectedly in places at a distance, which manifested a design of totally destroying the City, with numberless other circumstances of private misery and distress, made this one of the most tremendous and affecting Scenes I ever beheld.[17]

While the physical damage from the fire was enormous, its psychological impact ultimately had even greater repercussions. The fire introduced an element of paranoia and contributed to a siege mentality that made British commanders fiercely protective of the city. Accordingly, Tryon's letter assured Germain that what was left of New York City would be aggressively protected "and every measure pursued by General Robertson, commanding officer in New-York, assisted by myself, to establish such regulations and police as may ensure its future security."[18]

Even before the fire, the military authorities had struggled to house all of their soldiers, warehouse supplies, create hospitals, and accommodate an influx of loyalist refugees. The flames left thousands homeless, turning the existing shortage into an enduring crisis.[19] The hallmarks of the occupation over the next seven years—poverty and suffering made worse by a hypervigilant, dictatorial regime—quickly emerged in the wake of the disaster.

The fire helped convince the British commanders to keep martial law in place in the occupied city, rather than restoring the civil rights of the inhabitants—as they had hoped and expected when the rebels were driven out. "As this country is in the present period too much convulsed for the civil Government to act with any good effect, it is the opinion of both of his Majesty's Commissioners for restoring peace to the Colonies, that I should postpone any executive acts of Government, until the Province is more liberated from the control of the Rebels," Tryon wrote to Germain in the same letter of September 24. "I therefore have kept the executive powers of civil Government dormant, leaving everything in the direction of the military."[20]

For the moment, most loyalists were happy to have the army's protection and were willing to wait for a return to normalcy. They eagerly volunteered for military service in distinct loyalist companies that bolstered the British forces. Tryon told Germain that "General Oliver De Lancey, under General Howe's orders, is endeavouring to raise a brigade of fifteen hundred men for the defence of Long Island, and Major [Robert] Rogers a corps of Provincials for the war generally." The British in turn were happy to have the extra manpower. Tryon concluded his letter on a positive note, informing Germain that "the two New-York companies, under the Captains Campbell and Grant, have acquitted themselves in action so honourably as to obtain the General's thanks, transmitted to them in publick orders."[21] This approach of mustering the loyalists fit squarely with Germain's optimistic theory that they constituted a silent majority that he and the Howe brothers could mobilize to reconquer the colonies. General Robertson might have been speaking for the secretary of state when he said: "I never had an idea of subduing the Americans. I meant to assist the good Americans to subdue the bad."[22]

In establishing his position on Harlem Heights, one of Washington's priorities was to preserve American communications across the Hudson, as it was the link between New England and the rest of the colonies to the west and south of the river. Fort Washington, to the north of Harlem Heights—and Fort Constitution, directly across from it in New Jersey—had to be held to prevent the British from dividing the colonies in half by sending an army down from Canada for a rendezvous with General Howe at Albany, and controlling the entire Hudson River.[23]

To defend Harlem Heights, General Greene's division faced the British at the southern edge of the plateau with orders to check a British advance and fall back if necessary to the first line of fortifications half a mile north. Manhattan narrows sharply on its east side at this point, which enabled General Putnam's division to span the island with three redoubts and connecting trenches and breastworks. Farther north stood a second fortified line with four redoubts under General Joseph Spencer. A third line without redoubts remained incomplete roughly on the same parallel as Washington's headquarters.* The wooded hills of Harlem Heights concealed the American lines and encampments in a naturally strong defensive position.[24]

However, while some of Washington's generals thought Howe would attempt to storm the Heights, others warned that he would land troops behind the Americans at Kingsbridge (from the Hudson) or in Westchester (from Long Island Sound). In order to address all three contingencies with only 16,000 men actually present and fit for duty,† the generals settled on another precarious division, once again placing the Continental Army astride two rivers: Greene's division was ferried to Fort Constitution to secure communications across the Hudson and further harass British ships coming up the river, and a floating bridge was built across the Harlem River as an additional link for rapidly reinforcing—or evacuating—General Heath's units on the Westchester side of King's Bridge.[25]

Before the Kips Bay invasion, when the British were still on Long Island, Washington had sent a spy behind enemy lines, hoping to predict where Howe would land on Manhattan. There is no record to indicate that the commander in chief met with Nathan Hale to issue his instructions personally.[26] Nonetheless, on or about September 12, the young captain from Colonel Thomas Knowlton's Ranger corps exchanged his military uniform for the garb of his former profession of schoolmaster and left Harlem Heights to begin his secret mission. To complete his disguise as an unemployed schoolteacher searching for work at the beginning of the academic

---

*The three fortified lines corresponded approximately to today's 147th, 153rd, and 159th Streets. Fort Washington stood in the area of present-day 183rd Street.
†American forces totaled 25,000 men on paper, but sickness and desertion had taken their toll.

Captain Nathan Hale

year, he removed the fancy silver buckles from his shoes and took along his Yale diploma.[27]

Aside from Hale's attention to such details, in almost every other respect his mission was poorly planned. Still inexperienced, Washington was not yet thinking in terms of the elaborate, mutually supporting intelligence network that he developed in and around New York later in the war. He asked Knowlton to find only a single volunteer to go to Long Island, instead of sending a few to ensure that at least one would return safely with the information he needed. Hale apparently received no special training, no money, and no names of sympathetic Americans he could turn to for help once he arrived behind enemy lines. Like a diver without a lifeline, he had no planned means of communication with headquarters. Perhaps his handlers' worst omission was the failure to give him invisible ink, which the British had been using for at least a year, and for which the Americans had invented their own formula three years earlier.[28]

For his part, Hale's patriotic fervor and his highly developed sense of duty were remarkable, but he was otherwise a poor candidate for the job. As another Yale classmate, Captain William Hull, put it, "his nature was too frank and open for deceit and disguise."[29] Not only was Hale guileless, he had other liabilities as a spy. Scars on his face from a gunpowder explosion made it easy to remember him and track him down if his activity became suspicious, and his cousin, Samuel Hale, was the British army's deputy commissary of prisoners and could readily identify him.[30]

A lack of secrecy about the mission was another element of its unprofessional implementation, and when William Hull heard about it, he tried to dissuade Hale from going. Hull argued that the dangerous assignment could not be required of anyone, and that espionage carried a stigma of deceit and dishonor with it. According to Hull, his friend was so eager to perform some active and tangible service for the American army, that nothing could stop him. Hale countered Hull's objections by asserting that "every kind of service, necessary to the public good, becomes honorable by being necessary."[31]

Despite his friend's pleas and with his numerous disadvantages, Hale intrepidly set out to find a place where he could evade the cordon of British warships and their tenders in the East River. He had to travel as far as Norwalk, Connecticut, where on or about September 12 the armed sloop *Schuyler* took him across the Sound to Huntington, Long Island, where his mission began.[32]

While there is no known documentation of Hale's activity nor of the information he gleaned, he was back on Manhattan on September 21 when the fire broke out. After the invasion on the fifteenth, the devoted spy apparently chose to follow Howe's army to New York City instead of simply returning safely across the Sound and back to the American lines with outdated information. Hale probably crossed the East River and slipped into the city unnoticed as a hired hand on one of the market boats that brought provisions to New York from the farms on Long Island. It appears he then traveled north toward the front lines and would likely have noted Lord Hugh Percy's units stationed on the East Side not far above the city, Clinton's troops spread out in a line some three miles farther north, and Cornwallis's troops forming the vanguard on Bloomingdale Heights.* Hale apparently determined that he could not continue straight across the Hollow Way to the American lines and instead looked for a boat just above the British front line on the east side of Manhattan that would have dropped him off either on Long Island or on the Westchester or Connecticut shore.[33]

Unfortunately for Washington and for Nathan Hale, whatever information he had gathered was written down on paper concealed in his clothing, and the fire in the city sealed Hale's fate. The captain of the British man-of-war *Halifax*, stationed in the Sound off Whitestone Point, noticed the column

---

*The British positions corresponded to today's East 18th, West 91st, and West 106th Streets (Johnston, *Harlem Heights,* map, p. 47; Bakeless, p. 117).

of smoke rising from New York and set out in a small boat with some sailors to investigate, landing on Manhattan exactly where Hale hoped to depart. In the darkness, Hale evidently mistook them for Americans; according to a British account, his nervousness tipped them off and led to his arrest.[34]

When Hale was searched, the British discovered the incriminating notes and sketches. They took him to General Howe's headquarters at the Beekman mansion, where he confessed that he was an American officer in disguise. Because he was out of uniform behind enemy lines, and therefore de facto a spy, Hale had effectively forfeited the protection and decent treatment that his rank would have conferred had he been taken prisoner during the course of a battle. The rules of war entitled Howe to execute him without trial.[35]

Because the hanging was to take place the following morning at a British artillery park north of the Beekman House (near present-day Third Avenue and Sixty-sixth Street), on the night of the twenty-first the British kept Hale in the greenhouse attached to the mansion instead of sending him to the jail on the Common, down in the city.[36] Nonetheless, he had fallen under the jurisdiction of William Cunningham, the brutal provost marshal who had been appointed to his job in 1775 after he fled to Boston, vowing revenge against the American patriots who tormented him by dragging him across the Common in New York.

On the twenty-second Cunningham oversaw the execution and denied Hale both of his final requests, first for a clergyman to be present, then for a Bible. Fortunately for Hale, the British chief engineer, John Montresor, was stationed at the artillery park and, with Cunningham's permission, brought Hale into his tent during a delay before the hanging. Ever since the days of the Stamp Act riot, when he prepared the guns in Fort George at the foot of Broadway, Montresor's expertise with artillery had placed him at the center of events in New York. On this occasion, Montresor reportedly observed that Cunningham was "hardened to human suffering and every softening sentiment of the heart."[37] The engineer tried to compensate for the jailer's lack of decency.

According to William Hull (the classmate who had tried to dissuade Hale from his mission), Montresor later recounted that he "requested the Provost Marshal to permit the prisoner to sit in my marquee, while he was making the necessary preparations. Captain Hale entered; he was calm, and bore himself with gentle dignity, in the consciousness of rectitude and high intentions," Hull quoted. "He asked for writing materials, which I furnished him: he wrote two letters," one to his brother Enoch and one to his commanding officer. "He was shortly after summoned to the gallows," according to Hull. "But a few persons were around him, yet his characteristic dying words were remembered. He said, 'I only regret that I have but one life to lose for my country.'"[38]

The British left Hale's body hanging as a deterrent to others, which was a common practice after executions. Unusually gruesome, however, was the pleasure British soldiers took in creating a display out of the corpse. They found "in a rebel Gentleman's garden, a painted soldier on a board, and hung it along with the Rebel; and wrote upon it, General Washington," a British officer wrote in a letter to England, "and I saw it yesterday beyond headquarters by the roadside."[39]

It is entirely possible that Hale spoke the famous last words attributed to him. That they paraphrase a line from Joseph Addison's *Cato*, a classic English play that was widely read in America and often quoted in Washington's writings, lends credibility to this account. Frederick Mackenzie, however, the British officer who described the fire so vividly in his diary, recorded Hale's final words somewhat differently. "He behaved with great composure and resolution, saying that he thought it the duty of every good officer to obey any orders given him by his Commander in Chief; and desired the spectators to be at all times prepared to meet death in whatever shape it might appear."[40]

According to Mackenzie, Hale's "manly bearing and the evident disinterested patriotism of the handsome young prisoner, sensibly touched a chord of General Howe's nature; but the stern rules of war concerning such offenses would not allow him to exercise even pity."[41] That Howe chose to exercise his prerogative and deny Hale a trial is striking, however, since spies on both sides were often given the benefit of a court-martial during the Revolution and subsequent American wars.[42]

The swift, ruthless punishment of Hale has been ascribed to British anger over the fire in New York. Arguments have even been made asserting that Hale's real mission was to burn down the city. However, it would have made no sense for him to begin his mission on Long Island if he intended to burn New York City. At the time of his departure from Harlem Heights, on September 12, the Americans had begun to retreat, but they were still in possession of the city. If Hale had wanted to enter the town and prepare to destroy it, he might have simply headed south on the Post Road.[43] The British, furthermore, never accused Hale of arson, because they found papers on him that confirmed him to be a spy. Desperate for a conviction in the case of the fire, they would have trumpeted Hale's capture and execution had they believed he was responsible for an act that, according to one loyalist newspaper, rivaled the Gunpowder Plot* in its sinister intent and destructive potential.[44] Instead, they muted the story.

Cunningham apparently made sure that the letters Hale wrote in Montresor's tent never reached their intended recipients. Enoch Hale learned about them from an American prisoner who spoke with Cunningham shortly after the execution. "He saw my Brother's Diploma which the Provost Marshal showed him who also had two letters of his—one to me, the other to his commanding officer written after he was sentenced," Enoch wrote in his diary.[45] According to Hull, "The Provost Martial, in the diabolical spirit of cruelty, destroyed the letters of the prisoner, and assigned as a reason 'that the rebels should never know they had a man who could die with so much firmness.'"[46]

Again it was Montresor who tried to circumvent Cunningham's harshness. Hale was hanged at eleven A.M. on September 22, and that evening, Montresor arrived at the American lines under a flag of truce with a letter from General Howe to Washington about an exchange of prisoners. The shocking news of Hale's execution was not part of the official communication, but Montresor, who "seemed touched by the circumstances attending" the event, according to Hull, recounted what had transpired that morning.[47]

General Putnam, Captain Alexander Hamilton of the artillery, and Hull repeated "the melancholy particulars" that the engineer had given them, and feelings of anger—which had pervaded the British camp after the fire—soon spread through the American command as well.[48] "The General is determined, if he can bring some in his hands under the denomination of spies, to execute them," Washington's aide-de-camp, Tench Tilghman, wrote in a letter. "General Howe hanged a Captain of ours belonging to Knowlton's Rangers who went into New York to make discoveries. I don't see why we should not make retaliation."[49]

The death of one of his secret operatives, much as it may have outraged

*Guy Fawkes's Gunpowder Plot of November 5, 1605, an unsuccessful attempt by Catholic conspirators to blow up Britain's Parliament.

or saddened Washington, was naturally not something he chose to publicize and use for propaganda, especially since he immediately began sending out other spies and developing a more sophisticated—and less vulnerable— intelligence-gathering network in New York and on Long Island.[50] As a result, despite the account from Montresor, Hale's story remained little known for many years, as the British, particularly Cunningham, evidently preferred. It took almost five months for newspapers to publish confused versions of the events, and the first book of history to include Hale did not appear until 1799—almost twenty-three years later.[51]

On the day Hale was hanged, another execution of an American was scheduled to take place, this one by the Continental Army against one of its own— a soldier accused of desertion in the midst of the Battle of Harlem Heights on September 16. Ebenezer Leffingwell had been intercepted as he retreated from the fighting by Colonel Joseph Reed, Washington's adjutant. Leffingwell claimed he had been sent by his officers to procure more ammunition, and it is clear Joseph Martin and the rank-and-file soldiers believed him. Reed, however, accused him of deserting his post. The fragile harmony between the troops and their commanders that had resulted from the victory on the sixteenth was threatened on the twenty-second.

"[Leffingwell] remonstrated with the officer," Martin recalled,

> and informed him of the absolute necessity there was of obeying the orders of his own officers, that the failure of his procuring a supply of ammunition might endanger the success of the day. But all to no purpose. The officer would not allow himself to believe him, but drew his sword and threatened to take his life on the spot if he did not immediately return to his corps. The sergeant, fired with just indignation at hearing and seeing his life threatened, cocked his musket, and stood in his own defense. He was, however, taken, confined and tried for mutiny, and condemned to be shot.[52]

In Reed's version of the incident, Leffingwell was plainly running away, not carrying out a vital mission for his superiors, and the clash was far more violent. At the court-martial on September 19, Reed testified that he had just ordered Leitch and his men to reinforce Knowlton's flanking party: "[I] was going up to where the firing was, when I met the Prisoner [Leffingwell]

Colonel Joseph Reed

running away from where the firing was with every Mark of Trepidation & Fear." Then, Reed continued: "I followed him & ordered him back after striking him. He promised to return & went on into the Bushes. A little after I saw him running again, & pursued him with a Determination to mark him, & came upon him & struck him with my Hanger [sword] & wounded him in the Head & Hand."[53] Leffingwell was certainly a marked man at this point: One of his thumbs had been chopped off.[54] "He bid me keep off or he would shoot me," Reed testified. "He presented his Peice & I think snapp'd his Peice at me. I found him after this lying in a Ditch, on his seeing me he fell to bellowing out, & I should have shot him, could I have got my Gun off. He has since confess'd to me that he was running away at the Time I met him."[55]

Washington approved the sentence of the court-martial, and Leffingwell was brought before a firing squad on September 22. However, he was reprieved at the last minute, apparently because Washington sensed the growing anger of the troops. "The reprieve was read by one of the chaplains of the army," Martin wrote,

> after a long harangue to the soldiers setting forth the enormity of the crime charged upon the prisoner, repeatedly using this sentence, "crimes for which men ought to die," which did much to further the resentment of the troops already raised to a high pitch. . . . I believe it was well that he was [reprieved], for his

blood would not have been the only blood that would have been spilt: the troops were greatly exasperated, and they showed what their feelings were by their lively and repeated cheerings after the reprieve, but more so by their secret and open threats before it.[56]

CHAPTER 15

Throg's Neck and
the Battle of Pelham Bay

~⌒~

"I Plainly find that in order to Do my Duty as I would Chuse I want a Strong Constitution, as many times must be exposed to heavy fateague," Colonel William Douglas wrote to his wife from the Harlem lines on September 26. He had briefly mentioned a persistent cough in several previous letters, but mostly he focused on the plight of his troops. They had lost their baggage, clothing, and tents in the retreat; there were no proper hospital facilities in the camp; and the army was running out of medicines. He told his wife, "these things appear but Small at First (but men are not made of Steel) and those things have great wait in an army toward keeping up the Sperits of the troops, and if we conduct so as to Disparit our men we are Done."[1]

Congress was desperately short of funds and still had much to learn about creating an efficient supply system for an army. The commissaries struggled to buy provisions from hostile farmers who did not want to accept worthless Continental dollars and preferred to sell to the British. At the end of this disorganized supply chain, the soldiers went without food. Douglas, as usual, minimized his own discomfort and closed a letter to his wife in October by assuring her, "I am well all but a bad Cough, which troubles me much."[2]

Joseph Martin, like his regimental commander, detailed the hardships the men faced as summer turned to fall on Harlem Heights.

We remained here till sometime in the month of October without anything very material transpiring, excepting starvation and *that* had by this time become quite a secondary matter; hard duty and nakedness were considered the prime evils. . . . It now began to be cool weather, especially the nights. To have to lie as I did almost every night (for our duty required it) on the cold and often wet ground without a blanket and with nothing but thin summer clothing was tedious. I have often while upon guard lain on one side until the upper side smarted with cold, then turned that side down to the place warmed by my body and let the other take its turn smarting . . . till called upon to go on sentry, as the soldiers term it, and when relieved from a tour of two long hours at that business and returned to guard again, have had to go through the operation of freezing and thawing for four or six hours more. In the morning the ground as white as snow with hoar frost. Or perhaps it would rain all night like a flood; all that could be done in that case was to lie down (if one could lie down), take our musket in our arms and place the lock between our thighs and "weather it out."[3]

Since the British possessed New York City and loyalists had begun to return in late September, Governor Tryon and other officials expected William Smith, as a member of His Majesty's Council, to return home from exile at his country house on the Hudson. Instead, Smith moved his family deeper into rebel territory.[4] His eldest daughter, emotionally traumatized by the dislocation and strife brought on by the war, had just died suddenly from unexplained causes. During her bereavement Smith's wife, Janet, received a visit from her sister, Margaret Livingston. Margaret hoped a change of environment would do Janet good and urged her to visit Livingston Manor. Instead of returning to New York, the Smiths moved to the estate owned by one of New York's most prominent Revolutionary families, the bonds of marriage further complicating Smith's already ambiguous stance in the burgeoning conflict.

While his presence at Livingston Manor raised questions about his loyalty among the British, Smith's predictions that armed rebellion would fail did not ingratiate him to his host or to the other Revolutionary leaders who frequently visited the estate. At one point Robert Livingston and Smith stopped talking to each other for three months. After one of Robert's sons declared that the Americans should seek a peace agreement and then fled to

New England, and another son left for New York City to join the British, rumors abounded that Smith's presence had infected the Livingston family with a loyalist strain. Nonetheless, the Smiths remained at the manor, and the visit originally intended to distract Janet from her grief stretched out over most of the next two years.

By October 1776, for vastly different reasons, Lieutenant General Henry Clinton echoed Private Joseph Martin's complaint that weeks had passed without anything material transpiring between the two armies—except an improvement in Washington's defenses as a result of General Howe's habitual delays. This time, Howe hesitated to strike at Washington because he had received overly optimistic reports that the northern army under Sir Guy Carleton and his subordinate, General John Burgoyne, would soon reach Albany; he also expected help from a contingent of 8,000 more Hessians due to arrive from Europe.[5] Howe did not yet know that on October 11, in the Battle of Valcour Island, the two fleets constructed by Arnold and Carleton during the summer had finally clashed on Lake Champlain. Carleton was victorious, but with winter approaching, he made a fateful decision to postpone his thrust southward toward Ticonderoga until the following spring. "Gentleman Johnny" Burgoyne fled the Canadian winter for the high life in London.[6] Howe finally gave up waiting for support from Albany and looked at his remaining options for encircling the rebels.

Clinton's original plan to trap the Americans by reaching Kingsbridge ahead of them had been ignored, and he next proposed a landing farther north at New Rochelle in Westchester County at a safe distance from Kingsbridge. By doing so, he planned to cut off Washington's three lines of communication with the mainland—the two roads to Connecticut and the one to Albany—and pry him out of his stronghold and into a decisive battle on British terms, or force him to flee New York altogether. This, along with "the assistance of our armed vessels in the Hudson," Clinton wrote, "would enable us to embarrass the enemy's supplies both from the eastern and southern colonies."[7] Admiral Howe rejected this plan, however, since he thought the fleet would not be safe at New Rochelle. In the end, Clinton reluctantly agreed with the other British commanders to land farther south at Throg's Neck.[8] As he had with Grant and von Heister in Brooklyn, Howe left Lord Percy with three brigades in front of the American lines in Manhattan to hold their attention.

The third amphibious landing in New York by the British put on display all of Admiral Howe's expert seamanship, and Clinton came to respect the admiral as much as he disdained his brother. The army began to embark at Kips Bay at three A.M. on October 12, but the fleet did not sail up the East River until well after sunrise. Just as the ships entered the hazardous waters of Hell Gate, a thick fog wrapped them in complete darkness; the legendary rocks and whirlpools in the narrow channel suddenly became a grave threat to the eighty British vessels. Under Admiral Howe's direction, however, the nearly disastrous passage succeeded with minimal loss of life and equipment. Clinton reported that "the Admiral, who was present, persisted notwithstanding in the prosecution of the move at every hazard, and by his own excellent management and that of his officers the whole got through, almost miraculously, without any other loss than that of an artillery boat with a few men and three six-pounders, and even that by an accident not in the least imputable to his Lordship or the navy."[9]

By all accounts, it was a tremendous feat, especially in the eyes of local pilots, who knew firsthand the dangers of taking far smaller sailing vessels through Hell Gate. "Those men were in the utmost astonishment to see ships of war of 44 guns, frigates, transports full of troops, horses and waggons, and flat boats with troops and artillery, attempting and accomplishing so difficult an undertaking with such a trifling loss," Lieutenant Mackenzie wrote. "To any other nation the obstacles would have seemed insurmountable."[10]

The Throg's Neck Peninsula juts into Long Island Sound and was due east of Washington's army on Harlem Heights. That morning, the thick fog at first hid the British forces from view. Then as the sun rose and the fog lifted, fishermen on shore were astonished to see a frigate and barges full of soldiers, horses, and cannons all pulled in close for the landing. The boats filled the horizon all the way back to Hell Gate.[11] Clinton later recalled that the landing went smoothly at first, with only feeble resistance from a few Americans. The British formed ranks and immediately set out to secure the bridge at the village of Westchester, only to find that the Americans had already destroyed it.

Ten days earlier, General Heath had anticipated a possible British landing on the peninsula, which became an island at high tide, separated from the mainland by Westchester Creek and the marsh along its borders; only a causeway and bridge at one end, and a ford at the other, connected the peninsula to the mainland.[12] Near the bridge stood a mill and a woodpile "as advantageously situated to cover a party to defend the pass, as if constructed for the very purpose." Heath had ordered Colonel Hand to assign an officer and twenty-five of his best men to this naturally defensible spot "as their alarm-post at all times; and, in case the enemy made a landing on Frogs [Throg's] Neck, to direct this officer immediately to take up the planks of the bridge; to have everything in readiness to set the mill on fire; but not to do it, unless the fire of the riflemen should appear insufficient to check the advance of the enemy on to the causeway; to assign another party to the head of the creek; to reinforce both, in case the enemy landed."[13] Hand's men had been at their position for several days.

Some of the 4,000 British soldiers marching on the Throg's Neck Road split off onto the Pelham Road and headed for the ford. The main force reached the causeway and was stopped in its tracks on discovering that Hand's men had removed the planks from the bridge. Under attack from the riflemen behind the woodpile, the British pulled back and built an earthwork to cover themselves while they returned the American fire. Some of these shots, aimed across the creek, rained down on the village of Westchester, cracking the church bell and wounding civilians.[14] The other British detachment was stopped at the ford by American guards and also had to retreat. Temporarily, at least, the Americans had used New York's unique topography to offset the superior strength and numbers of the British forces.

The British, not for the first or last time in the New York campaign, had also helped the Americans by making a serious blunder. "There appears to me an actual fatality attending all their measures," William Duer, a member of the New York Provincial Congress, wrote shortly after the Throg's Neck landing. "One would have naturally imagined from the Traitors they have among them, who are capable of giving them the most minute description of the Grounds in the county of Westchester, that they would have landed much farther to the Eastward. Had they pushed their imaginations to discover the worst place, they could not have succeeded better than they have done."[15]

General Heath sent a messenger galloping from Kingsbridge to the Morris House with news of the British landing, but instead of retreating from Harlem Heights, Washington ordered Heath to reinforce both choke points on Throg's Neck with more men and artillery. As Washington explained in a letter to Congress, "The grounds [leading] from Frogs point [to Kings Bridge] are strong and defensible, being full of Stone fences, both along the road and across the adjacent Fields, which will render it difficult for artillery, or . . . [for a] large body of foot to advance in any regular order except through the main road," where they would be vulnerable to an American attack.[16] By evening, 1,800 Americans confronted the British at Throg's Neck. Instead of reembarking his men and landing farther east, Howe kept his army encamped on the island and lost several precious days waiting for additional supplies from Manhattan.

This latest of Howe's many delays gave Washington time to reorganize the American army and consider how to respond to the British threat on his left flank—and possibly on his rear. Charles Lee was back from the South, and Sullivan and Stirling, captured in the Battle of Brooklyn, had been released in an exchange of prisoners. On October 15, Washington created seven divisions in the American army under Greene, Lee, Heath, Sullivan, Putnam, Spencer, and Benjamin Lincoln. When he assigned Lee to the largest and strategically most important division—the army's left wing in the area north of Kingsbridge—Washington instructed him to spend two days becoming familiar with the terrain before actively assuming command.[17] The strongly opinionated Lee in turn had some immediate advice for the commander in chief: Make a full retreat from Harlem Heights to prevent an encirclement by the British.

Lee's reputation in the Continental Army was at its peak. The presence of the Englishman fueled the feeling that the battle for New York had so far been a victory in disguise, because they had outwitted and outmaneuvered the greatest army Britain could have possibly placed in the field. "The Enemy have made no move from Frog's Point," Tench Tilghman, Washington's aide-de-camp, wrote to William Duer of the New York Provincial Congress. "I don't know how it is, but I believe their design to circumvent us this time will prove as abortive as the former ones. If we can but foil Gen. Howe again, I think we knock him up for the Campaign. You ask if Gen. Lee is in Health and our people feel bold? I answer both in the affirmative. His appearance among us has not contributed a little to the latter."[18]

In a letter to his wife on October 15, Colonel William Douglas evinced that boldness. "Is he become tory because we have Lost a Little ground?" Douglas asked about a friend who had not responded to his letters. "Amarica will not yet be concored. God may Defeat us and Punish us for our Sins, untill we humble our Selves but he will not give up Amarica yet."[19]

Spurred by Lee's dire warnings, Washington convened a meeting of his generals at headquarters the following day; they voted to abandon Harlem Heights immediately and retreat to White Plains, while they could still get there first and entrench themselves in the hills. The terrain around the village offered a strong defensive position from which the Americans could fall back to the even more formidable hills at North Castle Heights to the north. An additional attraction at White Plains was a supply depot established by Governor Trumbull of Connecticut, who had sent barrels of flour and other stores there for Washington's use. Edward Hand's twenty-five riflemen behind the woodpile at Throg's Neck had stymied Howe's 4,000 troops just long enough for American reinforcements to arrive and block the British advance to Kingsbridge. The check at Westchester Creek, combined with Howe's delay to wait for supplies, and Lee's insistent advice, gave Washington a head start in the race for the hills above White Plains.

According to Joseph Reed, it was Lee's influence at this critical moment that saved the Continental Army.[20] Clinton also learned of Lee's role, and his assessment was essentially the same, with the addition of Howe's delay to resupply his troops as a crucial factor: "On our landing from Frog's neck Lee is supposed to have gone to Washington and prevailed on him to have moved. But had it been possible for us to have been at Rochelle . . . three days sooner, Washington must have attacked us on our own terms or lost all of his communication and laid down his arms, probably."[21]

General Greene's advice to Washington at this juncture was of more questionable value. He insisted that Fort Washington should be held despite the retreat—which would leave it isolated in enemy territory—arguing that the Americans needed a foothold on Manhattan to preserve a line of communication with New England across the Hudson; in concert with Fort Constitution, Fort Washington was a deterrent to British ships sailing up the river, he claimed. The commander at the fort, Colonel Robert Magaw, was convinced he could defend it against the British until December if necessary, and Greene assumed that in extremis, he could evacuate the men across the river to New Jersey. Washington had also received a request from Congress a few days earlier, urging him to obstruct the Hudson between Fort Constitution and Fort Washington as effectively as possible. (In late October, Fort Constitution was renamed Fort Lee in honor of Charles Lee.) In the face of this advice and pressure, Washington, nonetheless, had deep misgivings about such plans.[22] It was against his better judgment that he acquiesced in the decision of the war council to leave 1,200 men behind in the fort.*

As Washington headed north toward White Plains, General Howe belatedly realized that Throg's Neck had been a poor choice for a landing and reem-

---

*In addition to these 1,200 men, more than 1,500 would soon be sent to the fort.

barked for Pelham,* a true peninsula where there had been no American defenders. His delay, however, allowed deserters time to inform the Americans of Howe's intentions.[23]

On October 16, Heath wrote that the "General Officers of the army rode to reconnoitre the ground at Pell's Neck,† &c. and it was determined that the position of the American army should be immediately changed; the left flank to be extended more northerly, to prevent its being turned by the British."[24] The following day, roughly 1,000 men from Lee's division were dispatched to Pelham under Colonel John Glover. The Marblehead mariner's superb management of the boats during the retreat from Long Island had won him Washington's gratitude and confidence, and Glover was charged with protecting the retreating army by delaying the British should they land at Pelham.

By the eighteenth, a column of 13,000 American troops had been slowly and painfully set in motion from Manhattan into Westchester. As it struggled with a shortage of horses and wagons, the army had to drag much of its baggage and artillery by hand. The available wagons shuttled loads of supplies over King's Bridge, dumped them by the side of the road, and then returned to Manhattan for more.[25] To make up for lost time, Washington sought the shortest possible route to White Plains, keeping to the interior of Westchester County, close to the western bank of the Bronx River, instead of marching farther west along the Hudson at a safer distance from Howe's forces.[26]

Washington transferred his headquarters up to Valentine's Hill (about a mile and a half northeast of King's Bridge, near the Bronx River)‡ and sent his wagons of provisions and supplies ahead to the depot that had previously been established at White Plains. To occupy the strategic high ground, Washington dispatched Lord Stirling and his brigade to reach White Plains ahead of the army.[27] Whether Stirling arrived there ahead of General Howe, and whether the rest of Washington's army arrived there safely soon after him, depended to a large extent on the success or failure of the detached force from Lee's division that awaited the British landing at Pelham.

Early on the morning of October 18, as the American army left Kingsbridge, Colonel John Glover climbed a hill near the village of Eastchester, where his men were guarding the roads from Pell's Point to the interior of Westchester

---

*Part of present-day Pelham Bay Park in the Bronx.
†Present-day Rodman's Neck in Pelham Bay Park.
‡Today, in the vicinity of the Jerome Reservoir in the Bronx.

County. Through his spyglass, Glover spotted a number of ships in the Sound under way. "In a very short time I saw the boats, upwards of 200 sail, all manned and formed in four grand divisions," he wrote in a letter four days later. "I immediately sent off Major Lee express to General Lee, who was about three miles distant, and without waiting his orders, turned out the brigade I have the honour to command, and very luckily for us I did, as it turned out afterwards, the enemy having stolen a march one and a half miles on us."[28] Clinton and Cornwallis had managed to put 4,000 men on the Pelham shore before sunrise and advanced quickly along the road to Eastchester.

Outnumbered more than five to one, Glover nonetheless abandoned his camp and hurried to confront the British: "I marched down to oppose their landing with about seven hundred and fifty men, and three field-pieces, but had not gone more than half the distance before I met their advanced guard, about thirty men; upon which I detached a Captain's guard of forty men to meet them, while I could dispose of the main body to advantage."[29] Glover arranged three of his four small regiments (each consisting of roughly 200 men) at intervals behind the stone walls lining Split Rock Road, the narrow lane to the interior. As Washington had predicted with regard to the road from Throg's Neck, these walls, and more stone walls dividing the adjacent fields of Pelham, confined the regimented British column, with its long train of artillery and baggage, to the narrow road, where it had to run a gauntlet of American gunfire.[30]

Glover enhanced the destructive effect of his small force by coordinating a relay from one unit to the next: After a regiment popped up from behind the walls and fired several volleys at close range, it was to fall back to a new position, farther ahead of the British, while the next regiment, hidden on the opposite side of the road, took its turn firing at the enemy. Glover's own regiment with the three pieces of artillery stayed back on a hillside across Hutchinson's Creek from the scene of the ambush.[31]

"I did the best I could, and disposed of my little party to the best of my judgement," Glover wrote.

> Oh! the anxiety of mind I was then in for the fate of the day—the lives of seven hundred and fifty men immediately at hazard, and under God their preservation entirely depended on their being well disposed of; besides this, my country, my honour, my own life and everything that was dear, appeared at that critical moment to be at stake—I would have given a thousand worlds to have had General Lee, or some other experienced officer present, to direct,

Colonel John Glover

or at least to approve of what I had done—looked around, but could see none, they all being three miles from me, and the action came on so sudden it was out of their power to be with me.[32]

Reinforcements from the main body of British troops caught up to its advance guard, and Glover ordered his own patrol to retreat. Pressing their advantage and not knowing what lay in store, the British "gave a shout" and advanced on the heels of the retreating Americans. Glover's first concealed unit was "laying under cover of a stone wall undiscovered till they came within thirty yards, then rose up and gave them the whole charge; the enemy broke and retreated for the main body to come up."[33] The 4,000 British and Hessian troops appeared with seven fieldpieces and kept up a steady artillery barrage as they pressed forward. The Americans waited behind the same stone wall until the enemy had approached within fifty yards, when the whole battalion fired in unison. The British "halted and returned the fire with showers of musketry and cannon balls," Glover recalled. "We exchanged seven rounds at this post, retreated, and formed in the rear of Colonel [William] Shepherd and on his left."[34]

As Glover put his tactical relay into effect, falling back and alternating his attacks from one side of the road to the other, his men steadily poured an increasing number of rounds into the massive enemy column, which provided an easy target. Colonel Loammi Baldwin led the last regiment and reported that his men stayed "calm . . . as though . . . expecting a Shot at a flock of Pidgeons or Ducks."[35] Again Clinton's troops "shouted and pushed on," clearly expecting that this next charge would put a quick end to the fighting. Shepherd, "posted behind a fine double stone wall . . . fired by grand divisions, by which he kept up a constant fire, and maintained his part till he exchanged seventeen rounds with them, and caused them to retreat several times, once in particular so far that a soldier of Colonel Shepherd's leaped over the wall and took a hat and canteen off a Captain that lay dead on the ground they retreated from," Glover wrote.[36]

Despite the Americans' success, the overwhelming size of Clinton's army and its "heavy train of artillery" eventually forced Glover to retreat altogether. The first and second regiments fell back and formed behind the third, and the relay came to an end. Baldwin emphasized that this was no panicked flight. They retreated "with the greatest reluctance Immaginable though with as much good order and Regularity as ever they marched off a Publick Parade."[37]

As Clinton's column approached, the Americans escaped across the creek; since Glover had dismantled the bridge in the morning, the British ended their pursuit. Glover then gathered his men on the hillside where he had left his fieldpieces and his reserve corps. "The enemy halted and played away their artillery at us and we at them, 'til night, without any damage on our side and but little on theirs," Glover wrote.[38]

Remarkably, Glover calculated that he had suffered only twenty-one casualties—eight killed and thirteen wounded—in this extremely unequal contest. When General Howe reported only three of his own men dead and twenty wounded to Lord Germain in London, he followed the usual practice of excluding from his count the Hessians—who comprised three-quarters of the British force in the Battle of Pelham Bay. Casualty estimates from deserters suggested a much higher toll, from 200 up to 800 and even 1,000. Colonel Baldwin, who had led the rear guard of the American retreat and therefore had had the best view of Split Rock Road at the end of the battle, concluded, "From what I saw myself and good information . . . [the] enemy must have lost at least two hundred men dead."[39] When the number of wounded is added, the higher casualty figures of four or five times that number may not be exaggerated.[40]

The number of Hessian dead in the Battle of Pelham Bay remains conjectural and controversial, and some authorities assert that there is no hard evidence to support the higher estimates. Nonetheless, the tremendous strategic significance of the battle is beyond dispute. By obstructing the British advance for a day, Glover and his men helped Washington win the race to White Plains.[41] Notwithstanding his wish for a higher-ranking officer to guide him, it seems in retrospect that no general could have done better than Glover in his new role as a battalion commander.[42] One historian later quipped that it was fortunate for the American army that Charles Lee was not there, or he probably would have ordered Glover to retreat immediately.[43]

After dark Glover's men crept away from the hill and marched for three miles toward Dobbs Ferry on the Hudson before stopping for the night. The men were spent, but they had to endure a cold, sleepless night in the open, watching for the British.[44] As Glover wrote, "After fighting all day without victuals or drink, [we had to lie] as a picket all night, the heavens over us and the earth under us, which was all we had, having left our baggage at the old encampment we left in the morning."[45]

CHAPTER 16

The Battle of White Plains

~⁀

A t a high price in casualties, Clinton's landing at Pelham had placed the vital coast road along the Sound in British hands. "The Commander in Chief joined us here [at Eastchester] and, the rebels being forced to quit the high-road, the gross of our army lay this night on their great communication with New England," Clinton wrote.[1] The British stood poised to cut off the rest of Washington's communication and supply lines to the mainland as well.

Once again—as he had throughout the New York campaign—General Howe belatedly acceded to the commonsense advice that Clinton had given him from the start.[2] "Many plans for our further proceedings became now again the subject of deliberation," Clinton recalled. "Mine, still inclining for Rochelle, was at last adopted, and the grand depot removed in consequence to Myer's Neck. For, though Lord Howe had formerly objected to this place as dangerous for the ships, it was now, upon being examined more minutely, judged to be the most commodious that could be found; and all our supplies were accordingly landed there."[3] On October 19, the day after the Pelham landing, Howe left Eastchester and moved his army to New Rochelle, where he lingered for another three days, waiting to be reinforced by 8,000 Hessians under Lieutenant General Wilhelm von Knyphausen, who had recently arrived on Staten Island; it took until the twenty-second to transfer them to Westchester.[4]

· · ·

Two days after the Battle of Pelham Bay, as Howe moved to New Rochelle, Washington, himself unfamiliar with the terrain of Westchester County, dispatched his chief engineer, Colonel Rufus Putnam, on a reconnaissance mission to discover the British position and determine how soon they might reach White Plains.[5] "On my route I was liable to meet with some British or tory parties, who probably would have made me a prisoner (as I had no knowledge of any way of escape across the Brunx but the one I came out)," Putnam recounted later. "Hence I was induced to disguise myself by taking out my cockade, loping my hat and secreting my sword and pistols under my loose coat, and then had I been taken under this disguise, the probability is that I should have been hanged for a spy."

Without the benefit of a map, Putnam set off on horseback along a road that he guessed would take him in the direction of White Plains. He learned from a local resident that the British were at New Rochelle.

> On this information I turned and pursued my route toward White-plains (the houses on the way all deserted) until I came within three or four miles of the place; here I discovered a house a little ahead with men about it. By my glass I found they were not British soldiers; however, I approached them with caution. I called for some oats for my horse, sat down and heard them chat some little time, when I found they were friends to the cause of America, and then I began to make the necessary enquiries, and on the whole I found that the main body of the British lay near New Rochelle, from thence to White-plains about nine miles, good roads and in general level open country, that at Whiteplains was a large quantity of stores, with only about three hundred militia to guard them, that the British had a detachment at Mamaroneck, only six miles from White-plains, and from Whiteplains only five miles to the North River, where lay five or six of the enemies ships and sloops, tenders, etc.

It was clear that Howe had only to reach White Plains and proceed to a rendezvous with his brother's vessels at Tarrytown on the Hudson in order to encircle Washington's forces completely. Putnam immediately set off to inform Washington of his discoveries. After sunset, he encountered Lord Stirling at the head of the American column, refreshed himself, and then

Colonel Rufus Putnam

quickly covered the ten miles back to Washington's headquarters, still on Valentine's Hill: "[I followed] a road I had never travelled, among the tory inhabitants and in the night. I dare not enquire the way, but Providence conducted me."

The disturbing intelligence of Howe's proximity to White Plains spurred Washington to hasten the agonizingly slow retreat. After General George Clinton (who had known the area since childhood) confirmed the accuracy of Putnam's sketch of the countryside and his description of Westchester County, Washington dispatched the travel-weary Putnam back to Stirling, at the head of the column, with instructions for him to hurry to White Plains without delay to protect the army's supplies. "I arrived at his quarters about two o'clock in the morning. . . . Lord St[i]rling's division marched before daylight and we arrived at Whiteplains about 9 o'clock A.M. and thus was the American army saved (by an interposing providence from a probable total destruction)."

Putnam introduced a note of modesty into his account by blaming Howe's ineptitude and crediting his own valor to the workings of a higher power. "I may be asked wherein this particular interposition of providence appears," Putnam wrote. "I answer, first, in the stupidity of the British general, in that he did not early on the morning of the 20th send a detachment and take possession of the post and stores at Whiteplains, for had he done this, we must then have fought him on his own terms, and such disadvantageous terms on our part, as humanly speaking must have proved our overthrow; again when I parted with Col. Reed . . . as before mentioned, I have

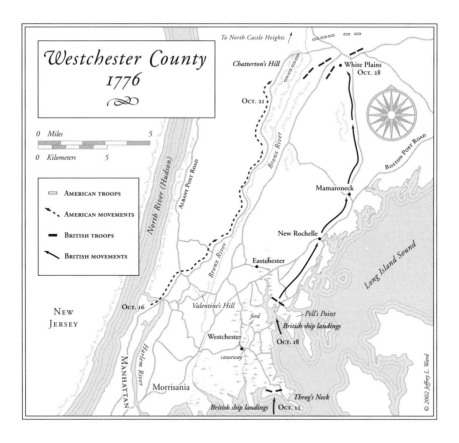

always thought that I was moved to so hazardous an undertaking by foreign influence."

While Putnam had nimbly traversed the county, Washington's famished, exhausted troops had continued their slow retreat. "We crossed Kingsbridge and directed our course toward the White Plains," Joseph Martin wrote. "We saw parties of the enemy foraging in the country, but they were generally too alert for us. We encamped on the heights called Valentine's Hill, where we continued some days, keeping up the old system of starving. A sheep's head which I begged of the butchers who were killing some for the 'gentlemen officers,' was all the provisions I had for two or three days."[6]

Eventually, Martin's hunger overtook his fear of a deadly encounter with the enemy, and he left the safety of the camp whenever possible in search of food. His encounter with an officer and a doctor after his return from one of these forays revealed the anger behind Martin's cynicism toward anyone in a position of authority in the army—and the sense of humor that apparently enabled him to endure his years of service.

While lying here I one day rambled into the woods and fields in order, if possible, to procure something to satisfy the cravings of nature. I found and ate a considerable quantity of chestnuts which are, as Bloomfield says of his acorns, "hot, thirsty food," which was I suppose the cause of our doctor's blunder, as I shall relate directly. I returned to camp just at sunset and met our orderly sergeant who immediately warned me to prepare for a two-days command. What is termed going on command is what is generally called going on a scouting party or something similar. I told the sergeant I was sick and could not go. He said I must go to the doctor and if he said I was unfit for duty, he must excuse me. I saw our surgeon's mate close by, endeavoring to cook his supper, blowing the fire and scratching his eyes. We both stepped up to him and he felt my pulse, at the same time very demurely shutting his eyes while I was laughing in his face. After a minute's consultation with his medical talisman, he very gravely told the sergeant that I was unfit for duty, having a high fever upon me. I was as well as he was; all the medicine I needed was a bellyful of victuals. The sergeant turned to go off for another man when I told him that I would go, for I meant to go; I only felt a little cross and did not know how just then to vent my spleen in any other way. I had much rather go on such an expedition than stay in camp, as I stood some chance while in the country to get something to eat. But I admired the doctor's skill, although perhaps not more extraordinary than that of many others of the "faculty."[7]

When Martin returned from detached duty, his regiment had already left Valentine's Hill for White Plains, so he marched with Heath's division, which began its all-night trek on October 21, arriving at White Plains at dawn on the twenty-second.[8] Washington had by then taken possession of the high ground, his lines extending from the steep and wooded Chatterton's Hill (on the right) to a nearby lake (on the left.) "Long poles with iron pikes upon them, supplied the want of bayonets," Benjamin Tallmadge recalled.[9] Some of the breastworks were improvised as well: Cornstalks pulled from the fields were stacked with the clods of earth on the bottoms facing the enemy, quickly creating defenses that looked much stronger than they were.[10]

"Cha[tt]erton's Hill was separated from the right of our intrenchment by a valley of some extent, with the river Bronx directly before it; but being within cannon shot of our intrenchment on the right, Gen. Washington thought it best to occupy it and ordered Gen. McDougall, with 800 or 1,000 men, to defend it, and if driven from it, to retire upon the right of the line," Tallmadge wrote.[11] Washington had already sent his ubiquitous chief engineer, Rufus Putnam, and two regiments of militia to fortify the hill.

After lingering for three days at New Rochelle, General Howe proceeded north to Mamaroneck, where, slow and deliberate, he paused for another four days. When the British finally moved again, Clinton, as usual, served as Howe's point man, striking out ahead of the main army, within three miles of the American position, to reconnoiter the ground and tighten the noose on Washington's supply routes. Clinton's advice was to follow a strategy similar to the one that had succeeded on Long Island: Perform extensive reconnaissance to become familiar with the roads as well as the terrain around White Plains and the American positions; fall back to New Rochelle while sending out diversionary detachments; and finally, march all night in order to launch a surprise attack on the American camp at dawn.[12]

"The General seemed at first to incline to my opinion," Clinton wrote. However, on the twenty-seventh, Howe changed his mind and sent Clinton forward to determine if an immediate attack seemed feasible. Clinton came back with a remarkably accurate assessment of the situation: "[I] could not from what I saw recommend a direct attack, as I suspected that the enemy's lines at the White Plains shouldered to the Bronx [River] and to the mountains, whereby their flanks were safe and their retreat practicable when they pleased."[13] Nonetheless, on the cold, bright morning of October 28, Howe ordered his entire force of 14,000 men forward to White Plains for an attack on the American lines. He did listen to one piece of Clinton's advice: The army should proceed in several columns, with Clinton leading the one farthest to the right, whose task would be to outflank the Americans while they fought the British column on the left.

By the time Howe's forces finally approached, Washington had been digging in and studying the terrain around the rural village for almost a week. General Heath later recalled that he was with Washington and Lee on horseback that morning, discussing which of the surrounding hills should be occupied, when a horseman came galloping up with the message that the British were bearing down on the American lines. Back at headquarters, they found the army primed for battle. According to Heath, Washington turned to his officers and said simply, "Gentlemen, you will repair to your respective posts, and do the best you can."[14] A detachment of about 1,500 men under General Spencer was sent to confront the British vanguard before it reached the American lines. Joseph Martin's and Benjamin Tallmadge's regiments were both assigned to this advance corps.

Martin and one of his messmates had just returned from an unofficial foraging expedition in which they had pilfered some turnips from a stingy farmer who would give them none unless they helped with the harvest. "When we arrived at the camp, the troops were all parading," Martin wrote. "Upon inquiry we found that the British were advancing upon us. We flung our turnip plunder into the tent, packed up our things, which was easily done for we had but a trifle to pack, and fell into the ranks. Before we were ready to march, the battle had begun. Our regiment then marched off, crossed a considerable stream of water [the Bronx River] which crosses the plain, and formed behind a stone wall in company with several other regiments and waited the approach of the enemy."[15]

The Hessian troops soon appeared in front of them on the slope of an apple orchard, Martin reported. "They would advance so far as just to show themselves above the rising ground, fire, and fall back and reload their muskets. Our chance upon them was, as soon as they showed themselves above the level ground, or when they fired, to aim at the flashes of their guns; their position was as advantageous to them as a breastwork. We were engaged in this manner for some time, when, finding ourselves flanked and in danger of being surrounded, we were compelled to make a hasty retreat from the stone wall."[16] Clinton's flanking column, so far, had worked just as he planned.

"We lost, comparatively speaking, very few at the [stone] fence, but when forced to retreat we lost in killed and wounded a considerable number," Martin wrote. "One man who belonged to our company, when we marched from the parade, said, 'Now I am going out to the field to be killed,' and he said more than once afterwards that he should be killed, and he was. He was shot dead on the field. I never saw a man so prepossessed with the idea of any mishap as he was. We fell back a little distance and made a stand, detached parties engaging in almost every direction."[17]

Tallmadge's regiment fell back as well, taking shelter behind stone walls and pouring "a destructive fire into the Hessian ranks. . . . It, however, became necessary to retreat wholly before such an overwhelming force," Tallmadge wrote, and in the process, he was nearly captured as he recrossed the Bronx River.

Major Benjamin Tallmadge

I being in the rear, and mounted on horseback, endeavored to hasten the last of our troops, the Hessians being then within musket shot. When I reached the bank of the river, and was about to enter it, our Chaplain, the Rev. Dr. [Benjamin] Trumbull, sprang up behind me on my horse, and came with such force [as] to carry me with my accoutrements, together with himself, headlong into the river. This so entirely disconcerted me, that by the time I reached the opposite bank of the river, the Hessian troops were about to enter it, and consider me as their prisoner. As we ascended the hill, I filed off to the right, expecting our troops on the hill would soon give them a volley. When they had advanced within a few yards of the stone wall, behind which Gen. McDougall had placed them, our troops poured upon the Hessian column . . . such a destructive fire, that they retreated down the hill in disorder, leaving a considerable number of the corps on the field.

Help from Captain Alexander Hamilton and his artillery corps also drove the Hessians off Chatterton's Hill. "This relieved me from my perilous situation," Tallmadge wrote, "and I immediately remounted my horse, and taking my course in the valley, directly between the hostile armies, I rode to Head Quarters, near the Court-house, and informed Gen. Washington of the situation of the troops on Cha[tt]erton's Hill. The enemy having rallied, and being reinforced, made a second attempt upon Gen. McDougall's detachment, who gave them a second warm reception."[18]

The struggle for Chatterton's Hill, where the most ferocious fighting of the day took place, was far more chaotic than Tallmadge could have known without being in the thick of it, and like the other battles in the campaign for New York, it engendered its share of frustration and controversy. Colonel John Haslet, whose regiment of Delaware Continentals had fought so well beside Lord Stirling and General Parsons during the Battle of Brooklyn, described in a letter to a friend the daunting view of Howe's army from the hilltop at the beginning of the battle, and the futile effort to keep the militia from panicking under an artillery attack, as it had at Kips Bay. "We had not been many minutes on the ground when the cannonade began, and the second shot wounded a militia-man in the thigh, upon which the whole regiment broke and fled immediately, and were not rallied without much difficulty."[19]

To Haslet's dismay with the poorly trained militia was added the decrepit condition of the American artillery: "so poorly appointed, that myself was forced to assist in dragging it along the rear of the regiment. While so employed, a cannon-ball struck the carriage and scattered the shot about, a wad of tow blazing in the middle. The artillerymen fled. One alone was prevailed upon to tread out the blaze and collect the shot. The few that returned made not more than two discharges, when they retreated with the field-piece."[20]

When the British column reached the Bronx River, the Hessians forded with great reluctance, according to an American captain named Samuel Smith, but the British grenadiers charged across and pressed on, despite fierce resistance, up the steep, densely wooded slope, where their own artillery's shells had ignited the dry autumn leaves and branches, and created a screen of smoke and fire that partially hid them from the American defenders on top of the hill. As the grenadiers ascended, however, they became the targets of their own artillery, which had to desist when the soldiers reached the top of the slope.[21] "It was a gallant sight to see them, steadily, without a falter, march up a very steep hill, exposed to a constant fire of cannon and musketry, until they attained the summit," Smith wrote with grudging admiration of the enemy. "The Americans, overpowered by numbers, were compelled to save themselves as best they could."[22]

As the militia bolted, Howe's forces gradually drove the Americans from Chatterton's Hill, but not before the steadiest troops—the same Continentals who had weathered the awful artillery barrage with Lord Stirling in August—exacted an exorbitant price in British and Hessian lives. "At this time the Maryland battalion was warmly engaged," Haslet wrote.

> The Militia regiment behind the fence fled in confusion, without more than a random, scattering fire. . . . The rest of General McDougall's brigade never came up to the scene of the action. Part of the first three Delaware Companies also retreated in disorder, but not till after several were wounded and killed. The left of the regiment took post behind a fence on the top of the hill with most of the officers, and twice repulsed the Light Troops and Horse of the enemy; but seeing ourselves deserted on all hands, and the continued column of the enemy advancing, we also retired. Covering the retreat of our party, and forming at the foot of the hill, we marched into camp in the rear of the body sent to reinforce us.[23]

The Americans suffered 175 casualties in the fight for Chatterton's Hill, later called the Battle of White Plains, but even by Howe's official estimate, they had inflicted more than 200 on the British and Hessians.[24] "We lost many men but from information afterwards received there was reason to believe they lost many more than we," Colonel Rufus Putnam wrote.[25] The high price that Howe paid for the hill was enough to discourage further aggression on his part.

"Every moment did we expect the enemy would have attempted to force us from our lines," Tallmadge remembered, but the British did not storm the American camp.[26] Howe's pattern of desisting from a frontal assault after a show of American resistance—even when he had the advantage—had by now become familiar. As Martin recalled: "The British were very civil, and indeed they generally were after they had received a check from Brother Jonathan for any of their rude actions. They seldom repeated them, at least not until the affair that caused the reprimand had ceased in some measure to be remembered."[27]

Instead, a heavy exchange of artillery fire continued throughout the day and took its toll, even as both sides remained in their respective positions. One soldier reported that "all the adjacent hills smoked as though on fire, and bellowed and trembled with a perpetual cannonade and fire of field pieces, howitzers and mortars. The air groaned with streams of cannon and musket-shot. The hills smoked and echoed terribly with the bursting of shells; the fences and walls were knocked down and torn to pieces, and men's legs, arms and bodies, mangled with cannon and grapeshot all around us."[28]

In the quiet after the heat of battle, the hardships of camp life reasserted themselves. "During the night we remained in our new-made trenches, the ground of which was in many parts springy," Martin wrote.

> In that part where I happened to be stationed, the water before morning was nearly over the shoes, which caused many of us to take violent colds by being exposed upon the wet ground after a profuse perspiration. I was one who felt the effects of it and was the next day sent back to the baggage to get well again, if I could, for it was left to my own exertions to do it and no other assistance was afforded me. I was not alone in misery; there were a number in the same circumstances. When I arrived at the baggage, which was not more than a mile or two, I had the canopy of heaven for my hospital and the ground for my hammock. I found a spot where the dry leaves had collected between the knolls. I made up a bed of these and nestled in it, having no other friend present but the sun to smile upon me. I had nothing to eat or drink, not even water, and was unable to go after any myself, for I was sick indeed. In the evening, one of my messmates found me out and soon after brought me some boiled hog's flesh (it was not pork) and turnips, without either bread or salt. I could not eat it, but I felt obliged to him notwithstanding. He did all he could do. He gave me the best he had to give, and had to steal that, poor fellow. Necessity drove him to do it to satisfy the cravings of his own hunger as well as to assist a fellow sufferer.[29]

After Howe's forces seized Chatterton's Hill, he had them continue working on the fortifications the Americans had begun while he once again waited for reinforcements, losing two more critical days in which he might have launched an attack. On October 30 Lord Percy arrived at White Plains with six regiments of Hessians and one of Waldeckers newly arrived in New York from Germany. When Howe was finally ready to advance on October 31, nature interceded once more on the side of the Americans: A heavy rainstorm lasting twenty hours canceled Howe's plans. The next day, poised to attack, Howe found that

Washington had moved his whole line back into North Castle Heights, where the hilly terrain made it too difficult to follow him.[30]

"The British made no other attempt on the Americans while they remained at White Plains," General Heath wrote. "The two armies lay looking at each other, and within long cannon shot. In the night time, the British lighted up a vast number of fires, the weather growing pretty cold. These fires, some on the level ground, some at the foot of the hills, and at all distances to their brows, some of which were lofty, seemed to the eye to mix with the stars, and to be of different magnitudes," as they flickered against the dome of the sky.[31]

CHAPTER 17

The Fall of Fort Washington

~⁀

T

he Liberty Poll erected some years ago in this City, and which remained as a monument of insult to the Government, and of li-
centiousness to the people, was . . . by my recommendation to
the Inhabitants, very properly and very quietly taken down and
removed by them," Governor Tryon wrote to Lord Germain regarding the pole's demise on October 28, 1776.[1] In the occupied
city, Isaac Sears and the other Sons of Liberty were nowhere to be
found, and the open-air meetings of the past decade and a half
had vanished with them. Though Washington had once again
slipped from Howe's grasp that same day in White Plains, New
York itself had not. The felled Liberty Pole affirmed that Howe
had at least accomplished his revised objective, which he had
clarified in mid-August, of driving the Americans out of the city
and controlling the vital strategic areas around it. Only Harlem
Heights and Fort Washington remained to be captured for the
British to possess all of Manhattan and begin to dominate the entire length of the Hudson River.

Howe ordered Lieutenant General Knyphausen and his
Hessians to strike their camp at New Rochelle and march to
Kingsbridge, where they arrived on November 2 and quickly
seized Fort Independence, guarding the northern approach to
King's Bridge across the Harlem River. Early in the morning on
November 5, the Americans at White Plains could hear the rum-
bling of wagons, and thinking that the British were advancing,
braced themselves for action. Instead of attacking, however, Howe

had finally given up the fitful chase that began on August 22 with the invasion of Long Island, and was withdrawing from White Plains to consolidate his grip on New York.[2]

As Howe's army headed west toward Dobbs Ferry, on the Hudson, General Heath's diary entries recorded the Americans' confusion about Howe's intentions, and their failure to realize how vulnerable his next target would be. They were also distracted from the British retreat by another fire, which had broken out at midnight in the village of White Plains. Clearly set by some marauding American soldiers, it infuriated Washington. "It is with the utmost astonishment and abhorrence, the General is informed, that some base and cowardly wretches have, last night, set fire to the court-house and other buildings which the enemy left," he wrote in his orders for November 6. "The army may rely upon it, that they shall be brought to justice, and meet with the punishment they deserve."[3]

Washington tracked Howe's movements by sending out a detachment to follow the British column and harass its rear guard; over the next two days, reports from these scouts and from British deserters confirmed that Howe was headed toward New York, but once again in his slow, desultory way. "The reconnoitring parties discovered them encamped near Dobb's Ferry. They were foraging grain and hay, and driving in the cattle," Heath wrote.[4] Nonetheless, at a war council on November 6, the American generals did not discuss Fort Washington. Instead they focused on the Hudson Highlands and on the danger that Howe might cross the river and march through New Jersey to capture Philadelphia.[5]

Washington had written to Governor Livingston that General Howe "must undertake something on account of his reputation," and to Greene that "they can have no capital object in view unless it is Philadelphia."[6] Washington asked Livingston to turn out the state's militia to replace the many soldiers—more than half the army—whose terms of enlistment were about to end. The persistence of sectional loyalties and conflict was evident in the war council's resolution "that the troops raised on either side of the Hudson river should occupy the side where they had been enlisted."[7]

While Washington told Congress that he "expected the enemy to lead their forces against Fort Washington, and invest it," before crossing into New Jersey, General Greene continued to argue that the fort could be defended successfully, and no move was made to evacuate it.[8] Yet Washington remained torn between his own best instincts and those of a trusted officer. General Putnam's attempts to sink obstructions in the Hudson had been ineffective, and on November 8 Washington wrote Greene: "If we can not prevent vessels passing up, and the enemy are possessed of the surrounding country, what valuable purpose can it answer to hold a post from which the expected benefit can not be had? I am therefore inclined to think it will not be prudent to hazard the men and stores at Mount Washington; but as you are on the spot, leave it to you to give such orders as to evacuating Mount Washington as you judge best."⁹

Acknowledging that the sunken obstructions had not worked, Greene wrote back the next day: "But upon the whole I cannot help thinking the garrison is of advantage, and I cannot conceive the garrison to be in any great danger; the men can be brought off at any time, but the stores may not be so easily removed; yet I think they can be got off in spite of them, if matters grow desperate. I was over there last evening; the enemy seems to be disposing matters to besiege the place, but Colonel Magaw thinks it will take them till December expires before they can carry it."¹⁰

At sunset on November 10, Washington arrived at Peekskill, eighteen miles north of White Plains, where he had stationed General Heath with about 4,000 troops to secure the overland routes between Albany and Manhattan. Washington had ordered 2,000 troops to cross the Hudson with him into New Jersey and join forces with 3,500 men under Greene's command at Fort Lee to contest Howe's expected incursion into the state.¹¹ General Lee remained at North Castle Heights with 7,000 men, with orders to remove the stores north of the Croton River and to be prepared for an attack in case "the threatened movement to New Jersey be but a feint."¹² However, if the British proceeded to New Jersey, Lee was to bring his troops across the Hudson to join Washington "with all possible dispatch."¹³

A week earlier, Magaw's adjutant, William Demont, had crept into Lord Percy's camp and given him the plans for Fort Washington along with information about the works and the garrison, which Percy had promptly passed on to General Howe. Lieutenant Mackenzie's journal indicates that Demont's debriefing gave the British a substantially accurate impression of the American forces, with only minor exaggerations.

> [Demont] says the rebels remaining on this island amount to about two thousand men, who, if they are obliged to abandon their advanced works, are to retire into fort Washington and defend it to the last extremity, having therein two months provisions, many cannon, and plenty of ammunition. He says there are great dissensions in the rebel army, everybody finding fault with the mode of proceeding, and the inferior officers, even ensigns,

insisting that, in such a cause, every man has a right to assist in council and give his opinion. They are much distressed for clothing. The people from the Southern colonies declare they will not go into New England, and the others that they will not march to the Southward. If this account is true in any degree, they must soon go to pieces.[14]

Since Greene, like Washington, fully expected the British to besiege Fort Washington, he had gradually increased the garrison under Colonel Magaw from 1,200 to 2,800 men. Greene had written to Washington on October 31 that this number was too large if they intended to hold only the fort itself, and far too small if they hoped to defend the entire northern end of Manhattan above the American fortified lines on Harlem Heights, constructed in September. According to Joseph Reed, no more than 1,400 men should have been stationed inside the fort, while a war council back in September had agreed that 8,000 troops were needed to secure the island between the three fortified lines and King's Bridge. Awaiting a reply from Washington, Greene had continued to enlarge the garrison, apparently hoping that Washington would opt to contest the whole area and send more troops. On this point, however, Greene was less confident and merely asked for the commander in chief's decision. Washington once again left the choice to Greene since he presumably had a more detailed knowledge of the ground. The final result of this indecisive exchange was Magaw's deployment of 2,800 men to defend a perimeter nearly five miles long—a job for which Greene knew he needed 10,000 troops.[15]

North of the American lines, Laurel Hill on the east and Mount Washington on the west dominated the island. The two long, narrow elevations, running north-south, were densely wooded and displayed steep, rocky cliffs to the Hudson and to the Harlem Rivers. Between the hills in the interior, the Post Road ran through the valley on its way to King's Bridge.[16] Facing south, Lieutenant Colonel Lambert Cadwalader and several detachments of Pennsylvania troops manned the original Harlem lines, while another detachment of Pennsylvanians under Colonel William Baxter guarded the northern end of Laurel Hill and looked east across the Harlem River toward Fordham Heights. This left a critical gap of a mile and a half along most of Laurel Hill all the way down to the Morris mansion, just above the fortified lines. To the west, a battalion of Maryland riflemen led by Colonel Moses Rawlings occupied a redoubt at the northern end of Mount Washington.* Half a mile south of the redoubt, Magaw commanded all of these outlying units from the main fort, with the expectation that they would all retreat there if necessary.[17]

Alexander Graydon, one of the Pennsylvanians who actually built Fort Washington back in August, considered the citadel itself to be the weak link in Greene's plan. Situated on the flat top of Mount Washington, it was easily accessible only from the gradual southern slope of the hill, the other three being steep and rugged. However, the vaunted pentagonal fortress, enclosing four acres of ground, was in fact nothing more than a large, crude earthwork, open to the sky and without proper barracks or magazines for ammunition; water had to be drawn from the Hudson, 230 feet below, because the fort had no well. Outside the walls, it had "ground at a short distance on the back of it, equally high if not higher," from which the enemy might fire into the fort. Aside from the small redoubt that Rawlings occupied, Fort Washington had neither outworks nor an adequate ditch around it, Graydon wrote; none of "those exterior, multiplied obstacles and defences . . . that could entitle it to the name of a fortress in any degree capable of sustaining a siege." Howe would not have to dig parallel trenches as he had on Long Island, because "the citadel was at once within reach of the assailants," if they arrived at the top of the hill. Given the weakness of the fort, Graydon concluded, Greene must have hoped the garrison, if besieged, "might have been snugly slipped over the Hudson, as erst we had been over the East river."[18]

On November 15, the adjutant general of the British army, Lieutenant Colonel James Paterson, and several other mounted officers approached Fort Washington with a white flag and a drummer "beating a parley" to demand its surrender.[19] It was Paterson who had so politely carried Admiral Howe's letters to Washington in July, seeking a peaceful settlement. Instead, at Fort Washington, he threatened death to all those captured if Magaw refused, and demanded an answer within two hours.

Magaw sent a note to Greene at Fort Lee and, without waiting for a reply, answered the British. In retrospect, Magaw's defiance may appear foolhardy, bolstered as it was by a tragically unprofessional assessment of the fort's strength. However, in the face of 8,000 British and Hessian troops and their

*Today Fort Tryon occupies the site of the redoubt, overlooking the Cloisters. On the elevation now occupied by the Cloisters, an additional redoubt, the Cock Hill Fort (also spelled Cox Hill), overlooked Spuyten Duyvil Creek.

traditional, but nonetheless grim, ultimatum, his reply evinced an astonishing amount of raw courage and an admirable purity of motive: "Sir: If I rightly understand the purport of your message from General Howe communicated to Colonel Swoope, this post is to be immediately surrendered or the garrison put to the sword. I rather think it a mistake than a settled resolution in General Howe to act a part so unworthy of himself and the British Nation. But give me leave to assure his Excellency that actuated by the most glorious cause that mankind ever fought in, I am determined to defend this post to the last extremity."[20]

After Greene instructed Magaw to stand firm and wait for further orders, he forwarded the news to Washington, who had established his New Jersey headquarters at Hackensack. Without waiting for a response, Greene then crossed the Hudson to Fort Washington. Arriving at Fort Lee at nine P.M., Washington found Greene had left and set out to join him on the New York side.[21] "I had partly crossed the North river when I met General Putnam and General Greene, who were just returning from thence, and they informed me that the troops were in high spirits and would make a good defense, and it being late at night, I returned," Washington recalled.[22] After the ultimatum, Howe had allowed the Americans a day and a night to evacuate the fort while he moved into position; early the next morning, November 16, his forces closed in.

In the predawn darkness, the Hessians marched southward through the mists of the Harlem River Valley, and Andreas Wiederhold, a Hessian captain, proudly recorded in his journal the parade of Germanic names of the regimental commanders: "Theyne, Bienau, Rall, Lossberg . . ."[23] General Knyphausen had asked Howe for the privilege of making the main attack with only Hessian troops, and Wiederhold led the first detachment of thirty men at the head of the advance corps. While the Hessians assaulted Rawlings's redoubt and proceeded to Fort Washington, another 3,000 troops under General Edward Mathew and Lord Cornwallis were to cross the Harlem River from the east and overwhelm Baxter's units on Laurel Hill. At the same time, Lord Percy's 2,000 troops, including some Hessians, were to storm the Harlem lines from the south. These three thrusts were designed to deliver all of northern Manhattan, including Fort Washington, into British hands. To confuse and possibly trap Cadwalader's men in the Harlem lines, Howe planned a fourth prong in the attack: Highlanders under Colonel Thomas Sterling were to cre-

The Battle
for Fort Washington
November 16, 1776

Spuyten Duyvil

KING'S BRIDGE

GEN. KNYPHAUSEN

0 Miles   1
0 Kilometers   1   2

196th St. —

British ships
(GEN. CORNWALLIS)

FORT
WASHINGTON

Mt. Washington

Laurel Hill

Fordham
Heights

NEW JERSEY

GEN. PERCY

British ships
(GEN. MATHEWS AND COL. STERLING)

FORT LEE

Pearl

North River (Hudson)

MORRIS
MANSION

Harlem River

159th St. —

153rd St. —

147th St. —

AMERICAN TROOPS
BRITISH TROOPS
BRITISH MOVEMENTS
BRITISH ARTILLERY
POSITIONS

© 2002 Jeffrey L. Ward

ate a diversion by crossing the Harlem River and landing at the southern end of Laurel Hill, just above the American lines.[24]

The battle began at seven A.M. with a massive two-hour barrage from British guns on the east side of the Harlem River and from the frigate *Pearl* in the Hudson "to divert the attention of the enemy, so that they should not know where the real attack was to be made," Wiederhold wrote.[25] However, the difficulty of coordinating Howe's complex plan initially threw his own forces into confusion. Wiederhold recalled that when he and his men were nearly halfway up Mount Washington, Howe had Knyphausen withdraw them because the attack on Laurel Hill by Mathew and Cornwallis had been delayed by the tides. "If we had continued in our charge at that time, we would not have suffered one third as great a loss as we did later on," Wiederhold wrote bitterly.[26] Graydon commented that, as the Germans "had been bought by his Britannic majesty, he had an unquestionable right to make a free use of them; and this seemed to be the conviction of General Howe."[27]

To the south, Percy's units were more fortunate. They had marched across Harlem Plains from their camp at McGowan's Pass, crossed the Hollow Way, and climbed up to the plateau of Harlem Heights, while exchanging artillery fire with the Americans. By 7:30, with only minor casualties, Percy had begun driving the Americans out of their trenches before he too was ordered to stop and wait in the woods until Mathew and Cornwallis crossed the Harlem River. If the attacks were pressed too hard, Howe believed, the Americans might fall back to the safety of the fort before the troops from the east could engage them on a third front or drive westward and block their escape.[28]

As Howe orchestrated his attack, the American commanders came over from Fort Lee and looked on helplessly; according to General Greene, they still did not realize that a major defeat was imminent. "General Washington, General Putnam, General [Hugh] Mercer, and myself, went to the island to determine what was best to be done," Greene reported, "but just at the instant we stepped on board the boat the enemy made their appearance on the hill." Despite the danger, the generals proceeded all the way across to the grounds around the Morris House. "There we all stood in a very awkward situation. As the disposition was made, and the enemy advancing, we durst not attempt to make any new disposition; indeed we saw nothing amiss."[29]

Washington, who had deep misgivings about defending the fort, at least had the presence of mind not to risk the lives of his generals in addition to the officers and troops of the garrison. "We all urged his Excellency to come off," Greene wrote. "I offered to stay. General Putnam did the same, and so did General Mercer; but his Excellency thought it best for us all to come off together, which we did."[30] Fifteen minutes later, the British captured the ground where they had stood.[31]

At eleven o'clock, the flatboats carrying two brigades of English troops finally came down the Harlem River and deposited Generals Mathew and Cornwallis with their troops on the Manhattan shore at the northern end of Laurel Hill.* Supported by their thundering guns on Fordham Heights, the British scrambled up the steep, wooded slope, despite the wet leaves that made the footing even more treacherous. The American commander, Colonel Baxter, was killed on the spot by a British officer, and the militia fled to the fort.[32]

*At today's 196th Street.

A view from the north of the British attack on Fort Washington,
November 16, 1776. Laurel Hill is to the left, Mount Washington
and the fort to the right.

At this point, the main attack, at the northern end of Mount Washington, also began. Wiederhold wrote, "We stood facing their crack troops
and their riflemen all on this almost inaccessible rock which lay before us,
surrounded by swamps and three earthworks, one above the other."[33] Then,
according to John Reuber, a soldier in Colonel Johann Rall's regiment, "[we]
marched forward up the hill and were obliged to creep along up the rocks,
one falling down alive, another being shot dead. We were obliged to drag
ourselves by the beech-tree bushes up the height where we could not really
stand."[34] Nonetheless, Wiederhold reported, "every obstacle was swept aside,
the earthworks broken through, the swamps waded, the precipitous rocks
scaled and the riflemen were driven out of their breastworks, from where they
had been seconded by their artillery."[35]

One of the deadliest gunners who opposed the Hessians on this hill
was America's first battlefield heroine, Margaret Corbin. She took her hus-

Margaret Corbin

band's place at his cannon when he was killed, and aimed with such accuracy that her position drew especially heavy fire from the Hessians' ten fieldpieces. A severe wound from grapeshot in her shoulder finally took her out of the action.[36]

Rall led his column up the northern end of Mount Washington from the west, while Knyphausen attacked the east side of the hill. The Hessians climbed over felled trees the Americans had placed in their path, and pressed forward under the hail of grapeshot and bullets from above. Knyphausen himself "at all times could be found in the thickest of the fight, where resistance and attack was the hottest, and he tore down the fences with his own hands to urge the men on," Wiederhold wrote. "He was exposed like a common soldier to the frightful cannon-and-shrapnell-fire, as well as to the rifle shots, and it is wonderful that he came off without being killed or wounded."[37] After two solid hours of fighting, with their rifles clogged from overuse, the Americans at Rawlings's redoubt retreated to the main fort.[38]

An exultant Wiederhold reported: "We gained this terrible height, pursued the enemy who were retreating behind the lines and batteries; routed them there also, took the batteries, one of which lay on the very top of the rock, and we followed the fleeing enemy to the fort proper. There we seated ourselves at the side of the precipitous mountain to protect ourselves from the cannonade from the fort. But only our regiment and that of Rall were here."[39] Rall's men were positioned behind a storehouse 100 yards from the fort.[40]

On Harlem Heights, Percy had resumed his attack; assured of Percy's progress, General Howe ordered the fourth prong, the diversionary force under Colonel Sterling, to cross the Harlem River and block Cadwalader's retreat to the fort. As Sterling's Highlanders arrived on the Manhattan shore just below the Morris mansion, Magaw sent a warning to Cadwalader and both commanders dispatched a combined force of 250 men to oppose the landing. They fired on the boats and hit 90 men, but the 800 Highlanders kept coming, backed up by cannon fire from the opposite side of the river. They climbed the steep slope up from the water's edge so quickly that they captured 170 Americans. Then they heard the shouts of their obese commander, Captain Murray, who had been left at the bottom of the hill, and they went back to pull him to the top.[41]

Percy kept up his attack, and Cadwalader retreated from the lines with his men before the Highlanders could cut them off. The Americans reached a wooded area just south of Mount Washington, where they were able to make a stand against the Highlanders, before following a narrow road along the Hudson that brought them up the gentle southern slope to the fort.[42] Most of Cadwalader's men reached the citadel, but as they crossed the open ground on the flat crest of the hill and approached the entrance, Rall's grenadiers sprang from behind the storehouse just to the north and attacked them.[43] Reuber later remembered that "Col. Rall gave the word of command, thus: 'All that are my grenadiers, march forwards!' All the drummers struck up the march, the hautboy-players blew. At once all that were yet alive shouted, 'Hurrah!' . . . Immediately all were mingled together, Americans and Hessians. There was no more firing, but all ran forward pell-mell upon the fortress."[44]

Having trapped some Americans against the wall of the fort and driven the others inside, Rall sent an English-speaking captain with a white cloth tied to a gun barrel and a drummer at his side to approach the fort with a demand for surrender.[45] Captain Hohenstein later recalled, "[The Americans] kept firing at me and the drummer until we came to the glacis, where the rebels led us off with our eyes bound."[46] He dictated Rall's terms to Magaw's second-in-command: The Americans must raise a white flag over the fort, come out immediately, lay down their arms, and turn over all ammunition, provisions, and other military supplies belonging to Congress. Even the most humble private, Rall promised, would be allowed to keep his personal effects. When the Americans asked for four hours to consider the demands, Hohenstein gave them just thirty minutes.[47]

With about 2,800 men crowded into a fort designed for half that number, a British bombardment would have meant the slaughter of everyone inside, but Magaw, encouraged by a note from Washington, tried to rally the men to defend the walls. "I sent a billet to Colonel Magaw directing him to hold out and I would endeavor this evening to bring off the garrison if the fortress could not be maintained, as I did not expect it could, the enemy being possessed of the adjacent ground," wrote Washington, who had witnessed the attack from New Jersey.[48] Washington's messenger went and came back safely, but Magaw had to face Colonel Rall, who refused to be kept waiting.

When Hohenstein returned at the end of the half hour, Magaw, evidently amazed by the capture of a fortress he once thought impregnable, muttered that "the Hessians make impossibilities possible." Hohenstein then said to him: "General von Knyphausen is a hundred paces off. Come with me, on my safe conduct, and see if he will give you better terms."[49] Knyphausen had come up with the other Hessian column soon after Rall, and Magaw surrendered his sword to him but received no better terms.

The Hessian regiments formed two lines facing each other, and the 2,800 Americans marched out between them to lay down their arms. The Hessian commanders did not keep their word, however. "To our shame, though [the Americans] capitulated for the safety of their baggage, they were stripped of their wearing apparel as they marched out by Hessians, till a stop was put to it by making them take a different route," Lieutenant Colonel Stephen Kemble wrote. "They were so thronged in the fort that they could not have subsisted there above three days."[50]

Not only did the fort lack adequate food, but the desperate condition of the American army and the toll the campaign had taken on the men was visible in every aspect of their appearance. "The rebel prisoners were in general but very indifferently clothed," Lieutenant Mackenzie reported. "Few of them appeared to have a second shirt, nor did they appear to have washed themselves during the campaign. A great many of them were lads under fifteen and old men, and few had the appearance of soldiers. Their odd figures frequently excited the laughter of our soldiers."[51]

"The loss of the Hessians in dead and wounded amounted to more than 300," Wiederhold wrote. "But I am still alive, thanks be to God! And have escaped unhurt, but for a little scratch in my face caused by a broken twig, although I led the van of this advance-guard, a body of thirty men. Here I thought of the old proverb, Weeds are never hurt—'Unkraut vergeht nicht.'" A battalion of Hessian grenadiers occupied the fort in the evening, and the rest of the Hessians went back to their camp, where, according to Wiederhold, "all those who were well, once more had cause enough to thank God for their preservation."[52]

For the Hessian survivors, there was also the pride of conquest. Fort Washington became Fort Knyphausen, and the smaller forts were also renamed. On Laurel Hill the redoubt became Fort George, and on the northern end of Mount Washington, the post defended by Rawlings and his riflemen, with help from Margaret Corbin, became Fort Tryon.*

In the storming of Fort Washington, as in the campaign for New York overall, more of Howe's troops lost their lives than did Americans. The British loss amounted to 78 killed and 374 wounded—mostly Hessians—while that for the Americans stood at 59 killed and 96 wounded. The American loss in prisoners, however, was staggering; 230 officers and 2,600 soldiers were marched out of the fort and brought down to the city, where they began their long ordeal of captivity in the city's jails and churches, and on infernally crowded, disease-ridden prison ships in the harbor.[53]

"I feel mad, vexed, sick, and sorry," Greene wrote to Henry Knox the day after the battle. "Never did I need the consoling voice of a friend more than now. Happy should I be to see you. This is the most terrible event: its consequences are justly to be dreaded." Greene evidently sensed that he would be blamed for the disaster and asked, "Pray what is said upon the occasion? A line from you will be very acceptable."[54]

Charles Lee was apoplectic. If it had been named Fort Lee, he fulminated, it would have been evacuated immediately and the terrible loss prevented. Four days later, on November 20, Lee's words were fulfilled. Admiral Howe had sent more flatboats up the Hudson, and, acting with uncharacteristic speed, General Howe dispatched Cornwallis to New Jersey with 6,000 men. As he crossed the Hudson and landed opposite Yonkers, most of the garrison fled Fort Lee and evaded capture with little time to spare.[55]

Exactly how serious a loss of military stores the Americans suffered at Fort Lee became a source of debate, when Greene claimed British estimates were exaggerated, and that he had decided to evacuate several days before Cornwallis landed.[56] Tradition holds, nonetheless, that the Americans left their pots boiling and meals unfinished in their flight. And the combined loss from Fort Washington and Fort Lee was undeniably a tremendous blow to

---

*Today the plaza in front of Fort Tryon Park and the roadway next to it bear Corbin's name. A large bronze tablet on the side of the fort tells her story. Congress voted Corbin a soldier's half-pay and the value of a suit of clothes annually as compensation for her service during the defense of Fort Washington, because she had been permanently disabled by her wounds (*American National Biography,* 5:499–501).

British troops scaling the Jersey Palisades.

the American cause: 146 cannons, 12,000 shot and shell, 2,800 muskets, and 400,000 cartridges. The British also captured other equipment, including tents and entrenching tools—items that had an enormous impact on the safety, comfort, and health of the individual soldier.[57]

Washington wrote to his brother: "What adds to my mortification is, that this post after the last ships went past it, was held contrary to my wishes and opinions, as I conceived it to be a hazardous one. . . . I did not care to give an absolute order for withdrawing the garrison till I could get round and see the situation of things, and then it became too late, as the fort was invested. . . . I had given it as my opinion to General Greene, under whose care it was, that it would be best to evacuate the place; but as the order was discretionary, and his opinion differed from mine, it unhappily was delayed too long to my great grief."[58] Washington's lapse of judgment, exacerbated by the practice of collective decision making through war councils, had led to a disaster.

"General Washington's own judgement seconded by representations from us would, I believe, have saved the men and their arms," Joseph Reed wrote to Charles Lee on November 21. "But, unluckily, General Greene's judgement was contrary. This kept the General's mind in a state of suspense till the stroke was struck. Oh! General—an indecisive mind is one of the greatest misfortunes that can befall an army. How often have I lamented it in this campaign."[59] Congress, by contrast, indulged in no hand wringing or censure of Washington and Greene. Instead, the delegates learned a lesson from Fort Washington and later authorized the commander in chief to act independently, as the circumstances of war often required.[60]

Until the loss of the fort, the campaign for New York had been for the Americans an extended and, on the whole, successful retreat, which had done at least as much to jeopardize General Howe's reputation as it had to demoralize the Americans. As Washington's aide-de-camp, Tench Tilghman, wrote to the New York Provincial Congress: "The loss of the post is nothing compared to the loss of the men and arms, and the damp it will strike upon the minds of many. We were in a fair way of finishing the campaign with credit to ourselves and I think to the disgrace of Mr. Howe, and had the General followed his own opinion the garrison would have been withdrawn immediately upon the enemy's falling down from Dobb's Ferry."[61]

Governor Jonathan Trumbull of Connecticut, who had supported Washington since the beginning of the war with troops and supplies and every other resource his state could provide, wrote to him and summed up the attitude Americans had to adopt if they intended to learn from the experience in New York and go on to win the war: "The loss of Fort Washington with so many of our brave men, is indeed a most unfortunate event. But though we are to consider and improve like disappointments, yet we are by no means to despair,—we are in this way to be prepared for help and deliverance."[62]

CHAPTER 18

Trenton and Princeton, the End of the Campaign

~⁓

They Cant keep the Ground when they have got it," William Douglas wrote to his wife on December 5, 1776, dismissing the British conquest of New York. "what Great things have they Done this year with the Best Army the King ever had. why they have Conker'd one Country that was their best frind but they cant keep but a small part of it through the winter and are oblige to Keep them Selves Close together. I hope the Cuntry will not be Discourag'd at our making some missteps at first. we are new but Shall be old in time as well as they."[1]

Douglas's prescience about the events of the winter and his fighting spirit aside, much of the country was deeply discouraged, as were Washington's 3,500 remaining troops, who retreated with him across New Jersey toward the Delaware River with Cornwallis aggressively in pursuit. Greene and his troops had fled westward from Fort Lee on November 20 and joined Washington at Hackensack. Together they marched west again to Acquackanonk on the far side of the Passaic River before following its course south to Newark, where they arrived, the troops disheartened and exhausted, on November 22.[2]

It was in New Jersey that the darkest gloom of the war had to be dispelled. It was there that Thomas Paine joined the army and wrote the series of pamphlets titled *The American Crisis*, the first of which was published on December 19, 1776. "These are the times that try men's souls," it famously began. "The summer soldier and the sunshine patriot will, in this crisis, shrink from the service of their country; but he that stands it *now* deserves the love and thanks of man and woman."[3]

On November 28, Washington's bedraggled column made another hairbreadth escape, leaving Newark just as Cornwallis's forces arrived. Continuing south past Elizabeth Town and Amboy, the Americans crossed the Raritan River and rested again at Brunswick* on the thirtieth.[4] Just as the Americans had delivered a strong counterpunch after the enemy's buglers taunted them on Harlem Heights in September, Washington sensed that British arrogance presented an opportunity to catch them off guard. "The advantages they have gained over us in the past have made them so proud and sure of success that they are determined to go to Philadelphia this winter," Washington wrote on the thirtieth to Charles Lee, who had not yet crossed the Hudson to New Jersey. "I have positive information that this is a fact and because the term of service of the light troops of Jersey and Maryland are ended they anticipate the weakness of our army. Should they now really risk this undertaking then there is a great probability that they will pay dearly for it and I shall continue to retreat before them so as to lull them into security."[5]

Washington expected Lee to follow his repeated orders to join him in New Jersey, but it soon became apparent that Lee, like the British, had become overconfident in the wake of the commander in chief's failure at Fort Washington. Joseph Reed's letter of November 21 not only criticized Washington but flattered Lee, urging him to hurry and join the main army, where he was sorely needed. The compliment had the opposite effect: Lee decided his own judgment was superior to Washington's, and that remaining in his current position would serve the vital strategic purpose of fending off a possible British incursion into New England. Of more immediate concern was the fact that Lee's men lacked shoes and blankets for the march. He requested supplies from officials in Connecticut and Massachusetts and lingered in Westchester instead of bringing his 4,000 remaining troops across the Hudson.[6]

Reed's letter suggests that Lee's reputation had reached its zenith, at the expense of Washington's: "I do not mean to flatter, nor praise you at the expense of any other, but I confess I do think that it is entirely owing to you that this army and the liberties of America so far as they are dependant on it are not totally cut off. You have decision, a quality often wanting in minds otherwise valuable, and I ascribe to this an escape from York Island—from

*Now called New Brunswick.

Kingsbridge and the Plains—and I have no doubt had you been here, the garrison at Mount Washington would now have composed part of this army." Washington needed Lee's "judgement and experience" to guide him, Reed implied. "Nor am I singular in my opinion," Reed added, "—every gentleman of the family [i.e., Washington's staff], the officers and soldiers generally have a confidence in you—the enemy constantly inquire where you are, and seem to me to be less confident when you are present."[7]

Lee wrote back and agreed with Reed about Washington's "fatal indecision of mind."[8] By chance, Reed was away from headquarters, and Washington opened the letter, thinking it was a piece of official correspondence. He immediately inferred from it the content of Reed's letter to Lee and wrote Reed on November 30 to explain what had happened, but received no reply for months and their relationship cooled considerably.[9]

In addition to creating ill will, Lee's insubordination compounded Washington's already critical shortage of men. On December 1, nearly 2,000 troops went home as their enlistments expired, cutting Washington's force in half. Desperate to shield his dwindling army from Cornwallis, Washington fled south again, toward Princeton and Trenton, hoping to escape across the Delaware River.[10]

Fortunately for Washington, General Howe had put Cornwallis on a short leash, forbidding him to go farther than Brunswick on the Raritan River, where he remained on December 1. Content to seize territory rather than destroy Washington's forces, Howe once again rejected Clinton's common-sense proposals for aggressively cutting off the American retreat. By sending the fleet up the Delaware River, while marching 10,000 men overland toward Philadelphia, the Howes might well have gotten ahead of Washington, enveloped his forces, and prevented their escape into Pennsylvania. If the British had simultaneously landed a detachment at the northern end of Chesapeake Bay to attack Philadelphia, they might have also taken the rebel capital.[11] If Washington managed to cross the Delaware, this detachment would have been waiting for him on the other side.

Instead, General Howe's priority, with the approach of winter, was to capture Rhode Island and establish an all-weather naval base at Newport, since New York's enclosed waters would soon freeze; he was hoarding his troops for that operation and for gathering forage both in Rhode Island and New Jersey before the first frost. Assigning Clinton to lead the Rhode Island expedition gave Howe yet another opportunity to get him out of the way.

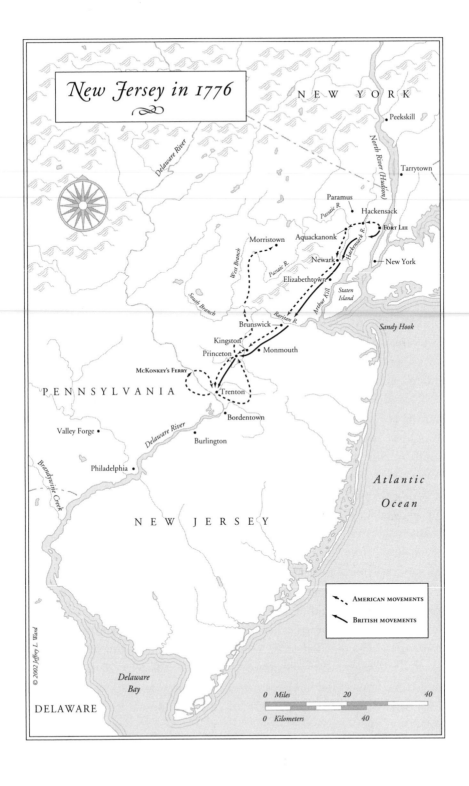

New Jersey in 1776

NEW YORK

Peekskill

Delaware River

North River (Hudson)

Tarrytown

Paramus

Passaic R.

Hackensack

FORT LEE

Morristown

Aquackanonk

Hackensack R.

West Branch

Passaic R.

Newark

New York

Elizabethtown

South Branch

Staten Island

Arthur Kill

Sandy Hook

Raritan R.

Brunswick

Kingston

Monmouth

Princeton

McKONKEY'S FERRY

PENNSYLVANIA

Trenton

Bordentown

Valley Forge

Delaware River

Burlington

Atlantic Ocean

Philadelphia

NEW JERSEY

Brandywine Creek

AMERICAN MOVEMENTS

BRITISH MOVEMENTS

© 2002 Jeffrey L. Ward

Delaware Bay

DELAWARE

| 0 | Miles | 20 | 40 |

| 0 | Kilometers | 40 |

Commanding the naval squadron that carried Clinton and his forces was none other than Commodore Sir Peter Parker, the man who had turned their joint mission against Charleston in June 1776 into a fiasco.[12]

When the weather remained warm and dry into December, however, Howe decided to proceed as far as the Delaware River, leaving open the option of capturing Philadelphia and bringing an even more triumphant end to the year's campaign.[13] On December 5 he left New York to join Cornwallis at Brunswick, arriving there the following day. At the head of the British vanguard, Cornwallis set out for Princeton on the seventh and again failed to overtake the Americans there by only a few hours. The next day, Washington's troops made an even narrower escape from Trenton and collected themselves in relative safety on the west bank of the Delaware, in Pennsylvania.[14] Putting the army's experience during the retreat from Long Island to use, Washington dispatched his trusted Marblehead mariner, Colonel John Glover, to bring over every small boat he could find for fifteen miles from the east bank and destroy any surplus vessels to prevent the British from crossing the river. Artillery mounted on the western shore also stopped the British advance at Trenton.[15]

Howe postponed the idea of taking Philadelphia and, ignoring Clinton's parting advice, set up a string of seven garrisons at Hackensack, Brunswick, Kingston, Princeton, Trenton, Bordentown, and Burlington to hold the southern half of New Jersey for the winter. Trenton was one of the smaller camps, manned by 1,400 Hessians under Colonel Johann Rall, who had demanded the final capitulation of Fort Washington. Satisfied with his arrangements, Howe left Trenton on December 15 and returned to Manhattan. After news arrived that Clinton had captured Rhode Island on the eighth, Howe considered the campaign of 1776 to be over and planned to start a new one in the spring.[16]

The major who had carried to London at the end of August the news of General Howe's triumph in the Battle of Brooklyn returned to New York in mid-December to announce that all of Britain was ecstatic, and the king had conferred a knighthood, the Order of Bath, on the commander in chief, henceforth to be known as Sir William.[17] With good news from every quarter, Howe settled comfortably into the elegant Beekman House, attended lavish parties in New York, and, with his mistress, indulged their penchant for gambling.

By December 8, when Washington crossed the Delaware River into Pennsylvania, Lee had finally crossed the Hudson with 4,000 troops and reached

Morristown, New Jersey. Over the next several days, Washington repeatedly sent instructions urging Lee to avoid the line of British garrisons, march across northern New Jersey, and join him in blocking a likely British advance toward Philadelphia. At this point Lee assumed correctly that Howe had given up on Philadelphia until the spring, and told Washington that instead of coming over to him, he would make a bold stroke on his own against Brunswick or Princeton, disrupt the British line of communications, and then dig in at Morristown, a hilly, readily defensible position. By attacking the British from the rear, he thought he might draw them away from Washington.[18]

Lee's men, however, many of them without shoes, were in no shape for such a maneuver, and on the night of the twelfth Lee seemed resigned to obey Washington. Assigning his second-in-command, General Sullivan, to set off for Pennsylvania the following day with the troops, Lee left their encampment in search of more comfortable quarters. He carelessly ensconced himself and his bodyguards at a country inn, dangerously far from the protection of his soldiers.[19]

In a letter to his close friend General Horatio Gates, written at Basking Ridge on December 13, Lee condemned the commander in chief even more strongly. "The ingenious manoeuvre of Fort Washington has unhinged the goodly fabrick we had been building. There never was so damned a stroke. *Entre nous*, a certain great man is damnably deficient. He has thrown me into a situation where I have my choice of difficulties. If I stay in this Province, I risk myself and army, and if I do not stay the Province is lost forever. I have neither guides, cavalry, medicines, money, shoes or stockings. I must act with the greatest circumspection."[20]

Lee was not careful enough, however. "General Lee was engaged in answering General Gates's letter," Captain James Wilkinson recalled in his memoirs,

> and I had risen from the table and was looking out of an end window down a lane about one hundred yards in length which led to the house from the main road, when I discovered a party of British dragoons turn a corner of the avenue at a full charge.
>
> Startled at the unexpected spectacle, I exclaimed, "Here, Sir, are the British cavalry!"
>
> *"Where?"* replied the general, who had signed his letter in the instant.

Lieutenant Colonel Banastre Tarleton

"Around the house;" for they had opened files and encompassed the building.

General Lee appeared alarmed, yet collected, and his second observation marked his self-possession: "Where is the guard?—damn the guard, why don't they fire?" and after a momentary pause, he turned to me and said, "Do, Sir, see what has become of the guard."

The detachment of British cavalry, sent out expressly to find Lee, fired through every window and door. Separated from the main body of Lee's troops by three or four miles, his guards quickly lost the ensuing shoot-out. When the British commander, Lieutenant Colonel Banastre Tarleton, threatened that "the house should be burnt and every person without exception should be put to the sword," unless Lee surrendered, he turned himself over to the sentry at the front door.[21]

"A general shout ensued," Wilkinson recalled, "the trumpet sounded the assembly, and the unfortunate Lee, mounted on my horse, which stood ready at the door, was hurried off in triumph, bareheaded, in his slippers and blanket coat, his collar open, and his shirt very much soiled from several days' use."[22] Wilkinson reportedly escaped by hiding in a chimney, and the British took only one other prisoner from Lee's entourage: a French cavalry officer who had recently arrived in America.[23]

Given Lee's inflated reputation, and Washington's presumed incompetence, Cornwallis and the Howes imagined they had dealt a deathblow to the

Continental Army. Tarleton could hardly believe the success of his mission. "This is a most miraculous event—it appears like a dream," he wrote to his mother.[24] When the news of Lee's capture spread, and people overcame their shock and disbelief, many on both sides of the conflict concluded that victory for the British was at hand.[25]

However much Lee was a trial to Washington, at the time of his capture the loss was mourned throughout the Continental Army; even General Greene, who had been sharply criticized by Lee for the loss of Fort Washington, called the Englishman "a most consummate general."[26] Washington, in a letter to his cousin Lund on December 17, ranked Lee's abduction as one of the main reasons the army might collapse: "The unhappy policy of short enlistments and a dependence upon militia will, I fear, prove the downfall of our cause, though early pointed out with an almost prophetic spirit! Our cause has also received a severe blow in the captivity of General Lee. Unhappy man!"[27]

Washington lamented to Lund in the same letter:

> A large part of the Jerseys have given every proof of disaffection that they can do, and this part of Pennsylvania are equally inimical. In short, your imagination can scarce extend to a situation more distressing than mine. Our only dependence now is upon the speedy enlistment of a new army. If this fails, I think the game will be pretty well up, as, from disaffection and want of spirit and fortitude, the inhabitants, instead of resistance, are offering submission and taking protection from Gen. Howe in Jersey.[28]

This widespread disaffection was fueled in part by Admiral Howe, who had resumed his peace efforts again on November 30 by issuing another proclamation, this one offering pardons and promising restitution of rebel property to anyone returning to British allegiance within sixty days. The response was meager, however, because such promises could only be fulfilled where recent British victories gave them lasting control of the area. Ironically, while Washington lamented the growing scourge of loyalism, Admiral Howe expressed disappointment that his efforts had not been more productive. In December his secretary, Ambrose Serle, recorded Howe's belief "that almost all the People of Parts and Spirit were in the Rebellion."[29]

Clearly, the ongoing effort by both sides to gauge the true mood and desires of the people throughout the colonies could never be more than a crude science. In practice, people were swayed by the instinct for self-preservation and the force of arms. Admiral Howe's remarks about New York and Washington's observations about New Jersey and Pennsylvania revealed that the residents of New York City and its environs, despite long-standing assumptions regarding their ingrained Tory character, behaved no differently than various other conquered cities during the war.[30]

"Will it not be possible, my dear General, for your troops, or such part of them as can act with advantage, to make a diversion, or something more, at or about Trenton," Joseph Reed asked Washington on December 22 in a letter from Bristol, downstream from the main American camp. Despite the recent friction between the two men, Reed expressed his esteem for Washington's "own good judgement" if he would not allow himself to be swayed by lesser men. "Something must be attempted," Reed insisted, "to revive our expiring credit, give our cause some degree of reputation, and prevent a total depreciation of the Continental money."[31] The Continental Army would disintegrate if morale were not raised by a decisive engagement, even a small one. They had nothing to lose by trying, Reed wrote.

Sullivan had brought Lee's remaining troops across to Pennsylvania after the latter's capture, but they were in terrible shape, and another wave of enlistments was due to expire after December 31. Reed also warned that the two-month amnesty offered by Admiral Howe had attracted New Jersey's militia officers and grew more dangerous with each passing day. Washington, with only 5,000 men, including the detachments under Reed, expected the British to attack him and then march against Philadelphia as soon as the ice thickened on the Delaware.[32] Washington intended to preempt them and told Reed on the twenty-third that "Christmas-day at night, one hour before day is the time fixed" for the American attack on Trenton.[33]

As snow and hail fell in the predawn darkness of December 26, the Continental Army crossed the icy Delaware and surprised the Hessian garrison at Trenton. After Glover's regiment rowed the army across, Sullivan and Greene led simultaneous attacks from different routes leading into Trenton from the north, while Hand's riflemen, who had blocked the British advance along the causeway at Throg's Neck in October, cut off the Hessians' escape route on the south side of the town. In forty-five minutes of fighting the Americans captured or killed almost 1,000 Hessians, suffered only five casualties themselves, and achieved a stunning victory.[34]

Governor Tryon was especially upset by the news of Trenton, realizing the Americans had given "life to their sinking cause" at a critical moment.[35] Without this bold stroke, Tryon, like many on both sides, believed the

Americans would have lacked the morale to rebuild the army. As the year ended, it was British morale that started to show signs of decline while the Americans' lifted. Lieutenant Colonel Stephen Kemble looked back on the New York campaign and vented his frustration with his commander in chief in his journal. He criticized the unnecessary "delay of [the British] Army under General Howe at New York Island," the botched landing at Throg's Neck, and the failure to reach White Plains before the Americans had time to dig in. Kemble also questioned British tactics in New Jersey and why Washington had not been pursued "with more Spirit" to cut off his retreat. He had no sympathy for Colonel Rall, the Hessian commander who was slain at Trenton, blaming him for the American victory and labeling him "Noisy . . . and a Drunkard."[36]

After the raid on Trenton, Washington took his prisoners back across the Delaware into Pennsylvania. However, on December 30, after the remaining Hessian outposts had been withdrawn from the river, Washington crossed into New Jersey again and dug in on the south side of Assunpink Creek, below Trenton. As the year ended, he was able to retain a force of some 5,000 troops with him in New Jersey only by personally making an urgent appeal for them to stay one month beyond the expiration of their original enlistments.[37]

Finally provoked to action by the recent American victory, Howe ended 1776 by dispatching Cornwallis with 8,000 troops to smash the remnants of Washington's army. Learning that Cornwallis had left only 250 men at his base in Brunswick, the Americans sent a detachment of horsemen at dawn on December 31 with orders to rescue General Lee from captivity. Only five miles from Brunswick, however, scouts reported to the cavalry that Cornwallis had reinforced the small garrison with 1,200 troops from Perth Amboy, and the mission was called off.[38]

Cornwallis was not so skillful when it came to attacking Washington, however. Arriving at Trenton on the evening of January 2, 1777, he ignored his quartermaster general's advice to attack immediately, and made his famous remark that he could "bag the fox" the next morning. During the night, Washington left enough men to keep the campfires burning while he slipped away with his main army around Cornwallis's left flank and headed north toward Princeton, where Cornwallis had left his rear guard.[39]

On January 3, Washington's forces collided with the British rear guard on its way south, and General Hugh Mercer, who led the advance corps, was killed. Washington then personally commanded the attack, and the Americans captured 50 prisoners, before moving on to storm Princeton, where they took 300 more. Colonel John Haslet was killed in the engagement, along with twenty-two other Americans, but British casualties were higher, and Princeton, like Trenton, proved to be another morale-building victory.[40]

Washington had wanted to continue on and attack Brunswick, but his men were in no condition to keep fighting. On the march to Princeton, one sergeant recalled, "the ground was literally marked with the blood of the soldiers' feet," because they had no shoes.[41] The hills above Morristown, where Lee had planned to hide after attacking the British, offered the best winter quarters, despite the long trek north from Princeton, and Washington set the army in motion, steering clear of Brunswick, which lay to the northeast. Stephen Moylan, one of Washington's staff and a friend of Charles Lee, regretted that with the move to Morristown "poor Naso" had to be left to his fate, a prisoner in Brunswick.[42]*

Lee's captivity, however, was luxurious compared to the lot of Washington's bleeding troops. Joseph Martin asserted that he suffered far more from the treatment inflicted on him by the army than he did at the hands of the British, and he returned home to Milford, Connecticut, temporarily after his enlistment expired in December.[43]

"Fighting the enemy is the great scarecrow to people unacquainted with the duties of an army," Martin wrote.

> To see the fire and smoke, to hear the din of cannon and musketry and the whistling of shot, they cannot bear the sight or hearing of this. They would like the service in an army tolerably well but for the fighting part of it. I never was killed in the army; I never was wounded but once; I never was a prisoner with the enemy; but I have seen many that have undergone all of these and I have many times run the risk of all of them myself. But, reader, believe me, for I tell the solemn truth, that I have felt more anxiety, undergone more fatigue and hardships, suffered more in every way, in performing one of those tedious marches than ever I did in fighting

*One of Lee's nicknames, among his fellow officers in the Continental Army, was "Naso"— Italian for *nose.*

the hottest battle I was ever engaged in, with the anticipation of all the other calamities I have mentioned added to it.[44]

Martin's former regimental commander, William Douglas, also left the army in December, but unwillingly and permanently.[45] He discovered that the cough, which had plagued him throughout the campaign in New York, was an indication of a serious medical condition. Douglas had written to his wife from Harlem Heights that he needed a stronger "constitution" to withstand the exhausting work of being in the army—the long marches without food or rest, and cold nights without the benefit of adequate shelter and clothing. Only the very strong, alert, and fortunate soldier survived the twin threats of the enemy and the deplorable conditions within the Continental Army. In failing health, Douglas had no choice but to return to his family in Northport, near New Haven, where he died in 1777, at the age of thirty-five.

As the campaign of 1776 came to a close in the first days of 1777, Washington hoped to keep Howe from sending reinforcements to his beleaguered troops in eastern New Jersey, and possibly even to draw the British units out of the state completely. Two days after the victory at Princeton, Washington instructed General Heath at Peekskill: "You should move down towards New-York with a considerable force, as if you had a design upon the city; that being an object of great importance, the enemy will be reduced to the necessity of withdrawing a considerable part of their force from the Jersies, if not the whole to secure the city."[46]

Washington's first experiment with this strategy—which he would later employ with increasing success—ended in humiliation for the Americans. Colonel Timothy Pickering, who served under General Heath, recalled in his journal the failed attempt to seize Fort Independence, just north of King's Bridge, a mission that unfolded like a parody of Howe's successful capture of Fort Washington.

> The expedition was disgraceful. We were to take Fort Independence, not by storm, for the whole army was militia, and the work was ditched, fraised, and surrounded by an abatis;* not by regular approaches, for we had not a single intrenching tool; not by cannonade, for we had only three six-pounders. And yet, on

*Abatis: a barrier of felled trees with sharpened branches.

General William Heath

the first morning we arrived, General Heath, with ridiculous parade and groundless, vain expectation, sent in a summons, demanding the surrender of the fort! The garrison must have been fools and arrant cowards to have regarded it.[47]

Washington also had harsh words for Heath, which he delivered directly to the general in a letter. "Your conduct is censured (and by men of sense and judgement who were with you on the expedition to Fort Independence) as being fraught with too much caution by which the Army has been disappointed, and in some degree disgraced. Your summons, as you did not attempt to fulfill your threats, was not only idle but farcical, and will not fail of turning the laugh exceedingly upon us."[48]

Admiral Howe's secretary, Ambrose Serle, took the opportunity to deride the lack of professionalism among the American generals, a charge that was true enough, since the Continental Army was a voluntary association drawing people, on an emergency basis, from other walks of life. Serle then proceeded, however, to his usual hyperbole. "One Heath, once a butcher, now a rebel general, has left the army in disgust, on account of some reflections thrown upon him by Washington for not attacking Fort Independence. He blamed his men, and his men, him; villains and cowards altogether!"[49]

The winter of 1776–77 and the early spring at Morristown, though less famous than the ordeal at Valley Forge the following year, were a time of similar privation and suffering for the Continental Army. However, Washington had chosen a naturally strong position surrounded by hills and forests, and by sending his men out to ambush and rob British foraging parties, he kept his greatly diminished force alive while Cornwallis remained nervously on the defensive. By spreading false reports about his troop strength, Washington also duped the British into believing he had far more than the five incomplete regiments at his disposal. With 10,000 fully equipped professional troops only a day's march from the American camp, the British might have wiped out Washington's forces.[50] Instead, Alexander Hamilton confirmed in more elegant prose what William Douglas had told his wife in early December: He witnessed the "extraordinary spectacle of a powerful army straitened within narrow limits by the phantom of a military force and never permitted to transgress those limits with impunity."[51]

CHAPTER 19

Occupied New York

~⌐

In the occupied city that the Americans had been forced to abandon, the remnants of Charles Lee's defense plan stood as monuments to his miscalculation. "If one was to judge from appearances, they would suppose the Rebels had intended to dispute every inch of ground with our troops," an English traveler named Nicholas Cresswell wrote in his diary in the spring of 1777. "In every street they have made ditches and barricades, every little eminence about the town is fortified, but they basely and cowardly deserted them all as soon as ever our people got ashore."[1] The sight and smell of the abandoned fortifications launched Cresswell on a vivid jeremiad about the evils of the great and fallen cosmopolitan city.

"Now all these Ditches and fortified places are full of stagnate water, damaged sour Crout, and filth of every kind," wrote Cresswell, a young aristocrat who had returned to New York after a sojourn in the colonies and was looking for a ship that would take him home to England.

> Noisome vapours arise from the mud left in the docks and slips at low water, and unwholesome smells are occasioned by such a number of people being crowded together in so small a compass almost like herrings in a barrel, most of them very dirty and not a small number sick of some disease,

the Itch, Pox, Fever, or Flux, so that altogether there is a complication of stinks enough to drive a person whose sense of smelling was very delicate and his lungs of the finest contexture, into a consumption in the space of twenty-four hours. If any author had an inclination to write a treatise upon stinks and ill smells, he could never meet with more subject matter than in New York, or anyone who had abilities and inclinations to expose the vicious and unfeeling part of human nature or the various arts, ways and means that are used to pick up a living in this world, I recommend New York as a proper place to collect his characters. Most of the former inhabitants that possessed this once happy spot are utterly ruined and from opulence reduced to the greatest indigence, some in the Rebels' Jails by force, others by inclination in their Armies.[2]

In contrast, the winter and spring of 1777 provided a busy social season for the British officers and affluent loyalists. By calling for a spree of merrymaking, General Howe, in effect, celebrated the capture of the city, if not the much bigger prize of Washington's army. "Toujours de la gaieté!" Howe ordered, in imitation of the king of Prussia, as he went from one banquet or ball to the next.[3] In addition to feasts at private mansions, twice a month the City Tavern on Broadway hosted the "Garrison Assembly," a dance where junior officers mingled with the belles of New York.[4]

Another favorite gathering place for loyalists and British officers was the Murrays' mansion at Inclenberg, where the soirees were "crowded with scarlet coats and powdered wigs."[5] Since most patriots had fled the city, and there was less competition, Robert Murray thrived as a purveyor of luxury items to the British. His son Lindley also participated in the family business as an agent for his father on Long Island. Robert's brother, John, made a show of breaking off his business ties in Philadelphia and returned to New York, where he too made a fortune feeding the frenzied demand for what had just recently been boycotted goods. Playing both sides, the Murray family's Hibernia Furnace in New Jersey continued to sell about 120 tons of cannonballs and grapeshot every year to the Continental Army.[6]

Howe and Betsey Loring continued to make a spectacle of themselves, according to Judge Jones, particularly at the gaming tables, where "the favorite sultana lost 300 guineas at a single sitting."[7]* Francis Hopkinson, a signer of the Declaration of Independence—and a musician and composer, among his other talents—was hardly alone when he suggested in a popular ballad that General Howe's carrying on with his mistress took its toll on the British war effort.[8] One verse in particular parodied Howe's soft lifestyle and his failure to pursue Washington aggressively:

> Sir William he, snug as a flea,
>   Lay all this time a-snoring,
> Nor dreamed of harm as he lay warm
>   In bed with Mrs. L——g

The commissary of prisoners—the highly paid position to which Howe had appointed Joshua Loring in exchange for his wife's favors—also offered lucrative opportunities for corruption. As a result, the soldiers captured at Fort Washington and seamen taken from American merchant ships were kept in hellish conditions.

Packed into the city's sugar refineries and churches, they lived without panes in the windows all winter; in the holds of prison ships anchored off the Brooklyn shore, only the fortunate ones had small portholes for ventilation. The *Jersey*, an old British man-of-war, held more than 1,000 men at a time belowdecks. Barely fed—on spoiled provisions—the prisoners quickly became "walking skeletons," dressed in rags and covered from head to toe with filth and lice. Racked by yellow fever, typhus, and dysentery, many died in their own bloody excrement and were buried a dozen at a time in shallow graves around Wallabout Bay.[9]

An estimated 8,000 to 11,000 of these men, like Benjamin Tallmadge's brother, William, died of starvation, disease, and exposure during the course of the war, while Loring reportedly sold off most of their rations and pocketed the proceeds.[10] Since Loring continued to bill the British government for the support of prisoners who had perished, he was said to have grown rich by "starving the living and feeding the dead."[11]

Loring's depravity was abetted by that of William Cunningham, the provost marshal, who confessed to starving "more than 2,000 prisoners . . . in the different churches, by stopping their rations, which [he] sold." He also secretly murdered hundreds of inmates (by hanging and by poison) "both

---

*This was an enormous sum. Her husband's exorbitant base salary as commissary of prisoners was reportedly a guinea a day (Bobrick, *Angel in the Whirlwind*, p. 308).

with and without orders from government."[12] The deliberate policy of making prison conditions unbearable was a form of "impressment": Enlistment in the British navy was offered as an alternative to captivity.

New Yorkers whose homes had burned down in the fire of September 21 and loyalist refugees from other colonies who began flooding into the city during the winter of 1776–77 did not fare well either. The tide of refugees had increased since mid-November, when Admiral Howe had issued his proclamation offering pardons to anyone returning to the royal fold within sixty days. They crowded into "Canvass-town," the foul-smelling, disease-ridden encampment that had grown up in the swath of charred ruins along the city's west side.[13] According to one memoir, the homeless found shelter by "using the chimneys and parts of walls which were firm, and adding pieces of spars, with old canvass from the ships, forming hovels—part hut and part tent."[14] The rest of the occupied city was dirty too, as residents routinely threw their garbage into the streets, and the military regime struggled with sanitation problems.[15]

While "Canvass-town" festered, Major General James Robertson, the commandant in charge of day-to-day operations in the city, confiscated houses the rebels had left empty and distributed them to British officers. The generals took the finest houses on the west side of Broadway just above Fort George, each one marked with the letters *G.R.* for George Rex. Loyalists also marked themselves, wearing red ribbons in their hats to proclaim their allegiance to the king and to place themselves under the protection of the British military.[16]

In the housing crisis created by the fire, and by the influx of refugees, Pastor Shewkirk fretted that his Moravian Church would be seized as barracks for soldiers "of whom more and more come in; as also many of their women and children." The British spared the Anglican churches that were still standing, but other public buildings were converted into prisons or sick infirmaries, "especially all the Dutch and Presbyterian churches, as also the French church, the Baptists, and new Quaker meeting." In the process, the interiors of these dissenting churches were totally destroyed. The Moravian meeting house was ultimately spared, according to Shewkirk, because it was the only church in the city where services were still being held.[17]

The quartering of troops in private homes was an even greater source of friction and resentment. Not only did martial law deprive residents of their basic civil rights under the English Constitution by shutting down the courts and legislature, it also forced them to house and feed arrogant occupying soldiers and their dependents. British garrison orders show that the commandant received "many and frequent complaints of the inhabitants being ill treated by officers and servants quartered upon their houses."[18] These protests were largely ignored by the military authorities, and without civil courts, the unwilling hosts had no other recourse.

Despite the imposition of martial law, crime was so prevalent that Lieutenant Johann Philipp von Krafft would not go out for an evening walk without two soldiers as bodyguards. He witnessed "theft, fraud, robbery and murder by the English soldiers, which their love of drink excited; and as they received but little money, they used these disgusting means" to obtain it.[19] Even when courts-martial found them guilty, British soldiers and officers were rarely punished, even for rape and murder. The municipal police court, which was expected to make up for the absence of civil courts, had no jurisdiction in capital cases.[20]

Many of the civil officials who once ran the city and province and tried such cases had been dispersed by the war. William Smith remained in retirement with his in-laws at Livingston Manor, hoping to extend his status as a neutral guest in rebel territory as long as possible. By contrast, Judge Thomas Jones—Smith's old antagonist on the royal Council—had been captured by the Americans and removed to Connecticut from his estate on Long Island. He awaited an exchange of prisoners that would bring him back to the British-controlled city. Like Governor Tryon, who had written to Lord Germain shortly after the fire about the need for martial law in the city, Admiral Howe told Germain that the restoration of civil government in New York would have to wait until the rebels were driven from the island and loyalists who had fled the city had a chance to return.

One group among the city's residents and incoming refugees whose lot had improved during the occupation was the population of free blacks and runaway slaves. The black regiment formed on Staten Island in August 1776 had fought in the Battle of Brooklyn, and other units such as the Black Pioneers, the Black Brigade, and the Royal African Regiment were organized later. According to disapproving Whig newspapers, these soldiers and tradesmen who served the king's army in combat and supporting roles even socialized with the British at "Ethiopian Balls," where black fiddlers and banjo players provided the music.[21]

As it had for decades, the Anglican Church continued to draw the city's growing number of blacks into its fold. Destroyed in the fire of 1776, Trinity

Church and its charity school for blacks reopened during the occupation. Marriage ceremonies for free blacks were also held there. Stephen Bleucke and his wife Margaret exemplified what Anglican missionaries hoped to achieve in converting blacks. Well-educated and articulate, Stephen had lived in New York since the 1760s and became the leader of the city's black loyalists during the Revolution.

By contrast, Peter Williams Sr., the highly regarded black sexton of the John Street Methodist Church, sided with the patriots. Williams nonetheless remained in the city throughout the war because he was a slave, owned by a loyalist tobacco dealer.[22] Despite a British proclamation later in the war promising freedom and equal opportunity to "every Negro who shall desert the Rebell Strandard," ultimately, more blacks in America served in the patriot forces during the war than for the British. Warnings from Washington and John Adams about slaves multiplying the British army's manpower caused Congress to lift its initial ban on enlisting black troops.[23]

Overcrowding, shortages, and prices all increased dramatically in 1777. The "markets were raised eight hundred percent for the necessaries of life"; and the landlords, "from the demand for houses, raised their rents on an average at four times the sum such houses had rented for previous to the rebellion," according to records published by the city government after the war.[24] General Robertson stepped in to put a ceiling on the price of bread, but he could not stop food producers from diverting goods into a flourishing black market. "This Town is filled by a Set of Villains and Harpies, who are enriching themselves," one resident complained.[25]

Adding to the atmosphere of crisis was the constant dread of another major fire; Robertson required everyone to serve on the nightly watch in each of the city's wards "to apprehend Incendiaries, and to stifle Fires before they rise to a dangerous Height."[26] On the very night that Robertson made this proclamation, however, John Montresor, the British engineer, had all of his buildings on Montresor's Island "burnt by the Rebels."[27]

While the military government waited for prominent Tories to return to the city, it also took control of the press. Admiral Howe assigned his secretary, Ambrose Serle, to the task of printing a newspaper, so Serle resumed publication of Hugh Gaine's *Weekly Mercury*, leaving Gaine's name on it in his absence. Gaine, a loyalist who had fled to Newark, then reopened his printing office on Hanover Square in November 1776. James Rivington, who had left for England after Isaac Sears raided his shop and took away his

James Rivington

type in November 1775, returned as the city's newly appointed "Printer to His Majesty the King" and resumed publication of his newspaper, which he soon renamed the *Royal Gazette*.

During the occupation Rivington enlisted the help of other printers to produce the first daily paper in America, in which they published numerous false reports designed to lift the flagging spirits of the impoverished loyalist refugees confined in New York. Such tales included Washington becoming a dictator with the title "Lord Protector," as well as news of both his death and his capture by the British. The *Royal Gazette* also announced that Benjamin Franklin had been assassinated, and that 36,000 Cossacks were on their way from Russia to fight alongside the British. The paper was so full of these baseless stories that Rivington gained a reputation throughout the colonies as a worse liar than even his British counterparts.[28]

The food and housing shortages in New York and the fear of rebel arsonists did not stop the military government from celebrating the queen's birthday in January 1777 with full pomp and circumstance. In fact, the event was moved to the winter from its actual date in the summer (also the season of the king's birthday) to provide some economic relief for the local tradesmen who would provision the festivities and sew the gala suits and dresses. The guns were fired at Fort George, and Montresor supervised a "very splendid Exhibition of Fire Works" at Whitehall Slip.[29] Residents all over the city illuminated their houses. After a ceremony in which Admiral Howe and General von Heister formally invested him with the Order of Bath, General Howe hosted "an elegant Ball and Supper in the evening."[30] Jabez Fitch, an American prisoner on parole in the city, wondered in his diary "whether it would not have been more Honourable to the British Army, to have had (at least) part of this Extraordinary Expence, bestow'd on the poor Prisoners who have perrished for want, in such vast numbers."[31]

The British did manage to mix entertainment with charity that same month when they reopened the John Street Theatre, which had been closed since the Continental Association labeled it a threat to public morals two years earlier. Renamed the Theatre Royal, it donated the ticket proceeds from an audience of about 750 people at each show to support the widows and orphans of British soldiers. Henry Fielding's *Tom Thumb* was the first of 150 productions, performed mostly by officers, which helped the British army pass the time while it remained idle in the city.[32] General Howe avidly supported the theater and commissioned a satire titled *The Battle of Brooklyn*, which, according to one historian, portrayed Washington as "a whoremongering barbarian and demagogue whose own (imaginary) mistress charged him $30 a night."[33]

In the middle of January, the British transferred their prize captive, Charles Lee, from Brunswick to New York and installed him comfortably in a suite of rooms at City Hall, where he was guarded constantly by fifty men. General Howe still hoped to convict the rebel general as a deserter and execute him, despite the legal obstacles arising from Lee's resignation from the British army.[34]

When rumors that Lee's life was in danger reached Congress, the delegates resolved to do all they could to help him. Since they had not yet captured a British major general, they offered to exchange six Hessian officers for Lee. They also threatened to retaliate against the six Hessians and one British officer if Lee were mistreated or harmed. Congress sent money to Lee to ensure that his needs were met, but his captors had already provided him with the same luxuries they enjoyed: firewood, candles, fine food and wine, and the company of officers and other guests. Eventually, Lee was even joined by one of his dogs and by his Italian servant, Giuseppe Minghini.

These creature comforts and the society of other Englishmen apparently reminded Lee of his native identity, and of the fact that while he was philosophically opposed to monarchy and tyranny, in practice he stopped short of being a republican. He ultimately regarded the war as a fight for improved status within a reunited British Empire. The test of Lee's commitment to the new American Republic came soon after his transfer to New York, when the

Howes tried to revive their peace mission by opening a dialogue with Lee about possible ways to end the war quickly and with a minimum of further bloodshed.

Employing one of Lord Howe's secretaries, Henry Strachey, as an intermediary, the Howes tried to manipulate Lee in much the same way they used General Sullivan after the Battle of Brooklyn, as a liaison to initiate peace talks, a proposal for which Lee sent in a letter to Congress via Washington.* The Howes may have initiated the discussions with Lee and may have implied his life would be spared if he cooperated; the record remains unclear. It is also possible that Lee, abandoning hope of an American victory without his generalship, tried to arrange the peace talks with the goal of securing leniency for himself and favorable terms for the Americans. In either case, Lee's actions helped put Congress back in the same public relations dilemma it had confronted in 1776: how to avoid playing into the hands of the Howes without appearing to be intransigent in the eyes of its war-weary constituents.

The mere resumption of negotiations, regardless of the terms, would have favored the British by dividing American opinion with the prospect of peace. Such talks would have also endangered the covert flow of French aid, which Congress hoped to turn into a formal alliance. After much debate, Congress decided on February 21 to inform Lee that it would continue every effort to protect him and gain his release, but no delegation would be sent to New York.

At the same time, Washington vehemently opposed the policy of retaliation as a means to shield Lee from mistreatment and force the British to classify him as an ordinary prisoner, eligible for exchange.[35] Washington warned that such threats would endanger the far more numerous American prisoners in British hands and freeze the process of exchanging them. He had even sent Nathanael Greene to argue the point in Congress. While the debate continued, Lee waited in New York to see if Congress would stand by him; Washington, hoping Congress might still reverse its policy of retaliation, did not inform Lee until April 1 that the delegates had voted on February 21 to

---

*After setting forth his critically important official business, the lonely and by all accounts perennially unhappy Lee concluded with another urgent request: "I am likewise extreamly desirous that my dogs should be brought as I never stood in greater need of their company than at present." Washington responded sympathetically about Lee's canine companions but told him it would take time to bring the hounds up from Virginia. Lee would have to wait, the commander in chief wrote, for the "satisfaction and amusements [he] hoped to derive from their friendly and companionable dispositions" (Alden, pp. 169–70).

protect him as aggressively as possible. Had Lee received the news just four days earlier, he might not have committed the act that branded him as a traitor when it came to light seventy years after his death.

On March 29, 1777, Lee submitted to Admiral Howe's secretary, Henry Strachey, a plan spelling out how the British could defeat the Americans in two months. Lee proposed that in addition to severing the colonies along the line of the Hudson, the British should sail to Chesapeake Bay with 4,000 men and cut the southern colonies off from the mid-Atlantic region. The suggestion in Lee's plan that the British also occupy Annapolis, Baltimore, and Alexandria would have dispersed British forces even farther and might well have weakened rather than strengthened their hold on the colonies. Since Lee gave the British no information about the American army, it is possible that he was not a traitor; that he was in fact trying to damage the British war effort and help the Americans. Lee agreed with the American strategy of avoiding a "general engagement" and knew Howe's army would be most formidable when gathered for such a major battle rather than diluted by holding various cities.

Given his willingness to lobby for peace talks, however, it is likely that Lee saw a British victory as inevitable—sooner or later—and that his plan was sincerely intended to end the war quickly for the benefit of both sides. Lee may also have been an opportunist, positioning himself to win favor from whichever side emerged victorious from the conflict. To his credit, Lee apparently was not motivated by money, unlike Benedict Arnold and others who neatly fit the profile of a traitor.

Whatever his true motives, Lee received no response from the Howes, and they never credited him with any influence over their decisions. In fact, in the months that followed, General Howe continued to request legal opinions from London that would enable him to prosecute Lee, who seemed to plead for mercy, writing in his plan that the Howes' "humanity will incline 'em to have consideration for Individuals who have acted from Principle."[36] Howe remained inactive and pessimistic, writing to Lord Germain: "I do not now see a prospect for terminating the war, but by a general action, and I am aware of the difficulties in our way to obtain it, as the enemy moves with so much more celerity, than we possibly can. Nor can we hazard a march at this unfavourable season with any hopes of making a stroke upon the enemy, in his present situation, that might turn the scale in our favour."[37]

Howe asked Germain for the resources and troops to fight a second campaign in the spring; "20,000 men," the general figured, "would by no means exceed our wants, yet 15,000 will give us a superiority . . . in the course of the campaign."[38] This enormous request for a second chance did not bode well, as Germain had already been "alarmed" by an earlier requisition from Howe, which he could not fill with "Hanoverians, or even with Russians in time."[39] Along with smaller numbers of troops, Germain sent cloth for uniforms along with camp equipment for the "Provincials," the loyalists in New York who were forming into companies under the direction of Tryon and other local leaders.

Howe wrote a secret letter to Germain in early April, saying that because of the small number of reinforcements agreed to, his "hopes for terminating the war this year are vanished."[40] Howe soon resorted to offering bounties of vacant land in the colonies to reward the loyalists who had already joined the various "Provincial Corps," and "as a further Encouragement to others to follow their laudable Example."[41]

While the city remained under British control and in the grip of martial law, New York's exiled Revolutionary leaders had begun to lay the foundations of a democratic government for the state. In April 1777, the Provincial Congress in Kingston adopted a written constitution: The governor would be elected, not appointed; the number of seats in the Assembly was doubled, while voting qualifications were reduced; secret ballots were introduced and civil rights guaranteed. The document was ratified by fiat, but elections were soon held, and George Clinton, then a brigadier general in the militia and an advocate for tenant farmers and artisans, defeated his aristocratic rivals to become the first governor of New York State.[42]

When it came to dealing with Tories, however, Governor Clinton and his supporters in the new bicameral legislature took a less democratic and more draconian approach. They created the permanent Commission for Detecting and Defeating Conspiracies and passed dozens of laws allowing it to prosecute proven or even suspected enemies of the Revolution. After having their civil rights revoked and their property confiscated and sold, hundreds of "inimicals" were driven out of the state. Those convicted of treason were marked for execution if they returned. New York's reputation for Revolutionary fervor had suffered before the war and would remain tarnished in subsequent centuries, but ultimately no other state did more to harass loyalists within its borders.[43]

In William Smith, however, New York State's new government had a special and very delicate case on its hands.[44] Governor Clinton had been one of Smith's law clerks and then his political protégé in the late 1760s. From

Governor George Clinton

his seat on the royal Council, Smith had coached Clinton and the other young Livingstonite assemblymen as they maneuvered to keep their majority against the De Lancey party. Moreover, Smith's former comrade in the Triumvirate, John Morin Scott, currently served on the Committee of Safety. Other prominent revolutionaries in New York, including Alexander McDougall, Gouverneur Morris, Philip Schuyler, and the entire Livingston family, remained Smith's friends. Indeed, Smith was still a guest of his in-laws at Livingston Manor, and Smith's acquaintances and relatives had even solicited his input when the framework for New York State's government was drawn up.

Given Smith's well-known conservatism—his fear of the "capricious wantonness of the Multitude" in a democracy—these requests were evidently motivated less by a desire to tap Smith's tremendous expertise in law and government and more by an intention to flatter him and win him over to the Revolutionary movement.[45] Smith had critiqued the plans for the state government and offered suggestions, even as he detected an attempt "to borrow my antient Popularity to support their Cause."[46] That old reputation, along with his retirement from public life, had buffered Smith from aggressive scrutiny since July 1776, when he had been allowed to evade the summons for a loyalty oath by merely giving his word,* in a letter to Gouverneur Morris, that he was a friend of America.

---

*His *parole*, meaning "word" in French; military prisoners were often exchanged only after giving their *parole*, signing an agreement not to serve in combat for a specified length of time after their release.

Early in 1777, however, New York State had begun to demand a more stringent oath of allegiance from all its citizens, and those who refused were exiled to occupied New York City. Despite Scott's protestations on behalf of his friend, the Committee of Safety voted to interrogate Smith in June. Scott tried to soften the blow by writing an apologetic cover letter for the summons, addressed to "My old Friend," in which he expressed his hope that the affair would turn out to be nothing more than "a political Farce."[47]

Smith's appearance before the panel did prove to be a performance of sorts, but not one that amused his inquisitors. When they pressed him for his views on American independence, Smith held forth for over an hour, using arguments he had been refining on paper for a year and rehearsing in after-dinner conversations at Livingston Manor. He asserted that the empire had to be preserved for the good of both sides, and that his views were shared by a majority of citizens in the province. Admitting that he still felt bound by his "oaths of fidelity to the crown," Smith declined to give the committee a sworn statement.[48] The atmosphere remained civil, and Scott even invited Smith to dine with the committee, but Smith graciously excused himself. In closed session, John Jay, who had spearheaded the vote to summon Smith in the first place, wanted him deported to New York City. On this round, however, Scott prevailed by arguing that the British would only be too glad to have such a talented jurist and propagandist at their disposal. Smith's retirement at Livingston Manor was therefore turned into a sort of house arrest: The committee agreed to release him, and he gave his word that he would not leave the grounds of the estate.

Despite the favorable weather, Howe's army remained inactive militarily during the spring and into the summer. However, the social activity among well-to-do residents and British officers in the city increased, along with the opportunities for genteel recreation. The occupiers rolled back the stern asceticism imposed by the revolutionaries and revived the very leisure activities proscribed by the Continental Association* during the past two years: billiards at the King's Head Tavern, horse racing at Hempstead Plains on Long Island, cricket at Bowling Green, fox hunting, golf, swimming parties, and outdoor concerts.[49]

As the heat of summer settled over New York City, however, the poor found no relief. The stench of "Canvass-town" only grew worse, and there

---

*The agreement drawn up by the Continental Congress in 1774.

were other—more gruesome—olfactory reminders of the terrible human toll exacted by the campaign of 1776. "This morning Captn. Scott and I hired a single horse-chaise and took a tour upon Long Island to Salisbury Plains through a little town called Jamaica, but returned in the evening," wrote Nicholas Cresswell, who was still stranded in New York. "Our noses were now and then regaled with the stink of dead Rebels, some of them have lain unburied since last August."[50] Staten Island too was littered with rotting corpses. "Almost bit to death with Mosquitoes and poisoned with the stink of some Rebels, who have been buried about three weeks in such a slight manner that waggons have cut up parts of the half corrupted carcases and made them stink most horribly," Cresswell complained.[51]

"When I see this once flourishing, opulent and happy City, one third part of it now in ruins, it brings sadness and melancholy upon my mind, to think that a set of people, who three years ago, were doing everything they could for the mutual assistance of each other, and both parties equally gainers, should now be cutting the throats of each other and destroying their property whenever they have an opportunity and all this mischief done by a set of designing villains," Cresswell wrote. "The reflection is too severe to bear with patience."[52] The "designing villains" were presumably the members of Congress: In his opinions, Cresswell echoed the insistent, wishful refrain of many Britons, including Lord Germain and the king, that a tyrannical few had forced the Revolution on a silent majority of loyal citizens.

CHAPTER 20

Philadelphia, Saratoga, and the Collapse of Britain's Grand Strategy

~◌

At the beginning of July 1777, Lieutenant General Clinton returned to New York as Sir Henry. He had done a professional job of seizing Newport, Rhode Island, and establishing a naval base there in December 1776, after which he went on leave to England, fixated—to the point of obsession by some accounts—on the slights, real and imagined, that General Howe had inflicted on him, and determined to resign as soon as he arrived.[1] "The many circumstances which occurred in the course of the last campaign to hurt my feelings made me very desirous of retiring," Clinton wrote plaintively in his account of the war.[2] However, the king welcomed him like a conquering hero and, conferring a knighthood on Clinton, asked him to remain in the service. Cajoled by the knighthood and by friends who appealed to his sense of duty, Clinton reluctantly agreed to recross the Atlantic and take up his old post in General Howe's army. "I was determined, however, to request I might not be forced to retain it any longer than the present campaign," Clinton noted.[3]

He would have preferred a separate command and had lobbied strenuously to replace Carleton at the head of the army in Canada. Burgoyne had reached London first, however, and submitted a plan for a march to Albany in 1777 that won him the post. Germain wanted to punish Carleton for failing to seize Ticonderoga in 1776, and he favored Burgoyne, who arrived at Quebec in early May. Carleton took the demotion gracefully and helped his successor prepare the fleet and army for the campaign.[4] By the end of June hundreds of British vessels, accompanied by Indian allies in canoes, set out across Lake Champlain toward Ticonderoga.[5]

In New York, Clinton was astonished to find that Howe's army had not struck out from the city even after months of good campaigning weather had gone by. Worse still, Clinton believed the move Howe was finally ready to make was a serious strategic blunder—one that promised to dismantle Britain's grand strategy of severing the colonies in two along the line of the Hudson River.[6] Instead of attacking the American forts in the Hudson Highlands and proceeding to Albany for a rendezvous with Burgoyne, Howe planned to set sail in mid-July for an assault on Philadelphia. By threatening the Highlands, Clinton argued later, Howe might have forced Washington to defend the vital waterway in the kind of "general action" he feared. Once again, however, Howe preferred the prospect of simply conquering more territory, where he believed numerous Tories eagerly awaited him. The news that Burgoyne had captured Fort Ticonderoga during the first week of July merely assured the commander in chief that the northern army could take care of itself without his help.[7]

Several weeks earlier, Howe had taken the precaution of transferring Charles Lee from his relatively luxurious abode at City Hall to close confinement on the British warship *Centurion*, anchored at a safe distance from shore in the harbor. Germain and the rest of the cabinet had so far been unable to confirm Lee's legal status as a deserter, but they had nonetheless ordered Howe to send him back to England for safekeeping and punishment; the move to the *Centurion* may have been a first step in carrying out that instruction. When Congress learned of the transfer, its renewed threats to retaliate against the Hessian officers in American custody convinced Howe to disobey Germain's order, as he could ill afford to create discontent—and perhaps a mutiny—among his German forces. In the next few weeks, Congress won the battle to secure Lee's standing as an ordinary prisoner, eligible for an exchange—which could occur whenever the Americans held a British officer of equal rank. This happened sooner than both sides expected. In a daring raid in July, the Americans captured the British commanding officer in Rhode Island, Major General Richard Prescott, and promptly offered to trade him for Lee. On the verge of embarking for Philadelphia, Howe was infuriated and ended up ignoring Washington's letter for several months, leaving Lee on the *Centurion*.[8]

Placing Clinton in command of New York and its environs with some 7,000 men fit for duty, Howe put the bulk of the army on his brother's fleet and sailed down to Sandy Hook at the entrance to the Lower Bay. After the British first amassed their great expeditionary force and seized New York in 1776, Admiral Howe drew steadily mounting criticism from First Lord of the Admiralty John Montagu, the earl of Sandwich, for dedicating too many ships to the support of General Howe's army and not enough to blockading the eastern seaboard. The strategy of severing the colonies along the Hudson was designed primarily to strangle New England, and stopping the region's trade was a vital component of the plan. After a base was established in New York, the Admiralty expected Admiral Howe to shift his emphasis from the army to the embargo. With his squadron of seventy-three warships, Howe was to patrol not only the Northeast but all 3,000 miles of coastline down to Florida. Sandwich was a longtime political enemy of Admiral Howe, and as the war progressed and his reprimands grew louder, he also deprived Howe of additional ships, even as the existing fleet fell into disrepair.[9]

Originally, the expensive strategy of raising a huge army for a land campaign was chosen in order to win the war quickly, before Britain's European enemies could intervene. The cheaper but slower approach of using a blockade was to follow if necessary.[10] After the campaign of 1776 failed to end the war in New York, the British eventually faced not only the demands of an embargo but the absolute necessity of deploying ships rapidly for naval combat. They soon discovered that the sandbar between Coney Island and Sandy Hook made New York's harbor the worst possible location for a naval base.[11] Day after day, the Howes' expedition to Philadelphia waited for a wind that would take the largest ships across the sandbar, and it finally departed on July 23, 1777—a portent of the critical delays the fleet would face in the future.[12]

After the winter and early spring at Morristown, Washington had expected General Howe to take advantage of the warm weather and march across New Jersey to Philadelphia, so on May 29 he moved his forces twenty miles south to Middlebrook in the Watchung Mountains, where he could monitor British movements closely and attack quickly if they set out from Brunswick toward the Delaware River.[13] Instead, Howe spent most of June performing a series of maneuvers designed to lure Washington out of the hills and into a "general engagement" on open ground, where the British would have a clear advantage. By the end of the month Howe had failed and withdrawn all of his forces from New Jersey.[14]

Reports in early July that Burgoyne was descending on Ticonderoga convinced Washington that the fleet in New York City had to be destined for Albany and a rendezvous with the northern army. However, still loath to leave Howe a clear overland route to Philadelphia, Washington took the main army only as far as Morristown and dispatched two brigades back across the Hudson to reinforce General Putnam, who had replaced Heath in May at Peekskill, the key to the passes through the Highlands.* The elaborate preparations in New York for the Howes' voyage suggested that they might be headed for Philadelphia or even Charleston, but news on July 12 that Burgoyne had taken Ticonderoga kept Washington poised to intercept a move up the Hudson.[15] Since Nathan Hale's death almost a year earlier, Washington's espionage network had improved considerably. Learning that the British fleet had sailed from Sandy Hook, Washington divided his forces to meet the threat, and Clinton reported the disposition of American troops to Howe by messenger.

"Mr. Washington, who had his spies in New York who gave him the earliest intelligence of all our movements, lost no time in putting his army into immediate motion," Clinton wrote in his narrative. "The gross of it marched with himself [from Morristown] directly toward the Delaware, after detaching a considerable body of men to join the northern corps under Schuyler; and Putnam was left with about 4000 at Peekskill, where on Rattlesnake Hill they had begun throwing up works for the defense of the Highlands on the east side [of] the Hudson."[16]

Clinton had begun to feel vulnerable with only 4,000 regular troops and 3,000 loyalists to defend Manhattan, Kingsbridge, Staten Island, Long Island, and Paulus Hook—far fewer men than the Americans had had for the same purpose in 1776.† A week after General Howe left New York, he infuriated Clinton again by writing to him with a vague promise of reinforcements as soon as he could spare them, and with the following suggestion: "If you can in the meantime make any diversion in favor of General Burgoyne's approaching Albany (with security to Kings Bridge), I need not point out the utility of such a measure."[17]

In Clinton's view, this contradicted Howe's parting admonition to stay put and protect New York until Howe had landed near Philadelphia and "Mr. Washington was decidedly gone to meet him."[18] Clinton therefore assumed the letter was a bureaucratic attempt by Howe to protect himself from the charge of neglecting Burgoyne in the event that the northern army

*Heath had been reassigned from the Highlands to Boston in March 1777.
†The naval base at Rhode Island, with additional men, was also part of Clinton's command.

Lord George Germain

ran out of supplies or was otherwise threatened. Clinton believed Howe had set him up to take any possible blame. Lord Germain, who bore ultimate responsibility for coordinating strategy, albeit from London, had written Howe on May 18 authorizing the move against Philadelphia, but admonishing him to return quickly and join forces with Burgoyne. This might have been possible if Howe had gone by land in both directions, an option discouraged by Washington's vigilance in New Jersey along the road to Philadelphia. By the time Howe received Germain's letter in August, he was already at sea and wrote back that he would not be able to support the northern army.[19]

Burgoyne's plan did not prescribe that Howe's forces should come all the way up to Albany to meet him, and until mid-August his dispatches contained no requests for help. However, on August 16, Burgoyne's march encountered its first severe setback: He allowed a Hessian foraging party of 1,600 men to search for horses and a rebel arms depot near Bennington, to the southeast, but the detachment was attacked and soundly defeated by an American force before it even reached the Vermont border. The engagement itself cost Burgoyne almost 1,000 men, and most of his 500 Indian allies deserted him in its aftermath. Soon after the battle Burgoyne received Howe's letter informing him of the expedition to Philadelphia.[20]

In New York, Clinton had barely enough troops to defend the city and far too few to carry out Howe's discretionary order that he protect King's Bridge and assist Burgoyne at the same time with an expedition up the Hudson. This became apparent when the ongoing battle for New York flared up again on August 23 and pinned Clinton's forces to the city. He couldn't venture north to make a diversion, Clinton wrote: "[This was] rendered manifest by the enemy's attacking me in three parts of my command at the same time."[21]

As Washington moved south toward Philadelphia, he detached Sullivan to Hanover, New Jersey, for an attack on Staten Island. Coordinated strikes at Kingsbridge, and at the east end of Long Island, timed to distract the British from Sullivan's assault, produced a far more credible show of force than Heath's fumbled mission in January.[22] According to Clinton, Tryon reported from Kingsbridge "that a considerable body of rebels [had] made their appearance near his foreposts and had cut off part of his advanced picket."[23] This turned out to be a feint, however, and more intense clashes took place at the other two points, where the units of die-hard loyalists that Tryon had enlisted in 1776 bore the brunt of defending New York.

"General Parsons' attack of the post at Setauket on Long Island was, after a brisk cannonade and five hours' perseverance, repulsed by Lieutenant Colonel Hewlett of [Oliver] De Lancey's [regiment], who commanded there with only 150 provincials," Clinton wrote.[24] The tenacious Richard Hewlett, a captain and the ringleader of the Long Island Tories who had survived both Charles Lee's and Nathaniel Heard's efforts to suppress him at the beginning of 1776, had been promoted by the British.

"But General Sullivan's descent on Staten Island, being made with less alarming preparation and in greater force, might have been attended with the most serious consequences," if the British had not responded as rapidly as they did, Clinton wrote.[25] Sullivan landed in two places at once, overwhelmed the loyalist units, set fire to their powder magazines, and had started to march toward the town of Richmond before British regulars drove him back and captured some of his men and boats.

Clinton's attitude toward the loyalists who were wounded or killed revealed that they, like the Hessians, were considered second-class citizens in the British military. Clinton's "satisfaction" with the repulse of the rebels was "heightened" by the fact that "the loss sustained was nearly confined to the provincials who had been swept off on the enemy's first landing."[26] Combined with the mistreatment and suffering of civilians in the city under martial law, this disdain for loyalist troops fomented resentment against the British in New York, which grew more bitter as the occupation continued.

The American attacks on New York "were certainly most admirably well combined," Clinton wrote in his narrative. "And, if Mr. Washington had made them with fourteen instead of seven thousand men, they might probably have succeeded" in capturing Staten Island or Long Island, or both.[27]* In a letter to Commodore William Hotham on August 27, Clinton implied that Washington would have done well to capitalize on Howe's blunder by ignoring his expedition to Philadelphia—a city that had symbolic but not strategic value. "If Washington is not a blockhead," Clinton wrote, "he will leave our chief where he is and exert his whole force against Burgoyne or me."[28]

The Howes' armada of 260 ships, carrying 13,000 men, spent more than a month at sea before it finally sailed up Chesapeake Bay and landed at the head of the Elk River on August 25. The Delaware River would have been a far shorter route, but General Howe had received exaggerated—albeit convincing—intelligence from a British ship at the mouth of the river warning of American fortifications and sunken obstructions on the route to Philadelphia. Howe also believed that by landing in the Chesapeake he would sever the link between the middle and southern states across the Susquehanna River; once he had seized Philadelphia, he expected to have an easier time clearing the Delaware and securing it as a supply line.[29]

Detachments from Washington's army of 8,000 Continentals and 3,000 Pennsylvania militia harassed Howe on his subsequent march to Philadelphia, and the main body of troops tried to stop him completely on September 11 at Brandywine Creek, about halfway to the capital city. As he had done in the Battle of Long Island, Washington left one of his flanks open, and Howe seized the opportunity to beat him: 1,000 Americans were wounded, killed, or captured.

Once again, however, Howe did not press his advantage, and Washington's army slipped from his grasp. As Washington retreated over the next two weeks, he tried to block the path to Philadelphia, but Howe outmaneuvered him and marched into the city on September 26. Congress had already fled to York, Pennsylvania, and Howe had to be content with the city itself as his prize, and with the cheers of the citizens who lined the streets.[30]

While Howe marched on and took Philadelphia, in the north Burgoyne's situation became critical, exacerbated by Clinton's hesitancy over diverting troops from New York City, and by the difficulty of communicating from the

*Clinton's estimates of American troop strength are generally exaggerated.

wilderness. In a letter to Burgoyne on September 11, Clinton had offered to make a diversion at the Americans' Highland forts in about ten days—a move, Burgoyne hoped, that would draw off some of the American forces that had begun to surround him.[31] On September 13 and 14, Burgoyne assembled a bridge of boats across a relatively narrow stretch of the Hudson below Saratoga, marched his army across to the west side of the river, and headed south toward Albany. However, General Horatio Gates, who had replaced Philip Schuyler at the head of the northern army in mid-August, stood directly in Burgoyne's path with 7,000 troops. On September 19, the armies clashed in the first of two battles at Freeman's Farm, just north of the American position. Burgoyne, who started the engagement with fewer than 6,000 troops, lost another 600 men.[32]

Gates, by contrast, had received an influx of volunteers eager to repel the British invasion, and his ranks quickly swelled to 11,000 men. One catalyst for these enlistments was the old feud between New York and New England. The appointment of Gates over Schuyler, his New York rival, elicited an enthusiastic response from the northernmost states, where Schuyler was blamed for the failure of the Canadian expedition and the loss of Fort Ticonderoga.[33] Even more powerful was the propaganda surrounding the murder of Jane McCrea, a twenty-three-year-old American woman who had been scalped by some of Burgoyne's Indian scouts on her way to marry her fiancé at the end of July. A letter of protest from Gates to Burgoyne found its way into every newspaper in the region, and McCrea was enshrined as a martyr of the Revolution. The fact that McCrea's fiancé was a loyalist serving under the British convinced Americans that Burgoyne could not guarantee their safety if they heeded his calls to join him or supply his army, and they fled behind the American lines.[34]

Clinton's promised attack on the Highlands was supposed to take place on or about September 21, the same day that Burgoyne received Clinton's encouraging letter. His supplies and salted provisions dangerously low, and his line of communications with Canada threatened, Burgoyne decided to let his troops recuperate instead of taking the offensive, hoping that Clinton's diversion might improve the situation. Instead, it grew steadily worse. Clinton was afraid to leave his base in New York exposed, so his offer to move up the Hudson was contingent on the arrival of reinforcements from England, which did not reach the city until September 24. Clinton also awaited a response from Burgoyne, which finally arrived on the twenty-ninth, because he hoped such a formal request for help would in some measure relieve him of responsibility for leaving New York City

The Hudson River in 1776

and putting it at greater risk. On October 3, Clinton belatedly sailed up the Hudson with 3,000 men.[35]

As Clinton prepared to seize the Highland forts,* he received a new letter from Burgoyne in which he tried to shift responsibility back to Clinton. Burgoyne enjoyed the power and prestige of an independent command in the north, but now that he was stuck, he suddenly wanted Clinton, who was more than 100 miles away and had no part in his campaign, to issue orders and take responsibility for whether he attacked "the enemy in his front or retreated across the lakes while they were clear of ice," Clinton wrote.[36]

The interplay of cautious and self-serving personalities within the British command structure—the bureaucratic game of enhancing and protecting rep-

---

*Fort Montgomery and Fort Clinton were on the west bank of the Hudson just north of Bear Mountain, about forty-five miles north of New York City. A third fort on an island a little north of West Point (five miles upriver) was known by Fort Lee's former name, Fort Constitution. On the east side of the Hudson, a few miles south of Fort Clinton, near Peekskill, stood Fort Independence, which shared the name with the fort near King's Bridge (Symonds, pp. 48–9).

Major General John Burgoyne

utations while avoiding responsibility for the fallout from military decisions—
had come full circle. Howe had shifted the burden of helping the northern
army to Clinton, as did Burgoyne in his turn, stipulating that if he did not hear
from Clinton by October 12, he would retreat to Canada by way of the lakes.[37]

Clinton did an exemplary job of capturing the forts in the Highlands
and clearing the river of American ships and obstructions by October 6.
When Clinton landed 1,000 men on the east bank of the Hudson, General
Putnam thought his position at Peekskill was under attack and retreated
northward in search of support. He commanded fewer than 1,500 troops at
this point, having sent reinforcements both to Gates in the north and to
Washington. Clinton's landing was a feint, however, and he deployed most of
his force on the west side of the Hudson to seize Fort Clinton (named for the
governor of New York State) and Fort Montgomery, where he overwhelmed
the 600 American defenders. Clinton also took a third fort farther upriver.[38]

"However, the small number of men which would remain to me for further operations, after garrisoning the extensive posts I had taken—which I
was obliged either to defend or dismantle—and securing my communications with New York, precluded every idea for the present of penetrating to
Albany," General Clinton wrote after the war to defend his actions. He had
not heard from Howe for more than a month and feared that Washington
might send a strong detachment, or even arrive with his whole army, to strike
below him on the Hudson and cut him off from the city.[39]

Abandoned, outnumbered, and trapped, Burgoyne despaired of hearing
from Clinton and recklessly launched an attack against the fortified American

position on October 7. In the Battle of Bemis Heights, the British were driven back to Freeman's Farm, lost another 600 men, and with them the last remnants of their morale. Benedict Arnold, who had commanded and fought brilliantly in the first battle at Freeman's Farm, was a hero of the second engagement as well.[40]

As Burgoyne's shattered army fled north toward Saratoga, Clinton dismantled one of the three forts he had captured so he could hold the Highlands with fewer men, and prepared to drop back down to New York. However, when he received word that 1,000 reinforcements could be spared from Rhode Island, he decided to make another effort to help Burgoyne. Returning quickly to the city, he ordered "six months' provisions" for Burgoyne's "five thousand men to be directly put on board vessels of proper draft for running up river to Albany." He then dispatched almost 2,000 men under General John Vaughan up the Hudson in galleys, "giving him orders to feel his way to General Burgoyne and do his utmost to assist his operations, or even join him if required."[41]

Vaughan reached Kingston on October 15 and burned it to the ground. He then proceeded as far as Livingston Manor, only forty-five miles south of Albany, at which point his pilots mutinied and American forces under Putnam, reinforced at this point by Parsons, blocked his advance. The final blow to Clinton's rescue effort, however, came from Howe himself. Vaughan had to be recalled and the Highlands abandoned completely on October 18, when the commander in chief ordered Clinton to send him additional troops on the Delaware and deploy his remaining forces to defend New York City.[42]

Howe called for reinforcements because Washington had proved to be far more aggressive than he expected. On October 4, while Clinton was in the process of occupying the Highland forts, Washington attacked the British encampments at Germantown, five miles north of Philadelphia. General Greene's units briefly put the redcoats to flight, but the morning fog and the overly complex battle plan led to a lack of coordination between the four American columns. Although American casualties were high, the troops had savored the sight of British regulars in full retreat. Another positive outcome was the replacement of an incompetent American general who had been drunk during the battle, by the marquis de Lafayette, a young Frenchman who had recently arrived in America to support the Revolution.*

---

*The twenty-one-year-old marquis de Lafayette, well connected at the French court, was given the rank of major general in the Continental Army, despite his lack of experience.

The attack at Germantown put Howe on the alert and forced him to consolidate his troops within a more defensible perimeter just north of Philadelphia. At the same time he had to contend with Washington's attempt to cut off his line of supply from the south. By occupying two forts several miles below the city—one on an island in the Delaware and the other across from it on the New Jersey shore—Washington was able to interdict all river traffic coming up from the Atlantic. By also controlling the roads in and out of Philadelphia, Washington had effectively besieged the city. Howe began attacking the forts in mid-October, but the Americans held them tenaciously.[43]

Joseph Martin was one of the defenders. He had given in to pressure from recruiters in the spring and reenlisted. Given that the war showed no signs of ending soon, and short-term enlistments would clearly not suffice, Congress had authorized a new system, under which soldiers were enrolled either for three years or for the duration of the war, however long that might be. Martin had no illusions about the soldier's life and was filled with dread, but he made the commitment to stay with the army until the bitter end.[44] As the British ships poured their fire into the forts on the Delaware, Martin later recalled, he survived by going without sleep and dodging cannonballs for fourteen days straight.[45] The siege continued, and residents of Philadelphia soon had to venture out into the countryside in search of food.

Howe's demand for reinforcements from New York ended Clinton's attempt to help Burgoyne, but that effort was already too late to be of any use. On October 17, Burgoyne surrendered his entire force to Gates at Saratoga. In the end, the only effect of Clinton's diversion at the Highlands was to make Gates rush somewhat during the negotiations that set the terms of Burgoyne's capitulation. Eager to close the deal quickly when he heard of Clinton's and Vaughan's forays up the Hudson, Gates accepted Burgoyne's demands for a "convention" instead of his surrender.[46]

This arrangement was supposed to allow the 5,000 captives to return to England on the condition that they not participate further in the current war. However, since their release would allow Britain to use them elsewhere around the globe, thereby freeing up an equal number of troops to fight in America, Congress eventually seized on a pretext to abrogate the convention. Burgoyne and his top aides returned to England, but the soldiers of the "convention army" spent the rest of the war as prisoners in Virginia.

News of Burgoyne's surrender at Saratoga—written on a piece of paper and baked into a large loaf of bread—was smuggled to American prisoners in New York City before most of the town had heard. When the entire prison on the Common resounded with cheers, the jailer burst in to see what had happened. He instantly branded the report a "damned Yankee lie," but when the news became official that the rebels had their hands on so many British soldiers, the treatment of the American prisoners in New York improved considerably.[47]

Even after the capture of the northern army, the British grand strategy would still have succeeded, Clinton argued later, if he had simply been allowed to keep enough men to preserve his hold on the Hudson Highlands. When Howe depleted the garrison in New York to bolster his campaign in Philadelphia, he also prevented Clinton from replenishing it by countermanding the transfer of the 1,000 troops from Rhode Island. Thus Howe not only doomed the attempt to help Burgoyne, Clinton wrote, but also threw away Britain's last real chance to win the war.

"I had . . . hope[d] that as soon as [Howe] found I had opened the important door of the Hudson, he would have strained to every nerve to keep it so and prevent the rebels from ever shutting it again—even though he had been obliged to place the back of his whole army against it." Clinton continued:

> And I hope I shall be pardoned if I presume to suggest that, had this been done, it would have most probably finished the war. And Sir William's southern move [to Philadelphia], instead of being censured, would perhaps have been extolled as one of the operative parts of a judicious and well combined plan, and even the loss of General Burgoyne's army looked upon as a necessary sacrifice, as having both essentially contributed to draw off the two grand armies of the enemy to a distance from that very strong and important hold [the Hudson Highlands], which might possibly have been placed beyond our reach had either remained in its neighborhood.[48]

Proud of his bold stroke against the Highland forts, and angry that Howe had not come back to support him in consolidating the British hold on the river, Clinton had relinquished the insight that he seemed to grasp fully during the campaign of 1776: that the only way to win the war was to capture or destroy Washington's army, not to seize a strategic waterway or piece of ground. This maxim applied to both sides in the conflict: Burgoyne's army, in fact, was not expendable under any circumstances.

In the world of international politics, the surrender at Saratoga could not simply be dismissed as a necessary cost of war. The American victory reverberated across the Atlantic, and by early December, the news had reached Paris. Two months later, encouraged by the former colonies' improved prospects, France formally recognized American independence and signed a commercial treaty with the United States. After the French declared war on Britain, Spain and the Netherlands eventually followed suit. The rebellion of thirteen colonies rapidly became a global conflict, which strained Britain's resources and ultimately brought down the ministry, ushering the opposition into power. The abandonment of Burgoyne had led to his surrender at Saratoga, which proved to be the great turning point of the American Revolution, and it was the misguided strategy of settling comfortably into America's two largest cities that brought it on. When word reached Benjamin Franklin in Paris that Howe had captured Philadelphia, he famously and presciently replied, "No, Philadelphia has captured Howe!"[49]

It was not until late November 1777—after a relentless bombardment of the American forts on the Delaware, and the arrival of reinforcements from New York—that Howe was able to lift the siege of Philadelphia. Washington pulled back and for several weeks maneuvered in and out of tense standoffs with Howe's army, hoping to end the year's campaign with some sort of victory before retiring to winter quarters. Howe did not take up the challenge, however; in December the British settled back into Philadelphia, and Washington took the army to Valley Forge. It was a less than ideal winter campground, but he hoped its proximity to Philadelphia would enable him to strike at Howe early in the spring.[50] Conditions were so desperate when the army first arrived that Joseph Martin spent his last few coins, "Pennsylvania currency," to buy a drink of water from two soldiers who had managed to fill their canteens at a distant spring.[51]

While the American troops endured famine and cold in the Pennsylvania hills, Howe finally responded to Washington's letters and went halfway toward exchanging Charles Lee for General Prescott: On December 27, he freed Lee from his six-month confinement on the *Centurion* and paroled him locally. From the ship he moved into "a handsome House. under the Care of 4 or 5 field Officers, who lived with him & Kept a genteel Table," according to an American visitor.[52] Caught up in the social whirl of the occupied city, Lee entertained various high-ranking guests, including his old acquaintance and adversary, Sir Henry Clinton. Lee wrote to Washington that he roamed New York and its suburbs with horses provided by Clinton and General James Robertson; shared lodgings with two British officers who were his best and oldest friends; and generally lived in a manner "as easy, comfortable and pleasant as possible for a man who is any sort of Prisoner."[53] Prescott, in turn, was granted similar freedom in Connecticut.

While eighteenth-century social and military conventions ensured that officers on both sides would live comfortably in captivity, the fate of ordinary soldiers was often horrific. During Lee's local parole, Washington sent a special envoy, Elias Boudinot, on an official tour behind enemy lines in New York City to investigate accounts from American escapees about British brutality in their prisons. In a letter to General Howe, Washington had protested the treatment of American prisoners in New York, calling it "shocking to humanity."[54] The British agreed to an inspection.

General Robertson and the notorious Commissary Loring greeted Boudinot courteously and gave him unlimited access to the prisoners.[55] At the jail on the Common, Boudinot encouraged the inmates to overcome their fear of retribution from the British officers present and to speak out about any abuses. They singled out the already infamous provost marshal, William Cunningham, as their chief tormentor, describing how he locked individual prisoners in a dungeon for months at a time as punishment for minor or even imagined infractions of his rules.

Boudinot had Cunningham brought into the room. The tall, ruddy Irishman wore his long hair in a ponytail with powdered "bat-wings" over his ears.[56] Confronted with the charges, Cunningham "with great Insolence answered that every word was true," and "swore that he was as absolute there as Gen'l Howe was at the head of his Army."[57]

Boudinot also learned that the 400 prisoners crowded into the French church "could not all lay down at once," and from October to January "never recd a single stick of wood, and that for the most part they eat their Pork Raw

When the Pews & Door & Wood on Facings failed them for fuel."[58] The British apparently did not show Boudinot the prison ships but sent him home with promises that conditions in the jails would improve. After he left New York, Boudinot continued his efforts to feed and clothe the prisoners by reminding Congress of their plight and advancing nearly $27,000 of his own money to purchase bread, beef, shirts, suits, and blankets for them through an agent in the city. For his part, Loring reported to General Howe that he had accompanied Boudinot on his inspection, and that everything was found to be satisfactory.[59]

By the end of January 1778 Howe and Washington had agreed to release captured officers "on general parole," meaning that as a group they could return to the comfort and safety of their own lines, but each signed a pledge not to perform active service in the war unless or until his final exchange for a specific officer considered to be of equal value was confirmed individually. Washington therefore sent Prescott to New York, but Howe, on the pretext that he wanted to receive Lee's pledge in person, insisted that he report to him in Philadelphia. In fact, Howe and Lee were both eager to resume their discussion, begun shortly after Lee was captured and transferred to New York, about engaging the Americans in peace talks.

Using Robertson as an intermediary, Lee had recently written a long letter to the Howes in which he proposed a framework for a negotiated settlement of the war and asked the brothers to deputize him to present the plan to the Americans. American independence would result in "confusion anarchy and civil wars," Lee predicted, while the British would go bankrupt seeking a military victory. Fearful that France was about to enter the war, the British government was eager for such a plan by which the Americans would renounce independence in exchange for greater freedom within the empire, and General Howe responded with enthusiasm to Lee's letter. On April 3, Howe and Lee had a friendly meeting in Philadelphia, in which the commander in chief, according to Lee, apologized for treating his prisoner so harshly and expressed regrets at having assumed the leadership of the British forces in America. Lee, in turn, assured Howe that he would use his influence to bring the Americans to the negotiating table.[60] Ezra Stiles, who had wondered in his diary if Lee was "a pimp for the ministry" after meeting him in 1774, in the end, had been justified in his doubts.

Lee signed his parole and departed for Valley Forge on April 5.

Washington sent out one of his aides and some mounted troops to escort Lee back to headquarters, where Mrs. Washington entertained them "with an Elegant Dinner" at which musicians serenaded the American generals, according to Boudinot. However, Lee took little interest in his hosts and their warm welcome, Boudinot wrote in his memoirs. Lee was given a room behind Mrs. Washington's sitting room, and the next morning "he lay very late. and Breakfast was detained for him," Boudinot recalled. "When he came out, he looked as dirty as if he had been in the Street all night. soon after I discovered that he had brought a miserable dirty hussy with him from Philadelphia (a British Sergeant's Wife) and had actually taken her into his Room by a Back Door and she had slept with him that night."[61]

Washington was more inclined to forgive the Englishman's behavior, including his insubordination in December 1776, shortly before his capture. Washington, whose reputation had suffered in Congress and in the army after the defeats at Brandywine and Germantown, hoped Lee might be an asset to the Americans in the campaign of 1778. The Continental Army needed victories, and Washington needed to silence his critics who argued that Horatio Gates—basking in the glory of his victory at Saratoga—would make a better commander in chief.[62]

Until his final exchange for Prescott was completed, however, Lee could not serve under Washington. So Lee, mounted on an old, worn-out horse, his own feet aching with gout, headed down to York to meet with members of Congress before proceeding to his estate in Virginia. In private conversations at York, the great pamphleteer of 1774—the champion of the American fighting-man who had stood up to the Reverend Myles Cooper—reversed himself. According to Henry Laurens, Lee tried to steer the delegates toward negotiations with Howe by warning them about the superiority of the British military, advising them against taking the offensive in the war, and suggesting that they give up full independence in the interests of peace. Lee also went beyond his promise to Howe and made disparaging remarks about Washington's ability to defeat the British.[63]

In mid-April, however, the basis of Lee's grim prognosis about British military might and his advice that the Americans pursue a defensive strategy suddenly unraveled. The British government, in a desperate attempt to forestall the entry of France into the war, had launched a concerted peace offensive. All of the laws dating back to 1763 that had provoked the American rebellion were repealed, and on April 13, the conciliatory bills introduced in Parliament by Lord North reached New York, where Tryon enlisted Rivington to print copies for distribution throughout the colonies. Three additional peace commissioners led by Frederick Howard, earl of Carlisle, were dispatched to the former colonies to assist the Howes in offering essentially the same terms that most Americans had demanded before 1774: substantial autonomy within the empire, including freedom from parliamentary taxation—except for the purpose of regulating trade. The proceeds from these duties would be used for the benefit of the colonies.[64]

On May 2 Congress learned from its envoys in Paris about the treaty of amity and commerce with France signed in February; two days later the delegates ratified that agreement along with a treaty of alliance, which was to be activated if France and Britain declared war on each other. Since the imminent entry of France into the war drastically shifted the balance of power, Congress had less incentive than ever to engage in talks with the British about relinquishing American independence. However, some Americans, including a minority of congressional delegates, preferred to negotiate a settlement with the British because they feared that France—the enemy they had driven from North America in the Seven Years' War—might try to impose its own tyrannical rule over the former British colonies.

Lee was among those who continued to hope for an Anglo-American reconciliation, and he maintained a secret correspondence with Clinton and Robertson on the subject over the next several weeks.[65] His exchange formalized, Lee stopped in York again on his way back to Valley Forge to ask Congress for a promotion, which would have made him the only lieutenant general in the Continental Army and given him an advantage over any other candidate to succeed Washington as commander in chief. Already besieged by requests for advancement from other officers, and doubtless influenced by Lee's disloyal views in conversations the month before, Congress turned Lee down.[66]

Lee reached Valley Forge on May 21, accompanied by "his usual train of dogs," according to Nathanael Greene.[67] Benedict Arnold arrived on the same day. Congress had originally promoted him to the rank of brigadier general in January 1776 after the failed attack on Quebec; raised him to major general after his defense of Danbury, Connecticut, in April 1777; and after Saratoga attempted to redress his accumulated grievances by issuing a new, backdated commission that gave him seniority over five generals he considered his inferiors and his rivals. Seriously wounded at Saratoga and unfit for a field command, Arnold was nonetheless at the height of his career in the Continental Army. The American troops—molded by this point into a much stronger and more efficient fighting force under drill-master Baron von Steuben—rejoiced at the sight of Lee and Arnold, two popular and respected generals.[68]

The top British commanders, by contrast, had given up hope of winning the war and had been lobbying for months for the king to accept their letters of resignation. In early December 1777, after Germain received definitive reports of the disaster at Saratoga, he began agitating for General Howe's removal. In London, however, the commander in chief's family and political allies criticized his detractors in the ministry and rallied the king to stand by him. At the same time Howe expressed his desire to resign and clear his name publicly in Parliament. Admiral Howe had spent the winter and early spring of 1778 at Newport, Rhode Island, dutifully and industriously using the base Clinton had established to run the coastal blockade; when he learned of the threat to his brother's career and reputation, he declared his intention to resign as well. The Howes made no further military plans as they waited for the official response to their letters of resignation and to Burgoyne's defeat.[69]

On his way to Philadelphia at the end of March, Admiral Howe stopped in New York, where on April 13 the *Andromeda* arrived from England with Parliament's conciliatory bills and news of Carlisle's peace commission, which Howe predicted would be futile, even as he and Tryon had the new measures printed up in the New York newspapers. The ship also brought long-awaited orders from the ministry: Clinton was to replace General Howe as commander in chief, and Admiral Howe would be assisted in America by Rear Admiral James Gambier and then by Commodore John Byron. Admiral Howe reached Philadelphia at the end of April and was soon informed that he could stay on as head of the North American squadron or resign and turn the command over to Gambier when he arrived in New York.[70]

In the midst of crisis, England's naval command in America was about to devolve on a series of obviously mediocre, if not incompetent, admirals.[71] As for the army's top post, no self-respecting military man wanted it, Clinton explained. "For neither honor nor credit could be expected from it, but on the contrary a considerable portion of blame, howsoever unmerited, seemed to be almost inevitable."[72] Unfortunately for the lieutenant general, Lord North was running out of talented commanders. The British public associated Cornwallis with Trenton and blamed Howe for not supporting Burgoyne, who was a prisoner in Boston. Once again Clinton bowed to pressure from friends and the ministry and took the job. "I was, notwithstanding, duly sensible of the confidence with which the King had honored me," Clinton wrote, "and I consequently prepared with all diligence to obey His Majesty's commands to the fullest extent of my ability."[73] The mercurial general, who had both coveted and dreaded an independent command, arrived in Philadelphia on May 11, 1778, to relieve Sir William Howe.

CHAPTER 21

The Return to New York City, the Fulcrum of the War

$\sim$

The day after my arrival in Philadelphia a frigate from England brought me two sets of instructions signed by His Majesty, dated the 8th and 21st of March," wrote Sir Henry Clinton, revealing yet again the challenge of communication the British faced, as the documents had been issued two months earlier.

The latter, which superseded the former, signified to me that, "in consequence of a treaty of amity and commerce entered into by the French King with the American states, a resolution had been taken to make an immediate attack on the Island of St. Lucia, and directing me to detach 5000 men to the West Indies for that purpose, so as to arrive there before the hurricane season set in. I was also desired to send at the same time 3000 men to St. Augustine and West Florida, and to return the 600 marines in garrison at Halifax to their respective ships. And, as my army would thus be much weakened by these detachments, etc., I was commanded to evacuate Philadelphia and proceed by sea with the remaining troops and stores to New York, there to wait the issue of a treaty to be proposed to the American Congress by Commissioners whom His Majesty had nominated for that purpose."[1]

With France one step from entering the war, Britain had abruptly shifted its attention away from the protracted series of inconclusive battles with the rebels on the American mainland and toward a contest for the valuable sugar islands in the West Indies. If the simultaneous peace offensive by the Carlisle Commission failed, Clinton was ordered "to endeavor without delay to bring Mr. Washington to a general action."[2] Failing that, the navy was to support Clinton in making destructive coastal raids against New England, and, after October, to maintain a blockade in the north while helping him conquer the South—especially Georgia and the Carolinas—where large numbers of loyalists were expected to turn out.[3]

In short, the British decided to retreat to New York for the same reasons they had captured it in the first place: its central location on the Atlantic seaboard. This time, however, they did not plan to use its position at the mouth of the Hudson to sever the colonies in two, but rather—if Clinton was unable to end the war sooner by luring Washington into a decisive battle—to use the harbor as a naval base for making direct attacks on both regions, North and South, in rapid succession. As the marquis de Lafayette remarked later in the war, New York was "the pivot on which turn the operations of the enemy."[4]

With the return to New York, the British were confronted with the fact that they had ultimately accomplished nothing in the two years since they captured the city in 1776. Before General Howe left for England at the end of May 1778, ending the nine months he and his officers had spent "playing in the drawing rooms, ballrooms, gaming rooms, and bedrooms" of Philadelphia, his officers threw him "the biggest bash the New World had ever seen. . . . It was called a Mischianza, meaning a medley or mixture of entertainments, a twelve-hour extravaganza that included a regatta of three divisions (each with a band) so big it clogged the river, triumphal arches, a tournament with jousting officers championing the cream of Loyalist girls in Turkish costumes and fantastic hair-dos, elaborate fireworks, a midnight banquet served by costumed slaves in a saloon over two hundred feet long, dancing till four in the morning—all in celebration of it was not clear what."[5]

Most bizarre of all was the participation of Admiral Howe in the festivities. Faithful, sober, and responsible, the admiral did not have a mistress and had lived in relatively Spartan quarters on his flagship when he presided over Newport's decidedly tamer social season from January through March. At the *mischianza*, the hollow, triumphal stage sets might well have seemed to mock

Admiral Howe's ambition of achieving peace through reconciliation, while providing an apt metaphor for both his brother's failure and his own.[6]

Sir Henry Clinton's aide-de-camp, Major John André, thought the party was a touching tribute. He wrote to a friend in London that it was "the most splendid entertainment . . . ever given by an army to their General."[7] In its sincere admiration, the letter unwittingly captured the grotesque excess—the advanced state of decadence—that already engulfed the British in Philadelphia and New York, where they soon returned.

In early June, Cornwallis returned from leave in England and became Clinton's second-in-command. Cornwallis had written to Clinton, "[I will] do all in my power to contribute to your ease in a situation which, I fear, you will not find a bed of roses."[8] His first act, however, was to attempt to resign, as soon as he landed and saw how hopeless the British position had become. The already beleaguered ministry predictably turned down his request.[9] The new peace commissioners also arrived in Philadelphia at the beginning of June, and when Congress refused to meet with them, the British envoys, along with 3,000 frightened loyalists in Philadelphia, prepared to leave for New York on Admiral Howe's fleet.

On June 18 Clinton evacuated Philadelphia but disobeyed Germain's instructions that he return to New York by ship. Embarking the whole army onto the fleet would have been a lengthy process, and Clinton feared that Washington might attack New York while the British were at sea. Admiral Howe and Clinton also disregarded the order to immediately dispatch ships and troops to the West Indies. Howe's North American squadron was dispersed along the length of the Atlantic seaboard, and he, like Clinton, wanted to regroup in New York before diluting his force even further.[10]

At the same time, Clinton suspected his Hessian troops would have taken the opportunity presented by an overland trek to desert him. Therefore, Admiral Howe's fleet carried the Hessians and the loyalist refugees while Clinton marched his army of 10,000 men across New Jersey in a column stretching for more than eight miles. Clinton hoped to lure the Americans into a decisive battle by parading across the state with a force significantly smaller than Washington's—but one that was far superior in skill and discipline. Washington's army had grown to nearly 13,000 men, and he could call on an additional 3,000 to 4,000 troops from the militias of the surrounding states; roughly 2,000 men under McDougall, who had relieved Putnam in the

Hudson Highlands in March, could have quickly joined the army in New Jersey as well, giving the Americans a two-to-one advantage.[11]

Given Clinton's apparent vulnerability, Washington was tempted to confront him. He followed Clinton's caravan and tried to defeat the British army at Monmouth, just east of Princeton, on June 28. In the last major battle in the North, Washington's offensive was blunted when Lee, who had been honored with the command of the army's vanguard, disobeyed the commander in chief's instructions to attack the British at a critical moment and ordered a retreat instead. Washington rallied the retreating troops to make an impressive stand and fought the British to a draw, despite the murderously hot day in the New Jersey pine barrens. Clinton suffered 1,200 casualties—including wounded, killed, and captured—to Washington's 300 or 400. It was the Continental Army's best performance so far in a full-fledged battle against the British. Whereas at Trenton and Princeton the Americans had attacked detached garrisons, at Monmouth Clinton's entire army was present, even if he did not send every unit into the fray.[12]

Lee's retreat, like the man himself, remains controversial. Many have condemned it as blatant insubordination, motivated by Lee's low estimate of the American soldier's chances in an open fight against British regulars. Others argue that fully engaging the British, as Washington tried to do, was folly: With French intervention coming soon, it made little sense to risk a defeat, and Lee saved the army from disaster, merely carrying out the wisdom of the war councils in the preceding days (which Washington apparently accepted and then chose to ignore) not to give Clinton the "general engagement" he wanted.[13]

Even Lee's defenders, however, agree that he made matters worse for himself in the aftermath of Monmouth. After Washington berated him on the battlefield, Lee wrote him two provoking letters and demanded a court-martial to clear his name. Theoretically, the tribunal could have handed down a death sentence, but instead convicted Lee on charges that included speaking disrespectfully to the commander in chief, and suspended him from command for a year. Lee's old friend from the days of fortifying New York, Lord Stirling, had presided at the tribunal. The punishment was damaging enough, since Lee never again served in the Continental Army.[14]

Washington chose not to pursue Clinton after the debacle at Monmouth and moved north instead, intent on sending some units across to the east side of the Hudson where they could bolster the camps in the Highlands, which would be under renewed pressure from the British after they resettled in New

York City. Two weeks later, at his new headquarters in Paramus, New Jersey, Washington received momentous news from Philadelphia: The French had arrived. A fleet of powerful warships under Vice Admiral Jean-Baptiste Charles Henri Hector Theodat, known more succinctly as the comte d'Estaing, had arrived from Toulon off the Virginia coast. The fleet would "destroy that of the English and block up the harbor of New York," the Philadelphia *Evening Post* predicted confidently on July 11.[15] As d'Estaing made his way toward Sandy Hook, Washington prepared to greet the admiral with a letter of welcome and a gift of livestock for his hungry men, who had been at sea for almost three months.[16]

Continuing toward New York after the battle at Monmouth, Clinton had headed for Sandy Hook on the New Jersey shore hoping to rendezvous with Howe's fleet, which arrived on cue on June 29. As he prepared to load Clinton's army the next day, Howe "was met at sea by the Grantham packet, express from England," according to Thomas O'Beirne, an officer in the fleet. It brought a warning that the French had entered the war and that the squadron of French ships sailing for America was "at no great distance from the coast."[17] Commodore John "Foul Weather Jack" Byron (the grandfather of the poet) had been dispatched from England with thirteen ships to reinforce Admiral Howe, but given the date of his departure, he was not expected to reach New York before the French fleet.

The delay of Byron's squadron reflected the defensive naval strategy Britain had adopted in response to French intervention in the war. Instead of blockading the French in their home ports of Brest (on the Atlantic) and Toulon (in the Mediterranean), the British nervously concentrated their ships to protect the English Channel and relied on piecemeal detachments to cope, belatedly, with challenges to their colonial possessions and vital trade routes. The dilemma of protecting the British Isles from invasion while fighting a global war was real: A significant number of ships had already been allocated to the North American squadron under Admiral Howe.

The problem required the audacity and risk-taking of a William Pitt, who led Britain to victory in the Seven Years' War. Lord Sandwich, at the helm of the Admiralty, and Admiral Augustus Keppel, the commander of the home fleet, made a far more cautious pair. Instead of sending ships to seal the Mediterranean at the Straits of Gibraltar, they allowed d'Estaing to escape, while they hung back to see if he would attack Britain or head for North America. This reactive policy and reliance on detachments of ships

Comte d'Estaing

carried its own risks. If d'Estaing reached New York before Byron, he might well overpower Howe's fleet and Clinton's army—and decide the outcome of the war.[18]

With the French bearing down on them, O'Beirne wrote, Clinton and Howe had to proceed with the "utmost expedition" to get the British troops, along with the "transports and victuallers," off the Jersey shore and up to Manhattan. A bridge of boats was positioned across the channel separating Sandy Hook from the mainland,* and the whole army proceeded onto the island; flatboats transferred the troops to the fleet without losing a single man. The flawless operation—a precision maneuver in treacherous waters—renewed the sailors' reverence for the man they called "Black Dick." O'Beirne noted that "Lord Howe attended in person, as usual; and by his presence animated the zeal, and quickened the industry, of officers and men."[19]

Reports came in on July 7 that the French fleet had moved up the coast to Chesapeake Bay and then to the Delaware River. On the eleventh its destination was finally confirmed by intelligence that "a fleet of 12 sail two-decked ships, and three frigates, appeared the evening before, under French colours, holding their course for New-York," O'Beirne reported. "At 12 o'clock the same day, a signal was made, from one of our frigates without the bar, that they had hove in sight; and in the afternoon they were observed to come to anchor off Shrewsbury inlet, about four miles from Sandy-Hook."[20]

The British were confronted with a much more powerful French fleet,

*Sandy Hook was an island at the time but is now connected to the mainland.

but the appearance of an ancient enemy, the stirrings of British chauvin-
ism, and a sense that the glory of empire hung in the balance seem to have
motivated the rank and file. As the men competed to serve on the fleet,
O'Beirne declared, "it was observed, with rapture, that the spirit which had
raised the British nation above the rest of Europe for so many ages past, was
not extinct; that it only wanted to be awakened, and properly directed, to
blaze out with as bright a luster as ever distinguished the most fortunate of
our days."[21]

Howe's flagship, the *Eagle*, and several other men-of-war were at Staten
Island taking on fresh water when the French ships arrived. Howe expected
them to cross the sandbar at Sandy Hook and attack immediately, so he raced
down to direct the ships he had stationed there; when the wind prevented him
from reaching Sandy Hook, "with all the expedition the danger seemed to
require, the vice admiral [Howe] quitted the *Eagle*, and throwing himself into
his barge, hastened to the ships below."[22]

The French, however, remained at anchor four miles away. Their enormous warships drew two or three feet more water than the British, and
d'Estaing did not want to risk running his vessels aground on the sandbar. At
high tide, they might have passed one at a time through the ship channel
closest to Sandy Hook, but that would have made them easy prey for Howe's
fleet. The solution was to have American pilots guide the ships collectively
across the bar at selected points.

Washington had dispatched his aide, John Laurens, to the Jersey shore
to greet d'Estaing; Laurens, who spoke fluent French, helped to arrange for
pilots and establish the signals that would be used to facilitate communication between the Americans and the French fleet. However, the pilots
Washington sent to d'Estaing claimed the French ships were too big. Even
when d'Estaing offered a reward of 50,000 crowns, he couldn't find a taker,
so he held back for several days, according to O'Beirne, "sounding the bar,
and wearing every appearance of a determination to enter and attack the
port."[23]

While the French were sailing north from Virginia, Washington had returned
to Westchester by crossing the Hudson well above New York City at King's
Ferry. "Each brigade furnished its own ferrymen to carry the troops across,"
Joseph Martin recalled. "I was one of the men from our brigade; we were still
suffering for provisions." Apparently, General Greene's reforms as the new

quartermaster had not yet trickled down far enough. However, Martin soon received an auspicious gift of food from an unexpected source.

> Nearly the last trip the batteau that I was in made, while crossing the river empty, a large sturgeon (a fish in which this river abounds) seven or eight feet in length, in his gambolings, sprang directly into the boat, without doing any other damage than breaking down one of the seats of the boat. We crossed and took in our freight and recrossed, landed the men and our prize, gave orders to our several messmates as to the disposal of it, and proceeded on our business till the whole of the brigade had crossed the river, which was not long, we working with new energy in expectation of having something to eat when we had done our job. We then repaired to our messes to partake of the bounty of Providence, which we had so unexpectedly received. Many of the poor fellows *thought* us happy in being thus supplied; for my part I *felt* happy.[24]

On reaching New York, Washington reflected on the futility of Britain's recent efforts: The British were back in New York and the Americans in Westchester. "It is not a little pleasing," Washington wrote, "nor less wonderful to contemplate that after two years Manoeuvring . . . both Armies are brought back to the very point they set out from."[25]

From King's Ferry the army proceeded to Tarrytown and from there to White Plains, where, according to Martin:

> We drew some small supplies of summer clothing of which we stood in great need. While we lay here, I, with some of my comrades who were in the battle of White Plains in the year '76, one day took a ramble on the ground where we were then engaged with the British and took a survey of the place. We saw a number of the graves of those who fell in that battle. Some of the bodies had been so slightly buried that the dogs or hogs, or both, had dug them out of the ground. The skulls and other bones and hair were scattered about the place.

The sight of the Hessians' remains provoked a primal fear of an anonymous death without a grave. "Here were Hessian skulls as thick as a bombshell," Martin wrote. "Poor fellows! They were left unburied in a foreign land. They had, perhaps, as near and dear friends to lament their sad destiny as the Americans who lay buried near them. But they should have kept at home; we should then never have gone after them to kill them in their own country."[26]

While d'Estaing hesitated at Sandy Hook, Howe spent the time "placing his ships in the strongest position the channel within the Hook would admit," O'Beirne observed. "He sounded its several depths in person; he ascertained the different setting of the currents, and from the observations thus made, formed different plans with a view to the points of wind with which d'Estaing might resolve to cross the bar."[27] The admiral also extended his line of warships by adding the *Leviathan*, a store-ship manned by volunteers and equipped with cannon from Clinton's artillery train.* John Montresor's engineers erected "a battery of two howitzers, and one of three eighteen pounders on the point round which the enemy must have passed to enter the channel; while four regiments . . . were ordered by General Clinton to the Hook, lest the enemy should attempt to possess it, and annoy us from so dangerous a quarter."[28]

D'Estaing was still a serious threat, if only because his fleet blockaded New York and captured about twenty merchant ships headed for the city. A British privateer with five captured American vessels "anchored in the middle of their fleet, during the night, thinking them to be British, and was boarded before he could discover the mistake," wrote an enraged O'Beirne. "A British fleet blocked up by a squadron of Frenchmen! and in our own harbour! Vessels, bearing English colours, daily captured in our sight!"[29]

Since Washington had moved down to White Plains, the city appeared to be caught in a vise, trapped on the narrow island of Manhattan. "By a person who came out of New York last Saturday," the *Pennsylvania Packet* announced on July 16, "we are informed the tories were in the greatest consternation.— Their insolence had quite vanished—and now they begin to send toast and

---

*Howe "had arranged his six largest ships in a line curving from the northernmost point of the Hook to the northwest, presenting a concave obstruction to anyone entering the channel from the sea," one historian wrote. "Because of the curvature of the line, each ship was able to bring its guns to bear both along and across the channel without masking the fire of any other; and by attaching a spring to its anchor cable, each ship could be trained about without regard to wind or tide" (Gruber, *Howe Brothers*, p. 309).

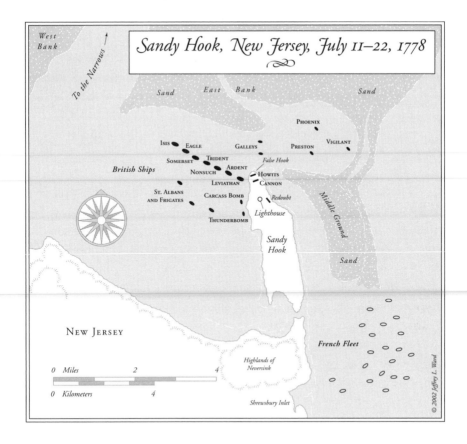

Map: *Sandy Hook, New Jersey, July 11–22, 1778*

butter to the prisoners by way of making fair weather for themselves against our army takes possession of that city, which time is near at hand."[30] The starving city might have been handed over without a shot within a month. D'Estaing, however, did not feel he had that long to wait, as Admiral Byron was expected from Halifax at any hour. On July 22, after eleven days at the Hook, d'Estaing finally made a decisive move.

"The wind blew fresh at north-east, and by eight o'clock D'Estaing, with all his squadron, appeared under way," O'Beirne recalled.

> He kept working to windward, as if to gain a proper position for crossing the bar by the time the tide should serve. The wind could not be more favourable for such a design; it blew from the exact point by which he could attack us to the greatest advantage. The spring tides were at the highest, and raised that afternoon thirty feet on the bar. We consequently expected the hottest day that had ever been fought between the two nations. On our side all

was at stake. Had the men of war been defeated, the fleet of transports and victuallers must have been destroyed, and the army, of
course, have fallen with us; yet, under Heaven, we had not the
least doubt of success. D'Estaing, however, had not spirit equal to
the risk; at three o'clock we saw him bear off to the southward,
and in a few hours he was out of sight.[31]

D'Estaing soon headed north, however, having decided to leave New
York and attack the British naval base in Rhode Island, which Clinton had
established in 1776. Washington had received the same suggestion in a letter
from Congress on July 17 and started marching detachments east on the
twenty-second. Employing two of his aides, Alexander Hamilton and John
Laurens, to communicate the plan to d'Estaing (they had been rowed to and
from the French flagship repeatedly during the past ten days, one going while
the other returned), Washington learned that d'Estaing had given up on
crossing the bar and decided on his own to set sail for Newport. By luck, the
allied movements were synchronized, but d'Estaing's delays and his abrupt
departure hinted that he would not be easy to work with.[32] In New York City,
residents heaved a sigh of relief that, for the moment, Admiral Howe's skill
and the great sandbar between Coney Island and Sandy Hook had lifted the
blockade.

In early August, just as General John Sullivan and d'Estaing began to coordinate their attacks on Newport by land and sea, Admiral Howe arrived to
challenge the French fleet. Displaying no lack of spirit, d'Estaing sailed out
to confront the British. Admiral Byron and most of his fleet had not arrived
yet, but a few ships had gotten ahead of the rest and they reinforced Howe,
who decided to engage the French even though he was still outgunned. Howe
succeeded in luring the French fleet southward, away from Newport, and
then doubling back to strike at them with the wind in his favor. The brilliant
maneuver promised Howe a final chance to redeem his diplomatic and military failures and change the course of the war. Just as he bore down on
d'Estaing, however, the storm that had been gathering steadily suddenly grew
so fierce that he had to call off the attack. The gale scattered and badly damaged the two fleets, the French ships sailing to Boston for repairs and the
British returning by ones and twos to New York.[33]

Howe's battered fleet found that the city had suffered serious damage
during its absence: At the beginning of August a second major fire had bro-

ken out, destroying more than sixty buildings. On the same day lightning struck a British ordnance sloop anchored in the East River near the Coffee House at the foot of Wall Street. The 248 barrels of gunpowder on board exploded, knocking people down in the streets, shattering windows, and damaging many roofs. These events, combined with the blockade by the French fleet in July, collectively afflicted the city's officials and residents with a siege mentality. Therefore, when Elias Boudinot returned to the city in August, he was able to procure a general exchange of American marine prisoners.[34]* John Holt's *New York Journal*, then being published in Poughkeepsie, described the atmosphere in the city as reported by a recently released prisoner. The freeing of the prisoners was "not from motives of generosity" but because of the panic induced by the appearance of the French fleet. The British did not want the expense of keeping the prisoners alive, and "under the apprehensions they [were] now in, of an attempt to dislodge them from that place, they thought themselves safer without such a body of Americans among them, though unarmed and confined."[35]

At Newport, the withdrawal of the French fleet had doomed the American attack by land, and an angry General Sullivan retreated, castigating d'Estaing in his general orders. Washington warned Sullivan to keep any disagreements with the French confined to the high command for the sake of the troops' morale, the French sense of decorum, and the delicate health of the new Franco-American alliance.[36] Howe repaired his fleet at Sandy Hook with extraordinary speed and set out to intercept d'Estaing's broken squadron on its way to Boston. Arriving on August 30, two days too late, Howe found the entrance to Boston's harbor heavily fortified and decided to return to New York via Newport. With the French holed up for lengthy repairs, the lull in the campaign gave Howe a welcome opportunity to finally resign his command.[37]

The day after the Battle of Monmouth, on June 29, the *New York Journal* had printed a letter allegedly addressed to Lord North and signed by William Smith, presenting a detailed plan for defeating the Americans by making territorial concessions to the French and then enlisting their aid to crush the rebellion. Holt agreed to print Smith's explanation of why the letter was a "wicked Forgery," but the publisher added his own note, which stated that

---

*Mariners of various types, including merchants, privateers, and the smaller category of soldiers and sailors captured aboard armed vessels constituting the rudimentary American navy such as it existed.

"no arguments or oaths will be effectual to restore to the love and confidence of his country a man who would do nothing to assist it in time of danger nor give it any satisfactory assurances that he would not join its enemies the moment he could do so with safety to his person and property."[38]

Holt was right on both counts. Smith had exhausted the goodwill of his friends, including Governor George Clinton, and they could no longer intercede to get him special treatment. It was also true that Smith had waited until the last possible moment to choose sides in order to diminish the chance that one or the other would confiscate his wealth. He finally asked for permission to leave for New York only after his house at Haverstraw had been plundered and his anxiety about his house in New York City became acute. Not only had Smith been concerned for his personal property in town since the fire of 1776, but he had secretly stored the city's chancery records in his home in an effort to protect them during the upheavals.

His old friend John Morin Scott was also correct, however, when he had warned that Smith was too valuable and influential to be handed over to the enemy. Smith's requests in recent months that he be allowed to return to New York had been turned down for fear that he, like the Howes, would formulate peace proposals that the British would use to divide public opinion in America. After Smith refused to take an oath of allegiance to New York State on July 7, for the third time in two years, the commissioners for conspiracies at Poughkeepsie again decided to keep him confined at Livingston Manor.

However, time had run out for the committee as well as for Smith. On August 11, Aaron Burr, who had risen to the rank of lieutenant colonel and become an aide to Washington, escorted Smith to the city under a flag of truce. Unlike most exiles to New York, whose belongings were confiscated, Smith was permitted to bring his furniture, a large, valuable library of books, a servant, and several horses. Fittingly, he made the journey in the company of another exile, Cadwalader Colden—the loyalist grandson of his old enemy during younger and more rebellious days.[39] The fifty-year-old Smith was so distinguished and accomplished and potentially valuable to either side that, according to rumor, Washington, Gates, and Governor Clinton had met to discuss his case before they reluctantly decided to deport him.

The Carlisle Commission, which had retired to New York to plot its next move after the snub by Congress, was eager to enlist Smith's help in the diplomatic maneuvering it hoped would end the war. On the earl of Carlisle's list of important Americans that he hoped to influence, Smith's name, like that of

Samuel Adams, was "heavily starred." However, the damning assessments of Smith by the commission's local advisers warned that he should be handled with caution. He "has more influence over the Rebels in the Province than any other Person—The titular Govr. *Clinton* was his Pupil and is his creature," wrote the Anglican minister John Vardill, whose enmity toward Smith went back to the days of the Triumvirate. "He is subtle, cool & persuasive. . . . He may be secured by an application to his *Ambition*."[40] Another loyalist described Smith in a letter to the commissioners as "a Lawyer of great intrigue and Subtlety . . . few Men so able, if he could be trusted."[41]

Once Smith joined his old enemies, however, he did not waver again. He began working for the Carlisle Commission, doing precisely what the revolutionaries had feared: The expert propagandist urged the members to disseminate their peace offer in a pamphlet to be distributed in rebel-controlled areas, and he told them how to write it. Smith also recommended that civil government be restored in New York in order to make the province a beacon for deluded Americans, demonstrating to them the advantages of the English Constitution over the new republican institutions that the revolutionaries had imposed. It was good advice that the British ignored at their peril, as New York became instead the embodiment of British corruption and the focus of loyalist resentment.

In the two years since the great fire of 1776, the British had done little to rebuild the lost housing, and many residents continued to live in "Canvass-town" while rents in actual buildings soared. Martial law continued, violent crime went largely unpunished, and a horde of petty functionaries enriched themselves by trafficking in the basic necessities of life, which were all scarce for ordinary citizens. Judge Jones's epic cataloging of these bureaucrats suggests the struggle for survival inhabitants faced in the occupied city, especially if they needed help from the military government. Jones complained of

> such a number of supernumerary barrack-masters, land commissaries, water commissaries, forage-masters, cattle commissaries, cattle feeders, hay collectors, hay inspectors, hay weighers, wood inspectors, timber commissaries, board inspectors, refugee examiners, refugee provision providers, and refugee ration deliverers, commissaries of American, of French, of Dutch, and of Spanish prisoners, naval commissaries, and military commissaries, with such a numerous train of clerks, deputy clerks, and other depend-

ents upon, the several offices aforesaid, with pensioners and placemen . . .

who drained the British treasury by their profiteering.[42]

With more refugees flowing in, and more hungry mouths to feed, the
city's food shortage reached a crisis by late August 1778: The army had only
five weeks of provisions left. On August 25, however, famine was averted by
a remarkable twist of fate. "This evening arrived the fleet of Victuallers from
Corke in most Excellent time," Lieutenant Colonel Stephen Kemble rejoiced
in his journal.[43] The timing of these supply ships from Ireland was fortunate
indeed. Had they arrived a little sooner, they would have been scooped up by
d'Estaing's squadron at Sandy Hook. It was only because the ships were mistakenly sent to Philadelphia, two months after it had been evacuated, that
they were fatefully delayed. This time, a lack of communication between the
departments of the British home government had been a gift.[44]

In the waning days of the summer William Smith took evening walks with
Sir Henry Clinton along the Battery, dined with him at headquarters, and
became his adviser and scribe, anonymously drafting numerous letters and
proclamations for the commander in chief. Smith had rapidly become an
integral part of the military administration in New York, but privately he was
as critical of the British leadership as he was of Congress. Even as he went
over to the British, Smith considered himself a moderate in the struggle, continuing to believe in a solution that would preserve both American rights and
the empire, and hoping to influence the outcome through his writing.[45]

By the end of 1778, however, the voices of reconciliation were falling
silent. Admiral Howe, after pursuing d'Estaing to Boston, had returned to
New York, resigned his command to Rear Admiral James Gambier on
September 11, and returned to England on the *Eagle*, to do battle with his
political enemies. In October the king's three remaining peace commissioners* made another futile overture, issuing a "Manifesto" to the members of Congress and the state legislatures. The *Pennsylvania Evening Post*
summed up the American reaction: "Why don't they go home and mind
their hardware and broadcloth, and not pester us with scribbling letters and
petitionery proclamations."[46] Several weeks later, the disheartened commis-

---

*Not including Henry Clinton, who, officially, was also a peace commissioner, authorized to
negotiate with the rebels.

sioners reluctantly took that advice, and the loyalists in New York lamented their departure. In reconciliation and peace they had hoped to regain their rights under the English Constitution that had been suspended during the war. The day the commissioners left, a printed handbill appeared containing an appeal by the aggrieved loyalists in the city for the restoration of civil government and an end to martial law, a proposition which looked increasingly unlikely.[47]

With France as an ally, Congress had less incentive than ever to negotiate with the British, who still refused to accept American independence. In Parliament and the ministry, many already saw clearly that Britain would soon lose the former colonies, since French intervention would dilute British strength in America by drawing forces away to other areas.[48] In early November, for example, Clinton finally carried out the orders Germain had sent him in March and dispatched General James Grant with 5,000 troops from New York to the West Indies, where he captured St. Lucia. At the same time, the British also shipped troops south to Florida and South Carolina. Clinton's struggle over the next two years to distribute his forces while protecting his base in New York would gradually take a toll on his already irritable nerves.

Washington was equally concerned about New York. In November he stationed the Continental Army for the winter of 1778–79 in a series of camps that went halfway to encircling the city and its environs. The six camps described an arc extending upward through their locations in Middlebrook, Elizabeth, and Ramapo, New Jersey, in the west, to West Point and Fishkill, New York, in the north and descending to Danbury, Connecticut, in the east.* This arrangement allowed Washington to detect and respond to any British forays toward Philadelphia, Albany, or New England, while keeping him poised for a joint attack on New York City with the French.[49]

The Connecticut end of the arc also served as a conduit to Washington's headquarters for intelligence gathered behind enemy lines. By the fall of 1778, Benjamin Tallmadge had risen to the rank of major and supervised the Culper

---

*The army had been reorganized in September into six divisions under Israel Putnam, Horatio Gates, Lord Stirling, Benjamin Lincoln, Baron Johann De Kalb, and Alexander McDougall. They were assigned singly or in pairs to the main outposts during the winter or to smaller bases in between.

Ring, a sophisticated spy network whose principal agents, code-named "Culper Sr." and "Culper Jr.," operated from New York City and Setauket, Long Island. Intelligence reports, many distilled from conversations with British officers at a coffeehouse run by the king's official printer, James Rivington, were transmitted orally or with invisible ink from the city to Long Island. A mariner who crossed the Sound from Connecticut then returned with the dispatches, and Tallmadge's horsemen relayed them to the commander in chief. Some of the Culper Ring's most daring and effective spies were women, who pretended to be visiting relatives in the city and composed coded messages by hanging a set number of petticoats and handkerchiefs on the clothesline of Mary Underhill's boardinghouse on Queen Street.[50]

Washington gained accurate information about British troop strength, supplies, and munitions, but little insight into Clinton's intentions. As he watched and waited, and Clinton remained in New York, showing no initiative, Washington declared that the British were "indecisive and foolish," and that their behavior in New York and Rhode Island defied "any rule of common sense."[51] Unfortunately for Washington, d'Estaing's actions were equally inscrutable: Without a word of explanation to his allies, he left Boston on November 4 with his entire fleet. Washington could only assume he was bound for the West Indies, a new focal point of the war.

Settling in for more inactivity, Washington's troops fared better than they had at Valley Forge a year earlier. The dispersal of the army to several compact outposts close to local supplies of food helped somewhat. However, it took the troops weeks to build log huts for their winter quarters, and they continued to suffer from a lack of blankets, hats, and shoes as well as food. The Continental currency, which Congress had printed in abundance, plummeted in value at an accelerated pace that winter, allowing the commissaries to buy less and less of the soldiers' basic necessities.[52]

In New York City, the inhabitants also struggled to feed and warm themselves during the harsh winter of 1778–79. In December, even the privileged William Smith wrote, "Winter has set in with uncommon severity: I write along-side a good fire, and yet the ink freezes in my pen."[53] The next day a snowstorm destroyed seven ships in the harbor, and three soldiers were found frozen to death in their guard boxes. By the middle of January 1779, firewood was "not to be got." Bread was so scarce and expensive that the military government imposed a price cap—twenty-two coppers—and a standard weight of two pounds per loaf, each of which had to be stamped with the baker's initials to discourage fraud.[54]

Major General James Robertson had appointed a number of leading citizens and created a vestry to run the almshouse, solicit charitable donations, and see to the needs of the poor in the city. In January 1779, a stern warning went out to the tenants of the houses from which the vestry collected rents to raise funds for the poor. It decried a practice that has been familiar to New Yorkers in every century since then: Tenants were admonished to stop taking advantage of desperate refugees from other colonies by subletting their houses to them at exorbitant rates.[55]

For some nine months, from the fall of 1778 through the spring of 1779, the two armies remained in a holding pattern—the British in, and the Americans around, New York City. However, clashes in the southern states soon had to be factored into Washington's strategic calculations: The lieutenant colonel dispatched by Clinton to Florida in November 1778 had taken his troops to Georgia instead and captured Savannah at the end of December. Congress asked Washington to administer this theater of the war too; while his priority remained the concentration of his army to attack New York and Rhode Island, he had to be prepared to dilute his strength there to cooperate with the Continental forces in the South.[56]

When a French representative came to his headquarters at Middlebrook, New Jersey, in late April 1779 to coordinate plans, Washington agreed that d'Estaing, who had indeed gone to the West Indies from Boston, should assist the Americans in Georgia to recover Savannah, before making his way north. Not until the French provided enough ships to guarantee naval superiority at New York and Rhode Island would Washington be eager to make another attempt at joint operations there.[57]

While the stalemate continued around New York in the spring of 1779, in London the Howe brothers had ignited a political war of words, a pitched battle between their camp and the ministry that lasted from April to June and was designed to rescue their reputations by examining the campaigns of 1776 and 1777 on the floor of Parliament. Thus, while the battle for New York paused on the front lines, witnesses called to testify by the Howes relived its initial phases. Montresor, for example, needing General Howe to sign off on his questionable accounts, testified to the formidable American lines on the neck of the Brooklyn peninsula. The battle would be continued in the London press and political pamphlets for another three years.[58]

. . .

On June 1, 1779, with summer approaching, Clinton broke the long period of inactivity in New York by capturing Stony Point and Verplanck's Point, which projected from opposite sides of the Hudson and formed the southern threshold of the Highlands. Clinton had hoped to provoke Washington into a "general action" by seizing these critical posts at either end of King's Ferry, a major link between New England and the states south of the Hudson. Washington deployed troops north of Stony Point to prevent Clinton from pushing on toward West Point but otherwise did not contest the British assault. At the approach of the overwhelming enemy force, the small American garrison at Stony Point set fire to the installation and fled, while the defenders at Verplanck's Point were captured.

Washington bided his time and six weeks later dispatched "Mad" Anthony Wayne on a daring raid, in which he took back Stony Point. Unwilling to spare the number of troops the post would require, Washington hauled away the captured supplies and artillery and razed the ramparts the British had just built. Clinton soon reoccupied the promontory and rebuilt the fort. Nonetheless, Wayne's successful raid had cost Clinton a good deal of time and effort and had boosted American morale. That his men had used bayonets to capture more than 500 British troops without firing a shot, and then spared their lives, won the admiration of both sides.

The second and final clash around New York between Washington's and Clinton's forces in 1779 took place on August 19 when Major Henry "Light Horse Harry" Lee attacked the British stronghold at Paulus Hook on the New Jersey shore directly opposite New York City.* Washington could not hope to keep a post so close to the occupied city, but in a year when the Revolution seemed doomed by inertia, the capture of 150 British troops, like the raid at Stony Point, helped revive the flagging spirits of the army and enabled Congress to submit another modest accomplishment to the American people. Washington moved his headquarters to New Windsor, farther up the Hudson, putting an end to Clinton's hope of a decisive battle in the Highlands.[59]

In September and October 1779, the Americans and the French joined forces in a second attempt to seize a British-held city, this time Savannah, Georgia. D'Estaing brought his fleet from the West Indies to Georgia to support the American siege, led by Major General Benjamin Lincoln, who had

---

*Henry Lee, the father of Robert E. Lee, was a friend of Charles Lee, but they were not related.

brought his Continental forces down from Charleston, South Carolina. On October 9, this attempt also failed, but with heavy losses, unlike the threat to New York a year earlier. D'Estaing left part of his fleet in the West Indies and returned to France with the rest; the Franco-American alliance seemed doomed to failure. However, the British victory at Savannah had an unexpected long-term effect: It misled Lord Germain into believing that numerous loyalists in Georgia were ready to support the king.[60]

Germain clung to this argument as the war became increasingly unpopular and drained the British treasury. The French strained Britain's resources by engaging in naval warfare not only in the Caribbean but in Europe and India as well. Spain also entered the war in the middle of 1779, which put Britain further on the defensive. In August a combined French and Spanish fleet made a serious bid to invade Britain itself. Privateers authorized by Congress also raided British home waters and took hundreds of ships as prizes. John Paul Jones made a circuit of the British Isles in September, where he plundered the coast and defeated the Royal Navy's ships.[61]

American forces remained concentrated in the Hudson Highlands, fortifying West Point and improving their skills under the stern eye of Baron von Steuben. As with the slow-moving Howe, parodied after the war as the "Duke of Dally, Lord Lingerloring," Clinton's reputation was "going down Hill," according to William Smith; Tryon thought the general had no clear plan of action and that the idle soldiers would soon mutiny.[62] To these restless troops were added the reinforcements Cornwallis had brought in August when he had returned to New York from leave in England with a dormant commission to replace Clinton as commander in chief.

The military government's poor management of the city had made people "disgusted and dispirited," Smith wrote. The "Season of Winter advances and the Town is destitute of Fuel."[63] Woodcutters on Long Island, like many others, were laid up by an epidemic of fever, and the rebels were capturing the wood boats in Long Island Sound. Above all, Smith cited Clinton's negligence and mismanagement in not stockpiling firewood during the summer.

The fuel situation was part of a larger pattern in which the British failed to use the occupation of New York to their advantage and gradually lost the allegiance of their natural supporters. Smith summed up the dynamic when he wrote that the loyalists "in general grow despondent. Of the Military Government all are impatient and regret the Delay of General Robertson."[64] Robertson had returned to England, where he was appointed to replace Tryon as governor of New York. Residents hoped his return to the city would inaugurate the restoration of their civil rights. A police court with no jurisdiction in capital cases was all the justice available under martial law. Smith blamed Germain for not instituting civil government a year earlier as he had planned and for not sending Robertson sooner. "Can it be that he dreads to offend Sir H Clinton and lose his services? That very Timidity shews him incompetent for his Station. . . . Nothing can be more injurious to the King's Interest than this negligent and untender Conduct of the Army. In the Despair arising from unfavorable Prospects as to the Issue of the Struggle, every Disgust works Disaffection."[65] By alienating its base of support, the military regime helped sustain the growing expectation that Britain would soon lose the former colonies.

CHAPTER 22

New York's Impact on the War in the South

~⌒

In the fall of 1779, Lord George Germain launched his last and most desperate effort to save himself politically and win the war in America.[1] Fortified by the victory in Savannah in October and bolstered by the Carlisle Commission, which had returned to England a year earlier bearing overly optimistic reports—many penned by William Smith—about the weakness of the rebel forces and the depth of loyalist support in America, Germain responded to the opposition in Parliament by arguing that the loyalists in the South merely needed British leadership and they would do most of the fighting. Accordingly, Clinton prepared to alter the strategy that had focused on New York as the sole hub of British operations and to create a second one in the South.[2]

By evacuating his posts at Stony Point and Verplanck's Point, and the base in Rhode Island, Clinton pulled together a force of almost 25,000 troops, including Hessians and Provincials and additional reinforcements from England—enough to defend New York City while preparing an expedition of 8,500 men to invade Charleston, South Carolina. As the major commercial port of the southern states, Charleston promised to be Britain's operational center for subduing the region.[3] With the reinforcements in August came Admiral Marriott Arbuthnot, Gambier's replacement. Arbuthnot was marginally more competent than Gambier but would never restore the excellent working relationship Clinton had enjoyed with Admiral Howe. Clinton called Howe's three immediate successors in America the "old women" of the navy.[4]

Washington remained at West Point through the fall. Expecting d'Estaing to return after his stop in Georgia, Washington wrote to him in early October with an ambitious plan for taking New York City. Washington promised to field an army of 25,000 men for the joint operation (using new powers vested in him by Congress to call out 12,000 militia for three months from adjacent states) if d'Estaing would commit his fleet to New York long enough for the harbor to freeze and close the port.[5]* However, in November Washington learned of d'Estaing's departure for France and reluctantly moved the main army to winter quarters at Morristown, still convinced that "something important and interesting, if not decisive might have been attempted against the Enemy in this Quarter, with a good prospect of success."[6] He left a semicircle of outposts around New York City—anchored at Morristown, West Point, and Danbury—intact but with fewer troops.

Clinton had also anticipated the return of the French fleet in the fall, and he delayed the southern campaign for months while he fortified New York against a possible attack. Having occupied New York, the British faced the same problem Lee, Stirling, and Putnam had struggled with almost four years earlier, in January of 1776; however, they focused their efforts on the critical choke points that Lee had ignored. They immediately sent ships down to Sandy Hook, where they prepared to sink transports in the channel at the first appearance of the French fleet.

"We have been indefatigable in making every Point of Defence as Strong as Time will permit, in raising a Battery at the Light House, lining the Heights of Staten Island & Long Island at the Narrows with Cannon, repairing all the Batteries at New York & planting the heavy Guns lately arriv'd, upon them, as likewise repairing the ruined Fortifications & Batterys, erected by the Rebels on Governor's Island," wrote General James Pattison on October 9. He had replaced Robertson as commandant in the city. Like the Americans in 1776, the British in 1779 faced a shortage of manpower because the troops were in "a very Sickly State," and because of the extensive waterfront that had to be secured. Once again the citizens of New York—including "the most Capital Merchants & Shop-keepers"—were called upon

---

*Despite the need to concentrate troops around New York City, Washington had sent Sullivan with a substantial force to devastate the fields and villages of the Indians of the Six Nations on the New York–Pennsylvania frontier during the summer. Sullivan was thorough and ruthless, as per Washington's orders, and returned with almost all of his troops by the fall, ready for joint operations with the French (Freeman, *George Washington,* 5:97).

to take up "the Spade & Pick-axe, to defend and secure their own Property," this time "against a Foreign Enemy."[7] Smith noted at the end of October that news of a threatened French invasion had increased the anger in the city over Clinton's failure to take the offensive.

Lieutenant Colonel Stephen Kemble's growing bitterness at the British high command spilled over in his journal when he wrote that Clinton was "despised and detested by the Army," because of "his unheard of Promotion to the first Departments of Boys not three Years in the Service, his neglect of old Officers, and his wavering, strange, mad Behaviour. If Government does not remove him soon, our Affairs in this Country will be totally undone." Kemble resigned at the end of November, and Captain John André became Clinton's new adjutant. "Nothing surely can be more shameful than our perfect inactivity during the whole summer and autumn," a loyalist wrote. "For God's sake let us have a man of resolution or abilities."[8]

Smith noted that most British officers had lost confidence in their capacity to subdue the rebels. When he argued that the rebels were a minority who ruled through their small army, and that the loyalists would rise up as soon as it was weakened, he found the officers "sighing with Impatience for a Return to Europe and the Reinjoyment of the Pleasures of London &c."[9] One disillusioned resident summed up the dawning realization that New York, despite its splendid harbor, was in fact a trap, and the worst possible choice for a naval base: "New York in itself seems as little worth consideration as any Place of an equal number of houses can possibly be. Entirely unfit for Ships of Force, on Acct of the Bar, which can only be passed at certain Times of Tide—the Ice in the Winter either Cuts them to Pieces or makes them entirely useless."[10]

Indeed, the winter of 1779–80 was one of the coldest in memory. The British army paid farmers on Long Island to cart wood into the city, but the soldiers still received barely enough fuel, while the poor froze. The garrison consumed 600 cords of wood per week, and by December was almost "destitute of Fuel," General Pattison wrote, so he dispatched hundreds of ax-wielding soldiers to northern Manhattan and to the woods near the ferry landings in Brooklyn.[11] Resentment of the commandant, the police, and the barrack master steadily grew with these attacks on private property, but Pattison contemplated going further and "taking from the private Stores of the Citizens in general," Smith wrote.[12]

People of every class suffered in the city from the cold, in diminishing proportion to their increasing level of wealth. Smith tried to keep writing. "The Ink freezes in my Pen. . . . I set before a large Coal Fire and within two feet of the Grait, and yet am not comfortably warm My Ink Stand is on the

Corner of the Grait. God have mercy on the poor. Many reputable People lay abed in these Days for Want of Fuel."[13]

The day after Christmas 1779, Clinton and Cornwallis finally sailed south with a fleet of fourteen warships and ninety transports, carrying 8,500 troops bound for Charleston, South Carolina. They left Knyphausen with more than 16,000 troops—but only a single frigate—to defend New York.[14] Chunks of ice floating in the rivers and bay were expected to deter a French naval invasion through the Narrows. Indeed, New York's waterways soon froze solid and almost prevented Clinton's expedition altogether. "In short Sir Henry tarried till the last Day of passing down to the Hook with Safety," Smith noted disapprovingly in his diary.[15]

While ships stood helplessly locked in the ice, New York suddenly became vulnerable to attack across the solid surfaces of its rivers. In mid-January 1780, Greene and Stirling led a raiding party of 3,000 men across the ice from the Jersey shore to Staten Island at two in the morning. They loaded up 300 sleds with "Salted Provisions, Clothing, Blankets and Household Furniture," and made off with their plunder.[16] At a cost of six men killed, the attack was less than a success, but New Yorkers started to panic. "If the Ice grows stronger and a Snow Storm rises, Washington may find us open to a Surprize on every Side," Smith wrote.[17]

Crossing the Hudson from Manhattan to Paulus Hook over the ice was "practicable for the heaviest Cannon, an Event unknown in the Memory of Man," General Pattison wrote to Germain. Numerous reports had convinced Pattison that Washington was "meditating a great Stroke upon New York, with his whole Force, by different Attacks."[18] To supplement the "Volunteer" and "Independent" companies, Pattison and Tryon drafted every male from seventeen to sixty years old, threatening them with prison or death if they failed to enlist and follow orders. Sailors were ordered to leave their ice-bound ships and guard the shores.[19]

Washington, however, did not attack. The most brutally cold winter of the war made the Continental Army's second stay at Morristown even more trying than the first, in 1776–77, and worse than the months at Valley Forge the next year. In the weeks it took to build log huts, the soldiers slept in tents, where some were "buried like sheep" by storms that dropped four to six feet of snow.[20] Dressed in rags and sometimes shoeless, the men subsisted for five days at a stretch on "half a pound of salt Beef and half a pint of Rice without any other kind of support whatever," according to one officer.[21]

Washington had long resisted the expedient of simply taking food from local inhabitants because he thought it was wrong and that despotic acts by the military would ultimately undermine popular support for the army and the cause. Nonetheless, he finally felt compelled to create and enforce a system by which every part of New Jersey according to its ability contributed grain and cattle to the army. By the end of January, this system had temporarily solved the problem of feeding 10,000 men, but the Continental dollar—in which farmers were promised future payments—continued to lose value, and the states responded less willingly in the coming months to appeals for food from the congressional Board of War. Soon it would take 20,000 Continental dollars to buy a single horse.[22]

The army's steadily dwindling muster rolls proved even harder to replenish than its stores of food. The three-year enlistments of many soldiers ran out on January 1, 1780, and some deserted before the end of their terms, making their way to New York City across the ice bridges.

Tryon sent many of these defectors to William Smith for interrogation, along with prisoners, loyalist refugees, and other new arrivals in the city, who had been in rebel territory. He produced numerous intelligence reports digesting their accounts, and he also developed his own spy ring with resident agents and a network of couriers. For Smith, the purpose of this information was to demonstrate that the rebels were weak militarily, had a narrow political base, and could be toppled with aggressive leadership from Britain's generals.

Smith's diligence, however, did not erase the distrust some loyalists continued to feel toward him. There were accusations that Smith spied for the Americans, too, to preserve his family ties and friendships as a hedge against possible British defeat. Stephen De Lancey—the son of Smith's nemesis on the governor's Council before the war—proclaimed that Smith disclosed military secrets to the rebel governor, George Clinton, his former political apprentice.[23]

Despite the extremis of the city, the garrison celebrated the queen's birthday more lavishly than ever on January 18, 1780.[24] Baroness Reidesel, the wife of a German commander, was the honorary queen of the ball, and her arrival at Hicks's Tavern, on Broadway, in a carriage with Tryon and Pattison was heralded by kettledrums and trumpets. She opened the ball at eight by dancing a formal minuet with one of the generals. At midnight she began the supper in the tavern's two "Long Rooms" with the first toast. Three hundred and eighty dishes were served until three in the morning, and the festivities cost the army "near 400 Guineas," Smith observed, which "would have been better laid out in Fuel for the Poor or in general Charity to the Plundered Inhabitants of Staten Island."[25]

Conditions improved somewhat in February when sleds crossed the Hudson and returned with loads of firewood. By the end of the month the rivers were navigable again. In March several of the hundreds of inmates on the prison ship *Good Hope* contributed to the thaw when they managed to start a fire on board. Only a few escaped, however; the rest were transferred to three other prison ships and after two months ended up on the infamous *Jersey*, which the British insisted had "a variety of apartments for officers and plenty of room between decks for the men."[26]

Smith saw the corruption, decadence, and ultimate collapse of the military regime in smaller, more trivial signs. Pattison chided him that he never attended the theater or other public entertainment. "I mortified him by saying my Wife and I thought ourselves too old. He was astonished, being himself near 70. I withdrew at 8 after a Coffee, and he sent his Aid de Camp after me to play a Rubber of Whist. I told him I never touched Cards. I suppose I have made a valedictory Visit. Heaven preserve a Nation of Triflers."[27]

Prospects for New York's residents brightened somewhat in the middle of March, when the Corke fleet arrived with provisions that helped relieve the food shortage. A week later Robertson returned from England as the new governor, and Tryon made plans to leave. Following instructions from Lord Germain, Robertson issued a lengthy proclamation in which he promised to restore civil government "as speedily as the public Exigencies will permit."[28]

Like most such documents at the time, its author was William Smith, who was sworn in as chief justice of New York in May. Lord Germain hoped to take advantage of the talent and connections of the respected lawyer to calm people's fears and bring them back from rebellion. Smith was a vocal proponent of restoring civil government, including civil courts, realizing that his role as chief justice remained a hollow ploy without these institutions.

However, Clinton did not want his military authority hampered by civil government, and Smith gradually came to see the benefits of the status quo; of using the promise of constitutional rights as a carrot and the military as a stick to win over the rebels. Neither Smith nor Robertson wanted to preside over a government and justice system that would condemn and execute rebels sent in by the army; both men had extensive landholdings in New York State that might have been confiscated as retribution for such verdicts.

Clinton, in turn, eventually realized that he wanted the option of passing such cases off to a civil authority, but when he asked Robertson to establish civil courts to alleviate the chaotic situation in the legal system (which was far worse than in any of the new rebel governments), the governor stalled. Smith did too. His delaying tactic was to argue that the colonial Assembly should be restored first: New laws for the changing times should be passed before the courts were reopened. As a result, martial law continued as the occupation wore on.[29]

"It begins to be surmised either that the British are tired or unwilling to terminate the war," Smith wrote in the middle of May. "If Great Britain recalled all her Generals and raised her Colonels, her Affairs would probably mend. Her principal Officers are the Plants of Corruption. Her Distresses must increase before Men rise by Merit for the Services of the Day. The Apology for our present Idleness is the Possibility of the French Fleet's appearance here before that expected under Greaves [the British admiral Thomas Graves]. We are therefore piddling in the Planting of Cannon on the Shores, and at the same Time amusing ourselves with Feasts, Plays, &c."[30] As Smith penned these words, however, Clinton had taken decisive action in the South.

Charleston, South Carolina, like New York City, had been built on the tip of a peninsula between two rivers. When he had arrived there in January 1780, Clinton, as commander in chief, did what he had repeatedly advised General Howe to do in New York in 1776: He besieged the rebel city by occupying the neck of the peninsula on which it stood. When Charleston fell to the British on May 12, 1780, Clinton achieved a victory the scale of which had completely eluded the Howes during the entire New York campaign. He captured 5,500 Americans and dealt the United States by far the worst single loss of the war.[31]

Clinton had established a base from which to subdue the South, but his preoccupation with defending New York soon overturned his plans for that theater of the war, just as it had kept him from assisting Burgoyne before Saratoga in the failed northern campaign. Alarmed by reports that a new French fleet was on its way to America, Clinton left Cornwallis in command at Charleston in the middle of June and returned to New York with 4,000 troops. Six weeks earlier, Jean Baptiste Donatien de Vimeur, the comte de Rochambeau, a lieutenant general leading 6,000 troops, had set sail from Brest aboard a fleet commanded by the admiral Charles Louis d'Arsac, chevalier de Ternay. After the failure of Franco-American military cooperation under d'Estaing, a new phase of the alliance had begun.[32] The British again played catch-up, as they had in 1778 after allowing d'Estaing out of the Mediterranean: This time they sent Admiral Thomas Graves racing to America with a detachment of six ships to counter the French.

Clinton's orders left Cornwallis considerable freedom to exercise his own judgment about how far to venture from Charleston in conquering new territory. However, the commander in chief emphasized that his subordinate should at all costs prevent the rebels from retaking the city, and that he should be careful not to cut himself off from the safety of his base. Cornwallis had his own agenda, however, and soon set out to establish a presence in both North Carolina and Virginia, dangerously far from Charleston, in effect creating a third British army—in addition to those left in New York and Charleston—and reconfiguring the strategic picture once more.[33]

Washington had kept up his vigil in the hills of New Jersey, the Hudson Highlands, and Connecticut, but he could not maintain the appearance of a credible threat against New York City indefinitely. By the late spring of 1780, the Continental Army was in fact on the brink of ruin once again. At Morristown, the harsh winter, illness, desertion, expired enlistments, and a dearth of new recruits left Washington with only 4,000 troops present and fit for duty. Half starved and despairing because the five months of back pay the army owed them was losing value with each passing day, two Connecticut regiments gathered on the parade ground on May 25 and threatened to desert or at least plunder civilian homes for food. Only a last-minute appeal from their officers dissuaded them and quelled the mutiny.[34] Five days later, Washington received a copy of Rivington's newspaper from New York, an extra edition with a report confirming the fall of Charleston to the British.[35] Delighted as he had been on May 10 when Lafayette brought him news that Rochambeau was on his way, Washington now wondered if his army could survive and hold back the British until the French arrived. "Indeed," he wrote at the end of May, "I have almost ceased to hope."[36]

Nonetheless, Washington did what Congress had empowered him to do: On June 2, 1780, he called for a draft of 17,000 militia from New England and the mid-Atlantic states in order to have 24,000 troops on hand by July 15, when the French would arrive to help recapture New York City. The states ultimately supplied only about 6,000 men in response to this draft; those who arrived, untrained and hungry, were more a burden than an asset to the army, and would soon be sent home or scattered to posts where food was available.[37]

Clinton returned to New York from Charleston in June 1780, seduced by the pleasures of the city as well as strategic considerations: by his own mistress, Mary Baddeley, the wife of a British officer who, like Loring, agreed to a mutually beneficial arrangement, and by the company of the young officers, like Major André, who were his protégés and intimate friends.[38] Clinton was also an avid patron of the Theater Royal, and its players came to be known as "Clinton's Thespians."[39] Unfortunately for the widows and orphans, the theater turned out to be a feeble attempt at charity: Most of the proceeds and donations were consumed by operating expenses.[40]

Soon after his return, Clinton tried to take advantage of Washington's precarious situation by sending General Knyphausen into New Jersey with 5,000 troops. To the surprise of many on both sides, the previously unreliable New Jersey militia turned out to harass the British on their march from Elizabethtown toward Morristown, and the militia's efforts, supported by 1,000 Continentals under General Greene, drove Knyphausen back to New York. Clinton had overestimated the inhabitants' disillusionment with the American cause and the willingness of Washington's troops to desert when confronted with a British show of force. In fact, the expedition backfired: Former New York governor William Tryon, now a brigadier general, accompanied Knyphausen and had his troops set fire to numerous American houses, a tactic that only strengthened local support for the Continental Army.[41]

Clinton had also misjudged the situation in the South, where a brutal, bloody summer of fighting—a staggering two dozen small clashes—erupted between June and September 1780. Before his departure for New York in June, Clinton had issued the last in a series of proclamations reversing his previous promise of royal pardons to all inhabitants who refrained from belligerence against the king's forces. Henceforth he required the active assistance of the loyalists to reestablish colonial governments in the region. Since neutrality would no longer be tolerated, the declaration forced every southerner to choose sides and enter the fray; the effect was cataclysmic.

While Clinton sailed north, the vicious civil war that was unleashed pitted neighbor against neighbor and cast aside the relatively civilized conventions of eighteenth-century warfare. The most dreaded of British officers was Lieutenant Colonel Banastre Tarleton, the zealous cavalry commander who had captured Charles Lee at Basking Ridge in 1776, and who set the standard of barbarism in the southern campaign when his loyalist dragoons massacred American troops at Waxhaws, South Carolina, on May 29. "Bloody Ban" later boasted that he had slaughtered more men and raped more women than anyone in America.[42]

Clinton's abandonment of Newport during the previous fall (so he could defend New York while capturing Charleston) also had unwelcome consequences. On July 10, 1780, Rochambeau and Ternay arrived at Newport with eight ships and quickly established themselves in its excellent harbor. Fortunately for Clinton, Admiral Thomas Graves arrived from England off Sandy Hook on the thirteenth with six battleships to reinforce Arbuthnot's fleet, and some fifteen British ships soon had the French hemmed in at Rhode Island. Lafayette had gone to Newport to welcome his countrymen, and Rochambeau encouraged Washington with assurances that more French ships carrying additional troops were on their way from Brest. The British, however, were positioned to give them a rude reception.[43]

Washington did not have enough horses and wagons to move his main army quickly east to reinforce the French at Newport, so instead he brought his troops across the Hudson and maneuvered as if to attack Manhattan. Clinton, who had sent troop transports east through Long Island Sound toward Newport, soon brought them back to New York, though he later claimed it was Arbuthnot's failure to coordinate with him for the attack at Rhode Island and not Washington's threat that influenced his action. When the transports returned to New York, Washington recrossed to the west bank of the Hudson to conserve his troops' strength and prepare for an attack on the city as soon as the promised second wave of French ships arrived to give them naval superiority in America.[44]

Clinton's concern about the expected joint French and American attack on the city was great enough that he developed a secret plan to counter it: He aimed to seize West Point and the other American forts in the Hudson Highlands—which he assumed would serve as the enemy's supply depots— in order to make Washington retreat abruptly from Kingsbridge and thus isolate the infantry that the French fleet would probably land on Long Island. The prospect of retaking the forts, which he had so reluctantly had to abandon at the end of the Burgoyne campaign, stirred Clinton's ambition to revive the original British strategy of joining forces with an army descending from Canada and controlling the Hudson.[45]

General Benedict Arnold

By the time he returned to New York from Charleston, Clinton had been conducting a clandestine correspondence with Benedict Arnold for more than a year. Arnold, unfit for active field duty because of his wounded leg, had been given the command in Philadelphia in June 1778, after the British evacuation. There he used his position to enrich himself by purchasing goods for speculation and by granting favors to the city's loyalists. In January 1780, after a drawn-out court-martial, Arnold got off with a reprimand for certain abuses but felt wronged that he had not been acquitted outright. He also claimed to be unhappy with the American decision to ally with the French, the old enemy whose imperial intentions he found suspect. His correspondence with Clinton began in May 1779, before the verdict of the court-martial.[46]

All in all, Arnold "was desirous of quitting the rebel service and joining the cause of Great Britain," Clinton wrote to Germain.

> The correspondence was continued up to July, 1780, when Major General Arnold obtained command of all the rebel forts in the Highlands,* garrisoned with near 4000 men. . . . The getting possession of these posts with their garrisons, cannon, stores, vessels,

---

*Arnold had asked Washington for the command at West Point because of his wounded leg. Washington valued Arnold's service and had used his influence with Congress to ensure that Arnold received the promotions he desired. Washington wrote the reprimand of Arnold that appeared in the general orders of the army and clearly regarded the offenses as minor (Boatner, pp. 27–29, 36).

gunboats, etc. etc., appeared to me an object of the highest importance, which must be attended with the best consequences to His Majesty's service—among others that of opening the navigation of the North River and the communication, in a certain degree, with Albany, as appears by the enclosed copy of a letter from G[eneral] [Frederick] Haldimand to me.[47] [Haldimand was then in charge of British forces in Canada.]

The timing seemed perfect for Arnold to deliver the forts to the British, Clinton told Germain, noting that the main rebel supply depot supporting their anticipated operations would be at West Point and its dependent forts. Clinton intended to wait until the Americans and the French had formed their depots and begun their attack on New York. Arnold "surrendering himself, the forts, and garrisons at this instant of time would have given every advantage which could have been desired. Mr. Washington must have instantly retired from Kings Bridge, and the French troops upon Long Island would have been consequently left unsupported and probably would have fallen into our hands. The consequent advantage of so great an event I need not explain."[48] Indeed, the capture of a large French force on Long Island might have gone far in answering the defeat at Saratoga. Clinton therefore quietly prepared to strike at West Point with "vessels properly manned and of a particular draft of water," which would allow them to move in close to the river's edge for a landing.[49]

At the end of August, while Clinton and Washington each waited for their plans to mature, the Americans received two devastating pieces of news in rapid succession. On August 25, Washington learned that British ships, in a rare and tardy burst of initiative, had blockaded the second division of the French fleet at Brest. Even if the French broke out, they would not arrive in America before October, and the attack on New York looked to be spoiled once again. Thoroughly discouraged, Washington had to start discharging the militia before they consumed any more of the army's provisions.[50]

As Washington moved the army back toward Hackensack, New Jersey, and urged Arnold to brace for a British assault on the Highlands, news arrived that on August 16 Cornwallis had smashed the Americans' southern army under Horatio Gates at Camden, South Carolina. Congress had appointed Gates to the southern command without consulting Washington, and the decision had proved disastrous. Gates, who never left the safety of his headquarters throughout the battles at Freeman's Farm near Saratoga, had rushed his exhausted and hungry troops onto the field at Camden and then fled on horseback when the battle turned into a rout—not stopping until he was miles away. It was a far more shameful performance than anything witnessed in the campaign of 1776 in New York, and the casualty figures (800 Americans killed or wounded and 1,000 captured) far exceeded those at the Battle of Brooklyn, an engagement with many more participants. With Cornwallis triumphant in South Carolina, an invasion of Virginia from the south seemed certain to follow.[51]

In New York, Clinton watched carefully to see how Washington would react to the news of Camden. "But he did not in the least alter his positions, or send a man to the southward," Clinton told Germain, "from whence I was led to imagine this place was still his object—in which, indeed, I was confirmed by intelligence from General Arnold."[52] Washington was contemplating the possibility that he would eventually have to move the whole army to the south to counter the British, but in the meantime he wanted to consult with the French before making any decisions.[53]

On September 14, the allies' hopes for naval superiority were dashed again by the arrival at Sandy Hook of a British fleet of twelve ships from the West Indies under Admiral George Rodney. How to regain the advantage was the theme of a meeting at Hartford, Connecticut, on the twentieth, when Washington met Rochambeau and Ternay in person for the first time. He found them very sympathetic, and the Frenchmen were likewise impressed with Washington. All agreed that recapturing New York should be their primary objective, because it was "the center and focus of all the British forces."[54] However, they also calculated that they would need 30,000 men to lay siege to the city, in addition to a blockade by the French navy. The only hope was to have the Comte de Guichen, a French admiral, come up from the West Indies with his fleet by October, or it would be too late in the season, and they agreed that any joint action later in the fall should be directed against the South. Washington returned to guarding the Hudson with his suffering troops, consoled by the hope of more French ships.[55]

With New York strongly garrisoned by a force of 12,000 British regulars, and an allied offensive against New York unlikely, Clinton decided he had better strike quickly at the Highland forts while he still had Arnold's assistance. "It became at this instant necessary that the secret correspondence under feigned names which had been so long carried on should be rendered

Comte de Rochambeau

into certainty," Clinton wrote. He wanted to confirm, with a face-to-face meeting, that the letter writer was in fact Arnold, and to make a "concerted plan between [them] that the King's troops sent upon this expedition should be under no risk of surprise or counterplot." According to Clinton, "[Arnold] required that my Adjutant General, Major [John] André, (who had chiefly conducted the correspondence with him, under the signature of John Anderson), should meet him for this purpose on neutral ground."[56]

Clinton had agreed to Arnold's suggestion that André "go to him by water from Dobb's Ferry in a boat which he would himself send for him under a flag of truce." As Clinton explained: "I could have no reason to suspect that any bad consequence could possibly result to Major André from such a mode, as I had given it in charge to him *not to change his dress or name on any account*, or possess himself of writings by which the nature of his embassy might be traced; and I understood that after his business was finished he was to be sent back in the same way."[57]

The conspiracy proceeded according to plan, and André met with Arnold. However, on September 23, probably "losing at the moment his usual presence of mind," Arnold abandoned the idea of sending André back by water and forced him "to part with his uniform, and under a borrowed disguise to take a circuitous route to New York through the posts of the enemy under the sanction of his passport," Clinton wrote. "The consequence was, as might be expected, that he was stopped at Tarrytown and searched; and, certain papers being found about him concealed, he was (notwithstanding his passport) carried prisoner before Mr. Washington, to whom he

Major John André

candidly acknowledged his name and quality." Arnold, "being fortunate enough to receive timely notice of Major André's fate," fled a meeting of generals at Washington's headquarters two miles from West Point and escaped by boat to the *Vulture*, a British warship which brought him down the Hudson to New York City.[58]

Young, eager, and dedicated to his country's cause, André not only fit the same profile as Nathan Hale but was captured and executed under strikingly similar circumstances. The major difference was that, unlike Hale, André had the benefit of a court-martial by a council of enemy officers, before he too was hanged—on October 3, 1780.* André's death aroused a similar wave of anger on the British side. William Smith was part of a delegation sent from New York that was still engaged in talks to gain André's release when its members learned of the execution. "The Rebel Generals who have shed his Blood ought to expiate it by their own," Smith wrote to William Eden on October 7.[59] Clinton mourned the personal loss of a "confidential friend for whom [he] had, very deservedly, the warmest esteem."[60]

Shortly after his arrival in New York, Arnold submitted a report to Lord Germain that included detailed information about the condition of the American army and its troubled finances. Smith wrote the first draft for Arnold along with an address, "To the Inhabitants of America," explaining

*Unlike Hale, André was also allowed to send some final letters; his body was returned to the British and buried with full state honors at Westminster Abbey; and the story of his untimely death appeared in every newspaper.

his reasons for defecting to the British cause. Rivington printed the address in the *Royal Gazette* and as a broadside on October 7. Two weeks later another proclamation written for Arnold by Smith appeared: Newly appointed a brigadier general by Clinton, Arnold urged American soldiers and officers to desert the Continental Army and offered them three guineas in gold to join a corps of cavalry and infantry under his leadership to fight for the British. Despite the additional incentives of ample food and clothing, he had few takers, and as a Provincial whose treason was clearly motivated by financial gain, Arnold also failed to win the trust of the British officer corps. The men for his brigade ultimately had to be drawn from one of the loyalist companies.[61]

Confident that Georgia and South Carolina were firmly under British control, Cornwallis had marched north toward Charlotte, North Carolina, in mid-September. Because of the civil strife that continued in the mountainous interior of South Carolina, Cornwallis also sent a contingent to the area under Major Patrick Ferguson to subdue the rebel frontiersmen. The demise of this British detachment at King's Mountain on October 7 was, according to Clinton, "an event which was immediately productive of the worst consequences to the King's affairs in South Carolina, and unhappily proved the first link in a chain of evils that followed each other in regular succession until they at last ended in the total loss of America."[62]

King's Mountain, in its impact on American morale, was to the war in the South what Trenton had been in the North. The relatively small battle drastically diminished the effect of the British victories at Charleston and Camden, and it "so encouraged that spirit of rebellion in both Carolinas that it never could be afterward humbled," Clinton wrote. "For no sooner had the news of it spread through the country than multitudes of disaffected flew to arms from all parts, and menaced every British post on both frontiers, 'carrying terror even to the gates of Charleston.'"[63] Clinton blamed Cornwallis for the key defeats that lost the war, implying clearly that had Clinton been there himself, instead of defending New York, the result would have been different. He may well have been right.

To justify his defensive posture in New York, Clinton had told Germain that Washington had not sent a single man southward in the wake of the American defeat at Camden in August. Belatedly, however, Congress had sought Washington's advice and agreed to replace Gates with Nathanael Greene, who arrived in Charlotte, North Carolina, on December 2, 1780, to command the 1,500 men who were still present and fit for duty. After learning of the King's Mountain fiasco, Cornwallis had retreated back across the border into South Carolina, where Greene followed him and initiated a series of maneuvers and subsequent clashes that eventually wore the British down while depriving them of a decisive victory.[64]

Greene's brilliant campaign in the Carolinas was threatened from the start, however, by the arrival in Chesapeake Bay of Brigadier General Benedict Arnold on December 30 with 1,600 men and support from several British frigates. Clinton had long recognized the strategic value of the Chesapeake and the rivers flowing into it as a means of dividing the colonies, similar to New York Bay and the Hudson; despite his reluctance to spare troops from New York, he dispatched Arnold, who arrived at Hampton Roads, Virginia, sailed up the James River, and burned much of Richmond. Greene suddenly found his lines of supply and reinforcement from the north all but severed while Cornwallis and Arnold were poised to close in on him from the south and the north simultaneously.[65]

Up on the Hudson, Washington faced the equally grave threat that the army might dissolve from within. The Continental troops remained in the crescent of positions established two years earlier above New York City, and the winter of 1780–81 at Morristown, West Point, and Danbury was no better than the previous three in all important respects: Food, clothing, and shelter were all sorely in short supply. Pay was promised but nonexistent, and the Continental dollar would be valued at zero in a few months.[66]

A larger and more serious mutiny than the previous year erupted on January 1, 1781, because the Pennsylvania troops believed their enlistment "for three years or during the war" meant they were free to leave after three years, even if the war had not ended. The army insisted the troops were bound by whichever period was longer, not shorter. This time the troops marched toward Philadelphia with some artillery in tow and were only brought back under discipline after a protracted negotiation in which the government promised to redress their grievances. Their success sparked a second revolt, but this time Washington drew the line by having the ringleaders executed.[67]

Greene's plight in the Carolinas concerned Washington greatly, but he resisted the idea of transferring the main army to Virginia, a trek of some 450 miles, which the British could swiftly counter with more detachments by sea. Only if the French could gather enough ships in one place to outnumber the British fleet and support Washington's army, even temporarily, would it be feasible to attack by land in the Chesapeake. In the meantime, Washington believed preying on Clinton's paranoia about the defense of New York City continued to be the best strategy.[68]

On January 22–23 a storm severely damaged the British squadron off Gardiner's Island at the eastern end of Long Island, leaving the French fleet unscathed in the sheltered waters of Rhode Island. The allies seized the moment to gain the upper hand in Virginia: The French sailed from Newport, and Washington, hoping to capture and execute Arnold, dispatched the marquis de Lafayette to the Chesapeake by land with 1,200 troops. However, the French admiral Charles Destouches (who had replaced Ternay after he had suddenly died) initially sent only a few ships, and when he finally sent the whole fleet in March, it turned back after a clash with Admiral Arbuthnot's fleet at the entrance to the bay.[69]

Lafayette, who had been waiting at the northern end of the bay to coordinate with the fleet, moved down to Virginia in mid-March and soon found himself outnumbered. Clinton had sent additional troops to Virginia—an expeditionary force of 2,600 men under Major General William Phillips—but Lafayette managed to reach Richmond by the end of April and dig in to protect what was left of the city.[70]

Greene, with the help of Brigadier General Daniel Morgan, had continued to elude Cornwallis in the first few months of 1781, inflicting heavy losses on him and his subordinate, Banastre Tarleton, at Cowpens and Guilford Court House. With his diminished army suffering from a lack of provisions, Cornwallis marched to the Atlantic coast at Wilmington, North Carolina, where he was resupplied by British ships, then north, still convinced that subduing Virginia would go far toward consolidating his hold on the Carolinas. Having ignored Clinton's emphatic admonitions not to overextend himself by straying too far from Charleston, Cornwallis left Lord Rawdon with 8,000 men in South Carolina and Georgia to hold those states, but these men were mostly loyalists dispersed at isolated outposts. Instead of pursuing Cornwallis, Greene headed south and succeeded in toppling these vulnerable garrisons one by one in the coming months, until the British held only Savannah and Charleston.[71]

Nonetheless, Virginia was vulnerable, with Cornwallis heading there to join forces with Phillips. Washington faced the prospect of them burning

Mount Vernon to the ground, yet he maintained that applying pressure at the mouth of the Hudson was still the best response. "You may be assured," Washington wrote to his friend Benjamin Harrison on March 27, "that the most powerful diversion that can be made in favor of the Southern States will be a respectable force in the neighborhood of New York."[72]

CHAPTER 23

New York's Role at Yorktown

~ɔ

I t may be declared in a word that we are at the end of our tether, and that now or never our deliverance must come," Washington wrote to John Laurens on April 9, 1781.[1] For nearly three years, the Continental Army had starved in its camps outside New York, while the well-equipped British forces enjoyed the relative comfort of the city. Despite the rags that barely covered his troops, Washington had managed to keep up the appearance of posing a serious threat and had kept Clinton on edge with the possibility that he might attack at any time. By the late spring of 1781, however, only 3,500 American troops remained in camp on the Hudson, hardly the "respectable force" Washington needed when compared to Clinton's 14,500 regulars.[2]

Lafayette's situation in Virginia had also become critical. On May 20, three weeks after Lafayette reached Richmond, Cornwallis met up with Phillips in Petersburg: Lafayette was suddenly faced with two British forces—and outnumbered six to one.* Lafayette pulled back to the Rapidan River, to the north, and prepared to skirmish with the British while buying time for reinforcements to arrive.[3] Congress did send him some troops from Pennsylvania, Delaware, and Maryland, but the delegates agreed with Washington that forcing Clinton to bring troops back from the Chesapeake for the defense of New York

* Phillips soon died at Petersburg, and Arnold briefly assumed command of his troops before returning to New York in June.

would be far more effective than marching large numbers of men by land to Lafayette's aid.[4]

In May a new infusion of French aid promised to give Washington his badly needed breakthrough. On the sixth, a single French vessel reached Boston, carrying the count de Barras,* who would replace Destouches at Newport, and Rochambeau's son, who brought good news from France: More French ships were on the way. Admiral François Joseph Paul de Grasse was en route from Brest to the West Indies with a powerful fleet including troop transports and had detached a few of them, escorted by a warship, to bring 600 soldiers to Newport. Distracted by developments in the Mediterranean this time, the British had neglected to blockade de Grasse, as they had failed to stop d'Estaing's departure from Toulon three years earlier.

Washington arranged a conference with the elder Rochambeau at Wethersfield, Connecticut, on May 21–23, to learn the particulars and to formulate a plan for renewed joint operations in America. Washington and the French commanders at Wethersfield agreed in the short term to combine their infantry and attack New York, while leaving enough French troops and American militia at Newport with Barras to protect the precious assortment of heavy siege artillery collected there. As for de Grasse, the allies agreed to urge him, through the French minister in America, to come to the American coast, but the choice of where he should meet them had to wait until they knew the size of his fleet, and where it would best offset British naval strength. For a start, Washington hoped he might come to New York, either to defeat Arbuthnot or to bottle his fleet up inside the harbor.[5]

Washington returned to his headquarters at New Windsor on May 25 only to be greeted with news that British forces from Canada under Haldimand had descended to Crown Point and might press farther south to the Mohawk Valley. The battle for the Hudson seemed ready to begin all over again, just when Washington needed every available man for the assault on Manhattan. He kept a small unit ready for deployment in the north, but continued his preparations for the New York operation with Rochambeau. The havoc in Virginia—where Tarleton had raided Charlottesville in early June, capturing seven of the state's assemblymen while Thomas Jefferson barely escaped—only affirmed Washington's conviction that an attack on New York was the best way out of the crisis.[6]

Even as he prepared for the allied offensive against Manhattan, the prospect of French naval superiority grew more likely, and Washington's

---

*Jacques-Melchior Saint-Laurent, Comte de Barras.

thoughts began to encompass other targets. On June 13, Rochambeau forwarded to Washington a letter from de Grasse, confirming what Congress had been hearing unofficially: The admiral had reached the West Indies with a fleet of twenty-five ships and would bring them to America in mid-July, but he did not say how long he would stay or where he would arrive on the Atlantic seaboard. Such a large fleet would tip the scales in the allies' favor, making Charleston and the Chesapeake good candidates for joint operations as well as New York. Washington realized that the allied troops on land had to be ready to adapt quickly if de Grasse chose the South as the next theater of operations, even if it meant a long and arduous overland march from New York to Virginia or South Carolina.[7]*

Through intercepted letters, Clinton had also learned of de Grasse's approach in mid-May and informed Germain that he intended to bring as many troops as possible back to New York to secure his principal base of operations and leave a small but strong outpost in the Chesapeake that could later serve as a naval station. Until the threat from de Grasse passed, Clinton wanted to curb Cornwallis's wandering in the South and his constant demands for more men, and he instructed Cornwallis to establish a single stronghold in a harbor on the Yorktown Peninsula before the French fleet could take shelter there. By the end of June, Lafayette's replenished force of 5,000 Americans had advanced against Cornwallis's army of more than 7,000 troops camped at Williamsburg on the neck of the peninsula.[8]

Assuming that Cornwallis did not need his whole force to man such an outpost, and detecting Rochambeau's departure from Newport to join Washington above New York, Clinton ordered Cornwallis to send him 3,000 men, if he felt he could spare them, and hoped to attack Rhode Island or Philadelphia to counter the imminent allied descent on New York. The long-simmering contest over strategy between the two British commanders finally boiled over with this request for troops: Cornwallis heatedly declared in a letter that if he could not keep all of his men, he would abandon the Chesapeake and, with Clinton's permission, return to Charleston.[9]

When the British began crossing the James River en route to Portsmouth, where Cornwallis planned to embark the troops for New York, Lafayette attacked, believing the British were in a vulnerable position. However, contrary

---

*De Grasse's decisions were constrained by timing and weather in conjunction with the French fleet's commitments in other theaters of the global war; the Americans had to adapt accordingly.

Major General Charles Cornwallis

to routine, the British baggage was sent across first, instead of last, and on July 6, the Americans suffered heavy casualties when they attacked what they thought was the rear guard, but encountered Cornwallis's main force instead.[10] Professing to be constrained by Clinton's strict orders, Cornwallis passed up a golden opportunity to crush the Americans and proceeded to Portsmouth.[11]

In fact, Cornwallis had misconstrued Clinton's order, which authorized him to keep his whole force if he needed it, and Clinton was flabbergasted at his subordinate's response. Clinton quickly retracted the request for troops and ordered Cornwallis back to the neck of the peninsula immediately, but it was too late: His movements had left Williamsburg to Lafayette's forces, which quickly camped across the neck of the peninsula between the York and James Rivers and cut off Cornwallis's escape by land.[12]

In scrambling to choose a new site for a base, Cornwallis decided he and his naval officers were free to use their discretion and disregard Clinton's choice of Old Point Comfort, where a beleaguered fleet might have stood a chance of evacuating the army by stealthy maneuvers. Instead, in early August they selected Yorktown—a port city on the York River, about ten miles east of Williamsburg—attracted by the shelter it afforded for the largest ships. Clinton reiterated his request for troops, if and only if Cornwallis could spare them, but the men were never sent to New York.[13]

While Lafayette skirmished with Cornwallis and positioned himself advantageously at Williamsburg, Washington, still waiting for news from de Grasse, had kept up his maneuvers against New York. By the first week in July, Rochambeau had marched his 4,000 troops from Newport to the Hudson; Washington mustered the local militia, and by the end of the month, the allies had a force of 9,000 men—half of them French and half American. Washington devised an ambitious plan to storm the northern end of Manhattan by simultaneously surprising the British garrisons at Fort Knyphausen (formerly Fort Washington), Fort Tryon, and Fort George on Laurel Hill. The works at Cox Hill at the mouth of Spuyten Duyvil and still others at Kingsbridge were also targeted—all of this despite the fact that Clinton's heavily fortified and well-manned lines were also surrounded on every side by rivers patrolled by British warships.[14]

The first phase of Washington's operation began on the night of July 1, when General Benjamin Lincoln came down the Hudson from Peekskill with 800 men in small boats and studied the Manhattan shore from the New Jersey side at Fort Lee. Lincoln's task was to land his men directly below Fort Knyphausen and then scramble up the steep slopes to the summit. At the same time, Washington and the allied forces were to attack from Westchester in two separate columns. However, when Lincoln saw that British ships in the river and troops on the far shore were in the way, he reverted to Washington's more modest backup plan, to capture or destroy James De Lancey's loyalist corps of mounted vigilantes, known as "Cowboys." For years they had disrupted American communications and supply routes and terrorized inhabitants by pillaging their farms in the "neutral zone" of Westchester—the no-man's-land between the American lines up the Hudson and the British lines just above Manhattan.[15]

Lincoln landed at Spuyten Duyvil on July 2. According to the Hessians' Lieutenant von Krafft, the Americans marched past Fort Independence "in whole regiments, flags flying and bands playing, down around the lower Courtland House."[16]* A skirmish ensued, and the British cavalry and Hessian riflemen drove off the Americans. "It remains doubtful . . . whose Loss is greatest," wrote William Smith, who continued to gather information compulsively through his intelligence network. "They have carried off the Cattle collected by the Refugees [De Lancey's Cowboys]. I believe we have near 40 wounded—40 or 5[0] killed. I don't learn of more than 21 of the Rebels left dead in different Places. They carried their wounded off in 9 Waggons."[17] The British had foiled Lincoln's attempt to coordinate with a detachment of allied troops marching

*The Van Cortlandt House, which is now open to the public in the Bronx.

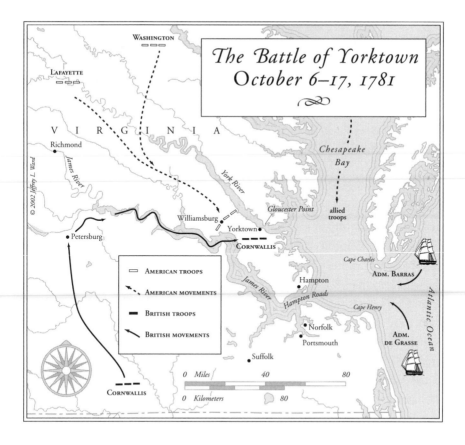

The Battle of Yorktown
October 6–17, 1781

WASHINGTON

LAFAYETTE

VIRGINIA

Richmond

James River

York River

Chesapeake
Bay

Williamsburg
Gloucester Point
Yorktown
CORNWALLIS

allied
troops

Petersburg

Cape Charles

AMERICAN TROOPS
AMERICAN MOVEMENTS
BRITISH TROOPS
BRITISH MOVEMENTS

James River

Hampton
Hampton Roads

ADM. BARRAS

Cape Henry

Atlantic Ocean

Norfolk
Portsmouth

ADM.
DE GRASSE

Suffolk

CORNWALLIS

0   Miles   40   80

0   Kilometers   80

© 2002 Jeffrey L. Ward

from Connecticut and with Washington, who swept down from Valentine's Hill in Westchester.

Washington took the opportunity to inspect the area around Kingsbridge for the future, and then retreated with the army to Dobbs Ferry, where Rochambeau's forces arrived a few days later. In late July, Washington and Rochambeau and two other French generals returned to Kingsbridge for four days to evaluate the strength of Sir Henry Clinton's defenses more thoroughly. One hundred and fifty Continentals guarded the generals, and 5,000 more troops formed a barrier between them and the enemy.[18] In his diary, Washington recorded every detail of the enemy forts, houses, huts, and tents as they might affect an allied attack.

He also noted that northern Manhattan had changed dramatically in the course of the war. "The Island is totally stripped of Trees, & wood of every kind; but low bushes (apparently as high as a mans waste) appear in places which were covered with wood in the year 1776." Any trees that had not been burned for fuel had gone to strengthen the British fortifications. "Forts

Tryon, Knyphausen & Fort George on Laurell [Hill], with the Batteries in the line of Pallisading across from River to river appeared to be well friezed, ditched and abattied—In a word to be strong and in good repair," Washington wrote.[19] The allied generals found no vulnerable points, and Rochambeau wrote to de Grasse suggesting that Chesapeake Bay might be a better location to coordinate a joint offensive.

New York remained virtually invulnerable, but Clinton's numerous plans for diversionary counterattacks had gone nowhere, much less to Newport or Philadelphia. Clinton could not bear to work with Arbuthnot and had threatened for months to resign unless the Admiralty replaced him; on July 4, Arbuthnot had finally sailed home and another unreliable, unimaginative admiral, Thomas Graves, temporarily took command in New York pending the arrival of Admiral Robert Digby from England. Despairing of cooperation from Graves, in July Clinton wrote to Admiral George Rodney, commander of the British fleet in the West Indies, sharing intelligence of de Grasse's approach and urging Rodney to come north to protect New York and attack Barras in Newport before the French fleets could join forces.[20]

Rodney was ill, however, and left for England with three warships two days before Clinton's letter arrived. Rodney also took with him a vital piece of information that might well have altered the course of the campaign and the war had he been well and not failed to share it with his successor, Sir Samuel Hood, or with Clinton and Graves. In July Rodney had learned of Rochambeau's letter to de Grasse, urging him to come to America and asking for a clarification of his plans. The message was sent on a French ship that also brought de Grasse thirty American pilots, specifically to guide him into Chesapeake Bay or the Delaware River. Rodney therefore knew, even before the Americans, that de Grasse's destination was not New York but the Chesapeake or Philadelphia. Moreover, the number of pilots might have tipped him off to the audacious gamble the Frenchman was about to take. For the sake of temporary naval superiority on the North American coast, de Grasse was willing to take his entire fleet of almost thirty ships there and leave his station in the West Indies at the mercy of the British. De Grasse apparently calculated that such a risky move would be inconceivable to the British, and he was right.[21]

After failing to carry out his various plans with Arbuthnot, Graves, and Rodney, Clinton clung to his strategy of retrenchment in New York and gradually descended into a state of passivity. Under the pressure of ultimate responsibility, the reclusive side of Clinton's personality also came to the fore. "He is incapable of Business. He consults No Body. All about him are Idlers and ignorants," William Smith railed against Clinton in his diary on July 4, 1781.[22] Another observer at headquarters denounced Clinton's indecisiveness, saying that he, "like the hungry ass between two bundles of hay, for want of preference starves."[23] Cornwallis, with his headstrong, if aimless and reckless, campaigning across the South became the darling of the ministry, while Germain's relationship with Clinton soured.[24]

When Smith didn't receive his salary, he suspected that London might be tired of him too. Despite the displeasure of the home government, he wrote, "I will persevere nevertheless in what I conceive to be the true Interest of the whole Empire and if possible bring in an American Parliament."[25] Smith continued to see himself as a moderate caught between the extremists on both sides—the House of Commons stubbornly insisting on its right to tax, and the American radicals who objected to British laws that imposed taxes and who thus rejected the supremacy of Parliament entirely. Smith clung to the idea of allowing the colonies to tax themselves through a separate legislature, a solution he had come up with during the Stamp Act crisis of 1765–66. By making a clear distinction between the power to tax and the legislative supremacy of Parliament, Smith still hoped, at this late stage, to overcome the all-or-nothing approach that had led to the war.[26]

On August 14, 1781, de Grasse's response to Rochambeau's letter of July at last reached Washington: The fleet in the West Indies would sail to the Chesapeake instead of coming to New York; de Grasse announced that he would arrive in August and stay only until mid-October. The time limit was a disappointment, but in addition to his twenty-eight ships, de Grasse would also bring 3,000 soldiers, who could reinforce Lafayette before Washington reached Virginia. The pronouncement from de Grasse resolved once and for all the lingering uncertainties that had plagued Washington since the alliance began: The time, the place, and a decisive naval advantage had been established.[27]

What remained was still a daunting task. Washington had two months to march and transport the allied forces with all of their equipment and supplies 450 miles to join Lafayette and coordinate with de Grasse for an attack on Cornwallis—while masking the movement from Clinton as long as possible. Since the army had no money or credit, Washington simultaneously had to call on the states for contributions of wagons and provisions and to muster the local militia to repair the roads leading to the Chesapeake, which

Comte de Grasse

were in terrible condition. Fortunately, Barras planned to sail his fleet from Newport to Virginia, ensuring French naval superiority and bringing the heavy siege artillery and cumbersome barrels of salted meat that would be crucial to the success of the land forces.[28]

Not until he received the October deadline from de Grasse did Washington finally, reluctantly "give up all idea of attacking New York," which had been his greatest goal since the retreat of 1776. In the end, he felt "obliged" to relinquish the prized city by circumstances beyond his control: de Grasse's timetable, the unwillingness of the French admirals to "force the harbor of New York," and the failure of the states to contribute enough troops to the effort.[29]

Keeping 2,500 men under General Heath just above New York and in the Highlands to occupy Clinton with the threat of an attack on the city, the allies crossed the Hudson to New Jersey and pretended to prepare for an invasion of Staten Island. They requisitioned boats along the shore from Newark to Amboy; openly displayed the pontoons that would be used to bridge the streams and rivers in the South, as if ready to span the Arthur Kill; and even built a bread oven in New Jersey, spreading the word that more were planned, to convince the British that they were digging in to the new staging area for a stay of many weeks. Loyalist spies promptly reported all of these details to the British.[30]

Washington marched his troops south through New Jersey at the end of August, in several columns, and made a feint toward Sandy Hook, as if to rendezvous for an attack at the entrance to New York's waters.[31] The elaborate subterfuge worked: Except for a buildup of forces on Staten Island, Clinton, with his 14,500 men, remained inactive in New York. He continued to believe the main march was a diversion to pry him from New York, where "there was imminent risk of losing all."[32] Finally, on September 2, he belatedly informed Cornwallis that Washington's army, which had already reached Philadelphia, was headed his way.

"The deception has proved completely successful," James Thacher, a physician who had been with the Continental Army throughout the war, exulted in his journal. Between New York and Yorktown, Clinton was caught on the horns of a dilemma. "His Excellency General Washington, having succeeded in a masterly piece of generalship, has now the satisfaction of leaving his adversary to ruminate on his own mortifying situation, and to anticipate the perilous fate which awaits his friend, Lord Cornwallis, in a different quarter."[33]

Washington had much cause for anxiety too, however, as he moved south from Philadelphia in early September toward the northern end of the Chesapeake, where the allied troops would embark on a fleet of small vessels for the last leg of the trip to Virginia: He still had no news from the two French fleets that were to converge at the lower end of the bay. As reports came to him from the New Jersey shore of British ships coming and going at Sandy Hook, Washington could only wonder if Barras and de Grasse had reached their destination or had been attacked and defeated en route.[34] De Grasse had left Cap François in Haiti on August 5 with twenty-eight ships of the line. Admiral Hood, who had assumed command of the British Caribbean squadron at Antigua, set off after him with only half as many ships, mistakenly assuming de Grasse would leave part of his fleet behind. Hood was an aggressive commander, but in this case, his energy and initiative worked against him: Arriving at the Chesapeake before de Grasse and seeing no French ships in the bay, he proceeded to New York on August 25, hoping to overtake the French if they were headed there,[35] and to combine his own fleet with that of Admiral Graves.

Once again, New York drew the British away from the point where their strength was needed most. De Grasse, who had stopped in Havana, Cuba, arrived at the Chesapeake on August 30 and met no resistance. Not only did his ships control the waters around Yorktown, but he landed his 3,000 troops to reinforce Lafayette on the neck of the peninsula, further hemming in Cornwallis while Washington and Rochambeau marched on with the allied army of 2,000 Americans and 4,000 French troops.[36]

When the details of de Grasse's arrival reached Washington on the road just south of Chester, he was ecstatic. He turned his mounted entourage around so he could greet Rochambeau, who was traveling to Chester by way of the Delaware River instead. As his boat pulled up to the dock, the French general was shocked to see the reserved American commander wildly waving his hat and handkerchief with both arms, and when Rochambeau debarked, Washington gave him a hug that lifted him off the ground.[37] The allied generals proceeded through Maryland, crossed the Potomac into Virginia, and made a quick stop at Mount Vernon—which Washington had not visited at all since the war began. They then headed south to Williamsburg to join Lafayette.

As de Grasse sailed into the Chesapeake, Admiral Hood had arrived in New York at the end of August and immediately realized the French were not aiming there, but rather at the Chesapeake after all. Graves sent a note down to Sandy Hook casually inviting Hood to bring his fleet across the bar for protection while he waited for the New York squadron to join him. Instead Hood jumped into a small boat and quickly had himself rowed up to Denyse's Ferry on the Long Island shore at the Narrows, where Graves and Clinton were having one of their leisurely conferences. Hood burst into the room: "Whether you attend the army to Rhode Island or seek the enemy at sea, you have no time to lose," he shouted at the commanders in chief. "Every moment is precious." They had to combine their fleets immediately and destroy Barras's squadron at Newport or return directly to the Chesapeake, Hood insisted.[38]

"The Town much agitated this morning because No Troops are in Motion to stay the Progress of the Rebels Southwardly. No French Fleet in the Chesapeak last Sunday. Ours can't leave the Hook yet for Head Winds ever since the Night before last," Smith wrote with evident frustration.[39] Graves and Clinton were, as usual, apprehensive about leaving New York exposed, but on September 1, Graves finally took five ships across the bar at Sandy Hook to join Hood, and the fleet of nineteen ships headed south in search of de Grasse. "A Week will decide perhaps the Ruin or Salvation of the British Empire!" Smith wrote when news of the French fleet's arrival in Virginia reached New York during the first week of September.[40]

At dawn on September 5, the British fleet arrived off Cape Charles at the mouth of the Chesapeake. Since Barras was still en route from Newport carrying Rochambeau's siege artillery, de Grasse ordered all of his ships out into the Atlantic to draw the British away from the harbor. The French began to form a line of battle, and to Hood's dismay, Graves ordered the British ships into a line almost parallel to the French, giving them time to close their line, instead of bearing down on them while there were still gaps in the formation. The lead ships in each line battered each other for two hours, and then the two sides disengaged; for the next five days they maneuvered in the Atlantic without resuming the battle. On September 10, de Grasse took his fleet back into the Chesapeake to discover that Barras's eight ships had quietly sailed into the bay during the battle. Rochambeau's siege artillery was soon in place, and the sight of the enlarged French fleet of thirty-six ships left Graves little choice but to sail his battered squadron back to New York, where he arrived on the nineteenth, hoping to make another attempt to rescue Cornwallis after Digby arrived from England with more ships. The Battle of the Virginia Capes had preserved the French navy's grip on the Chesapeake and closed the trap on Cornwallis's army.[41]

Washington and Rochambeau reached Williamsburg ahead of the army on September 14 to find that Lafayette still had Cornwallis's forces bottled up on the peninsula. While the allied troops moved down the Chesapeake in small vessels from Head of Elk over the next ten days, Washington visited de Grasse on his flagship and persuaded him to keep his fleet in the bay long enough to ensure the success of the joint maneuvers. On September 28, the complete allied army of some 14,000 men set out from Williamsburg to lay siege to Yorktown, where Cornwallis commanded a little more than half that number.[42]

Cornwallis's situation deteriorated steadily over the next two weeks. Relying on a recent letter from Clinton that promised him 5,000 troops, Cornwallis gave up the weaker outer defenses of the city (small earthworks) and concentrated his men inside the main fortifications. Banastre Tarleton and other aggressive young officers had been telling Cornwallis, before Lafayette was reinforced, that to expect help was absurd under these conditions; the only answer was to fight their way out at the neck of the peninsula. Cornwallis, however, like Burgoyne exactly four years earlier, chose to rely on Clinton's promises, enabling him to transfer the blame for his own ill-advised adventure onto someone else.[43]

After camping outside the city and sending a detachment to surround Tarleton's position on Gloucester Point on the other side of the York River, the allies began siege operations on October 6, advancing toward the city with a series of trenches—the same kind of "regular approaches" that General Howe had begun on the neck of the Brooklyn peninsula in 1776. Two days later they carried out an all-night bombardment that took a heavy toll on the city, the

British forces, and Cornwallis's confidence. A smallpox epidemic also ravaged the army within the walls. After a second all-night barrage on October 10, Cornwallis wrote to Clinton that he couldn't hold out much longer.[44]

By mid-October, loyalists in New York were horrified by the grim news from Yorktown and furious about the divided and ineffectual command exercised by their generals. "The Enemy within 600 yards. About 100 men lost by their Fire from 40 Pieces of Cannon and 17 Mortars," William Smith recorded in his diary. "The *Charon* Ship of 44 Guns blown up by a red hot Ball." And still Clinton remained in New York with the fleet, preparing for the expedition. "The Populace rave at the Navy who have been refitting here since 23 September."[45] Despite the urgency of the situation, Clinton had decided to wait until October 13 to sail south and rescue Cornwallis, reasoning that "before the 13th of October, there will be a great risk in getting over the Bar," at Sandy Hook, presumably because of the tides and weather.[46] Clinton felt sure that Cornwallis had enough provisions to last until the end of October.

Smith sensed the pessimism of the British commanders in New York and thought it was "a bad Symptom." He noted that Governor Robertson "talks in this pitiful Strain. He is a Dotard and abandoned to Frivolity. He has Parties of Girls in the Fort Garden, in the Midst of his own Fears, and the Anxieties of this Hour."[47]

When the allies were only 250 yards from the British lines, Cornwallis wrote to Clinton that the situation was "very critical." The younger officers at Yorktown pressured their chief to take some decisive action and break out of the allied encirclement. Perhaps the memory of Washington's astonishing escape from Brooklyn to Manhattan in 1776 inspired Cornwallis's next move. He commandeered as many boats as he could find and planned to evacuate his army across the York River to Gloucester Point, where he hoped to break through the allied forces camped in front of Tarleton's position and march back to New York.[48]

He began the escape on the night of the sixteenth by ferrying his wounded and 1,000 troops to Gloucester Point, but where the elements had conspired to assist Washington in 1776, they failed Cornwallis utterly in 1781. The boats never even made it back to Yorktown for a second load of troops: A sudden, violent storm dispersed them, and Cornwallis finally gave up. On the morning of October 17, a drummer beating a parley appeared on the British ramparts but could not be heard over the roar of the bombardment. However, when an officer with a white handkerchief came out, he was quickly blindfolded by the Americans and taken off to present Cornwallis's letter of surrender to Washington.[49]

"Our fleet, which received considerable damage in their spars and rigging in the last engagement off Chesapeak, are now perfectly refitted," a New Yorker wrote to London on October 18, not realizing the irony of his words. Once again, the winds held back the ships at Sandy Hook. "Upwards of 5000 troops are embarked on board the men of war, and wait only for a fair wind to sail to the assistance of our Southern Hero."[50] The following day, Cornwallis signed the capitulation and the surrender at Yorktown became official, just as the fleet left New York.

Clinton and Graves reached the Chesapeake on October 24 and could only guess what had happened at Yorktown, where all was quiet. Over the next five days small boats reached the British fleet with partial reports suggesting that Cornwallis had surrendered. The sight of the French ships in the bay confirmed that nothing could be done, and the British returned to New York on the twenty-ninth.[51]

The day after the surrender, Cornwallis wrote a damning letter to Clinton, blaming him for the defeat and claiming that he, Cornwallis, would never have dug in and tried to defend a weak position like Yorktown without Clinton's letters promising him support from both the army and navy. Had he not been assured repeatedly that help was on the way, Cornwallis wrote, he might have avoided disaster by attacking the Americans in the open, or attempting an escape to New York by land. Clinton in turn wrote to Germain a few weeks later and justified himself by saying that if the fleet had been able to leave on the day it was originally supposed to, the rescue would have worked. The delay, he implied, was beyond his control.[52] "I have been of opinion that operations should not be undertaken in the Chesapeake without a naval superiority in these seas," he later wrote to Germain, "and to the want of it, and perhaps that alone, we are to impute our late misfortunes in that quarter." His warnings to the ministry that Cornwallis was vulnerable without a fleet had met with unfulfilled promises to send one, Clinton asserted. "We, however, had it not, and the consequences were such as I predicted."[53]

As if to compound the irony of Britain's vast resources and terrible timing, as Yorktown fell on October 19, a fleet from London arrived in New York with a staggering amount of food: enough provisions to feed 30,000 men for six months.[54]

CHAPTER 24

The Colonies Lost,
New York Regained

⁓

I have no doubt but that by the concurrence and support of my Parliament, by the valour of my fleets and armies, and by the vigorous, animated and united exertion of the faculties and resources of my people, I shall be able to restore the blessings of a safe, and honourable peace to all my dominions," King George III proclaimed in his speech at the opening of Parliament on November 27, 1781.[1] He considered the defeat at Yorktown a setback, not an end to the war, even as he looked forward to its peaceful resolution. After all, the French naval advantage was temporary, and the British still held New York City, Charleston, and Savannah with a powerful fleet and army. Word of the king's speech took weeks to reach New York, however, and the loyalists there waited anxiously to hear that they had not been abandoned.[2]

Like the patriots who had risked their lives and property for the cause of American independence, the Tories had done the same for their king. Washington's refusal to consider the Provincial troops who fought at Yorktown as ordinary prisoners of war, leaving them open to arrest and execution as traitors, showed they had reason for concern. In a gesture of leniency, Washington had allowed Cornwallis to load a single sloop with men of his choosing and send it to New York; after several piecemeal reports, the arrival of these grateful but frightened Provincials proved to incredulous New Yorkers that the disaster at Yorktown was real indeed.[3]

Cornwallis himself arrived in New York on parole on November 19 and met with Clinton, whom he had not seen since their conquest of Charleston a year and a half earlier. On the surface, the session was friendly, with both agreeing that King's Mountain had been the final blow to Germain's strategy of enlisting loyalist support, and both willing to lay the blame for Yorktown on Admiral Rodney's failure to provide a covering fleet. Clinton then questioned parts of Cornwallis's letter from Yorktown but did not challenge him to retract it; when Clinton in his distraction forwarded the letter to the ministry, he sowed the seeds of his own defeat in the political battle to assign blame for the fiasco in Virginia. Cornwallis departed for London a month later, where his powerful friends ensured that he received a warm welcome from the king and that Clinton became the scapegoat.[4]

In New York, Clinton believed Governor Robertson was scheming to replace him as commander in chief, and suspected he was behind the government's investigation of expenses during Clinton's term—an inquiry that led to accusations of fraud and waste. Clinton had not enriched himself through dishonest means, but he tolerated corrupt practices in his administration, arguing apathetically that there was no way to stop them, and that they were a fact of life in every war in history. Between his two large salaries as commander in chief and peace commissioner, Clinton was paid well enough and saved enough to be financially independent after the war, despite the poor start and the debts his father had left him. Eager for retirement and a reunion with his family in London,* Clinton resigned but then had to wait several months for his replacement. He remained in New York reeling from the loss of one third of his army at Yorktown and expecting the city to be attacked in the spring.[5]

His prediction about the threat to New York was correct. Washington's immediate objective after Yorktown was to enlist de Grasse's help in capturing Charleston before he took his fleet back to the West Indies. By the following June, Washington hoped—as he had since d'Estaing first appeared off Sandy

---

*By this time Mary Baddeley had borne him the first of several children. Her husband continued to be grateful for their financial arrangement and departed cheerfully to the South when Clinton had him transferred. Clinton felt guilty when Baddeley died of fever shortly afterward, and struggled to dispel the appearance that he had dispatched him to a hardship post to eliminate him. After returning to London, Clinton supported both families and divided his time between them (Willcox, *Portrait*, pp. 470–71).

Hook in 1778—to concentrate the allied forces at New York for a victory comparable to that at Yorktown. Washington calculated that if the planned siege went well, New York would fall in six weeks.[6]

De Grasse, however, was anxious to be on his way, and the attack on Charleston was scrapped; the plans for New York would depend on how many ships returned in the spring. Fortunately for Washington, de Grasse was still in the Chesapeake on October 28 when twenty-six British battleships, part of the fleet of almost 100 vessels belatedly dispatched from New York to rescue Cornwallis's army, arrived outside the bay. Admiral Graves maneuvered for two days before leaving on the twenty-ninth, and Washington, under the protection of the French, prepared his army for the trip back to the Hudson. The supplies and men were embarked and moved up the bay on November 3. Washington left the next day for a stopover at Mount Vernon, while Rochambeau and his army, along with some American units, were to remain in Virginia for the winter.[7]

At the end of November Washington arrived in Philadelphia, where congressional delegates, much to his relief, declared themselves ready to pressure the states for contributions to the continuing war effort. Washington feared that the victory at Yorktown would lead straight to defeat if Americans became complacent and let their guard down while the British looked for an opportunity to attack and recoup their losses. Washington's worries were confirmed on January 1, 1782, by a report that another British fleet had left New York, probably bringing troops to Charleston. Since he had already sent some reinforcements to Greene in South Carolina, and Rochambeau's forces guarded Virginia, Washington remained in Philadelphia, where he wrote letters to the states urging them to fulfill their quotas of men, money, and supplies for the ongoing struggle.[8]

By early January, Germain had also begun planning the next campaign. He was still encouraging Clinton to muster the loyalists, warning that the commander in chief would only receive reinforcements equal to the number of men he had lost, but allowing that he would be expected only to make raids along the Atlantic coast, not fight a land war. However, a storm of criticism after Yorktown soon forced Germain to resign, clearing the way for the acceptance of Clinton's resignation and the eventual appointment of Sir Guy Carleton as commander in chief in America. Clinton, despite his disagreements with the secretary of state for the American colonies, was undeniably the instrument of his failed strategy, and Germain had been Carleton's nemesis ever since he failed to take Ticonderoga after the Battle of Valcour Island in 1776. Before Germain stepped down in February, he informed Clinton that his resignation had been accepted, and that Robertson was to take his place until a successor was named.[9]

Traveling on the same fleet with Cornwallis, Benedict Arnold also arrived in London in early February 1782, far from convinced that the war was over. Exasperated with Clinton's inaction, he had come to present his own "Plan of Operations" to the British government; he also carried a second document titled "Considerations on the American War." Both were essentially the work of his ghostwriter, William Smith, with whom he had collaborated since his defection and escape to New York in September 1780. The plans called for an end to martial law in New York and the resumption of civil government under the direction of a viceroy, a "lord lieutenant," who could make new laws by decree and control the appointment of all Crown officers in North America.

A similar potentate had been described in Smith's proposals for an American Parliament back in the 1760s, during the Stamp Act crisis. Only with drastic measures, with a comprehensive plan carried out by such a soldier-statesman, could the empire be saved, Smith's pen proclaimed in its usual anonymous fashion. However, the moment for the descent of the *"deus ex machina"* had passed.[10]

Carleton was appointed in early March, but by this time there were strong indications that the new commander in chief would not be launching a military campaign, but rather cutting the army's losses and extricating it from America. By the time Arnold crossed the Atlantic, news of the surrender at Yorktown, which had reached London at the end of November 1781, had already provoked calls to end the war and sparked intense debate in Parliament. At the end of February 1782, the House of Commons passed a resolution to unilaterally suspend all offensive military operations in America. The news reached New York by packet boat from Falmouth, England, on March 28.

Five weeks later the city's distressed loyalists learned that Lord North's ministry had fallen from power. A new administration was soon formed under the marquis of Rockingham,* the man who had proposed the repeal of the Stamp Act in Parliament. The new ministers were members of the

---

*Charles Watson-Wentworth.

General Guy Carleton

opposition who had always denounced the war and the policies that triggered it; unlike the outgoing ministry's peace commissioners, they were ready to accept American independence.[11]

Washington had returned to the Hudson by the beginning of April, establishing his headquarters at Newburgh, not far north of his previous post at New Winsdsor on the west side of the river. While the soldiers, militia, and citizens in New York were again enlisted in a continuing effort to fortify the city and the entire island of Manhattan, Washington waited for the return of the French fleet and plotted small raids. He authorized an attempt to kidnap Admiral Digby and Prince William Henry, the first member of the royal family to visit America. The young prince was a naval officer, and the two had quarters in Hanover Square. However, the prince was heavily guarded, and when the British doubled the sentries outside his door, the plan for a night raid in whaleboats from New Jersey was abandoned.[12]

On May 5 Sir Guy Carleton arrived in New York to replace Clinton, who left a week later for England, where he lived comfortably but embarked on an obsessive and largely futile quest to rehabilitate his reputation. "Your Grace and I may say with Macbeth, 'thou canst not say I did it,'" he wrote to Lord Percy, while he pinned the blame for losing the war on every other general and admiral. He used the quotation repeatedly but seems to have realized it was a device for coping with his own sense of failure. "I admit there has been blame," he wrote to a friend a few years after his return. "I admit also I may have had my share. God knows there is enough for us all."[13]

Carleton forwarded copies of the votes of Parliament to Washington but also strengthened the city's fortifications. The new commander in chief's management style was the antithesis of Clinton's: He rooted out corruption and instituted reforms designed to save the government about one million pounds a year in expenses. He replaced intrigue and paranoia among his officials with openness.

Before dawn every morning Carleton was on his horse, riding for miles to get acquainted with Manhattan and with the problems of the inhabitants. Even the American prisoners benefited a little from Carleton's arrival: After visiting the prison ships, Carleton ordered that during the heat of summer, the inmates were to spend the daylight hours on Blackwell's Island.* The army respected him, and the loyalists adored him.[14] He fit William Smith's ideal of the "lord lieutenant," the kind of powerful figure Smith had always attached himself to and tried to influence; this time he found that Carleton also shared his vision of the future. Both men believed the United States had to be brought back into the empire, even if Britain had to make substantial concessions at the negotiating table.[15]

In late May news that Admiral Rodney, returned from sick leave, had demolished the French fleet in the Caribbean and captured de Grasse sent the city into a brief paroxysm of joy, complete with a military parade and the illumination of every window with candles or lanterns.[16] When Washington received the news at Newburgh on June 2, he redoubled his efforts to prepare for another campaign. While still hoping for an opportunity to attack New York, he realized a reduced French naval force might be more effective in the South. He also traveled to northern New York State at the end of the month; finding that the British, along with Indian allies and loyalist refugees, had raided the Mohawk Valley, he began planning another Canadian expedition to stamp out the threat once and for all.[17]

Returning to Newburgh for the Fourth of July, Washington learned that the French were sending another fleet to arrive in July or August. Rochambeau came north to meet with Washington in Philadelphia on the sixteenth, and they planned the alliance's next joint operation. As before, Washington put New York City at the center of his strategic considerations: Attacking New York should be the top priority, he argued, but if the fleet arrived too late in the season or did not have enough ships for a decisive advantage over the

*Now called Roosevelt Island.

British, then Charleston should be the target. They agreed that Rochambeau should begin marching his forces from the Chesapeake to the Hudson River, where the threat to New York would prevent the transfer of British troops to the West Indies for use against the French. Rochambeau's presence would also have allowed Washington to invade Canada, if that were necessary. The city at the mouth of the Hudson, linked to Canada by the river, remained, as it had in 1776, a "key to the continent," for the Americans and the British alike. By the first week of August, however, Washington had returned to Newburgh, where he learned that the marquis de Vaudreuil had arrived in the Chesapeake with a fleet of thirteen warships—too few, as he had feared, for a concentration of allied forces at New York.[18]

The loyalists' last hope that Admiral Rodney's success would inspire the king to resist American independence was crushed at the end of July 1782 when a packet arrived from England with mail from May and June: In anticipation of peace talks begun in Paris, the king had taken the initiative to recognize the independence of the United States. In return he stipulated only that loyalists should be protected and their property restored, a proposition which, in practice, was unenforceable.[19] As one New York Tory noted grimly, "the Loyalists of America" were "to depend upon the mercy of their enemies for the restoration of their possessions, which we are assured they will never grant, the greatest part of the estates that have been confiscated by them are already sold."[20] Broadsides, once a popular medium for the revolutionaries' political screeds, became an outlet for the loyalists' rage and despair: "Papers are every night stuck up in every quarter of the town with the most vindictive fury against those who advised our Sovereign to accede to the independence of this country," another New Yorker wrote.[21]

When Carleton broke the news to Smith, he was flabbergasted. He envisioned civil war in England, the ministers who had granted independence assassinated in the streets. When Carleton had first arrived in New York and wanted to restore civil government, Smith, in his role as chief justice, had continued to stall. He had wanted to avoid handling a particularly prominent case in which a loyalist was accused of murdering an American prisoner of war. For political reasons, Smith would have had to acquit the loyalist and anger the revolutionaries. Once he managed to transfer the case to New Jersey (on the basis that the crime was committed there) Smith was finally ready to stand behind his words and restore civil rights to New

York's aggrieved and embittered residents. By this time, however, it was too late.[22]

With his industrious gathering of scraps of intelligence about the rebels, Smith had focused on the weakness of Washington's army and convinced himself that the British were in a better position than they had been five years earlier. Until this moment, he saw Carleton's combination of magnanimity and strength as the final ingredient that would bring the rebels back into the royal fold.[23] Smith's hand trembled as he wrote in his diary, "This information struck me as the Loss of all I had in the World and my Family with it." By the next day he was deep in denial: The recognition of independence, he felt, had to be a "State Artifice to discover Secrets or to gain Time."[24]

After appealing to Carleton and Digby to plead their case with King George III, the city's loyalists also drafted a petition and sent William Franklin, New Jersey's last royal governor, to London, where he delivered it to the king and the prime minister in person, impressing on them the dire circumstances of George's American subjects. Back in New York, the months passed in harrowing uncertainty, as they waited for word of a peace treaty. Assuming the worst, those who could afford to—the wealthy merchants and Mayor David Matthews—booked passage to England for themselves and their families, and the exodus of refugees from New York's harbor grew steadily.[25]

While New York's loyalists panicked, Washington remained cautiously pessimistic about the probability of peace on favorable terms for the United States. When news arrived that Rockingham, the leader of the new coalition government, had died on July 1, the commander in chief was inclined to believe that negotiations in Paris would unravel. At the end of August, he moved the army down to Verplanck's Point, closer to New York City, where it could strike quickly if the British made hostile maneuvers.

In mid-September, Rochambeau's forces completed their march from Virginia and crossed the Hudson at King's Ferry for a joyful reunion at Verplanck's with the American troops who had fought beside them at Yorktown. Awaiting further developments in Paris, the allies remained near there throughout September, while Carleton pulled in his outposts and retrenched in the city. Carleton's defensive maneuvers suggested that the evacuation of New York was only a matter of time, and under orders from the French government, Rochambeau's forces departed gradually, marching first to Boston and embarking for the West Indies from there at the end of October.[26]

At about this time, Washington received word that following a sudden illness, Charles Lee had died in Philadelphia on October 2. After his court-martial, Lee had tried vainly to salvage his own reputation through letters and articles in which he questioned Washington's capability as a military commander. Had Lee resisted and been killed when Tarleton's cavalry surrounded him at Basking Ridge in 1776, or if General Howe had executed him as a deserter, he probably would have been enshrined by Americans as a Revolutionary hero and a peer of the founding fathers.[27] Instead, he died amid unconfirmed accusations that he had been plotting with the British in eastern Virginia the previous year, and his name is largely forgotten. Washington expressed no feelings whatsoever on learning of Lee's death, just as he had refrained from responding publicly to Lee's provocative insults.[28]

In November, Washington gave in to the cold weather and withdrew his army from the lower Hudson up to winter quarters at Newburgh.

Between the peace negotiations in Europe, and the Continental Army's dismal finances, Washington's planning for a military campaign in 1783 proceeded in an atmosphere of uncertainty.[29] On November 30, 1782, the negotiators in Paris had signed provisional articles "for treating of peace" between Britain and the United States, articles that were to be included eventually in a definitive treaty. This led to the signing of preliminaries for a general peace between Britain, France, and Spain at Versailles two months later, in January of 1783.

In February King George III at last proclaimed a "Cessation of Arms" between England, Spain, the Netherlands, and the United States. Washington, who had learned on January 22 that the British had evacuated Charleston, did not have news of developments in Europe until the end of March. Even then, he focused on the fact that a final treaty remained just out of reach and continued to assume the British would have to be expelled by force from New York, their last bastion in the United States.* Lacking the resources and French commitment to prepare actively for an offensive, Washington nonetheless estimated the quantities of men and matériel he

*The British had ended their occupation of Savannah, Georgia, on July 11, 1782.

would need in order to invest the city and drive the British out. He wrote to Henry Knox, by this time a major general, asking what the "Ordnance and Artillery Department" would need "to carry on an Offensive and vigorous Campaign; considering the Siege of New York as a probable Operation."[30]

Washington's extreme caution was matched on the loyalist side by William Smith's stubborn optimism: He convinced himself and tried to persuade others that the real mission of the American delegation in Paris—which included Benjamin Franklin and John Adams, almost seven years after they had refused Admiral Howe's peace terms at their meeting on Staten Island—was to achieve a reunion with Britain. Otherwise, he wrote in the *Royal Gazette*, America would become "thirteen petty nations with jarring interests controlled by a majority that leaves real sovereignty to none. . . . And at the same time, suppose [the remaining colonies] Canada, Nova Scotia, and the two Floridas, monopolized the fostering care of the mother country . . . to make them and such others as she may be induced to plant all along the western frontiers, the objects of your envy, and perhaps of your dread." When Carleton informed Smith that the preliminaries had been signed and a cease-fire was coming soon, he again told himself it must be a stratagem to trick the Americans, a "Ruse de Guerre."[31]

Nonetheless, it was real: After the general peace reached New York late in March, the "Cessation of Arms" was read in front of City Hall at noon on April 8, 1783. Sources told the *Pennsylvania Packet* that the crowd did not rejoice, but instead "groans and hisses prevailed, attended by bitter reproaches and curses upon their king, for having deserted them in the midst of their calamities. The greatest dispair is depicted in every countenance, and the little comfort they can possibly experience in the desarts of Nova Scotia will tend to heighten their distress. It is said that the number of persons last embarked for that country amount to near four thousand."[32] Smith, apparently stunned by these developments, did not write a word in his diary for the next three weeks.[33]

On April 6 and 9, all the prisoners of war in the city, on Long Island, and on board the prison ships were released. According to a British official, he provided six vessels under flags of truce which "took the whole of the prisoners on board and carried them to their respective places of abode to save them expence and the fatigue of long marches—excepting about 18 or 20 sick and wounded who cou'd not be removed with safety."[34] Presumably, many of those who were delivered to their destinations would have been too weak from starvation and disease to make the journey on their own.

To the dismay of the loyalists, as the prisoners left, Americans poured into the city from the countryside. "I must confess though I stood prepared for bad terms, yet I did not think it was in the power of the greatest villains on earth to place us in so humiliating a situation," one New Yorker wrote to a friend in London. "Even the Rebels affect to pity our case. . . . All accounts from the country bespeak the utmost violence. Threats are thrown out, and vengeance denounced against all here. The town now swarms with Americans, whose insolence is scarce to be borne. . . . should the troops be hastily withdrawn from this place, a scene of confusion and distress will take place that words cannot describe."[35]

Another resident wrote that many loyalists "have lost their senses, and are now in a state of perfect madness. Some have put a period to their miserable existence by drowning, shooting, and hanging themselves, leaving their unfortunate wives and helpless infants destitute of bread to support them."[36]

"As little doubt could be entertained but that peace would soon follow," Benjamin Tallmadge wrote, "I found it necessary to take some steps to insure the safety of several persons within the enemy's lines, who had served us faithfully and with intelligence during the war." After Nathan Hale's death, Tallmadge had been instrumental in establishing and running Washington's network of spies in New York. Because some of them had played their parts as Tories so convincingly and would be subject to reprisals by New Yorkers after the British army left, Tallmadge "suggested to Gen. Washington the propriety of being permitted to go to New York, under the cover of a flag," to see to their welfare.

"This he very readily granted," Tallmadge reported,

> and I proceeded to New York, where I was surrounded by British troops, tories, cowboys, and traitors.
>
> By the officers of the army and navy I was treated with great respect and attention, and especially by the Commander-in-Chief, Gen. Carlton, at whose table I dined with the commanding officers of the navy, and others of high distinction. It was not a little amusing to see how men, tories and refugees, who a little before uttered nothing but the terms *rebels and traitors to their King*, against all the

officers of the American army, would now come around me while in New York, and beg my protection against the dreaded rage of their countrymen. But I knew them too well to make any promises. . . . I saw and secured all who had been friendly to us throughout the war, and especially our emissaries. . . . Having accomplished all my business in New York, I returned again to the army, and made my report to the Commander-in-Chief. The troops now began to be impatient to return to their respective homes, and those that were destined for that purpose, to take possession of the city. Gen. Washington now dismissed the greater part of the army in so judicious a way that no unpleasant circumstances occurred.[37]

Tallmadge did not mention that the troops' seething resentment about the conditions they had endured and the army's broken promises about their back pay erupted in yet another mutiny in June 1783, when 500 Pennsylvania troops marched with fixed bayonets from Lancaster to Philadelphia, surrounded the building where Congress convened, and prompted them to take up new temporary quarters in Princeton. Joseph Martin was never a mutineer, but his account of the common soldier's discharge from the army differs dramatically from Tallmadge's and expresses what drove others to desperate acts. "Starved, ragged and meager," he wrote, the men had "not a cent to help themselves with. . . . This was appalling in the extreme."

When the soldiers enlisted, Martin continued,

they were promised a hundred acres of land, each, which was to be in their own or the adjoining states. When the country had drained the last drop of service it could screw out of the poor soldiers, they were turned adrift like old worn-out horses, and nothing said about land to pasture them upon. Congress did, indeed, appropriate lands . . . but no care was taken that the soldiers should get them. . . . no one ever took the least care about it, except a pack of speculators, who were driving about the country like so many evil spirits, endeavoring to pluck the last feather from the soldiers. . . .

Had I been paid as I was promised to be at my engaging in the service, I needed not to have suffered as I did. . . . there was enough in the country and money would have procured it if I had had it. It is provoking to think of it. The country was rigorous in exacting *my* compliance to my engagements to a punctilio, but equally careless in performing her contracts with me, and why so? One reason was because she had all the power in her own hands and I had none. Such things ought not to be.[38]

At the beginning of May 1783, Washington and the governor of New York State, George Clinton, hosted the British commanders, Carleton and Digby, at a conference at Tappan, just north of the New Jersey border, to discuss a timetable and other conditions for the British evacuation. The victorious Americans entertained their guests lavishly and ran up a bill for 500 pounds from the caterer, the famous tavern owner Sam Fraunces.[39] The British contingent included William Smith, who initially thought it would be humiliating and inappropriate for him, as chief justice, to have to negotiate the terms of surrender with Governor Clinton, "a Man who was once my Clerk." Nonetheless, he attended, and the meals and discussions proceeded without incident; Smith even managed to draw the conclusion from these meetings that Washington might be part of a faction in Congress that was working to "bring about a Reunion" at the Paris talks.[40]

Washington opened the first meeting at Tappan by spelling out three priorities: The British were not to destroy or steal American property as they left, especially not black slaves; a timetable was needed for completing the evacuation; and the authority of New York's state government should be extended as far as possible, bringing it right up to the British lines before the withdrawal was complete to ensure a seamless transfer of power and avoid the disorders that might otherwise break out.

Carleton responded that he would not return the thousands of blacks leaving for Nova Scotia, but he had created a registry of their identities and would reimburse their owners. The British had guaranteed the slaves their freedom if they would abandon the rebel cause, and they intended to keep their word, he told Washington. This theft of American property seemed to be a violation of the peace treaty, Washington replied. Carleton insisted that the treaty should not impinge on Britain's national honor, which required keeping its promises to people of all races.[41] Ironically, the American Revolution, which began with the colonists' assertion that all men were created equal, ended with their commander in chief bickering with the British in an attempt to deny freedom to blacks.

Washington and Thomas Jefferson, like many otherwise humane Americans from Georgia to New York, were both slave owners. Elias Boudinot, who had extended himself on behalf of the American prisoners of war, like Washington saw blacks as simply another form of private property and apparently never equated the institution of slavery with the brutal confinement and impressment practiced by the British. In June Boudinot wrote to Benjamin Franklin that Americans were furious about the "cruelties, ravages, and barbarisms of the refugees and loyalists." New Yorkers, he said, "are kept out of their city, and despoiled daily of their property by the sending off their negroes by hundreds, in the face of the treaty."[42] British protestations about national honor, on the other hand, were also susceptible to charges of hypocrisy: Freeing blacks was a convenient form of revenge on the enemy.

In the middle of August, Carleton assured Boudinot, then president of Congress, that he was proceeding with the evacuation of refugees and military personnel as quickly as possible. He had received final orders from London about the evacuation, Carleton wrote, which was proof that the British had every intention of abiding by the terms of the peace treaty. However, Carleton also said that it would be impossible to specify an exact date for completing the withdrawal, because the number of refugees pouring into New York had increased dramatically. This he blamed on the failure of Congress to stand by the treaty and protect loyalists from the organized and violent retribution that was breaking out across America, "even at Philadelphia, the very place which the Congress has chosen for their residence."[43] He could not, he asserted, be expected to leave behind a single loyalist who wished to leave the country. Any delays were the responsibility of Congress and the state and local legislatures, because it was in their power to reduce the multitude of emigrants by seeing to their needs and calming their fears.

As wealthy loyalists liquidated their assets—their homes in town and in the country along with furniture and other contents—New York became the scene of endless auctions and a magnet for thieves. Even with British sentries stationed every 100 yards or so, the *Pennsylvania Packet* claimed it was "unsafe to walk the streets in the night, or be in a crowd in the day. . . . The inhabitants have formed associations for a nightly watch."[44]

Many who had lost their land, possessions, and livelihoods to the rebels petitioned the British government to resettle them in Nova Scotia, the St. John River in Canada, or the West Indies; the first of many such convoys, carrying almost 500 refugees and stocked with enough provisions for their first year, had sailed from New York in early October 1782. Successive fleets in April and September 1783 were much larger, transporting thousands of emigrants and soldiers (including blacks) as well as artillery and supplies in dozens of ships. By mid-October the new arrivals had swelled the existing settlements in Nova Scotia and created entirely new ones. Towns with names like Carleton and Clinton sprang up, in addition to the city of Shelburne with a population of 9,000 whites and a separate district for 1,200 free blacks who had fought for the British. In all, more than 29,000 refugees left from New York for Nova Scotia and St. Johns in the space of a year.[45]

Smith thought Nova Scotia was fine for the lower classes but regarded the rugged existence there as simply out of the question for a man of his stature. Pamphlets against New York's loyalists had begun to circulate, threatening Smith by name if he should remain in the city after the British evacuation. Fortunately for him, Carleton came to his rescue by recommending him to the British government for the post of chief justice in Quebec. Carleton's support may have been self-serving, prompted by his desire to be appointed, in effect, viceroy for North America, a position Smith strongly advocated.[46]

While Stephen Bleucke, the leader of the city's black loyalists, went into exile with them, Peter Williams, the sexton of the John Street Methodist Church, managed to remain in New York. The trustees of the church bought Williams from his Tory master as the latter prepared to flee the city. A few years later, Williams repaid the debt and gained his freedom. According to his son, Williams always remembered the departure of the loyalists and the British as an event that "gave double joy to his heart, by freeing him from domestic bondage and his native city from foreign enemies."[47]

The definitive peace treaty was signed on September 3, 1783, and by the end of October, Cornelius Bradford had returned and resumed ownership of the Merchants' Coffee House. A month later, Hugh Gaine's loyalist *Weekly Mercury* shut down, and Samuel Loudon, who had been publishing the *New York Packet* in Fishkill during the war, restarted the paper in the city, maintaining the prewar subscription price of three dollars a year. A week later, John Holt also revived his weekly paper, which he had published in Kingston and Poughkeepsie during the war; formerly called the *Weekly Gazette or Post-Boy*, and then the *New York Journal*, it fittingly became the *Independent New-York Gazette*. Amid the competition of some entirely new papers, Holt sought readers by reminding them that when the war broke out his paper had loudly urged Americans to fight for their rights, and had published the views of Revolutionary leaders despite threats from the powerful Tory establishment in New York. On the same day that Holt resumed publication, James Rivington dropped the word *Royal* and renamed his paper *Rivington's New York-Gazette*.[48]

In November, Carleton finally gave Washington and Governor Clinton a precise date for the withdrawal of British troops from New York, writing that he planned to evacuate northern Manhattan and eastern Long Island on November 21, to leave Paulus Hook on the twenty-second, and finally to evacuate the city and Brooklyn at noon on the twenty-fifth if the wind and weather were favorable.

Washington and Clinton met at Tarrytown on the nineteeth and proceeded to Harlem on the twenty-first, extending their authority, as Washington had insisted, right up to the British lines. They stayed at a tavern, then nine miles north of the city, with an entourage that included army officers and members of the state senate and assembly. American troops were also stationed around McGowan's Pass, and some scouts had gone ahead to within five miles of the city, near the Dove Tavern.[49]*

Despite fears that the town would be pillaged amid widespread violence, incidents were relatively minor. The following day some patriots in New York prepared in advance for Washington's triumphal entry into the city by raising an American flag over their houses. This provoked the dreaded William Cunningham to march over with his sword drawn, leading a gang of enforcers and determined to remain in control until the moment of evacuation. After he "pronounced some scores of double-headed Damns, besides the genteel epithets of Rebel Bitches, &c. without number," he tore down the flag and stalked off with it.[50] As noon approached on November 25, Mr. and Mrs. Day ran up the Stars and Stripes over their tavern on Murray Street in anticipation of the appointed hour when the Continental Army would repossess the city. Even this was too early for Cunningham, who came over to remove the flag. Mrs. Day, a "stout, athletic woman," answered the door and refused to let him in. When he started to force his way into the house, "she boxed his ears warmly, made the powder fly from his hair, and caused him to beat a hasty retreat, amid the jeers and laughter of some few spectators who were present at the scene."[51]

The British soldiers departing from Fort George at the southern tip of Manhattan had more success than Cunningham. Before relinquishing the last patch of occupied soil in the United States, they sabotaged and greased the flagpole. The American procession into the city was delayed briefly while someone ran to an ironmonger's workshop in Hanover Square to fetch a saw,

---

*The tavern stood at present-day 126th Street near Frederick Douglass Boulevard. McGowan's Pass was at the northern end of today's Central Park. The Dove Tavern was at today's Third Avenue and Sixty-sixth Street.

Washington and his troops entering New York City,
November 25, 1783.

a board, a hammer, and nails. With these a young sailor fashioned cleats, which he nailed into the flagpole as he climbed to the top and set the rope back in the pulley.[52] Only then did the American flag finally wave above the fort for the first time since it had been torn down on September 15, 1776, when the Howes captured the city and Pastor Shewkirk rejoiced as loyalists trampled on the rebel colors.

With the flag raised, cannon booming, and crowds cheering, the Americans marched into the city without further incident, Benjamin Tallmadge reported, with his usual pride.

> Gen. [Henry] Knox, at the head of a select corps of American troops, entered the city as the rear of the British troops embarked; soon after which the Commander-in-Chief, accompanied by Gov. Clinton and their respective suites, made their public entry into the city on horseback, followed by the Lieut.-Governor and members of the Council. The officers of the army, eight abreast, and citizens

on horseback, eight abreast, accompanied by the Speaker of the Assembly, and citizens on foot eight abreast, followed after the Commander-in-Chief and Gov. Clinton. So perfect was the order of march, that entire tranquility prevailed, and nothing occurred to mar the general joy. Every countenance seemed to express the triumph of republican principles over the military despotism which had so long pervaded this now happy city.[53]

In his upbeat style, Tallmadge captured the spirit if not the appearance of the island (stripped of its trees and fences), the battered mansions, the war-torn city, and the lean American soldiers returning after seven years. "The troops just leaving us were as if equipped for show," another eyewitness wrote, "and with their scarlet uniforms and burnished arms, made a brilliant display. The troops that marched in, on the contrary, were ill-clad and weather-beaten, and made a forlorn appearance. But then they were *our* troops, and as I looked at them, and thought upon all they had done for us, my heart and my eyes were full, and I admired and gloried in them the more because they were weather-beaten and forlorn."[54]

New York also had its church bells back from storage in Newark and used them, as in the days of the Stamp Act's repeal. One Hessian soldier recalled the ecstatic mood in the city, and the desolation on the British vessels in the harbor. "On all corners one saw the flag of thirteen stripes flying, cannon salutes were fired, and all the bells rang. The shores were crowded with people who threw their hats in the air, screaming and boisterous with joy, and wished us a pleasant voyage with white handkerchiefs. While on the ships, which lay at anchor with the troops, a deep stillness prevailed as if everyone were mourning the loss of the thirteen beautiful provinces."[55]

At Fraunces Tavern that evening, Tallmadge recalled, "Governor Clinton gave a public dinner, at which Gen. Washington and the principal officers of the army, citizens, etc. were present," the first of many banquets that week. The following morning, Washington completed the work that Tallmadge had begun, of paying the spies who had remained in the city during the occupation, and revealing their identities. First, Washington had breakfast with Hercules Mulligan, the tailor who had helped remove the guns from the Battery in 1775 and during the intervening years eavesdropped on British officers and soldiers when they entered his shop, passing along vital information to his old King's College roommate, Alexander Hamilton. Lest anyone should mistake him for a Tory, Washington publicly proclaimed Mulligan, "a true friend of liberty."[56]

Washington also paid a visit—and a bag of gold coins—to James Riving-ton, the printer who, like so many other devoted loyalists in occupied New York, had become disaffected under the military regime. When Rivington had tried to criticize the Howes in his newspaper for their disastrous conduct of the war, British censorship and threats had silenced him. Apparently, they also drove him to offer intelligence to the Americans and seek assurances that he would be allowed to stay in the city if and when they took it back.[57] In addi-tion to his newspaper, Rivington had operated a coffeehouse where British officers relaxed and unwittingly provided him with valuable information. The king's official printer was above suspicion, and even managed to steal the British fleet's signal book, which the Americans delivered to de Grasse in 1781, before the Battle of the Virginia Capes.[58]

The festivities continued as Washington secured this network of agents in the city that had been critical to his success. The following Tuesday evening, Tallmadge wrote, "there was a most splendid display of fireworks, at the lower part of Broadway, near the Bowling Green. It far exceeded anything I had seen in my life."[59]

"The time now drew near when the Commander-in-Chief intended to leave this part of the country for his beloved retreat at Mount Vernon," Tallmadge wrote. On December 4, his officers gathered at Fraunces Tavern, where Washington took his final leave of them. After Washington gave a toast to them collectively, "every officer in the room marched up to, kissed, and parted with his General-in-Chief," Tallmadge wrote. "Such a scene of sorrow and weeping I had never before witnessed." Washington left the tavern and "passing through a corps of light infantry who were paraded to receive him, he walked silently on to Whitehall [Slip], where a large barge was in waiting. We all followed in mournful silence to the wharf, where a prodigious crowd had assembled to witness the departure of the man who, under God, had been the great agent in establishing the glory and independence of these United States. As soon as he was seated, the barge put off into the river, and when out in the stream, our great and beloved General waived his hat, and bid us a silent adieu."[60]

Tallmadge, who considered himself "a singular instance of the divine protection and care," because he had been on the front lines of so many bat-tles without receiving "a dangerous wound" or "a single bone broken," con-tinued to lead a charmed life after the war.[61] After the tearful parting at Fraunces Tavern, Tallmadge left Manhattan to visit his birthplace, still his father's home, on Long Island. In Brookhaven, which had been behind enemy lines for seven years, residents celebrated the liberation of New York by roasting a whole ox on the village green, a scene reminiscent, on a smaller scale, of the feast on the Common in Manhattan after the repeal of the Stamp Act seventeen years earlier. Tallmadge was appointed master of ceremonies. "When the ox was well roasted, the noble animal on his spit was removed to a proper place, and after a blessing from the God of Battles had been invoked by my honored father, I began to carve, dissect, and distribute to the multitude around me."[62]

Tallmadge received a hero's welcome as he traveled the length of Suffolk County, particularly in the home of his future father-in-law. Among his other blessings, Tallmadge also found true love. These visits, he wrote, "secured to me a *companion and friend*, the most desirable, in my view, had I been privileged with a choice from her whole sex."[63] The couple had seven children. Tallmadge prospered in business and represented Connecticut in Congress for sixteen years before he died in 1835, at the age of eighty-two.

Eager to return to private life, Washington had left several army units under General Henry Knox to patrol New York's southern counties and the city's streets and departed from Whitehall Slip right after the British commander in chief, Sir Guy Carleton, and his remaining forces set sail on December 4.[64] William Smith, whose appointment as chief justice of Quebec had not yet been confirmed, took Carleton's advice and went with him to London, never to return to the city where he was born and raised and where he had played such an active, albeit often anonymous, role in public affairs.[65]

Presumably because Governor Clinton had been his protégé, Smith was one of the few loyalists in New York State whose property was not confiscated. However, as an exile in London, Smith found that the contortions he had gone through to avoid personal responsibility for condemning rebels in a civil court worked against him. On the one hand, when he petitioned the government for his unpaid salary as chief justice, the Treasury scoffed that a garrison town like New York didn't need such an official, and pointed out that he had never actually presided in that capacity. Then when Smith, with his bubble of self-importance deflated, joined the flood of other refugees and requested compensation for lost income resulting from his loyalty to the king, and for support until he was resettled, he was told to make do with the sixty pounds he received annually from his investments in land in New York.

Smith spent three dreary, bitter years in London, much of them in the waiting rooms of government offices, before he finally became chief justice of Quebec and was reunited with his family. Carleton received a peerage and became the governor of Quebec. He relied on the advice of his chief justice, and Smith once again came to control the levers of power. This time, however, Smith was unable to remain aloof, because his legal opinions and verdicts gave him immense influence over land grants and the future settlement of Canada, and thrust him into the center of the fierce conflict between its Anglo and French populations. While Smith's ideas had lagged behind the revolutionary changes in the United States, he was a generation ahead of his time in Canada. His constitutional framework for autonomy within the empire, which he had hoped the thirteen states would embrace, prefigured Canada's dominion status as it was implemented in the nineteenth century.

In his youth, Smith had envisioned a comfortable retirement on an estate in New York. Instead, he spent his final years trying to attract English settlers to Canada—to make it the envy of the United States, a nation that he expected would not last long. In the end, the former prankster, Presbyterian propagandist, and firebrand of the Whig Triumvirate, who had fought the Church of England tooth and nail for most of his life, was buried in 1793 in an Anglican cemetery.

Epilogue: Reconciliation, Rebirth, and Remembrance

∼

I n short, the Mob now reigns as fully and uncontrolled as in the Beginning of our Troubles," a frightened loyalist wrote to a friend after the British evacuation of New York in 1783.[1] Isaac Sears had returned to the liberated city and, with the second fortune he made as a privateer in Boston, installed himself in a mansion facing Bowling Green; with Marinus Willett and John Lamb he revived the Sons of Liberty and the tactics they had employed during the Stamp Act crisis. At the end of March 1784, they rallied an enormous crowd on the Common to demand the expulsion of any remaining Tories from the state by May 1 and to call for harsher penalties against those who might choose to stay. The Sons tapped the fury of residents whose jobs, houses, and farms had been taken over by Tory neighbors or refugees for the past seven years. The demonstration grew out of several months of mass meetings and increased violence against loyalists: tarring and feathering, beatings, and other forms of physical abuse and intimidation.[2]

In the postwar city, however, the radicals encouraged these methods not from outside the legal framework of government but from official positions of power. Governor George Clinton's inflammatory denunciations of the Tories in January seemed to trigger and condone the new wave of reprisals, and the Sons of Liberty had won enough seats in the state legislature during the December elections to pass a raft of hostile, punitive laws. Loyalists could not hold public office, and anyone accused of

Toryism by a single witness could be deprived of the vote. Ignoring the Treaty of Paris, the radicals called for loyalist property to be confiscated and immediately sold at auction, and imposed an exorbitant tax on residents of the state's southern counties, who had remained and collaborated with the occupying army.[3] In the heat of political vengeance, the irony that the war had been fought to free Americans from a tyrannical legislature seemed lost on the radical lawmakers. With Lamb appointed as collector of the port, Willett as the city's sheriff, and a Common Council dominated by ardent Whigs, the conservative mayor, James Duane, seemingly had little room to maneuver, politically or physically: Both the state and city governments met at the crowded City Hall, where Congress also took up its sessions in 1785, pending the selection of a permanent national capital.[4]

The radicals not only directed their wrath at individuals but tried to settle old scores with the city's Anglican corporations as well. In this continuing struggle for the spiritual and educational bastions of the new republic, the radicals abolished the Board of Governors of King's College and renamed it Columbia College, placing it under a larger Board of Regents and absorbing it into a new entity, the University of the State of New York.[5]

The decades-old clash over Trinity Church also entered another round when the Council for the Southern District, the transitional government for the state's southern counties established by the legislature, placed the church under the control of nine Whig trustees, including Sears and Duane. The legislature then issued a new charter in order to control appointment of the rector and sued the corporation to gain title to its extensive real estate. Initially it remained unclear whether this lawsuit would succeed and open the floodgates to the radicals' entire populist, egalitarian agenda.[6] In the meantime, Alexander McDougall, now a state senator and once again politically estranged from Sears and Lamb, had accomplished his more moderate goal of separating church and state: disestablishing the Anglican Church, eliminating the tax to support its ministry, and aligning its charter with the religious freedoms guaranteed in the state constitution.[7]

McDougall, the former street agitator and anonymous pamphleteer of 1769, and Alexander Hamilton, a prosperous lawyer and dyed-in-the-wool elitist, were unlikely allies, but both believed in political reconciliation for the sake of the city's economic future. Maritime trade, the basis of the city's wealth, had been completely disrupted by the war: The merchants' ships had been captured or destroyed, and the infrastructure of the East River waterfront deteriorated rapidly during the occupation. Britain placed severe restrictions on American trade with the West Indies, which had been a vital part of the city's commerce before the war, while France and Spain—no longer enemies of the British—excluded Americans from markets that had been open to them temporarily during the conflict. At the same time, English creditors pressed Americans for payment of prewar debts. Not surprisingly, New York stood in dire need of money as a basic medium of exchange as well as capital for resuming business activity.[8]

Economic recovery had to go hand in hand with the city's physical rehabilitation. Large areas remained charred ruins after two major fires in seven years, while excavations, forts, and barricades still marred the city's beauty and choked circulation through its dirty, heavily damaged streets with fractured pavements and broken lamps. The interiors of houses and churches whose structures survived were worn down and covered in filth after years of use as barracks and stables. The collapse of municipal services during martial law left the streets clogged with garbage and other refuse.[9] One returning resident described the "gloom" of the "Burnt District," which extended "up both sides of Broadway to Rector Street. . . . No visible attempts had been made since the fire to remove the ruins," and the charred façade of the old Trinity Church "still reared its ghastly head."[10]

In February 1784 McDougall presided over two large public meetings that resulted in the creation of the city's first commercial bank, the Bank of New York. By making short-term loans and issuing notes backed by gold and silver, the bank fueled the city's economic recovery while avoiding the problems of unlimited paper money that had plagued the country throughout the war. Alexander Hamilton, who had hoped to start a bank in connection with Robert Morris's Bank of North America, instead teamed up with McDougall, and the enterprise also became an instrument of political rapprochement: Its officers and shareholders represented the entire spectrum from radical Whigs like Sears to Tories and opportunists like Robert Murray.[11]

Murray had performed a political tightrope act during the war, but he had helped establish the city's Chamber of Commerce in 1768, and its members, mostly Tories themselves, supported his continuing presence in the city after Evacuation Day. Mayor James Duane, Murray's neighbor, was also a powerful ally. Duane presided over the mayor's court, which confiscated loyalist property, and it is likely that he brokered the final arrangement by which Robert and John Murray were allowed to keep their property and remain in New York. Duane asked for Robert Murray's involvement in rebuilding the city as part of their quid pro quo. With the mayor, Murray served as a governor of New York

Hospital, which had burned down during the war, and as a commissioner of the Bridewell Alms House, formed to help the numerous poor and homeless residents in the city.[12]

Many of them were artisans and tradesmen returning to the city in search of housing and employment only to fall into debt—people McDougall struggled, unsuccessfully, to assist by proposing laws protecting debtors from imprisonment.[13] In the two years after Evacuation Day, 12,000 people flowed back into New York City, bringing its population back to the prewar level of almost 25,000.[14] The influx also included Whig businessmen, entrepreneurs, lawyers, and other professionals of a moderate or conservative stripe who saw opportunities in the war-ravaged city and worried that the radicals' political dominance would stifle economic growth. The harassment and expulsion of Tories, they argued, would drain wealth and talent from the city, undermine social stability, and alienate potential European supporters of the rebuilding process and of the new nation.[15]

Whereas McDougall, writing as "A Son of Liberty," had galvanized the city's Revolutionary movement before the war with his anonymous broadside "To the betrayed inhabitants of the city and colony of New York," it was his new ally, Alexander Hamilton, under the pseudonym Phocion, who called for reconciliation in two pamphlets in January and April 1784, which laid the groundwork for organized opposition to the radicals and their legislative program over the next few years.* A champion of federal authority, Hamilton argued in "A Letter from Phocion to the Considerate People of New-York" that punishment of Tories and confiscation of their property violated the Treaty of Paris, a contract entered into by Congress, whose laws should override those of individual states. Hamilton also warned that the assault on New York's Tories subverted the underlying principles of the Revolution. His view of natural rights, however, was essentially conservative: In order to maintain social harmony, government should remain in the hands of upper-class gentlemen, not the democratic rabble that backed the radicals.[16]

By the early spring of 1784, international trade had resumed to and from New York Harbor, and the city's merchants began to rebound. The first American ship carrying goods to east Asia left New York that season, bound for China, whose markets had been monopolized by the British East India Company before the war. In the former Walton mansion on Pearl Street, the Bank of New York was open for business with McDougall as president, despite

---

*After helping to defeat the Macedonians in 339 B.C., the Athenian general Phocion espoused a policy of reconciliation (Burrows and Wallace, p. 274).

its lack of a charter from the legislature. Isaac Sears was named vice president of the largely Tory Chamber of Commerce, a further sign that both sides were willing to lay aside wartime feuds for the sake of economic revitalization.[17]

During the summer, Hamilton also advanced his drive for reconciliation by winning a partial victory in a contentious court case. He defended a Tory who was being sued for damages and rent under the Trespass Act of 1783 by a brewery owner who had fled in 1776. Hamilton argued that the Trespass Act, a creation of the state legislature, had no legal validity because it violated international law and the will of Congress as embodied in the Treaty of Paris. Mayor Duane presided in the case and awarded some damages while excluding others, a verdict that infuriated radical Whigs, who saw in it a dangerous erosion of the legislature's power as well as a reprieve for New York's Tories.[18]

By this time, however, the Sons of Liberty had helped set the stage for their own defeat by committing a major blunder. Sears, Lamb, Willett, John Morin Scott, and others were exposed for buying up soldiers' pay certificates and state securities from their cash-poor owners at depressed prices and using them to speculate in forfeited Tory property. Since the state laws were designed to help impoverished soldiers get back on their feet after the war by favoring holders of these certificates in such land transactions, the public regarded this kind of speculation as the height of venality and cynicism. As a result, Sears and the radical majority took a beating at the polls in the Assembly election of June 1784 and saw their seats go not only to moderate and conservative Whigs but to Tories as well. By the following year, Sears was deeply in debt and sailed to China to avoid arrest. He hoped a brief stay in Canton would replenish his fortune, but he died and was buried there in 1786.[19]

Over the next few years, Governor Clinton's protectionist policies were also responsible for driving artisans and tradesmen, the radicals' traditional supporters, into Hamilton's capacious political tent, which embraced a growing alliance of conservative Whigs and Tories. The British responded to Clinton's high taxes on imports, especially on those from the British West Indies, by dumping huge quantities of cheap British manufactured goods on the New York market. The situation was not unlike pre-Revolutionary times, and it seriously undercut the city's workers. By issuing paper money and having the state assume war debts, Clinton also seemed bent on having New York go its own way rather than strengthening the national union.[20]

Consequently, in the Assembly elections of 1785, artisans and tradesmen became the swing vote ushering in more moderate and conservative Whigs and Tories. Hamilton, who was married to Philip Schuyler's daughter, had the perfect entrée to New York's other landowning families, the Livingstons and Van Cortlandts, and he had set about quelling their habitual factionalism and drawing them into his coalition as well. In 1786, this conservative alliance finally achieved a solid grip on the Assembly, with Hamilton himself winning a seat, and repeated the performance the following year. Within five years of the British evacuation of the city, the radicals had lost their influence once again. While Governor Clinton continued to win reelection for six terms, the legislature repealed its anti-Tory laws and many exiles returned from England, Canada, and the Caribbean. Those not banished by name were restored to full citizenship by 1786, and by 1788 the state struck from the books all statutes that conflicted with the Treaty of Paris. Four years later, even those prominent Tories who had been singled out for expulsion were allowed to return if they agreed not to contest the previous forfeiture of their property.[21]

The social and political consensus that evolved in postwar New York left the city's major institutions in the hands of a moderate and conservative ruling class, as Hamilton believed they should be. Even Trinity and Columbia escaped the radicals' clutches. One of Hamilton's law clerks unearthed the church's deed, which quashed any further attempt to seize its real estate. While Columbia remained part of the new state university, with help from Hamilton, Duane, and John Jay, the college regained its own Board of Governors. A loyalist, William Samuel Johnson, the son of the first president of King's College, was soon installed as the school's president.[22]

Nonetheless, during the course of the Revolution and its immediate aftermath, the manor lords and the merchant princes had lost many of their traditional privileges and had seen a broader electorate organize itself and use its influence to determine the outcome of political races; the old system of threatening tenants and employees, bribing them with drinks and money at the local tavern on election day, or simply assuming their obedience, had been transformed to the point where the establishment now reached out to voters and addressed their concerns.[23]

While the living settled their differences and healed old wounds, they also failed to give the dead their due. A city and a nation hurtling toward a prosperous future were reluctant to commemorate the atrocities that took place during the long, dark struggle for their freedom. The prison ship *Jersey* "being considered unfit for use, was abandoned where she lay," a former prisoner, Captain Thomas Dring, recalled.

The dread of contagion prevented every one from venturing on board, and even from approaching her polluted frame. But the ministers of destruction were at work. Her planks were soon filled with worms, who, as if sent to remove this disgrace to the name of common humanity, ceased not from their labour until they had penetrated her decaying bottom, through which the water rushed in, and she sunk. With her went down the names of many thousands of our countrymen, with which the inner planks and sheathing were literally covered; for but few of her inmates had ever neglected to add their own names to the almost innumerable catalogue. Could these be counted some estimate might now be made of the whole number who were there immured; but this record has long since been consigned to eternal oblivion.[24]

Based in part on the bones that were collected twenty years after the war's end, most authorities agree that 11,000 men perished on the prison ships.[25] In 1803, when work began on the Brooklyn Navy Yard, the banks of Wallabout Bay were cut away, and the skeletons of many prisoners buried by the British were discovered. Congress declined to provide funds for a tomb and monument on the site, but five years later, Dring recalled, "the bones were interred under the direction of the Tammany Society of New York, attended by a solemn funeral procession, in the presence of a vast concourse of citizens; and the cornerstone of a Monument was laid (to use the impressive words which are inscribed upon it), '*in the name of the Spirits of the Departed Free.*'"[26]*

The common soldier who fought the battle for New York was left in most cases with only depreciated pay certificates—"paper bubbles," as Hamilton called them—which he sold for hard cash to speculators like the Sons of Liberty in the belief that the government would never redeem them.[27] After his discharge from the army, Joseph Martin moved briefly to a Dutch community in upstate New York, where he worked for one winter as a schoolteacher. Still waiting for his bounty land from Congress, Martin then settled

*Today the completed Prison Ship Martyrs' Monument, a 148-foot Doric column, towers over the crypt in the center of Fort Greene Park.

in Massachusetts on land granted to stimulate a migration to this northern frontier (later the state of Maine). He built a cabin on the rugged coast near the mouth of the Penobscot River and made a modest living as a farmer and day laborer. Ten years later he married and moved to a larger house in what became the town of Prospect, where he served as a selectman and justice of the peace on and off during the next twenty-five years.[28]

In 1797 Martin finally received his 100 acres of bounty land in Ohio, as promised when he reenlisted in the Continental Army at the age of sixteen. However, Martin apparently sold the land to a speculator, and at the age of fifty-nine, in failing health, he had to request a government pension to support himself, his "sickly and rheumatic" wife, and his five children, the eldest "an idiot from birth," according to his application.[29]

Congress passed a bill in 1818 to support "the poor old decrepit soldiers," as Martin called them. "President Monroe was the first of all our Presidents, except President Washington, who ever uttered a syllable in the 'old soldiers'' favor," Martin wrote.

> President Washington urged the country to do something for them and not to forget their hard services, but President Monroe told them how to act. He had been a soldier himself in the darkest period of the war, that point of it that emphatically "tried men's souls," was wounded, and knew what soldiers suffered. His good intentions being seconded by some Revolutionary officers then in Congress, brought about a system by which . . . many of the poor men who had spent their youthful, and consequently their best, days in the hard service of their country, have been enabled to eke out the fag end of their lives a little too high for the groveling hand of envy or the long arm of poverty to reach.[30]

To those who murmured that the pensions were undeserved, Martin declared: "Those men whom they wish to die on a dunghill, men, who, if they had not ventured their lives in battle and faced poverty, disease, and death for their country to gain and maintain that Independence and Liberty, in the sunny beams of which, they, like reptiles, are basking, they would, many or most of them, be this moment in as much need of help and succor as ever the most indigent soldier was before he experienced his country's beneficence."[31] With these words, Martin seemed to fling Gouverneur

Morris's famous, scornful description of the lower classes as reptiles, back in his face.*

With a pension of eight dollars a month added to his earnings from occasional manual labor and service as town clerk, Martin not only subsisted but remained gregarious, energetic, and intellectually curious into old age. He read classical literature and history, drew from nature, and wrote verse well into his eighties. When he lost his vision at the age of eighty-nine, Martin's charm and sense of humor reportedly remained intact. He had not prospered financially, but he also did not die as he dreaded—anonymously, in battle, far from home. After he passed away in 1850, six months short of his ninetieth birthday, the town of Prospect placed a monument at his grave with the epitaph: "A Soldier of the Revolution."[32]

Martin had received little formal education, but he made the deficit a virtue when he summed up his experience in the war and—with both wit and conviction—restored the battle for New York to its proper place in the chain of events leading to the triumph of the American Revolution:

> I never studied grammar an hour in my life; when I ought to have been doing that, I was forced to be studying the rules and articles of war. As to punctuation, my narrative is in the same predicament as it is in respect to the other parts of grammar. I never learned the rules of punctuation any farther than just to assist in fixing a comma to the British depredations in the state of New York; a semicolon in New Jersey; a colon in Pennsylvania, and a final period in Virginia;—a note of interrogation, why we were made to suffer so much in so good and just a cause; and a note of admiration to all the world, that an army voluntarily engaged to serve their country, when starved and naked and suffering everything short of death (and thousands even that), should be able to persevere through an eight years war, and come off conquerors at last![33]

---

*On May 20, 1774, Gouverneur Morris warned that the growing political activity of common "tradesmen, etc." would soon lead to mob rule: "The mob begin to think and reason. Poor reptiles! It is with them a vernal morning; they are struggling to cast off their winter's slough, they bask in the sunshine, and ere noon they will bite, depend on it" (quoted in Kammen, *Colonial New York*, p. 344).

APPENDIX

A Walking Tour of the Battle for New York

~⌐

In 1789 New York City became the nation's capital, and Washington was inaugurated as the first president at City Hall, on the site now occupied by Federal Hall at Wall and Broad Streets. Had New York remained the capital—a place devoted to the symbolic and ceremonial preservation of the nation's heritage—in addition to resuming and expanding its role as an international center of commerce, there might well be more plazas and traditional monuments commemorating the city's central role in the Revolution.[1] Nonetheless, there is a wealth of sights to see that recall the Revolutionary battlefields in our midst—and even one solemn monument on a grand scale, thanks largely to the long and determined activism of Walt Whitman.

A full century passed between the interment of the prison ship inmates' bones in 1808 and the dedication of the towering Prison Ship Martyrs' Monument that stands in Fort Greene Park in Brooklyn today. During his boyhood in the 1820s, Walt Whitman still came upon some of these bones when they were exposed or washed up on the shores of Wallabout Bay, and he later played a leading role in the movement for a suitable memorial.[2] In the *Brooklyn Daily Eagle* editorial of August 27, 1846, he asked his readers if they were "apt enough to keep the memory of these things—with which the *very soil* we daily tread is so closely identified." Could they not "reserve at least *one spot* as a visible token" of the Battle of Brooklyn?[3]

As an antidote to the strife of the Civil War years, Whitman continued to point out the common heritage of Southerners and Northerners who had been comrades in arms during the Revolution.[4] In 1888, four years before his death, he wrote "The Wallabout Martyrs,"[5] a poem which continued his call for a monument and more broadly suggested that the darkest realms of the nation's history are no less its source of greatness than the clear-cut victories.

Greater than memory of Achilles or Ulysses,
More, more by far to thee than tomb of Alexander,
Those cart loads of old charnel ashes, scales and splints of mouldy bones,

Once living men—once resolute courage, aspiration, strength,
The stepping stones to thee to-day and here, America.

ITINERARY FOR THE WALKING TOUR

The following is a partial list of the sights included on the complete Walking Tour, available at www.thebattlefornewyork.com. The Web site provides detailed instructions, phone numbers, and other information for a tour through all five boroughs and Westchester following the entire route of the armies in the campaign of 1776—all accessible on foot and on public transportation.[6] The Web site also correlates the tour with the narrative in the book, enabling the reader to review appropriate passages and gain a fuller appreciation of what took place at each stop on the tour.

The Bastions of Authority (pages 11–24)

Lower Manhattan: The Common, the triangular block where the Stamp Act protesters gathered in 1765, is now the site of City Hall, the Tweed Courthouse, and City Hall Park. The Liberty Pole and other structures that occupied the Common in the eighteenth century are marked today by plaques and architectural footprints. Nathan Hale was executed elsewhere, but a statue next to City Hall honors him. Other sights on the way down to South Ferry include: St. Paul's Chapel; John Street; Golden Hill; Trinity Church and its graveyard; Bowling Green, where the Stamp Act rioters burned Lieutenant Governor Colden's carriage on the lawn. Here Colden dedicated the equestrian statue of King George III in 1770, and the iron fence that now surrounds the green was installed in 1771. After the reading of the Declaration of Independence on July 9, 1776, the crowd toppled the equestrian statue and knocked or hacked off the original gilded crowns that topped the fence. The jagged tops of the fence posts are a vivid, tangible trace of the moment when the Revolution became a reality for New Yorkers.

From Bouweries to Barricades (pages 69–81)

The Battery; sites related to the fortification of New York before the British invasion; the Fraunces Tavern Museum; Coenties Slip; Hanover Square; the waterfront, the commercial center of colonial New York, where Isaac ("King") Sears reigned and the Sons of Liberty drew their political support; the South Street Seaport Museum's pier, where tourists can board nineteenth-century sailing vessels.

The British Juggernaut Reaches Full Strength
(pages 112–125)

From South Ferry the tour continues to Staten Island, the staging area for the British invasion of Long Island, with views of Governors Island en route. The main attractions on Staten Island are Historic Richmond Town and the Conference House, where Adams, Franklin, and Rutledge met with Admiral Howe on September 11, 1776.

The Invasion of Long Island (pages 126–140)

Views of the Narrows while crossing the Verrazano Bridge; on the Brooklyn side: Fort Hamilton and the Harbor Defense Musem; views of Gravesend Bay; Dyker Beach Park, the landing site of the British; the site of their encampments at the village of New Utrecht; New Utrecht Reformed Church and the oldest Liberty Pole in continuous use since the Revolution; the original church cemetery with a monument to General Nathaniel Woodhull; Milestone Park, the oldest mile marker in New York City; the sites of more British camps in the neighborhoods of Gravesend and Flatlands; the route of the British flanking maneuver on August 26, 1776; the Flatlands Reformed Church; the Pieter Classen Wycoff House Museum, a Dutch farmhouse of the period (the oldest house in the city and the city's first landmark); the site of the Rising Sun Tavern near the Jamaica Pass; the Rockaway Path through the Cemetery of the Evergreens, including the grave of William Howard, the tavern owner's son.

The Battle of Brooklyn (pages 141–154)

The site of Bedford village; Prospect Park, including the Lefferts homestead; Battle Pass (marked by the Dongan Oak Monument, the historic marker of Battle Pass, and a bronze tablet at the northern end of the pass); Lookout Hill; and the Maryland Monument. The tour continues at Green-Wood Cemetery, including Battle Hill, the statue of Minerva, and the Altar to Liberty; the Vechte farmhouse, known as the Old Stone House Historic Interpretive Center; Gowanus Canal, following the line of American forts guarding the Brooklyn peninsula; the Prison Ship Martyrs' Monument; the site of Cobble Hill Fort; the Brooklyn Heights Promenade, near the site of the war council before the retreat to Manhattan; the site of Fort Stirling; and Fulton Ferry Landing, where Washington conducted his miraculous retreat.

The Invasion of Manhattan (pages 179–193)

Site of the Kips Bay invasion; site of the Murray mansion at Thirty-seventh Street and Park Avenue; site of Nathan Hale's execution, on the path of the old Post Road, which was the route of the American retreat to Harlem Heights; McGowan's Pass at the northern end of Central Park; views of Harlem Plains.

The Battle of Harlem Heights (pages 194–203)

Site of Nicholas Jones's house, where the battle began and ended; the route of the old Bloomingdale Road; plaques and signs in memory of the battle at and near Columbia University; Claremont and the Hollow Way (the valley that is now 125th Street); plaques marking the three American fortified lines on Harlem Heights; the Morris-Jumel mansion and Roger Morris Park, the site of Washington's headquarters during the battle.

Throg's Neck and the Battle of Pelham Bay
(pages 219–230)

Views of Hell Gate and Throg's Neck on Long Island Sound; Pelham Bay Park and the bridle path that was once Split Rock Road, where General John Glover ambushed the British on October 18, 1776; Split Rock itself; views of the salt marsh along the Hutchinson River; St. Paul's Church National Historic Site in Mount Vernon (which was used as a Hessian field hospital after the battle), including the visitors' center and historic burial ground.

The Battle of White Plains (pages 231–242)

The view from Chatterton's Hill (now Battle Hill), along with plaques and signs explaining the battle; Purdy's Hill and the Purdy House (Washington's headquarters); the Miller farm-house in North White Plains, which was also Washington's headquarters; the bronze tablet and the remains of the trenches on Miller Hill; and monuments at Horton's Pond (now Silver Lake), which was the Americans' left flank.

The Fall of Fort Washington (pages 243–257)

The Bronx: A series of historic markers on University Heights showing the sites of American forts in a line leading up toward the Jerome Reservoir and the plaque for Fort Independence; the Van Cortlandt House; the plaque for the "Negro Fort" in St. Stephens Church in Marble Hill; the tablet showing the site of the original King's Bridge, where Spuyten Duyvil Creek has been filled in, at 230th Street. Manhattan: The site of the Cock (or Cox) Hill fort in Inwood; the Dyckman House, including its Relic Room and Hessian log hut; Laurel Hill, the eastern edge of the battlefield; bronze tablet at George Washington High School, honoring Colonel William Baxter; a view of the steep terrain in High Bridge Park; Colonel Robert Magaw Place and the plaque in his honor on the Fort Washington Collegiate Church; Bennett Park, including the marble monument and granite tablet marking the site of the fort, along with granite blocks in the ground in the center of the park, at the summit of Manhattan, the highest point on the island; Fort Tryon Park, including the bronze tablet honoring Margaret Corbin, America's first battlefield heroine.

The Colonies Lost, New York Regained (pages 360–380)

The seven years of British occupation are eloquently memorialized by the Prison Ship Martyrs' Monument in Brooklyn, earlier in the tour. After the Americans' triumphant return to the city on Evacuation Day in 1783, Washington said farewell to his officers at Fraunces Tavern (at Pearl and Broad Streets) and then to the crowd at Whitehall Slip, today's Whitehall Street at South Ferry.

$\mathcal{N}$otes

All works are cited by author's name and a short title for the first reference. Titles are repeated for subsequent references only in cases where authors have more than one book listed in the bibliography. Full titles and bibliographical information appear in the bibliography.

ABBREVIATIONS

N.Y. Col. Docs.: O'Callaghan, *Documents Relative to the Colonial History of the State of New York.* 15 vols.
NYHS: New York Historical Society
NYHSQ: New York Historical Society Quarterly
NYPL: New York Public Library
NYPL, RBM: New York Public Library, Rare Books and Manuscripts

PROLOGUE: RETHINKING NEW YORK CITY'S PLACE IN THE AMERICAN REVOLUTION

1. Both quotations are from the *Brooklyn Daily Eagle,* August 27, 1846. Whitman's crusade in the pages of the newspaper and his family history (in the following paragraph): Reynolds, *Walt Whitman's America,* pp. 11–15.
2. All quotations from the poem are from Whitman, *Complete Poetry,* pp. 211–15.
3. New York's exports, imports, and balance of trade: Tiedemann, *Reluctant Revolutionaries,* p. 16; Wertenbaker, *Father Knickerbocker Rebels,* pp. 4–5. Pickled oysters: Parry, *Life at the Old Stone House,* p. 17.
4. Wertenbaker, pp. 4–5.
5. Mackesy, *The War for America,* p. 65.
6. Number of ships and men: Gruber, *Howe Brothers,* p. 101. Comparison to Philadelphia's population: McCullough, "What the Fog Wrought," p. 191. Population of Philadelphia in 1775 was 34,000 to 38,000: Boatner, *Encyclopedia,* p. 856.
7. Both quotations are from Collier, "To My Inexpressible Astonishment," pp. 298–99. Contents of transport vessels: Field, *The Battle of Long Island,* pt. 1:149.

8. Gruber, "America's First Battle: Long Island, August 27, 1776," p. 1.
9. Gallagher, *The Battle of Brooklyn, 1776,* p. 2. However, casualties were higher in other battles: Peckham, *The Toll of Independence,* p. 22.
10. Tilley, *The British Navy and the American Revolution,* p. 84.
11. Ward, *The War of the Revolution,* 1: 205; Tiedemann, pp. 13, 16.
12. Augustyn and Cohen, *Manhattan in Maps,* pp. 84–87; Johnston, *Campaign,* pt. 1:40.
13. The following account of the city's geological prehistory is drawn from Burrows and Wallace, *Gotham,* pp. 4–5.
14. Manders, *The Battle of Long Island,* p. 8.
15. Bushnell, ed., *The Adventures of Christopher Hawkins,* note on pp. 287–88.
16. Burrows and Wallace, p. 15.
17. Quoted in Young, *Revolutionary Ladies,* p. 61.
18. Quoted in ibid., p. 63.
19. The marquis de Lafayette called New York the "pivot" of British operations: quoted in Stokes, *Iconography,* 5:1114.
20. Quoted in McCullough, *John Adams,* p. 15.
21. Wertenbaker, p. 1.
22. Tiedemann, pp. 1, 88–89.

I. THE BASTIONS OF AUTHORITY

1. My account of the Stamp Act riot in New York is drawn from the following sources: letter from an eyewitness dated November 2, 1765, in Dawson, *New York City During the American Revolution,* pp. 44–48; Montresor, *Journals,* pp. 336–337; *New York Post-Boy,* Nov. 7, 1765; Dawson, "The Park and Its Vicinity," in Valentine, *Manual of the Common Council,* p. 439; Decker, *Brink of Revolution,* p. 55; Wertenbaker, p. 1; Burrows and Wallace, p. 199; Tiedemann, pp. 1–2.
2. Burrows and Wallace, p. 196.
3. Bailyn et al. *The Great Republic,* 1:227–29.
4. Dawson, *New York City During the Revolution,* p. 16.
5. Gilje, *The Road to Mobocracy,* p. 47.
6. Montresor, p. 337.
7. Wertenbaker, p. 17.
8. Tiedemann, pp. 20, 22; Wilkenfield, "Revolutionary New York, 1776," p. 62.
9. Ibid., p. 53.
10. Burrows and Wallace, p. 214.
11. Discussion of Amsterdam and New Amsterdam: ibid., pp. 16, 22, and 37–39.
12. Tiedemann, p. 22.
13. Burrows and Wallace, p. 209.
14. Tiedemann, p. 22.
15. This description of New York's elites is drawn from Bonomi, *A Factious People,* pp. 56–75; Tiedemann, p. 32; and Wertenbaker, pp. 16–17.
16. Upton, *The Loyal Whig,* p. 5.
17. Tiedemann, p. 27.
18. Structure of New York's colonial government: Upton, pp. 6–7.
19. Anglican/Presbyterian conflict in New York politics: ibid., pp. 24–34, and Tiedemann, p. 23.

20. "Soaking at Tavern . . . Fops": Upton, p. 19; toasts to heroes, Nelson, *William Alexander,* p. 12; wig burning: Upton, p. 19.
21. William Smith, *Historical Memoirs,* October 30, 1776; quoted in Upton, p. 19.
22. Long-term influence of the *Independent Reflector*: Burrows and Wallace, p. 180.
23. Quoted in Upton, p. 24.
24. Burrows and Wallace, p. 180.
25. For William Smith's transformation: Upton, pp. 41–50.
26. For Smith's dilemma and his activities during the Stamp Act crisis: ibid., pp. 51–60.
27. Ibid., p. 54.
28. Quoted in Middlekauff, *The Glorious Cause,* pp. 74–75.
29. Tiedemann, pp. 88–89.
30. Upton, p. 54. Champagne, pp. 14–15, points out that McDougall, influenced by Smith, was more moderate than Sears and Lamb at this point. McDougall was not active in the Sons of Liberty between November 1765 and May 1766. The rift between them lasted for the next four years.
31. Smith's self-image as mediator and his role in tribunal for tenant uprising: Upton, pp. 54–56.

2. THE MONSTER TYRANNY BEGINS TO PANT

1. *New York Post-Boy,* May 22, 1766, quoted in Stokes, 4:765.
2. Burrows and Wallace, p. 203.
3. The maypole . . . traditional springtime fertility symbol: Gilje, pp. 52–53. Ancient Roman liberty pole . . . Seven Years' War: Bobrick, *Angel in the Whirlwind,* p. 63.
4. *New York Post-Boy,* August 14, 1766, quoted in Stokes, 4:768.
5. Montresor, p. 382.
6. *New York Post-Boy,* August 14, 1766.
7. *New York Gazette* (Weyman), March 30, 1767, quoted in Stokes, 4:774.
8. *New York Journal,* March 26, 1767, quoted in Stokes, 4:774.
9. Upton, p. 57.
10. Political developments from 1767 to 1769: Burrows and Wallace, p. 207; Upton, pp. 64–66.
11. Family politics and combustible issues: Upton, pp. 61, 71.
12. Burrows and Wallace, p. 207.
13. Broadside, December 16, 1769, in NYPL, RBM.
14. *Assembly Journal* (1769–70), 42–43, quoted in Stokes, 4:800.
15. Upton, pp. 68–69.
16. Broadside, January 15, 1770, by "Brutus" in NYPL, RBM.
17. *New York Post-Boy,* February 5, 1770.
18. Broadside, January 15, 1770, by "Brutus" in NYPL, RBM.
19. Broadside, January 15, 1770, by the "Sixteenth Regiment of Foot," in NYPL, RBM.
20. The following account of the "battle" is from the *New York Post-Boy,* February 5, 1770.
21. Stokes, 4:803.
22. "Ill humour . . . and the soldiers": *N.Y. Col. Docs.,* 8:208, quoted in Stokes, 4:803.
23. *New York Journal,* February 8, 1770, quoted in Stokes, 4:805.
24. *New York Journal,* February 15, 1770.
25. Champagne, *Alexander McDougall,* p. 14; Burrows and Wallace, pp. 200–201.

26. Champagne, p. 8; Burrows and Wallace, pp. 200–201.
27. *New York Journal,* February 15, 1770.
28. Burrows and Wallace, p. 210.
29. *New York Post-Boy,* February 19, 1770. Second Jacobite Rebellion: Boatner, p. 312.
30. Upton, p. 70.
31. Burrows and Wallace, p. 212.
32. Stokes, 4:812.
33. *New York Mercury,* July 16, 1770, cited in ibid.
34. Upton, p. 72.
35. Stokes, 4:813.
36. Quoted in ibid.
37. Ibid.
38. William Smith, *Historical Memoirs,* February 16, 1771, quoted in Upton, p. 75.
39. Burrows and Wallace, p. 213.
40. William Smith, *Historical Memoirs,* March 5, 1772, quoted in Stokes, 4:826.
41. Upton, p. 73.
42. Burrows and Wallace, p. 213.
43. This biographical sketch of Washington is largely from Boatner, pp. 1166–67.
44. Washington's stopover with Stirling: Nelson, p. 51. The quest for the earldom: ibid., pp. 31–51.
45. Washington's visit to New York: Stokes, 4:837. Newspaper quoted in Freeman, *George Washington,* 3:323.
46. Colonial reaction to Tea Act and New York's tea party: Wertenbaker, pp. 31–34.
47. *New York Journal,* April 21, 1774, quoted in Wertenbaker, p. 33.
48. Quebec Act: Boatner, p. 909; Faragher, pp. 348–49.
49. William Smith, *Historical Memoirs* (1969), May 18, 1774, p. 186.
50. Letter in the Bancroft Collection, NYPL, quoted in Stokes, 4:853 and 982.
51. Stokes, 4:982.
52. Broadside, May 16, 1774, in NYHS, quoted in ibid., p. 853.
53. William Smith, *Historical Memoirs* (1969), May 18, 1774, p. 186.
54. Wertenbaker, pp. 36–37.
55. Ibid.
56. Ibid., p. 38.
57. *New York Mercury,* September 5, 1774, quoted in Stokes, 4:865.
58. *Journals of the Continental Congress,* quoted in Stokes, 4:866.
59. Tiedemann, p. 16; Bailyn et al, 1:238 (graph). Total colonial imports from Britain in 1774 were valued at about 2 million pounds sterling.
60. Quoted in Alden, *General Charles Lee,* p. 29. The following section on Lee is drawn from Alden, pp. 1–83, and Chidsey, *The Tide Turns,* pp. 1–4.
61. The classical Greek history of the Peloponnesian War by Thucydides: Chidsey, p. 1.
62. Quoted in Alden, p. 55.
63. Quoted in ibid., p. 64.
64. Quoted in ibid., p. 63.
65. Association agreement: quoted in Burrows and Wallace, p. 218.
66. Quoted in Monaghan, *The Murrays of Murray Hill,* p. 55. Details of the *James* and *Beulah* incidents: ibid., pp. 43–58.
67. Quoted in ibid., p. 56.

3. A GENERAL INSURRECTION OF THE POPULACE

1. Gruber, *Howe Brothers,* p. 54.
2. Quoted in Russell B. Adams, Jr., ed., *The Revolutionaries,* p. 98.
3. All quotes in this paragraph are from Mackesy, *The War for America,* pp. 20–21.
4. North was a masterful politician: ibid., p. 20. North was a moderate, willing to compromise: Gruber, *Howe Brothers,* p. 53.
5. Ibid., p. 52.
6. "Black Dick": ibid., p. 45. Leadership style: ibid., p. 52.
7. Ibid., p. 46.
8. Admiral Howe's physical traits: ibid., p. 45. King chided him: ibid., p. 47.
9. Ibid., pp. 54–55.
10. Ibid., p. 55.
11. Ibid.
12. Stokes, 4:872; Wertenbaker, p. 44.
13. Letter, quoted in Stokes, 4:872.
14. Quoted in ibid., p. 876.
15. Quoted in ibid.
16. *Rivington's Gazetteer,* March 9, 1775, quoted in ibid., p. 877.
17. "New York in the Revolution," *Scribner's Monthly,* January 1876, p. 309.
18. Extract of a letter, quoted in Dawson, *New York City During the American Revolution,* p. 54.
19. William Smith, *Historical Memoirs* (1969), April 29, 1775, p. 222.
20. "Col. Marinus Willett's Narrative," in Dawson, *New York City During the American Revolution,* p. 54.
21. Sears's house became the de facto seat of government: Burrows and Wallace, p. 224.
22. Militia mostly Liberty Boys: Upton, p. 95.
23. Thomas Jones, *History of New York During the Revolutionary War,* quoted in Stokes, 4:882.
24. Quoted in Stokes, 4:882.
25. William Smith, *Historical Memoirs* (1969) April 29, 1775, p. 222.
26. Quoted in Stokes, 4:882.
27. Willett in Dawson, *New York City During the American Revolution,* p. 55.
28. *New York Journal,* May 4, 1775, in Stokes, 4:883–84.
29. *New York Mercury,* May 8, 1775, quoted in ibid., p. 885.
30. *N.Y. Col. Docs.,* 8:297–98, footnote.
31. Quoted in Tiedemann, p. 224.
32. Middlekauff, p. 276.
33. Willett in Dawson, *New York City During the American Revolution,* p. 65.
34. Ibid., p. 58.
35. John Adams, *Autobiography,* quoted in Burnett, ed., *Letters of Members of the Continental Congress,* p. 130.
36. Letter from John Adams to Mrs. Adams, June 17, 1775, quoted in Burnett, p. 130.
37. Ford, ed., *Journals of the Continental Congress,* 1:92.
38. Ward, 1:101.

39. Quoted in Burnett, p. 132.
40. Quoted in Gruber, *Howe Brothers,* p. 25.
41. Quoted in ibid., p. 56; Howe opposed the war . . . Germain's support: ibid., pp. 58–59.
42. Ibid., p. 27.
43. John Adams to Washington, January 6, 1776, letter in the *George Washington Papers at the Library of Congress* (online presentation).
44. Washington, *Writings,* 4:399.
45. Wilcox, *Portrait,* p. 44. Clinton was practically a New Yorker: Sabine, *Murder,* p. 22.
46. Clinton, *The American Rebellion,* pp. xlv, xlviii.
47. Ibid., pp. xvii–xviii.
48. *Journal of the Provincial Congress,* 1:54, quoted in Stokes, 4:894.
49. William Smith, *Historical Memoirs* (1969), June 25, 1775, p. 228d.
50. Quoted in Stokes, 4:895.
51. Washington's task of disciplining the Continental Army: Ward, 1:103–21.
52. Butterfield, ed., *Diary and Autobiography of John Adams,* 2:162.
53. Quoted in Stokes, 4:898.
54. Canadian expedition: Ward, 1:163.
55. This account of the episode at the Battery is drawn from Bliven, *Under the Guns,* pp. 35–39; Manders, p. 5; and Stokes, 4:900.
56. Pastor Shewkirk, *Diary,* p. 103.
57. Quoted in Stokes, 4:901.
58. Burrows and Wallace, p. 227; Stokes, 4:902.
59. Howe's efforts to win appointment as naval commander: Gruber, *Howe Brothers,* pp. 59–63.
60. North's efforts to expand the powers of the peace commission: ibid., pp. 35–38.
61. Ford, 3:280.
62. Manders, p. 5.
63. Montresor, p. 357.
64. *Pennsylvania Journal,* December 6, 1775, quoted in Stokes, 4:905–6.
65. Quoted in Stokes, 4:908.
66. Quoted in Ward, 1:120.
67. Quoted in ibid., p. 121.
68. Sears's warnings got the attention of General Lee in Cambridge: Manders, p. 6.
69. Lee to Washington, January 5, 1776, quoted in ibid. His mission to Newport: ibid.
70. Quoted in ibid. Details of intelligence about a British fleet: ibid.
71. Quoted in Freeman, 4:80. Lee wanted a separate command: Manders, p. 6.
72. Quoted in Freeman, 4:80.
73. Quoted in Alden, p. 9. The story of the name is according to Lee.
74. Quoted in Manders, p. 6.

4. FROM *BOUWERIES* TO BARRICADES

1. Lee's gout and his plans to enter New York: Alden, pp. 96–97; Manders, p. 7; Champagne, p. 99.
2. Women and children fleeing . . . in the dead of winter: Johnston, *Campaign,* pt. 1:52.
3. Quoted in Charles Moore, *The Treason of Charles Lee,* p. ix.

4. His height was an illusion . . . attenuated limbs: Chidsey, p. 1; Russell Adams, Jr., p. 91.

5. Quoted in Dann, *The Revolution Remembered,* p. 105.

6. Lee's past: Alden, pp. 1–33; Chidsey, p. 4. Like Frederick the Great and his hounds: Alden, p. 73.

7. The problem of jurisdiction: Champagne, p. 99.

8. The confrontation and solution: ibid., pp. 99, 101. Lee on a litter, escorted: Manders, p. 7.

9. Andrew Allen, Letter to "My Dear Sally," February 5, 1776, in the Chalmers Collection, NYPL, RBM.

10. Mayor rowed out to see Clinton: Sabine, *Murder,* p. 22.

11. Clinton's arrival and talks with Tryon; revealed destination: Manders, p. 7.

12. Montgomery's reputation and the invasion of Canada: Ward, 1:135–95; Middlekauff, pp. 304–8. McDougall's sons: Champagne, pp. 92–94; Burrows and Wallace, p. 228.

13. Letter of March 22, 1776, quoted in Kelby, *Centennial Notes,* p. 7.

14. Provocative steps by the Provincial Congress to prepare for war: Manders, p. 9. Manders makes the important point that the New York authorities were not spineless—as Lee, the other colonies, and historians have widely interpreted them to be, much to the detriment of the city's reputation in the Revolution—and consequently to the popular neglect of this portion of New York's history. Johnston makes the same argument in *Campaign of 1776,* pt. 1:51–53, where he quotes a letter from the Committee of Safety to Lee, enumerating the quiet preparations it has made while keeping up appearances for the threatening warships.

15. The need to take action against royalists: Manders, p. 12.

16. William Smith, *Historical Memoirs,* quoted in ibid., p. 9.

17. Movement of the ships: Manders, p. 9.

18. Quoted in Sabine, *Murder,* p. 22.

19. Manders, pp. 8–9. The engineer was Captain William Smith, not to be confused with the lawyer.

20. Quoted in Johnston, *Campaign,* pt. 1:54.

21. Quoted in ibid., p. 57.

22. Ford, 4:44–45, quoted in Stokes, 4:911.

23. Letter, Holt to Samuel Adams, quoted in Stokes, 4:912.

24. The following account of Lee's plans: Manders, pp. 8–10; Johnston, *Campaign,* pt. 1:54–57.

25. Johnston, *Campaign,* pt. 1:44.

26. Ibid.

27. Manders, pp. 8–10.

28. The following description of the roads on Manhattan, including the correlation with modern streets (in the footnotes), is drawn from Johnston, *Harlem Heights,* p. 47 (map); Johnston, *Campaign,* pt. 1:40–43; Bliven, *Battle for Manhattan,* endpaper maps and pp. 25–26, 34–35; Martin, *Private Yankee Doodle,* p. 34, note 17 and p. 35, note 18; Augustyn and Cohen, pp. 70–87; *New York City Five Borough Pocket Atlas.*

29. Johnston, *Harlem Heights,* p. 47 (map).

30. *WPA Guide,* p. 273.
31. Manders, pp. 9–10.
32. The following account of Howe's progress in London is from Gruber, *Howe Brothers,* pp. 64–77.

5. WE EXPECT A BLOODY SUMMER AT NEW YORK

1. Quoted in Alden, p. 108. Lee's departure for the South: ibid., pp. 104–9.
2. Stirling's promotion and previous career: Nelson, pp. 71, 73.
3. Stirling appeared to accept Parliament's supremacy: ibid., pp. 49–50. His financial problems: ibid., pp. 52–60; a fortune of 100,000 pounds: ibid., p. 43.
4. Ibid., pp. 61–62.
5. Quoted in ibid., p. 63.
6. Stirling to Philip Schuyler, March 20, 1776, *Stirling Papers,* 4, NYHS.
7. Quoted in Manders, p. 13.
8. Stirling to Hancock, March 17, 1776, quoted in Force, 4ᵗʰ Ser., 5:247–48, cited in Manders, p. 13, note 29.
9. Stirling to Washington, April 1, 1776, quoted in Kelby, p. 10.
10. Washington to Stirling, March 19, 1776, quoted in ibid., p. 8.
11. The following account of the army's move to New York: Manders, pp. 13–14.
12. Stirling's efforts in New Jersey: ibid., p. 13.
13. Washington, *Writings,* 4:398–99.
14. Logistics of the army's move to New York: Manders, pp. 13–14.
15. Desire for reconciliation: Gruber, *Howe Brothers,* p. 97. Timing of transatlantic mail: p. 357.
16. Ibid., pp. 95–96.
17. Quoted in Kelby, pp. 5–6.
18. Manders, p. 12.
19. Quoted in Kelby, p. 7.
20. Ibid., p. 8.
21. Washington to John Adams, April 15, 1776, in Washington, *Writings,* 4:483–84.
22. Upton, p. 102.
23. Quoted in Kelby, pp. 16–17.
24. Tales of "Old Put": Bliven, *Battle for Manhattan,* pp. 51–52; Newton, *Once Upon a Time,* pp. 81–93.
25. Putnam to Hancock, April 7, 1776, quoted in Kelby, p. 13.
26. Quoted in ibid., pp. 15–16.
27. Wertenbaker, p. 79.
28. Manders, p. 31 and Appendix A, p. 57.
29. Bangs, *Journal,* p. 64.
30. Smallpox: Wertenbaker, pp. 79–80. Unregulated inoculation spread the disease more rapidly. However, when combined with quarantine, inoculation was effective: Fenn, *Pox Americana,* pp. 82–83.
31. Additional labor on the forts . . . shortage of firearms: Manders, p. 15.
32. Proclamation, April 29, 1776, quoted in Kelby, p. 21.
33. Whittemore: "John Sullivan: Luckless Irishman," pp. 137–8. Quotes: pp. 141–2.

34. Results of Washington's trip to Philadelphia: Manders, p. 16–17.
35. Item from London, February 18, 1776, quoted in Kelby, p. 27.
36. The king's efforts to enlist foreign troops: Johnston, *Campaign,* pt. 1:28–31.
37. Howe's army takes shape: Willcox, *Portrait,* pp. 94–95.
38. Papers copied by clerks: Gruber, *Howe Brothers,* p. 77.
39. Admiral Howe's voyage: Ibid., p. 88.
40. Washington, *Writings,* 5:91–93.

6. A MIGHTY FLEET OF SHIPS OUR ENEMIES HAVE GOT

1. Washington, *Writings,* 4:498.
2. Ibid., 5:123.
3. Tryon's plot: ibid., p. 182; Manders, p. 18; Bakeless, *Turncoats,* pp. 93–109.
4. Quoted in Bakeless, p. 108.
5. De Lancey's escape: Sabine, *Murder, 1776,* p. 29; and Stokes, 5:935.
6. Quoted in Upton, p. 106.
7. Quoted in ibid., p. 107.
8. The story of the Lorings: Young, pp. 57–86.

Elizabeth Loring's maiden name was Lloyd, and she was born into a wealthy Anglican family on Long Island in 1752; Lloyd's Neck, the site of Lloyd Manor, was a 3,000-acre peninsula jutting into Long Island Sound just east of Oyster Bay. After her father died when she was an infant, her mother remarried and they moved to Boston. At seventeen, "Betsey" married Joshua, who was eight years her senior. When they arrived in New York on the *Crawford* with General Howe's fleet, she was all of twenty-four—more than twenty years younger than the commander in chief.

This femme fatale of the American Revolution has been described in historical works, novels, plays, and verse over the centuries as a beautiful, blue-eyed blonde. However, Philip Young, a literary scholar and a distant relation of the Lloyds on his mother's side, pointed out that even contemporary writers, like Judge Thomas Jones, who ranted about Elizabeth Loring's dissipating effect on General Howe, probably never actually saw her in the flesh. Young claimed that a pair of portraits he was allowed to study—"held very privately by descendants in England," and attributed by these owners to John Singleton Copley—depict the real Elizabeth and her husband, Joshua, whose father is the subject of a well-known Copley canvas.

"These paintings do not look at all like Copleys. But whoever the artist, they are without question portraits of the commissary and his wife," Young wrote. "Joshua presents, as Ethan Allen conceded, a 'phiz of humanity'—gentle, affable, fine-featured, an eerie, plumper duplicate of his father. But it is Elizabeth's likeness that is compelling. Different people looking at the same picture see different things, even under a realistic brush. Yet it is safe to say that the lady, although regal, was not conventionally beautiful: nose and chin a little prominent (that is the Lloyd look, exactly my mother's), mouth a bit too wide, forehead very high with a great crest of hair a la mode above it. She is viewed from the hip up in profile, chin in graceful hand, dressed in a jacket with lace blouse and cuff that leave only hand, face, and throat exposed. She is looking off to the left for what appears to be a long way, but with an eye that seems to permit a long look in. The look about the eye is truly beautiful: gentle, vulnerable, compassionate. The eye itself does not seem to have any dominant color. The hair is brown" (Young, pp. 85–86).

9. Quoted in ibid., p. 61.
10. William Douglas, "Letters," *NYHSQ,* 13:37.
11. Ibid., p. 37.
12. Ibid.
13. Biographical sketch of William Douglas: William Douglas, *NYHSQ,* 12:149.
14. Quoted in Freeman, 4:127.
15. Admiral Howe's voyage to New York: Gruber, *Howe Brothers,* pp. 89–91.
16. Quoted in Stokes, 4:933.
17. Quoted in Commager and Morris, eds., *The Spirit of 'Seventy-six,* p. 422.
18. Burrows and Wallace, p. 233; Sabine, *Murder,* p. 30.
19. Background of French alliance: Bobrick, pp. 190–95.
20. This account of New York's delay in signing: Wall, "New York and the Declaration of Independence," pp. 25–31; Stokes, 4:930, 932, 937–40; Sabine, *Murder,* p. 30.
21. Bangs, p. 57.
22. The fate of the statue's head: Montresor, pp. 123–24; and Stokes, 5:992–93. (The horse's tail can be seen today in a glass case at the New York Historical Society's Henry Luce III Study Center.)
23. Washington, *Writings,* 5:250.
24. Bangs, pp. 59–60.
25. Shewkirk, pp. 110–11.
26. Ibid.
27. Letter, July 17, 1776, quoted in Dawson, *New York City During the American Revolution,* p. 102.
28. Koke, "The Struggle for the Hudson," p. 44.
29. Serle, *Journal,* pp. 28, 30.
30. This account of Admiral Howe's peace effort: Gruber, *Howe Brothers,* p. 93.
31. Quoted in Commager and Morris, pp. 426–27.
32. Washington's rejection of the series of letters: Freeman, 4:138.
33. Quoted in Commager and Morris, p. 427.
34. Quoted in ibid.
35. Gruber, *Howe Brothers,* p. 98.
36. Quoted in ibid., p. 99.
37. All quotes from Franklin's letter: Commager and Morris, pp. 449–50.
38. Gruber, *Howe Brothers,* p. 99.
39. Ibid., p. 100.
40. Letter to "My Dear Son," in the Gilder Lehrman Collection at the Pierpont Morgan Library.

7. THE BRITISH JUGGERNAUT REACHES FULL STRENGTH

1. Details of Parker's fleet: Field, pt. 1:129.
2. Clinton accepted Parker's vague proposal: Clinton, pp. xix–xxii.

3. Moultrie, not Lee, emerged as the hero at Charleston: Ward, 2:676–78; Alden, p. 129.

4. Gruber, *Howe Brothers,* p. 101.

5. Details of Hessians' arrival: Gruber, *Howe Brothers,* p. 101; Collier, p. 300.

6. Collier, p. 298.

7. Stone, trans., *Letters of Brunswick and Hessian Officers,* p. 194.

8. Ibid., p. 185.

9. Blacks joined the British: Burrows and Wallace, p. 248; Hodges, *Root and Branch,* p. 144; Fenn, *Pox Americana,* pp. 55–60. Dunmore quoted in ibid., p. 55.

10. The British force had reached full strength: Gruber, *Howe Brothers,* p. 101.

11. Both quotes are from Douglas, *NYHSQ,* 13:80.

12. Koke, pp. 65–66.

13. Both Hale quotes are from Nathan Hale to Enoch Hale, August 20, 1776, letter in the collection of the Sons of the Revolution in the State of New York.

14. Collier, pp. 300–301.

15. Shortage of British ships and men and need to capture Washington's army: Gruber, *Howe Brothers,* pp. 102–4.

16. The following account of General Howe's change of plans is from ibid., pp. 104–7.

17. The fortification of northern Manhattan: Gallagher, p. 74; Manders, pp. 17, 27–28.

18. Augmentation of Brooklyn defenses . . . sealing off peninsula: Johnston, *Campaign,* pt. 1:67, 73.

19. Brooklyn forts: ibid., pp. 68–77; Manders, p. 16; and Gallagher, pp. 78–80.

20. Nathanael Greene's background: Russell Adams Jr., pp. 131–32.

21. Quoted in Gallagher, pp. 70–71.

22. Details of "putrid fever": Manders, p. 31 and Appendix A, p. 57.

23. Quoted in Dawson, *New York City During the American Revolution,* p. 105.

24. *Journal of the Provincial Congress,* 1:568, quoted in Manders, p. 31.

25. The final collapse of the Canadian expedition: Whittemore, pp. 140–41; Boatner, pp. 173–79.

26. Sullivan's promotion: Whittemore, p. 142.

27. Quoted in ibid., pp. 141–42.

28. Sullivan's fateful decision to defend Gowanus Heights: Manders, pp. 33–34.

29. Fertile outwash plain: Gallagher, p. 82.

30. "Deep winding cut": Field, pt. 1:160.

31. Quoted in Manders, p. 34.

32. Bakeless, p. 111.

33. Details of agent's report: Manders, p. 34.

34. The following account of the storm is quoted in Field, pt. 2:348–52 (document 15).

8. THE INVASION OF LONG ISLAND

1. At nine A.M. Admiral Howe . . . contingent of flatboats: Field, pt. 1:148; Manders, p. 34.

2. To escort the seventy-five flatboats . . . the shore: Field, pt. 1:148; Manders, p. 34; Gallagher, p. 88.

3. Manders, p. 34.

4. Serle, pp. 72, 74.

5. The beauty of the landing . . . in the east: Manders, pp. 34–35; Johnston, *Campaign,* pt. 1:141–42.
6. Field, pt. 1:153.
7. Quoted in Commager and Morris, p. 429.
8. Washington received an inaccurate estimate of 8,000 British troops: Manders, p. 35.
9. Quoted in ibid., p. 34.
10. Quoted in ibid., p. 35.
11. William Douglas, *NYHSQ,* 13:81.
12. American skirmishers brought back a Hessian corpse: Johnston, *Campaign,* pt. 1:147.
13. Quoted in Manders, p. 35.
14. Washington began daily trips to Long Island and sent reinforcements: ibid.
15. Washington, *Papers,* 6:126.
16. Quoted in Manders, p. 36.
17. Quoted in Johnston, *Campaign,* pt. 2:29.
18. Biographical sketch of General Samuel Parsons: Boatner, pp. 833–34.
19. Quoted in Manders, p. 36.
20. William Howe, "A Proclamation, August 23, 1776," in the Gilder Lehrman Collection at the Pierpont Morgan Library.
21. Manders, p. 35.
22. Ibid., p. 37.
23. William Douglas, *NYHSQ,* 13:82.
24. Estimate of 9,000 American troops: Manders, p. 37.
25. Manders, pp. 31, 37.
26. Ibid., p. 37.
27. Quoted in Johnston, *Campaign,* pt. 2:35.
28. Manders, pp. 37–38.
29. Quoted in Johnston, *Campaign,* pt. 2:61.
30. Quoted in ibid., pt. 1:194, footnote.
31. Reasons that more cavalry was not available to Sullivan: Manders, p. 37.
32. Quoted in Johnston, *Campaign,* pt. 2:63–64.
33. Quoted in Manders, p. 37.
34. Washington, *Papers,* 6:109–10.
35. Clinton, p. 39.
36. Ibid.
37. Ibid., p. 41.
38. Ibid., p. 41, footnote 3.
39. Quoted in Willcox, *Portrait,* p. 105. Reaction of Grant and others at headquarters: ibid., and Fleming, *1776,* p. 311.
40. Fleming, *1776,* p. 311.
41. Clinton, p. 41, note 3.
42. Ibid., p. 42.
43. Field, pt. 1:159.
44. Clinton, p. 42.
45. Firing probably from sentry posts . . . Woodhull was unaware: Manders, p. 39; Stokes, 5:1003.
46. Clinton, p. 42.

47. Johnston, *Campaign,* pt. 1:177–78.
48. Clinton, p. 42.
49. The British interrogated Howard and forced him to act as their guide: Gallagher, pp. 105–6; Onderdonk, ed., *Revolutionary Incidents,* pp. 138–39. In these two accounts, the tavern owner's son claims that General Howe did the interrogating, but Clinton's narrative, p. 42, rules that out, because Howe was too far behind him to be in the area of the roadhouse at that time.
50. "New Utrecht, Long Island, August 26, 1776, After Orders," in *British adjutant's orderly book, 1776–1777,* in the Gilder Lehrman Collection at the Pierpont Morgan Library.
51. Quoted in Gallagher, p. 107.
52. Field, pt. 1:289.
53. Bobrick, pp. 213–14.
54. Parry, pp. 22, 24.
55. Quoted in Field, pt. 2:372 (document 21).
56. Quoted in ibid., p. 373.

9. THE BATTLE OF BROOKLYN

1. Gallagher, p. 102.
2. Manders, p. 40.
3. Putnam's response . . . elite troops under Stirling: Manders, p. 40; Johnston, *Campaign,* pt. 1:163.
4. Quoted in ibid., pt. 2:35.
5. Letter from Stirling to Washington, August 29, 1776, quoted in Washington, *Papers,* 6:159.
6. Stirling positioned his men: Onderdonk, p. 141.
7. Johnston, *Campaign,* pt. 1:167.
8. The Americans' motley collection of firearms: Ward, 1:31; Peterson, *Continental Soldier,* p. 23.
9. Sawyer, *Firearms,* 1:70–72.
10. Discussion of the rifle: Peterson, pp. 38–44.
11. The musket ball stayed in the body: Neumann, "A Revolutionary Soldier's Life."
12. Discussion of the musket: Peterson, pp. 24–29; Frey, *The British Soldier,* pp. 96–103.
13. Discussion of the bayonet: Ibid.
14. Field tactics: Peterson, p. 26. British variations on the bayonet attack: Neumann, "A Revolutionary Soldier's Life."
15. Quoted in Onderdonk, p. 147.
16. Stirling detected the encirclement: Manders, p. 43; British losses were highest at Battle Hill: Johnston, *Campaign,* pt. 1:172.
17. Manders, p. 40.
18. Quoted in Johnston, *Campaign,* pt. 2:62.
19. Manders, pp. 41–42.
20. Ibid.
21. Quoted in Onderdonk, p. 138.
22. Lurid tales of slaughter were greatly exaggerated: Johnston, *Campaign,* pt. 1:186, 206; Stevenson and Wilson, *The Battle of Long Island,* p. 13.

23. Quoted in Onderdonk, p. 135.
24. Clinton, p. 43.
25. Ibid., p. 44.
26. Ibid., p. 44, footnote 7.
27. "Stormed with rage": quote from the *London Chronicle,* in Onderdonk, p. 138.
28. Stevenson and Wilson, p. 14.
29. Manders, p. 45.
30. Quoted in Stevenson and Wilson, p. 14.
31. Quoted in ibid.
32. Nelson, p. 88.
33. Martin, *A Narrative,* pp. 18–19. (*A Narrative* refers to the original 1830 edition.)
34. Ibid., p. 19.
35. Ibid., p. 20.
36. Ibid.
37. Ibid., p. 21.
38. Movement of Admiral Howe's ships: Onderdonk, pp. 132–33; Manders, p. 46. Washington's decision to come over to Brooklyn: Ibid.
39. Quoted in Onderdonk, p. 148.
40. Most of the Marylanders were captured, not killed: Johnston, *Campaign,* pt. 1:188; Stevenson and Wilson, p. 16.
41. Stirling to Washington, Washington, *Papers,* 1:159–61.
42. Manders, pp. 45–46; Johnston, *Campaign,* pt. 1:190.
43. Casualty figures: Johnston, *Campaign,* pt. 1:195, 202–6; Manders, Appendix E, pp. 62–63.
44. Quoted in Johnston, *Campaign,* pt. 1:202.
45. Quoted in ibid., pt. 1:204.
46. Several modern authorities agree: Johnston, in ibid., pt. 1:202–6, argues that Washington's figure of 1,000 captured and killed was correct; Peckham, p. 22, lists 897 captured and 200 killed; Manders, in appendix E, pp. 62–63, estimates a total of 800 to 900 captured and killed. Stevenson and Wilson, on p. 16, support Johnston's numbers for those captured as well as for the total number of Americans killed and wounded.
47. Johnston, *Campaign,* pt. 1:180.
48. Quoted in ibid., pt. 2:38.
49. Quoted in ibid., pt. 2:36.
50. Quoted in Scheer and Rankin, *Rebels and Redcoats,* p. 175.
51. Expecting the British . . . settle down for the night: Manders, p. 47. Number of grenadiers: Stiles 1:286, note 1.

10. A WISE AND MOST FORTUNATE RETREAT

1. Tallmadge, *Memoir,* p. 9.
2. Biographical sketch of Tallmadge and the quote: ibid., p. 6.
3. Ibid., p. 9.
4. Ibid., p. 10.
5. Ibid.
6. Mifflin's background: Boatner, pp. 704–5.

7. The "amphibious units" raised morale: Billias, *General John Glover*, p. 99.

8. Graydon, *Memoirs*, p. 164.

9. Biographical sketch of Glover: Billias, *General John Glover*, pp. 16–18, 73–75.

10. Manders, p. 47.

11. Quoted in Johnston, *Campaign*, pt. 1:210.

12. Martin, *A Narrative*, pp. 21–22.

13. On Wednesday evening . . . their advancing trench: Manders, p. 47.

14. Gordon, *History*, 2:102–4.

15. Quoted in Johnston, *Campaign*, pt. 1:218.

16. Secrecy was vital to the retreat: ibid., pp. 219–21.

17. Heath, *Memoirs*, p. 49.

18. Quoted in Johnston, *Campaign*, pt. 1:218.

19. Orders went out a little before noon: ibid., p. 219, note 1.

20. Stiles, 1:284–85, note 3. He argues convincingly that the Cornell-Pierrepont mansion was the site of the war council. However, Johnston, *Campaign*, pt. 1:213, footnote 1, cites a letter from John Morin Scott as evidence that it took place at Philip Livingston's mansion on Hicks Street. (The letter is in pt. 2:36–37.) The location of the council therefore remains a matter of debate.

21. Johnston, *Campaign*, pt. 1:216.

22. Quoted in ibid., pt. 2:37–38.

23. Intelligence from General Heath: Onderdonk, p. 162.

24. Martin, *A Narrative*, pp. 22–23.

25. Ibid., p. 23.

26. Graydon, pp. 166–67.

27. Gordon, 2:102.

28. McDougall's attempt to call off the retreat: ibid. Eleven round-trips: Gallagher, p. 149.

29. Gordon, 2:103.

30. Manders, p. 48.

31. Quoted in Onderdonk, p. 158. Gunwhales within three inches of the water: ibid.

32. Graydon, p. 167.

33. Gordon, 2:103.

34. Tallmadge, p. 10.

35. Manders, p. 48.

36. Tallmadge, p. 10.

37. Graydon, p. 167.

38. Quoted in Scheer and Rankin, pp. 170–71.

39. Why the British failed to act remains a mystery: Manders, p. 48. Stiles, 1:289, quotes a British account in the *Parliamentary Register*, vol. 13, which asserts only that "pickets marched twenty-five minutes after" the lines were found to be empty. It does not explain why General James Robertson did not hear of the retreat until seven A.M. His brigade "was ordered to march at eight; but while marching to the ferry, he was ordered towards Hell-Gate to meet Lee, reported to be landing there with an army." Perhaps Washington had spread some disinformation of his own.

40. Gallagher, p. 151; Hibbert, *Redcoats and Rebels*, p. 124.

41. Quoted in Stiles, 1:287, note 1.

42. Tallmadge, pp. 10–11.

43. Gordon, 2:104.
44. Washington, *Papers,* 6:177.
45. Gordon, 2:104.
46. Tallmadge, p. 11.
47. Quoted in Wheeler, *Voices of 1776,* p. 138.
48. Quoted in ibid.
49. Collier, p. 304.

II. THE FIRST SUBMARINE, A PEACE CONFERENCE, AND A SECOND RETREAT

1. Shewkirk, p. 115.
2. Washington, *Papers,* 6:199–201.
3. Quoted in Johnston, *Campaign,* pt. 2:65.
4. Quoted in ibid., pp. 65–66.
5. Washington, *Papers,* 6:199–201.
6. Peterson, pp. 1–18.
7. William Douglas, *NYHSQ,* 13:119.
8. Johnston, *Campaign,* pt. 1:226.
9. William Douglas, *NYHSQ,* 13:121.
10. Quoted in Johnston, *Campaign,* pt. 1:229.
11. Ibid., p. 230.
12. Disposition of American troops: ibid., p. 228.
13. Quoted in ibid., pp. 226–27.
14. Washington's support of Bushnell: *Naval Documents,* 6:1499–1500.
15. Ibid., p. 1502.
16. Quoted in Stokes, 5:997.
17. Quoted in ibid.
18. Quoted in ibid.
19. Ibid.
20. The torpedo: ibid., p. 998.
21. Quoted in *Naval Documents,* 6:1508.
22. Stokes, 5:998.
23. Quoted in ibid.
24. Quoted in ibid.
25. Bushnell's conclusion as to what foiled the mission: *Naval Documents,* 6:1506.
26. Quoted in Stokes, 5:998.
27. Quoted in ibid., p. 997.
28. Quoted in *Naval Documents,* 6:1511.
29. Collier's *Journal,* quoted in Field, pt. 2:413–14.
30. Washington, *Writings,* 5:507, footnote 31.
31. The following account of the conference by Adams is quoted in Commager and Morris, p. 455.
32. Quoted in Russell B. Adams Jr., p. 99.
33. Johnston, *Campaign,* pt. 1:230.
34. Howe's preparations for the invasion: Gruber, *Howe Brothers,* pp. 120–21.

12. THE INVASION OF MANHATTAN

1. Quoted in Stokes, 5:1011.
2. Clinton, pp. 44–45.
3. Quoted in Paltsits, "The Jeopardy of Washington," p. 255.
4. Martin, *Private Yankee Doodle*, p. 32, footnote 15.
5. Martin, *A Narrative*, pp. 25–26.
6. Bliven, *Battle for Manhattan*, p. 32.
7. Martin, *A Narrative*, p. 26.
8. Quoted in Stokes, 5:1012.
9. Shewkirk, p. 117.
10. Quoted in Hibbert, p. 126.
11. All quotes in this paragraph are from Martin, *A Narrative*, pp. 26–27.
12. Bliven, *Battle for Manhattan*, pp. 37–38.
13. Ibid., p. 39.
14. Quoted in Hibbert, p. 126.
15. Clinton, pp. 46–47.
16. Paltsits, p. 268; Bliven, *Battle for Manhattan*, p. 47.
17. Heath, p. 52.
18. Quoted in Johnston, *Campaign*, pt. 2:93.
19. Quoted in Paltsits, p. 265.
20. Quoted in ibid., pp. 262–63.
21. Quoted in ibid., p. 263.
22. Force, ed., *American Archives*, 5th ser., 2:1013–14.
23. Quoted in Stokes, 5:1014.
24. Martin, *A Narrative*, p. 27.
25. Ibid., pp. 27–28.
26. Ibid., p. 28.
27. Ibid., pp. 31–32.
28. William Douglas, *NYHSQ*, 13:122.
29. Washington and Putnam in today's Times Square: *New York Herald*, November 26, 1893. The article describes a series of plaques installed around the city by the Sons of the Revolution to celebrate the 110th anniversary of Evacuation Day. The plaque in Times Square, which is no longer there, described the meeting of the two generals. Putnam and Burr rounded up troops in the city: Bliven, *Battle for Manhattan*, pp. 52–53.
30. Bliven, *Battle for Manhattan*, p. 57.
31. Details of the column's route up the West Side: Johnston, *Campaign*, pt. 1:238–39; Bliven, *Battle for Manhattan*, pp. 53–54, 57–58.
32. Quoted in Johnston, *Campaign*, pt. 2:89.
33. Ward, 2:937–39; Bliven, *Battle for Manhattan*, p. 58.
34. Mary Murray a "warm Whig": Monaghan, p. 68–69.
35. Ibid., pp. 21–22.
36. Ibid., p. 67; Ward, Appendix D, 2:937–39.

37. Bliven, *Battle for Manhattan,* p. 61; Stokes, 5:1012.
38. Shewkirk, p. 17.
39. Quoted in Stokes, 5:1012.
40. Smallwood's tactics at McGowan's Pass (including footnote): Bliven, *Battle for Manhattan,* pp. 62–64.
41. Quoted in Johnston, *Campaign,* pt. 2:90.
42. Quoted in ibid.
43. Ward, 1:244; Bliven, *Battle for Manhattan,* p. 65.
44. Quoted in Commager and Morris, p. 467.
45. Quoted in Johnston, *Campaign,* pt. 2:90.

13. THE BATTLE OF HARLEM HEIGHTS

1. Shewkirk, pp. 117–18.
2. Stokes, 5:1026.
3. Shewkirk, pp. 117–18.
4. Quoted in Stokes, 5:1015.
5. Quoted in ibid., 5:1016.
6. Shewkirk, p. 118.
7. Johnston, *Harlem Heights,* p. 51.
8. Washington, *Papers,* 6:314.
9. Johnston, *Harlem Heights,* pp. 46–48.
10. Washington, *Papers,* 6:314.
11. Quoted in Johnston, *Harlem Heights,* pp. 55, 195. Knowlton's background: Bliven, *Battle for Manhattan,* pp. 85–86; Johnston, *Harlem Heights,* pp. 53–55.
12. Bliven, *Battle for Manhattan,* p. 86.
13. First encounter at Jones's farmhouse: Johnston, *Harlem Heights,* p. 59.
14. Washington, *Papers,* 6:331.
15. Force, 5th ser., 2:443–45.
16. Washington, *Papers,* 6:331; Washington's plan of attack: Johnston, *Harlem Heights,* pp. 68–69.
17. Quoted in Scheer and Rankin, p. 185.
18. Johnston, *Harlem Heights,* p. 76.
19. Force, 5th ser., 2:444.
20. Martin, *A Narrative,* p. 32.
21. Montresor, p. 121.
22. Martin, *A Narrative,* p. 33.
23. Quoted in Johnston, *Campaign,* pt. 2:87.
24. Johnston, *Harlem Heights,* p. 59.
25. Martin, *A Narrative,* p. 32.
26. Washington, *Papers,* 6:325.
27. Ibid., 6:333.
28. Ibid., 6:346.
29. Quoted in Johnston, *Campaign,* pt. 2:91.
30. Clinton, p. 47.
31. Martin, *A Narrative,* p. 33.

32. Ibid., p. 33.

33. Ibid., pp. 33–34.

14. THE GREAT FIRE AND THE EXECUTION OF NATHAN HALE

1. Colden's death: *N.Y. Col. Docs.*, 8:685–86.

2. Quoted in Stokes, 5:1024.

3. Maps of fire damage: Tiedemann, p. 255; Burrows and Wallace, p. 243.

4. Force, 5th ser., 2:462.

5. Ibid., pp. 493–94.

6. *Naval Documents,* 6:930.

7. Force, 5th ser., 2:493–94.

8. Ibid.

9. *Naval Documents,* 6:930.

10. Ranlet, *New York Loyalists,* p. 76.

11. Quoted in Stokes, 5:1023.

12. Quoted in ibid., 1024.

13. Stokes, 5:1023.

14. Force, 5th ser., 2:524.

15. Washington, *Papers,* 6:369.

16. Ibid., pp. 493–95.

17. *Naval Documents,* 6:931.

18. Force, 5th ser., 2:493–94.

19. Wertenbaker, p. 98.

20. Force, 5th ser., 2:493–94.

21. Ibid.

22. Quoted in Mackesy, p. 88.

23. Johnston, *Harlem Heights,* p. 48.

24. Fortifications and disposition of troops on Harlem Heights, ibid., pp. 48–50.

25. Heath, p. 53; Scheer and Rankin, p. 187.

26. Bakeless, p. 113.

27. Hale's disguise: Shelton, "Mission of Nathan Hale," p. 283.

28. Poor planning for Hale's mission: Bakeless, pp. 113–15.

29. Quoted in ibid., p. 114.

Hale's personality was apparently so delightful that despite his occasionally severe moral tone, he was tremendously popular with his peers and his troops. Lieutenant Elisha Bostwick, a close friend in the same regiment, described Hale as "a little above the common stature in height, his shoulders of a moderate breadth, his limbs strait and & very plump: regular features—very fair skin—blue eyes—flaxen or very light hair which was always kept short—his eyebrows a shade darker than his hair & his voice rather sharp or piercing—his bodily agility was remarkable I have seen him follow a football & kick it over the tops of the trees in the Bowery at New York, (an exercise which he was fond of)—his mental powers seemed to be above the common sort—his mind of a sedate and sober cast, & he was undoubtedly Pious; for it was remarked that when any of the Soldiers of his company were sick he always visited them & usually prayed for and with them in their sickness." Bostwick also recounted an incident in which Captain Hale discovered some of his troops "in a bye place Playing Cards." According to Bostwick, Hale announced, "This won't do,—give me your Cards," and "chopd them to pieces, & it was done in such a manner that the men were rather pleased than otherwise." Quoted in Stokes, 5:1025.

30. Bakeless, p. 113.
31. Quoted in ibid., p. 114.
32. Ibid., p. 115.
33. Hale's probable route north and disposition of British troops: ibid., p. 117.
34. Hale's capture: ibid., pp. 117–19; Pennypacker, *George Washington's Spies,* pp. 28–29.
35. Hale had returned to Manhattan with intelligence: Bakeless, p. 117. Hale concealed papers in his clothes: Hull's memoirs, quoted in Commager and Morris, p. 476.
36. Bakeless, p. 119. The story of Hale's detention overnight in the greenhouse is often repeated but remains undocumented.
37. Hull's memoirs, quoted in Bakeless, p. 120.
38. Ibid.
39. Quoted in Shelton, "Mission of Nathan Hale," p. 270.
40. Quoted in Commager and Morris, pp. 475–76.
41. Quoted in Bakeless, p. 119.
42. Spies court-martialed then and in subsequent wars: ibid.
43. Hale is an unlikely culprit because of his route: Pennypacker, pp. 27–28, footnote.
44. The fire rivaled the Gunpowder Plot: quoted in Shelton, "Mission of Nathan Hale," p. 277.
45. Quoted in Bakeless, p. 122.
46. Quoted in ibid., p. 122.
47. Ibid., p. 120.
48. Ibid.
49. Quoted in Pennypacker, pp. 20–21.
50. Washington's spy network: Bakeless, pp. 122–83; Pennypacker, pp. 30–31.
51. Delay in dissemination of Hale's story: Pennypacker, p. 21.
52. Martin, *A Narrative,* p. 34.
53. Washington, *Papers,* 6:366, footnote 3.
54. Thumb chopped off: Reed to Mrs. Reed, Force, 5th ser., 2:444.
55. Washington, *Papers,* 6:366, footnote 3.
56. Martin, *A Narrative,* p. 35.

15. THROG'S NECK AND THE BATTLE OF PELHAM BAY

1. William Douglas, *NYHSQ,* 13:158.
2. Ibid., p. 159.
3. Martin, *A Narrative,* pp. 35–36.
4. The following account of the Smiths' move to Livingston Manor: Upton, pp. 107–10.
5. Gruber, *Howe Brothers,* p. 157.
6. Boatner, p. 132.
7. Clinton, pp. 47–48.
8. Ibid., pp. 48–49.
9. Ibid., p. 49.

10. Quoted in Commager and Morris, p. 485.
11. Hufeland, *Westchester County,* p. 111.
12. Ward, 1:255.
13. Heath, pp. 59–60.
14. Hufeland, p. 112.
15. Quoted in Johnston, *Campaign,* pt. 1:265–66, note 1.
16. Quoted in Billias, "Pelham Bay," p. 23.
17. Heath, p. 63.
18. Quoted in Johnston, *Campaign,* pt. 1:270–71.
19. William Douglas, *NYHSQ,* 13:160.
20. Reed and others credited Lee with saving the army: Alden, pp. 144, 330, note 20.
21. Clinton, p. 49, footnote 3.
22. Fort Washington held, despite misgivings: Ward, 1:269–70; Alden, p. 141.
23. Billias, "Pelham Bay," p. 26.
24. Heath, p. 63.
25. Ward, 1:256–57.
26. Carrington, *Battles,* p. 236. The army screened itself from the British with entrenched positions along the Bronx River.
27. Ward, 1:256-57.
28. Force, 5th ser., 2:1188.
29. Ibid.
30. Billias, "Pelham Bay," p. 30.
31. Glover devised a relay to ambush the British: ibid., pp. 30–31.
32. Force, 5th ser., 2:1188.
33. Ibid.
34. Ibid.
35. Quoted in Billias, "Pelham Bay," p. 36.
36. Force, 5th ser., 2:1188.
37. Quoted in Billias, "Pelham Bay," p. 34.
38. Force, 5th ser., 2:1188.
39. Quoted in Billias, "Pelham Bay," p. 35.
40. Casualty estimates: ibid., pp. 35–36.
41. Ibid., pp. 36–38. David Osborn, site manager of the St. Paul's Church National Historic Site in Mount Vernon, N.Y., is one authority who disputes the high Hessian casualty figures suggested by Billias. The Hessian wounded were brought to the church after the battle, and the dead were buried in the adjacent graveyard.
42. Ibid., pp. 35–36.
43. Abbatt, *Battle of Pell's Point,* p. 1.
44. Billias, "Pelham Bay," p. 34.
45. Force, 5th ser., 2:1188.

16. THE BATTLE OF WHITE PLAINS

1. Clinton, p. 50.
2. Ibid., pp. xxiii–xxiv.
3. Ibid., p. 50.
4. Ward, 1:260–61.

5. The following account of Putnam's mission is quoted from Johnston, *Campaign,* pt. 2:137–39.
6. Martin, *A Narrative,* p. 38.
7. Ibid., pp. 38–39.
8. Martin, *Private Yankee Doodle,* p. 52, note 25.
9. Tallmadge, p. 13.
10. Ward, 1:267.
11. Tallmadge, p. 13.
12. Clinton, p. 51.
13. Ibid.
14. Heath, p. 69.
15. Martin, *A Narrative,* p. 40.
16. Ibid., p. 40.
17. Ibid., pp. 40–41.
18. Tallmadge, p. 14.
19. Quoted in Commager and Morris, pp. 489–90.
20. Quoted in ibid.
21. Samuel Smith, "Autobiography," p. 4; Ward, 1:264–65.
22. Samuel Smith, "Autobiography," p. 4.
23. Quoted in Commager and Morris, p. 490.
24. Casualty figures: Ward, 1:266.
25. Quoted in Johnston, *Campaign,* pt. 2:139.
26. Tallmadge, p. 14.
27. Martin, *A Narrative,* p. 41.
28. Force, 5ᵗʰ ser., 3:474.
29. Martin, *A Narrative,* pp. 41–42.
30. Ward, 1:267.
31. Heath, p. 73.

17. THE FALL OF FORT WASHINGTON

1. Quoted in Stokes, 5:1032.
2. Capture of Fort Independence: Carrington, p. 242. British withdrawal: Heath, pp. 74–75.
3. Quoted in Heath, p. 75.
4. Ibid.
5. Ward, 1:268.
6. Both quotes are in Carrington, p. 243.
7. Quoted in ibid., pp. 242–43.
8. Quoted in ibid., p. 242.
9. Quoted in ibid., p. 243.
10. Quoted in ibid., pp. 244–45.
11. Precarious division of the army: Scheer and Rankin, p. 196.
12. Instructions to Lee: Quoted in Carrington, p. 245.
13. Ibid.
14. Quoted in Commager and Morris, pp. 491–92.

15. Indecisive exchange about number of men needed: Ward, 1:270–71; Freeman, 4:246–48; Commager and Morris, p. 498.
16. Topography of northern Manhattan: Ward, 1:268; Carrington, p. 248.
17. Disposition of American forces: Carrington, p. 248; Ward, 1:271.
18. Graydon's assessment of the fort: Graydon, pp. 186, 193.
19. Quoted in Scheer and Rankin, p. 198.
20. Quoted in Johnston, *Campaign,* pt. 1:278.
21. Freeman, 4:249.
22. Quoted in Carrington, p. 249.
23. Wiederhold, "Capture of Fort Washington," pp. 95–96.
24. Howe's strategy: Ward, 1:271; Carrington, pp. 249–50; Scheer and Rankin, p. 197.
25. Wiederhold, p. 96.
26. Ibid.
27. Graydon, p. 197.
28. Howe's plan: Ward, 1:271; Carrington, pp. 249–50.
29. Quoted in Stokes, 5:1035.
30. Quoted in ibid.
31. Graydon, p. 200.
32. Ward, 1:272.
33. Wiederhold, p. 96.
34. Quoted in Commager and Morris, p. 494.
35. Wiederhold, pp. 96–97.
36. Plaque at Fort Tryon Park; *American National Biography,* 5:499–501.
37. Wiederhold, pp. 95–96.
38. Ward, 1:273.
39. Wiederhold, p. 97.
40. Ward, 1:274.
41. Attack of the force under Sterling: Ward, 1:273–74; Graydon, pp. 200–201.
42. Ibid., p. 201.
43. Reuber's account of the attack, in Commager and Morris, p. 494.
44. Quoted in ibid.
45. Hohenstein's account of the demand for surrender, in Lowell, *The Hessians,* p. 81.
46. Quoted in ibid.
47. Ibid.
48. Quoted in Carrington, p. 250.
49. Quoted in Lowell, pp. 81–82.
50. Quoted in Scheer and Rankin, p. 200.
51. Quoted in ibid.
52. Wiederhold, pp. 96–97.
53. Casualty figures: Ward, 1:274.
54. Quoted in Scheer and Rankin, p. 200.
55. Cornwallis took Fort Lee on November 20: Ward, 1:276–77.
56. Carrington, pp. 251–52.
57. Amounts of military supplies lost: Ward, 1:274.
58. Quoted in Carrington, p. 252.

59. Quoted in Commager and Morris, p. 498.
60. Carrington, p. 253; Bobrick, p. 229.
61. Quoted in Johnston, *Campaign,* pt. 1:284–85.
62. Quoted in Carrington, p. 253.

18. TRENTON AND PRINCETON, THE END OF THE CAMPAIGN

1. William Douglas, *NYHSQ,* 14:42.
2. Symonds and Clipson, *Battlefield Atlas,* pp. 30–31; Ward, 1:280.
3. Quoted in Commager and Morris, p. 505.
4. Symonds, pp. 30–31.
5. Quoted in Commager and Morris, p. 499.
6. Heath, p. 87; Alden, p. 154.
7. Quoted in Commager and Morris, p. 498.
8. Quoted in ibid.
9. Alden, pp. 149–150.
10. Symonds, pp. 30–31.
11. Clinton, pp. xxiii, 55; Gruber, *Howe Brothers,* pp. 128, 135–36.
12. Ibid., p. 135.
13. Ibid., pp. 147–48.
14. Ibid.
15. Ibid., p. 148.
16. Ibid. Clinton's parting advice to General Howe: Clinton, p. 56.
17. Stokes, 5:1040.
18. Alden, pp. 153–54.
19. Ibid., p. 155.
20. Quoted in Commager and Morris, p. 500.
21. Quoted in ibid., p. 502.
22. Wilkinson's account of Lee's capture: quoted in ibid., p. 504.
23. Alden, pp. 157, 158.
24. Quoted in Commager and Morris, p. 502.
25. Alden, p. 161.
26. Ibid., p. 159.
27. Quoted in Commager and Morris, p. 504.
28. Quoted in ibid.
29. Howe's proclamation: Gruber, *Howe Brothers,* pp. 146–47, 149–50. The quote by Serle is in Ranlet, p. 77.
30. Ranlet, p. 77.
31. Quoted in Commager and Morris, p. 510.
32. Reed's letter of December 22 in Commager and Morris, p. 510; Symonds, p. 31.
33. Quoted in Commager and Morris, p. 511.
34. Attack on Trenton: Symonds, pp. 30–31; Commager and Morris, pp. 507–8.
35. Quoted in Stokes, 5:1041.
36. Quoted in ibid.
37. After the appeal, Washington had about 5,000 troops: Bobrick, p. 234.
38. Alden, p. 162.

39. "Bag the fox": quoted in Commager and Morris, p. 518.
40. Number of prisoners and casualties at Princeton: Symonds, pp. 32–33.
41. Quoted in Commager and Morris, p. 519.
42. Quoted in Alden, p. 162.
43. Martin, *Private Yankee Doodle,* pp. 57–58.
44. Martin, *A Narrative,* pp. 209–10.
45. Douglas's return to his family: William Douglas, *NYHSQ,* 12:149.
46. Quoted in Heath, p. 97.
47. Quoted in Commager and Morris, p. 532.
48. Quoted in ibid., p. 530.
49. Quoted in ibid.
50. Privation at Morristown similar to Valley Forge: Symonds, p. 35. Washington's position and tactics: Bobrick, p. 237.
51. Quoted in Bobrick, p. 237.

19. OCCUPIED NEW YORK

1. Cresswell, *Journal,* p. 244.
2. Ibid., pp. 244–45.
3. Quoted in Bobrick, p. 238.
4. Burrows and Wallace, p. 247.
5. Quoted in Monaghan, p. 69.
6. Ibid., pp. 74–75.
7. Quoted in Young, p. 61.
8. Quoted in Frank Moore, *Diary of the American Revolution,* p. 282.
9. Prison conditions: Wertenbaker, pp. 163–67; Burrows and Wallace, p. 253.
10. Death toll on prison ships: Greene, *Recollections of the Jersey,* p. viii; Stokes, in 5: 1160, questions generally accepted estimates.
11. Quoted in Young, p. 71.
12. Quoted in Onderdonk, p. 246. The story that Cunningham, after this confession, was hanged for forgery is often repeated but was never documented. Boatner, p. 312, cites Lossing, who points out that the British prison records make no mention of Cunningham.
13. "Canvass-town": Quoted in Stokes, 5:1022.
14. Quoted in ibid., pp. 1021–22.
15. Sanitation problems: Burrows and Wallace, pp. 111, 184–85, 229, 251; Cresswell, pp. 244–45.
16. Houses were marked *G.R.* for George Rex; red ribbons: Stokes, 5:1026.
17. Shewkirk, p. 120.
18. Quoted in Stokes, 5:1097.
19. Quoted in ibid., 5:1083. Two bodyguards: 5:1082.
20. Police court's jurisdiction: Upton, pp. 123–24.
21. Burrows and Wallace, pp. 248–49; Hodges, p. 151.
22. Bleucke and Williams: Hodges, pp. 142, 147; Ottley and Weatherby, eds., *The Negro In New York,* pp. 53–54.
23. Quoted in Hodges, p. 150. More blacks fought as patriots: Bobrick, p. 162.
24. Quoted in Stokes, 5:1042.

25. Quoted in Ranlet, p. 78.
26. Quoted in Stokes, 5:1044.
27. Quoted in ibid.
28. Newspapers during the occupation: Stokes, 5:1027, 1034, 1056–7; Burrows and Wallace, p. 245.
29. Quoted in Stokes, 5:1044.
30. Quoted in ibid.
31. Fitch, *Diary,* p. 103.
32. Details about the Theater Royal: Burrows and Wallace, p. 247; Stokes, 5:1045.
33. Bobrick, p. 238.
34. The following account of Lee's captivity is drawn from Alden, pp. 166–69.
35. Washington's opposition to helping Lee and details of Lee's alleged treason: ibid., pp. 170–79.
36. Quoted in George Moore, *The Treason of Charles Lee,* p. 85.
37. Quoted in Stokes, 5:1045.
38. Quoted in ibid.
39. Quoted in ibid., p. 1044.
40. Quoted in ibid., p. 1048.
41. Quoted in ibid., p. 1050.
42. Details of New York's state government: Stokes, 5:1049; Burrows and Wallace, pp. 256–58.
43. New York's severe measures against Tories: Burrows and Wallace, p. 258.
44. The following account of Smith's relations with the state government is in Upton, pp. 111–17.
45. Quoted in ibid., p. 112.
46. Quoted in ibid., p. 114.
47. Quoted in ibid., p. 115.
48. Quoted in Stokes, 5:1051.
49. Lifting of the Association's asceticism; list of pastimes: Burrows and Wallace, p. 247.
50. Cresswell, p. 231.
51. Ibid., p. 240.
52. Cresswell, pp. 243–44. Wishful refrain of many Britons (below): Middlekauff, p. 434.

20. PHILADELPHIA, SARATOGA, AND THE COLLAPSE OF BRITAIN'S GRAND STRATEGY

1. Clinton's obsession with his grievances: Clinton, pp. xxiv–xxv; Ward, 2:514.
2. Clinton, p. 61.
3. Ibid.
4. Boatner, pp. 133–35.
5. Symonds, p. 39.
6. Clinton, pp. xxv, 61–62.
7. Ibid.; Gruber, *Howe Brothers,* pp. 230–33.
8. The transfer of Lee to the *Centurion,* negotiations for his release: Alden, pp. 181–84.
9. Howe and the Admiralty; fleet in disrepair: Gruber, *Howe Brothers,* pp. 136–42, 221, 273–74.
10. Willcox, *Portrait,* p. 42.

11. Tilley, p. 84.
12. Delays at Sandy Hook: Stokes, 5:1054; Gruber, *Howe Brothers,* p. 234.
13. Ward, 1:325.
14. Ibid., pp. 325–28.
15. Ibid., pp. 328–31.
16. Clinton, p. 66.
17. Quoted in Clinton, p. 66.
18. Ibid.
19. Howe's abandonment of Burgoyne and Germain's role: Ibid. p. 67.
20. Details of battle near Bennington: Symonds, p. 45.
21. Clinton, p. 67.
22. Freeman, 5:464.
23. Clinton, p. 67.
24. Ibid., p. 68, footnote 20.
25. Ibid.
26. Ibid.
27. Ibid., p. 68.
28. Ibid., p. 69, footnote 22.
29. Ward, 1:331–33.
30. Battle of Brandywine; British capture of Philadelphia: Symonds, pp. 53, 55.
31. Clinton, pp. 70–72.
32. Symonds, p. 47.
33. Influx of volunteers for Gates: Ward, 2:498, 524; Symonds, p. 47.
34. American reaction to McCrea incident: Ward, 2:496–98; Symonds, p. 47.
35. Clinton, pp. 70, footnote 26; 72; Symonds, p. 49.
36. Burgoyne's sudden desire for help: Clinton, pp. 73; 74; 75, footnote 35; 82–83; quote on p. 73.
37. Ibid., pp. 73–74.
38. Symonds, p. 49.
39. The quote is in Clinton, p. 79. Clinton's fear of Washington cutting him off from the city: ibid., pp. xxvi–xxviii; 79, footnote 43.
40. Arnold's role in the battles was heroic, but because of friction between him and Gates, his behavior was also the subject of controversy. See Boatner, pp. 27, 977–78.
41. Clinton, pp. 79–80.
42. Howe, in Philadelphia, drew men from New York: Clinton, pp. 80–81.
43. Details of Germantown and siege of Philadelphia: Symonds, pp. 57, 59.
44. Martin, *Private Yankee Doodle,* p. 61, note 2.
45. Ibid., p. 89.
46. Ward, 2:537.
47. Quoted in Wertenbaker, p. 139.
48. Clinton, pp. 81–82.
49. Quoted in Boatner, p. 865.
50. Siege of Philadelphia lifted . . . Americans at Valley Forge: Symonds, p. 59.
51. Martin, *Private Yankee Doodle,* p. 103.
52. Boudinot, *Journal,* p. 73.
53. Lee entertained high-ranking guests: Alden, p. 185; quoted in ibid.

54. Quoted in Stokes, 5:1057.
55. This account of Boudinot's visit to New York is drawn from Boudinot, pp. 12–19.
56. Description of Cunningham, with "bat-wings": quoted in Stokes, 5:1174.
57. Boudinot, pp. 16–17.
58. Ibid., pp. 18–19.
59. Loring's report to General Howe: Stokes, 5:1062.
60. Parole of officers, Lee's proposal and meeting with Howe: Alden, pp. 185–88.
61. Boudinot, p. 78. Alden (p. 190) notes that Boudinot hated Lee and is therefore an unreliable source. Boudinot's *Journal* is, nonetheless, an eyewitness account—exaggerated as it may be.
62. Washington's motives for excusing Lee's behavior: Alden, p. 189.
63. Lee's trip to Virginia; his stop in York: ibid., pp. 190–92.
64. British peace offensive: Alden, p. 195.
65. Treaty with France; American distrust of French; Lee's secret correspondence: ibid., pp. 195–96.
66. Lee's request for promotion turned down: ibid., pp. 194–95.
67. Quoted in ibid., p. 197.
68. Arnold's promotion: Boatner, pp. 26–29. Improved condition of Continental Army: Symonds, p. 61.
69. Germain's and Howe brothers' responses to Saratoga: Gruber, *Howe Brothers,* pp. 273–74, 287–88.
70. Ibid., pp. 293–94.
71. Mediocre admirals: Wilcox, "Arbuthnot, Gambier, and Graves," p. 260.
72. Clinton, p. 85.
73. Ibid., pp. 85–86.

21. THE RETURN TO NEW YORK CITY, THE FULCRUM OF THE WAR

1. Clinton, p. 86.
2. Ibid., p. 87.
3. Middlekauff, pp. 434–35.
4. Quoted in Stokes, 5:1114.
5. Young, p. 67.
6. Gruber, *Howe Brothers,* pp. 287, 298–99.
7. Quoted in Young, p. 67. Andre's description of the *mischianza*: Commager and Morris, pp. 657–60.
8. Quoted in Clinton, p. 88, footnote 5.
9. Ibid.
10. Gruber, *Howe Brothers,* pp. 299–300.
11. Evacuation of loyalists and the army from Philadelphia: ibid., pp. 300–301. Size of Washington's force: Clinton, p. 89; Freeman, 5:7.
12. Details of Monmouth: Freeman, 5:43.
13. Lee's defenders are Alden, pp. 194–227, and Shy, "Charles Lee: The Soldier as Radical," pp. 22–48.
14. Lee's court-martial: Alden, pp. 228–58; Shy, pp. 45–46; Nelson, pp. 131–33.

15. Arrival of the French, newspaper quote: Freeman, 5:45, 46.
16. Ward, 2:587.
17. O'Beirne, *Narrative*, p. 9.
18. Britain's defensive strategy: Willcox, *Portrait*, pp. 212–19.
19. O'Beirne, *Narrative*, pp. 9–10.
20. Ibid., p. 11.
21. Ibid., p. 13.
22. Ibid., p. 14.
23. D'Estaing's attempts to find pilots to cross the bar: Freeman, 5:49–50; Ward, 2:588. The quote is in O'Beirne, *Narrative*, p. 14.
24. Martin, *A Narrative*, p. 97.
25. Quoted in Martin, *Private Yankee Doodle*, p. 134, note 14.
26. Martin, *A Narrative*, p. 97.
27. O'Beirne, *Narrative*, pp. 14–15.
28. Ibid., p. 15.
29. Ibid., p. 20.
30. Quoted in Stokes, 5:1070.
31. O'Beirne, *Narrative*, p. 16.
32. Freeman, 5:50–51.
33. Gruber, *Howe Brothers*, p. 316.
34. Fire, explosion, siege mentality, and prisoner exchange: Stokes, 5:1072–73.
35. Quoted in ibid., p. 1073.
36. Ward, 2:593.
37. Gruber, *Howe Brothers*, pp. 319–20.
38. "Wicked Forgery": quoted in Stokes, 5:1068. Holt quoted in Upton, p. 118. The following account of Smith's return to New York is in ibid., pp. 118–19.
39. Smith traveled with Colden's grandson: William Smith, *Historical Memoirs* (1971), p. 2, note ii.
40. Quoted inUpton, p. 121.
41. Quoted in ibid.
42. Quoted in Ranlet, p. 164.
43. Quoted in Stokes, 5:1074.
44. Fateful delay was a gift: ibid.
45. Ibid.
46. Quoted in ibid., p. 1076.
47. Ibid., p. 1078.
48. Middlekauff, p. 432.
49. Ward, 2:594; Freeman, 5:87.
50. Culper Ring: Bakeless, pp. 182, 227–28. Female spies: Burrows and Wallace, p. 255.
51. Quoted in Freeman, 5:86
52. Ward, 2:595.
53. Quoted in Stokes, 5:1080.
54. Seven ships destroyed . . . three soldiers frozen: William Smith, *Historical Memoirs* (1971), p. 59. Firewood was "not to be got" and regulations on sale of bread: Stokes, 5:1081, 1082.
55. Ibid., p. 1082.

56. Freeman, 5:134–36.
57. Ibid., p. 136.
58. Middlekauff, pp. 436–38; Gruber, *Howe Brothers,* pp. 338–49.
59. Accounts of Stony Point and Paulus Hook: Symonds, p. 69; Ward, 2:596–610.
60. Symonds, p. 75.
61. Global war: Symonds, pp. 61–62, 77.
62. "Duke of Dally, Lord Lingerloring"; quoted in Young, p. 79; "going down Hill": quoted in Stokes, 5:1092.
63. William Smith, *Historical Memoirs* (1971), pp. 156, 172–73. Sabine transcribes the phrase "destitute of Fuel" as "destitute of Trade." Stokes, 5:1094, quotes the manuscript as "destitute of Fuel."
64. William Smith, *Historical Memoirs* (1971), p. 173.
65. Ibid.

22. NEW YORK'S IMPACT ON THE WAR
IN THE SOUTH

1. Germain's desperate effort: Symonds, p. 79; Middlekauff, p. 435; Upton, p. 127.
2. Clinton, p. xxxiii; Symonds, p. 79.
3. Symonds, p. 83; Ward, 2:695–96; Clinton, p. xxxiv.
4. Wilcox, "Arbuthnot, Gambier, and Graves," p. 260.
5. Freeman, 5:137.
6. Quoted in Ward, 2:611.
7. Quoted in Stokes, 5:1094.
8. Quoted in ibid., pp. 1095, 1097.
9. William Smith, *Historical Memoirs* (1971), p. 183.
10. Quoted in Stokes, 5:1096.
11. "Destitute of Fuel": ibid., p. 1099.
12. William Smith, *Historical Memoirs* (1971), p. 197.
13. Ibid., p. 211.
14. Symonds, p. 83; Stokes, 5:1099.
15. Quoted in ibid.
16. William Smith, *Historical Memoirs* (1971), p. 216.
17. Ibid.
18. Quoted in Stokes, 5:1101.
19. Ibid.
20. Quoted in Ward, 2:612.
21. Quoted in ibid., p. 613.
22. Ibid., p. 614.
23. Smith's intelligence network and De Lancey's suspicions: Upton, pp. 127–28.
24. Details of the celebration for the queen's birthday: Stokes, 5:1100–1101.
25. William Smith, *Historical Memoirs* (1971), p. 217.
26. Quoted in Stokes, 5:1104.
27. William Smith, *Historical Memoirs* (1971), p. 247.
28. Quoted in Stokes, 5:1106.

29. Smith wrote Robertson's proclamation . . . martial law continued: Stokes, 5:1106–07; Upton, pp. 123–25.
30. William Smith, *Historical Memoirs* (1971), pp. 261, 265.
31. Clinton, p. xxxiv; Symonds, p. 83.
32. Freeman, 5:161.
33. Clinton, p. xxxiii.
34. Ward, 2:621.
35. Freeman, 5:167.
36. Quoted in ibid.
37. Freeman, 5:168–69, 178, 186.
38. Wilcox, *Portrait*, pp. 60, 69; Clinton, p. xliv; Young, pp. 47; 48, footnote.
39. Burrows and Wallace, p. 247; Bobrick, p. 372.
40. Theater's expenses: Broadside, "New-York, Theatre, 1782: General Account of Receipts and Disbursements for the last Seasons." In the exhibition, "Independence and Its Enemies," (2001) at the NYHS.
41. Ward, 2:621–23.
42. Civil war in the South, Clinton's proclamations, and "Bloody Ban": Symonds, p. 80.
43. Freeman, 5:179–81.
44. Ibid., pp. 181–82.
45. Clinton, p. 463.
46. Boatner, pp. 27–29.
47. Clinton, pp. 462–63.
48. Ibid., p. 463.
49. Ibid., p. 463–64.
50. Freeman, 5:180.
51. Symonds, p. 87.
52. Clinton, p. 464.
53. Freeman, 5:189–90.
54. Quoted in Stokes, 5:1116.
55. Freeman, 5:192–94.
56. Clinton, p. 215.
57. Ibid., p. 216.
58. Ibid.
59. Quoted in Upton, p. 128.
60. Clinton, p. 216.
61. Upton, pp. 128–29; Boatner, p. 29.
62. Clinton, p. 226.
63. Ibid., p. 228.
64. Symonds, pp. 91–97.
65. Clinton saw value of Chesapeake: Wilcox, *Portrait*, p. 63. Greene's supply lines: Freeman, 5:252–53.
66. Ward, 2:624.
67. Ibid., pp. 624–26.
68. Freeman, 5:254, 270.

69. Ibid., pp. 255–72.
70. Symonds, p. 99.
71. Ibid., pp. 91–95.
72. Quoted in Freeman, 5:270.

23. NEW YORK'S ROLE AT YORKTOWN

1. Quoted in Freeman, 5:278.
2. Symonds, p. 101. "respectable force": quoted in Freeman, 5:270.
3. Symonds, p. 99.
4. Freeman, 5:288, 293.
5. Ibid., pp. 285–89. British distracted in Mediterranean: Willcox, *Portrait,* p. 393.
6. Freeman, 5:290–91, 301; Symonds, p. 99.
7. Freeman, 5:296–97.
8. Wilcox, *Portrait,* pp. 393–94; Symonds, p. 99.
9. Wilcox, *Portrait,* p. 404; Symonds, p. 99.
10. Symonds, p. 99.
11. Wilcox, *Portrait,* p. 404.
12. Symonds, p. 99.
13. Wilcox, *Portrait,* pp. 405–408.
14. The following account is from Ward, 2:880–81 and Carrington, pp. 619–20.
15. Carrington, p. 618.
16. Quoted in Stokes, 5:1132.
17. William Smith, *Historical Memoirs* (1971), p. 426.
18. Ward, 2:881.
19. Quoted in Stokes, 5:1132.
20. Wilcox, *Portrait,* pp. 400–402.
21. Ibid., pp. 409–10, 411–12.
22. William Smith, *Historical Memoirs* (1971), p. 426.
23. Quoted in Wilcox, *Portrait,* p. 398.
24. Ibid., pp. 405–406, 443.
25. William Smith, *Historical Memoirs* (1971), p. 426; Stokes, 5:1132.
26. Upton, p. 51; Stokes, 5:1074.
27. Ward, 2:881–82; Freeman, 5:309.
28. Freeman, 5:309–12.
29. Quoted in ibid., p. 310, note 68.
30. Ibid., pp. 312–13.
31. Ibid., p. 317.
32. Quoted in Wilcox, *Portrait,* p. 418.
33. Quoted in Stokes, 5:1135.
34. Freeman, 5:318–19.
35. Symonds, pp. 101–03; Wilcox, *Portrait,* p. 420, footnote 5. Willcox defends Hood against critics who argue that he left the Chesapeake prematurely and failed to find de Grasse. Hood's proper mission, according to Willcox, was to combine his fleet with that of Graves as quickly as possible in order to match or outnumber the French ships.
36. Symonds, p. 101.
37. Freeman, 5:322; Symonds, p. 101.

38. Hood's arrival in New York; Hood's words: in Wilcox, *Portrait,* p. 421.
39. William Smith, *Historical Memoirs* (1971), p. 435.
40. Ibid., p. 438.
41. Symonds, p. 103.
42. Ibid., p. 105.
43. Wilcox, *Portrait,* pp. 427–29.
44. Symonds, p. 105.
45. William Smith, *Historical Memoirs* (1971), p. 459.
46. *Lloyd's Evening Post,* quoted in Stokes, 5:1135.
47. William Smith, *Historical Memoirs* (1971), p. 441.
48. "Very critical": quoted in Symonds, p. 105; plan of escape: Ward, 2:893.
49. Symonds, p. 105; Ward, 2:894.
50. Quoted in Stokes, 5:1138.
51. Wilcox, *Portrait,* p. 439.
52. Cornwallis to Clinton; Clinton to Germain: Stokes, 5:1138–39.
53. Quoted in Wertenbaker, pp. 245–46.
54. Stokes, 5:1138.

24. THE COLONIES LOST, NEW YORK REGAINED

1. Quoted in Wertenbaker, p. 249.
2. Ibid.
3. Ibid., pp. 244–45, 253.
4. Wilcox, *Portrait,* pp. 447–48, 451–52, 459, 461.
5. Ibid., pp. 448–50.
6. Freeman, 5:398.
7. Ibid., pp. 399–401.
8. Ibid., pp. 403–6.
9. Wilcox, *Portrait,* pp. 457, footnote 4; 458–59; 462.
10. Smith's role as Arnold's ghostwriter: Upton, p. 129. Desire for a viceroy: ibid., and William Smith, *Historical Memoirs* (1971), pp. 414–15.
11. Developments in London in two preceding paragraphs: Wertenbaker, pp. 250–51.
12. Stokes, 5:1145.
13. Both quotations in Wilcox, *Portrait,* pp. 490–91.
14. Carleton's style: Wertenbaker, pp. 248–49; Upton, p. 136; Stokes, 5:1148–49, 1150.
15. Carleton shared Smith's vision of reuniting the empire: Upton, p. 137.
16. Wertenbaker, p. 251.
17. Freeman, 5:416–17.
18. Ibid., pp. 417–20.
19. Wertenbaker, p. 251.
20. Quoted in ibid.
21. Quoted in ibid.
22. Upton, p. 139.
23. Ibid.
24. William Smith, *Historical Memoirs* (1971), pp. 541, 542. Smith's hand shook: Upton, p. 140.

25. Wertenbaker, pp. 253–54.

26. Freeman, 5:422–25.

27. Alden, p. 158. Circumstances of Lee's death: ibid., pp. 293–99.

28. Washington learned of Lee's death: Freeman, 5:424–25.

29. Ibid., p. 429.

30. Ibid. Letter to Knox: Washington, *Writings,* 26:88.

31. Quoted in Upton, pp. 141–42.

32. Quoted in Stokes, 5:1159.

33. Upton, p. 141.

34. Quoted in Stokes, 5:1159.

35. Quoted in ibid.

36. Quoted in ibid.

37. Tallmadge, pp. 61–62.

38. Martin, *A Narrative,* pp. 202, 205, and 208.

39. Stokes, 5:1161.

40. William Smith, *Historical Memoirs* (1971), pp. 584, 588.

41. Details of the negotiations at Tappan: Stokes, 5:1162.

42. Quoted in ibid., p. 1165.

43. Quoted in ibid., p. 1166.

44. Quoted in ibid., p. 1167.

45. Details of emigration: Wertenbaker, pp. 260–65; Stokes, 5:1168, 1172.

46. Upton, pp. 142–43.

47. Quoted in Ottley and Weatherby, eds., p. 54. Bleucke's career: Hodges, *Root and Branch,* pp. 147; 316, note 35; and Hodges, ed., *Black Loyalist Directory,* pp. xxiii–xxv, xxxiv, 88. Spelled "Blucke" in *Black Loyalist Directory.*

48. The return of newspapers to New York City: Stokes, 5:1170, 1172.

49. Details of British plans to evacuate New York and approach of Americans: ibid., 5:1171–74.

50. Quoted in ibid., 5:1172.

51. Quoted in ibid., 5:1174.

52. Details of raising the flag at Fort George: Wertenbaker, p. 268; Stokes, 5:1174.

53. Tallmadge, p. 62.

54. Quoted in Burrows and Wallace, p. 260.

55. Quoted in Ranlet, p. 169.

56. Quoted in O'Donnell, *1001 Things,* pp. 199–200. Breakfast with Mulligan: Bakeless, p. 358.

57. Ibid.; Ranlet, pp. 84–86.

58. Bakeless, p. 228; Fleming, "George Washington, Spymaster," p. 51.

59. Tallmadge, p. 63.

60. Ibid., pp. 63–64.

61. Ibid., p. 67.

62. Ibid., p. 65.

63. Ibid., p. 66.

64. Freeman, 5:465; Champagne, p. 203.

65. Smith's final years: Upton, pp. 146–60, 161, 163, 166, 187, 202, 217, 221, 222.

EPILOGUE. RECONCILIATION, REBIRTH, AND REMEMBRANCE

1. Quoted in Ranlet, p. 167.
2. The return of Sears and the tactics of the Sons: Burrows and Wallace, pp. 267, 276; Champagne, p. 203.
3. Clinton's denunciations and the new punitive laws: Burrows and Wallace, p. 267.
4. Lamb, Willett, Duane: functions of City Hall: ibid., pp. 266–67.
5. Ibid., p. 268.
6. Ibid., p. 269.
7. Champagne, pp. 203, 213.
8. Economic problems: ibid., p. 206–8.; Burrows and Wallace, p. 265.
9. Physical condition of the city: ibid.; Champagne, p. 201.
10. Quoted in Stokes, 5:1179.
11. Bank of New York: Burrows and Wallace, p. 277; Champagne, pp. 207–9; Monaghan, p. 86.
12. The fate of the Murrays after the war: Monaghan, pp. 84–87.
13. Champagne, pp. 209–10.
14. Population: Burrows and Wallace, p. 270.
15. Ibid., pp. 270–74.
16. Hamilton writing as Phocion: ibid., pp. 274–75.
17. Ibid., pp. 275–77.
18. Ibid., p. 278.
19. Ibid., pp. 282–83, 276; Ranlet, p. 172.
20. Ibid., p. 279.
21. Hamilton's coalition grew; anti-Tory laws repealed: ibid., pp. 278–79, 280–81.
22. Ibid., p. 281.
23. Ibid., p. 283. Old voting system of bribery and intimidation: Wertenbaker, p. 17.
24. Quoted in Greene, pp. 145–46.
25. Estimates of deaths on prison ships: ibid., p. viii; Stokes, 5:1160.
26. Quoted in Greene, pp. 146–47.
27. "Paper bubbles": quoted in Ranlet, p. 172.
28. Details of Martin's life after the war: Martin, *Private Yankee Doodle,* pp. xiii–xiv.
29. Quoted in ibid., p. xv.
30. Martin, *A Narrative,* pp. 211–12.
31. Ibid., p. 212.
32. Martin, *Private Yankee Doodle,* pp. xv–xvi.
33. Martin, *A Narrative,* p. iv.

APPENDIX. A WALKING TOUR OF THE BATTLE FOR NEW YORK

1. New York would have more monuments to the Revolution if it had remained the capital: Kenneth Jackson, interviewed in Ric Burns, *New York: A Documentary Film.*

2. Reynolds, p. 14.

3. *Brooklyn Daily Eagle,* August 27, 1846.

4. Reynolds, pp. 14–15.

5. Quoted in ibid., p. 14.

6. Sources for the Walking Tour include the following: *City Hall Park: New York's Historic Commons; Landmarks of New York; WPA Guide;* Stember, *Bicentennial Guide;* and Wolfe, *New York: A Guide to the Metropolis.*

$Bibliography$

ABBREVIATIONS

NYHS: New York Historical Society
NYHSQ: New York Historical Society Quarterly
NYPL: New York Public Library
NYPL, RBM: New York Public Library, Rare Books and Manuscripts

Abbatt, William. *The Battle of Pell's Point (or Pelham), October 18, 1776. Being the Story of a Stubborn Fight.* New York: W. Abbatt, 1901.

Abbott, Wilbur C. *New York in the American Revolution.* New York: Scribner's, 1929.

Adams, Russell B., Jr., ed. *The American Story: The Revolutionaries.* Alexandria, Va.: Time-Life Books, 1996.

Alden, John Richard. *General Charles Lee: Traitor or Patriot?* Baton Rouge: Louisiana State University Press, 1951.

Allen, Andrew. Letter to "My Dear Sally," February 5, 1776. Chalmers Collection, NYPL, RBM.

American National Biography. New York and Oxford: Oxford University Press 1999.

Anderson, Fred. *Crucible of War: The Seven Years' War and the Fate of Empire in British North America, 1754–1776.* New York: Knopf, 2000.

Augustyn, Robert T., and Paul E. Cohen. *Manhattan in Maps: 1527–1995.* New York: Rizzoli, 1997.

Bailyn, Bernard, et al. *The Great Republic: A History of the American People.* Lexington, Mass. and Toronto: Heath, 1992.

Bakeless, John. *Turncoats, Traitors, and Heroes: Espionage in the American Revolution.* New York: Da Capo Press, 1998.

Bangs, Isaac. *Journal of Lieutenant Isaac Bangs, April 1 to July 29, 1776.* New York: New York Times and Arno Press, 1968.

Barck, Oscar. *New York City During the War for Independence.* New York: Columbia University Press, 1931.

Becker, C. L. *The History of Political Parties in New York, 1760–1776.* Madison: University of Wisconsin Press, 1909.

Billias, George Athan. *General John Glover and His Marblehead Mariners.* New York: Holt, 1955.

———. "Pelham Bay: A Forgotten Battle." *NYHSQ* 42 (January 1958), pp. 20–38.

———, ed. *George Washington's Generals and Opponents.* New York: Da Capo Press, 1994.

Bliven, Bruce, Jr. *Battle for Manhattan.* New York: Holt, 1955.

———. *Under the Guns: New York, 1775–1776.* New York: Harper and Row, 1972.

Boatner, Mark. *Encyclopedia of the American Revolution.* New York: David McKay, 1974.

Bobrick, Benson. *Angel in the Whirlwind: The Triumph of the American Revolution.* New York: Simon and Schuster, 1997.

Boudinot, Elias. *Journal or Historical Recollections of American Events During the Revolutionary War.* New York: New York Times and Arno Press, 1968.

British Adjutant's Orderly Book, 1776–1777. In the Gilder Lehrman Collection at the Pierpont Morgan Library.

Broadsides in the NYPL: December 16, 1769, by "A Son of Liberty"; January 15, 1770, by "Brutus"; January 19, 1770, by the "Sixteenth Regiment of Foot."

Brooklyn Daily Eagle, August 27, 1846. NYPL, microfilm.

Burnett, E. C., ed. *Letters of Members of the Continental Congress.* Gloucester, Mass.: Peter Smith, 1963.

Burns, Ric. *New York: A Documentary Film.*

Burrows, Edwin, and Mike Wallace. *Gotham: A History of New York City to 1898.* New York and Oxford: Oxford University Press, 1998.

Bushnell, Charles, ed. *The Adventures of Christopher Hawkins.* New York: New York Times and Arno Press, 1968.

Butterfield, L. H., ed. *Diary and Autobiography of John Adams.* Cambridge, Mass.: Belknap Press of Harvard University Press, 1961.

Carrington, Henry B. *Battles of the American Revolution, 1775–1781.* New York: Promontory Press, 1973. Originally published in 1877 and 1881.

Champagne, Roger J. *Alexander McDougall and the American Revolution in New York.* Schenectady, N.Y.: New York State American Revolution Bicentennial Commission/Union College Press, 1975.

Chidsey, D. B. *The Tide Turns: An Informal History of the Campaign of 1776.* New York: Crown, 1966.

City Hall Park: New York's Historic Commons. New York: Parks Department booklet, 1999.

City History Club Historical Guide to the City of New York. New York: Frederick Stokes, 1909.

Clinton, Sir Henry. *The American Rebellion: Sir Henry Clinton's Narrative of His Campaigns, 1775–1782, with an Appendix of Original Documents.* William B. Willcox, ed. New Haven: Yale University Press, 1954.

Collier, Sir George. "'To My Inexpressible Astonishment': Admiral Sir George Collier's Observations on the Battle of Long Island." *NYHSQ* 48 (October 1964), pp. 293–305.

Commager, Henry Steele, and Richard B. Morris, eds. *The Spirit of 'Seventy-six: The Story of the American Revolution as Told by Participants.* New York: Da Capo Press, 1995.

Cresswell, Nicholas. *The Journal of Nicholas Cresswell, 1774–1777.* Port Washington, N.Y.: Kennikat Press, 1968.

Cumming, William P., and Hugh F. Rankin, eds. *The Fate of a Nation: The American Revolution Through Contemporary Eyes.* London: Phaidon, 1975.

Dann, John C., ed. *The Revolution Remembered: Eyewitness Accounts of the War for Independence.* Chicago and London: University of Chicago Press, 1980.

Dawson, Henry B. "The Park and Its Vicinity." In Valentine.

———, ed. *New York City During the American Revolution: Being a Collection of Original Papers (Now First Published) from the Manuscripts in the Possession of the Mercantile Library Association of New York City.* New York: Mercantile Library Association, 1861.

Decker, Malcolm, *Brink of Revolution: New York in Crisis, 1765–1776.* New York: Argosy Antiquarian, 1964.

De Lancey, Edward F. *The Capture of Mount Washington, November 16, 1776: The Result of Treason.* New York: NYHS, 1877.

Delaney, Edmund T. *New York's Turtle Bay, Old and New.* Barre, Mass.: Barre Publishers, 1965.

Dictionary of American Biography. New York: Scribner's 1933.

Dolkart, Andrew. *Morningside Heights: A History of Its Architecture and Development.* New York: Columbia University Press, 1998.

Douglas, Charles Henry James, comp. and ed. *A Collection of Family Records, with Biographical Sketches, and Other Memoranda of Various Families and Individuals Bearing the Name Douglas, or Allied to Families of That Name.* Providence: E. L. Freeman, 1879.

Douglas, William. "Letters Written During the Revolutionary War by Col. William Douglas to His Wife Covering the Period July 19, 1775, to Dec. 5, 1776." *NYHSQ* 12–14 (1928–29).

Faragher, John Mack, ed. *The Encyclopedia of Colonial and Revolutionary America.* New York: Da Capo Press, 1996.

Fenn, Elizabeth. *Pox Americana: The Great Smallpox Epidemic of 1775–82.* New York: Hill and Wang, 2001.

Field, Thomas W. *The Battle of Long Island.* Brooklyn, N.Y.: Long Island Historical Society, 1869. Contents: pt. 1, the narrative; pt. 2, documents.

Fitch, Jabez. *The New-York Diary of Lieutenant Jabez Fitch.* Ed. W. H. W. Sabine. New York: New York Times and Arno Press, 1954.

Fleming, Thomas. *1776: Year of Illusions.* Edison, N.J.: Castle Books, 1996.

———. "George Washington, Spymaster." In *American Heritage,* February/March 2000.

Foner, Philip S. *Labor and the American Revolution.* Westport, Conn.: Greenwood Press, 1976.

Force, Peter, ed. *American Archives: A Collection of Authentick Records, State Papers, Debates, and Letters and Other Notices of Publick Affairs.* 4th ser., vol. 5 and 5th ser., vols. 2, 3, Washington, D.C., 1837 and 1839.

Ford, W. C., ed. *Journals of the Continental Congress.* Washington, D.C.: Government Printing Office, 1905.

Freeman, Douglas Southall. *George Washington: A Biography.* 7 vols. New York: Scribner's, 1948–54.

Frey, Sylvia. *The British Soldier in America: A Social History of Military Life in the Revolutionary Period.* Austin: University of Texas Press, 1981.

Gallagher, John J. *The Battle of Brooklyn, 1776.* New York: Sarpedon, 1995.

Gephart, Ronald M. *Revolutionary America, 1763–1789: A Bibliography.* Washington, D.C.: Library of Congress, 1984.

Gilje, Paul. *The Road to Mobocracy: Popular Disorder in New York City, 1763–1834.* Chapel Hill: University of North Carolina Press, 1987. Published for the Institute of Early American History and Culture at Williamsburg, Virginia.

Gordon, William. *The History of the Rise, Progress and Establishment of the Independence of the United States of America: Including an Account of the Late War; and of the Thirteen Colonies, from their Origin to that Period.* 4 vols. London: Printed for the author; sold by Charles Dilly and James Buckland, 1788.

Graydon, Alexander, *Memoirs.* New York: New York Times and Arno Press, 1969.

Greene, Albert, ed. *Recollections of the Jersey Prison Ship from the Manuscript of Captain Thomas Dring.* New York: Corinth Books, 1961.

Gruber, Ira. *The Howe Brothers and the American Revolution.* New York: Atheneum, 1972. Published for the Institute of Early American History and Culture.

———. "America's First Battle: Long Island, August 27, 1776." In Charles Heller and William Stofft, eds. *America's First Battles, 1776–1965* (Lawrence, KS: University Press of Kansas, 1986).

Hale, Nathan. Letter to Enoch Hale, August 20, 1776. Collection of the Sons of the Revolution in the State of New York.

Heath, William. *Memoirs of Major-General William Heath.* ed. William Abbatt. New York: New York Times and Arno Press, 1968.

Heller, Charles, and William Stofft, eds. *America's First Battles, 1776–1965.* Lawrence, Kans.: University Press of Kansas, 1986.

Hibbert, Christopher. *Redcoats and Rebels: The American Revolution Through British Eyes.* New York: Avon Books, 1991.

Higginbotham, Don. *War and Society in Revolutionary America: The Wider Dimensions of Conflict.* Columbia, S.C.: University of South Carolina Press, 1988.

Hodges, Graham Russell. *The Black Loyalist Directory: African Americans in Exile after the American Revolution.* New York: Garland Pub. in association with the New England Historic Genealogical Society, 1996.

———. *Root and Branch: African-Americans in New York and New Jersey, 1613–1863.* Chapel Hill and London: University of North Carolina Press, 1999.

Hufeland, Otto. *Westchester County During the American Revolution, 1775–1783.* Harrison, N.Y.: Harbor Hill Books, 1974.

Jackson, Kenneth T., ed. *The Encyclopedia of New York City.* New Haven: Yale University Press, 1995.

Jay, John. *Commemoration of the Battle of Harlem Plains on Its One Hundredth Anniversary by the New York Historical Society.* New York: NYHS, 1876.

Johnston, Henry Phelps. *The Battle of Harlem Heights.* New York: AMS Press, 1897 and 1970.

———. *The Campaign of 1776 Around New York and Brooklyn.* Brooklyn, N.Y.: Brooklyn Historical Society, 1878 and 1971. Contents: part 1, the narrative; part 2, documents.

Jones, David E. *Women Warriors: A History.* London and Washington: Brassey's, 1997.

Jones, Thomas. *History of New York During the Revolutionary War.* New York: NYHS, 1879.

Kammen, Michael. *Colonial New York: A History.* New York: Scribner's, 1975.

Keegan, John. *Fields of Battle.* New York: Random House, 1995.

Kelby, William, comp., and John Austin Stevens, ed. *Centennial Notes: New York City One Hundred Years Ago, 1776–1876.* A scrapbook of clippings from the *New York Evening Mail,* March 13–November 20, 1876. NYHS Library. "Centennial Notes" was a weekly series of columns, which reprinted items from the New York newspapers of 1776 for the same week. In the eighteenth century, before the advent of modern journalism, letters were often printed in newspapers as sources for current events.

Klein, Milton. "Why Did the British Fail to Win the Hearts and Minds of New Yorkers?" *New York History* 64 (October 1983), pp. 356–75. Cited in Burrows and Wallace.

Koke, Richard J. "The Struggle for the Hudson." In *Narratives of the Revolution in New York,* pp. 36–79.

Landmarks of New York. New York: City History Club, 1923.

Lowell, Edward J. *The Hessians and Other German Auxiliaries of Great Britain in the Revolutionary War.* Port Washington, N.Y.: Kennikat Press, 1965.

Mackesy, Piers. *The War for America, 1775–1783.* Cambridge, Mass.: Harvard University Press, 1964.

Manders, Eric. *The Battle of Long Island.* Monmouth, N.J.: Philip Freneau Press, 1978.

Martin, Joseph Plumb. *A Narrative of Some of the Adventures, Dangers, and Sufferings of a Revolutionary Soldier; Interspersed with Anecdotes of Incidents That Occurred Within His Own Observation. Written by Himself.*
"Long sleepless nights in heavy arms I've stood;
"And spent laborious days in dust and blood."—Pope's Homer
Hallowell, Maine: Glazier, Masters, 1830. NYPL, Rare Books and Manuscripts.

———. *Private Yankee Doodle: Being a Narrative of Some of the Adventures, Dangers, and Sufferings of a Revolutionary Soldier.* Ed. George F. Scheer. Boston: Little, Brown, 1962.

McCullough, David. *John Adams.* New York: Simon and Schuster, 2001.

———. "What the Fog Wrought." In Robert Cowley, ed., *What If? The World's Foremost Military Historians Imagine What Might Have Been,* pp. 189–200. New York: Putnam, 1998.

Middlekauff, Robert. *The Glorious Cause.* New York: Oxford University Press, 1982.

Monaghan, Charles. *The Murrays of Murray Hill.* Brooklyn, N.Y.: Urban History Press, 1998.

Montresor, John. *Journals of Capt. John Montresor.* Ed. G. D. Scull. New York: NYHS Collections, 1881.

Montross, Lynn. *Rag, Tag, and Bobtail: The Story of the Continental Army, 1775–1783.* New York: Harper and Brothers, 1952.

Moore, Frank. *Diary of the American Revolution.* New York: Washington Square Press, 1968.

Moore, George. *Mr. Lee's Plan—March 29, 1777. The Treason of Charles Lee, Major General, Second in Command in the American Army of the Revolution.* Port Washington, N.Y.: Kennikat Press, 1970.

Narratives of the Revolution in New York: A Collection of Articles from the New York Historical Society Quarterly. New York, 1975.

Naval Documents of the American Revolution. Ed. William Bell Clark. Washington, D.C.: Naval History Division, 1964–.

Nelson, Paul David. *William Alexander, Lord Stirling.* University, Ala.: University of Alabama Press, 1987.

Neumann, George. "A Revolutionary Soldier's Life." Lecture at the NYHS, July 24, 2001.

Newton, Caroline Clifford. *Once Upon a Time in Connecticut.* Boston: Houghton Mifflin, 1916.

New York City Five Borough Pocket Atlas. Maspeth, N.Y.: Hagstrom, 1999.

New York Gazette, (Weyman). March 30, 1767. NYPL, microfilm.

New York Herald, November 26, 1893. Original clippings in NYPL.

New York Journal, March 26, 1767; February 8, 15, 1770. NYPL, microfilm.

New York Mercury, July 16, 1770; May 8, 1775. NYHS, photostats.

New York Weekly Post-Boy, November 7, 1765; August 14, 1766; and February 5, 19, 1770. NYHS microfilm.

O'Beirne, Thomas. *A Candid and Impartial Narrative of the Transactions of the Fleet, Under the Command of Lord Howe, from the Arrival of the Toulon Squadron, on the Coast of America, to the Time of His Lordship's Departure for England. With Observations. By an Officer Then Serving in the Fleet.* London: printed for J. Almon, 1779. NYPL, RBM.

———. *Narrative of the Fleet Under Lord Howe.* New York: New York Times and Arno Press, 1969.

O'Callaghan, E. B., ed. *Documents Relative to the Colonial History of the State of New York: Procured in Holland, England, and France by John Romeyn Brodhead.* 15 vols. Albany: Weed, Parsons, 1853–87.

Onderdonk, Henry, Jr., ed. *Revolutionary Incidents of Suffolk and Kings Counties.* Port Washington, N.Y.: Kennikat Press, 1849 and 1970.

O'Donnell, Edward. *1001 Things Everyone Should Know About Irish American History.* New York: Broadway Books, 2002.

Ottley, Roi, and William J. Weatherby. *The Negro in New York: An Informal Social History.* New York and Dobbs Ferry, N.Y.: NYPL and Oceana Publications, 1967.

Paltsits, Victor H. "The Jeopardy of Washington: September 15, 1776." *NYHSQ* 32 (October 1948), pp. 253–68.

Papers of the Lloyd Family of the Manor of Queens Village, Lloyd's Neck, Long Island. New York, 1654–1826. Vol. 2, 1752–1826. New York: NYHS Collections, 1927.

Parry, William J. *Life at the Old Stone House, 1636–1852: A History of the Farm and Its Occupants.* New York: First Battle Revival Alliance, 2000.

Peckham, Howard, ed. *The Toll of Independence: Engagements and Battle Casualties of the American Revolution.* Chicago: University of Chicago Press, 1974.

Pennypacker, Morton. *George Washington's Spies on Long Island and in New York.* Brooklyn, N.Y.: Long Island Historical Society, 1939.

Peterson, Harold L. *The Book of the Continental Soldier.* Harrisburg, Pa.: Stackpole Books, 1968.

Ranlet, Philip. *The New York Loyalists.* Knoxville: University of Tennessee Press, 1986.

Ratzer, Bernard. Map of New York City in 1776. Collection of the NYHS.

Rawson, Jonathan A., and George G. Ruben. *Riding into the Past by Motor Coach.* New York: Fifth Avenue Coach Company, 1926. 150th anniversary commemorative pamphlet/map, in the NYHS.

Reynolds, David. *Walt Whitman's America: A Cultural Biography.* New York: Knopf, 1995.

Rochambeau, Marshal, Count de. *Memoirs of the Marshal Count de Rochambeau, Relative to the War of Independence of the United States.* New York: New York Times and Arno Press, 1971.

Sabine, William H. W. *Murder 1776 and Washington's Policy of Silence.* New York: Theo. Gaus' Sons, 1973.

Sauthier, C. J. Map of New York City in 1776. Collection of the NYHS.

Sawyer, Charles. *Firearms in American History, 1600–1800.* Norwood, Mass.: Plimpton Press, 1910.

Scheer, George F., and Hugh F. Rankin. *Rebels and Redcoats: The American Revolution Through the Eyes of Those Who Fought and Lived It.* New York: Da Capo Press, 1987.

Scribner's Monthly, January 1876, "New York in the Revolution." pp. 305–22.

Serle, Ambrose. *The American Journal of Ambrose Serle.* San Marino, Calif.: Huntington Library, 1940.

Shelton, William Henry. "Nathan Hale Execution and the New York Fire." *New York Times,* September 22, 1929.

———. "What Was the Mission of Nathan Hale?" *Journal of American History* (1915), pp. 269–89.

Shewkirk, Ewald. "Diary of Rev. Mr. Shewkirk, Pastor of the Moravian Church, New York." In Henry Phelps Johnston, *The Campaign of 1776 Around New York and Brooklyn.* Brooklyn, NY: Brooklyn Historical Society, 1878 and 1971, pt. 2: 101–27.

Shy, John. "Charles Lee: The Soldier as Radical." In Billias, ed., *George Washington's Generals and Opponents,* pp. 22–53.

Silliman, Gold Selleck. Letter to "My Dear Son," July 27, 1776. Gilder Lehrman Collection at the Pierpont Morgan Library.

Singleton, Esther. *Social New York Under the Georges, 1714–1776.* New York: D. Appleton, 1902.

Smith, Samuel. "Autobiography of General Samuel Smith." In *The General Samuel Smith Papers.* Columbia University Rare Book and Manuscript Library.

Smith, William. *Historical Memoirs of William Smith from 16 March 1763 to 25 July 1778.* Ed. W. H. W. Sabine. New York: New York Times and Arno Press, 1969.

———. *Historical Memoirs of William Smith from 26 August 1778 to 12 November 1783.* Ed. W. H. W. Sabine. New York: New York Times and Arno Press, 1971.

Stedman, C. *The History of the Origin, Progress, and Termination of the American War.* New York: New York Times and Arno Press, 1969. Originally published in London in 1794.

Stember, Sol. *The Bicentennial Guide to the American Revolution.* Vol. 1, *The War in the North.* New York: Saturday Review Press/Dutton, 1974.

Stevenson, Charles G., and Irene Wilson. *The Battle of Long Island* ("The Battle of Brooklyn"). Brooklyn, N.Y.: Brooklyn Bicentennial Commission, 1975.

Stiles, Henry. *A History of Brooklyn.* 3 vols. Bowie, MD: Heritage Books, 1993.

Still, Bayrd. *Mirror for Gotham: New York as Seen by Contemporaries from Dutch Days to the Present.* New York: New York University Press, 1956.

Stirling Papers, vol. 4. NYHS, microfilm.

Stokes, I. N. Phelps. *The Iconography of Manhattan Island, 1498–1909: Compiled from Original Sources and Illustrated by Photo-Intaglio Reproductions of Important Maps,*

Plans, Views, and Documents in Public and Private Collections. 6 vols. Union, N.J.: Lawbook Exchange, 1998.

Stone, W. L., trans. *Letters of Brunswick and Hessian Officers During the American Revolution.* New York: Da Capo Press, 1970.

Symonds, Craig L., and William J. Clipson. *A Battlefield Atlas of the American Revolution.* Baltimore: Nautical and Aviation Publishing Company of America, 1999.

Tallmadge, Benjamin. *Memoir of Colonel Benjamin Tallmadge.* New York: New York Times and Arno Press, 1968. First published in 1858.

Tanner, Stephen. *Epic Retreats from 1776 to the Evacuation of Saigon.* Rockville Center, N.Y.: Sarpedon, 2000.

Tiedemann, Joseph. *Reluctant Revolutionaries: New York City and the Road to Independence, 1763–1776.* Ithaca, N.Y., and London: Cornell University Press, 1997.

Tilley, John A. *The British Navy and the American Revolution.* Columbia, S.C.: University of South Carolina Press, 1987.

Upton, L. F. S. *The Loyal Whig: William Smith of New York and Quebec.* Toronto: University of Toronto Press, 1969.

Valentine, D. T. *Manual of the Common Council of the City of New York.* New York, 1855.

Wall, Alexander. "New York and the Declaration of Independence," in *Narratives of the Revolution in New York.*

Ward, Christopher. *The War of the Revolution.* 2 vols. New York: Macmillan, 1952.

Washington, George. *The Papers of George Washington.* Ed. Dorothy Twohig. Revolutionary War Series. Charlottesville and London: University Press of Virginia, 1994.

———. *The Writings of George Washington, from the Original Manuscript Sources, 1754–1799.* Ed. John C. Fitzpatrick. 39 vols. Washington, D.C.: U.S. Government Printing Office, 1931–34.

Weiderhold, Andreas. "The Capture of Fort Washington, New York," *Pennsylvania Magazine of History and Biography,* 23 (1899), pp. 95–97. Cited in Scheer and Rankin.

Wertenbaker, Thomas Jefferson. *Father Knickerbocker Rebels.* New York: Scribner's, 1948.

Wheeler, Richard. *Voices of 1776: The Story of the Revolution in the Words of Those Who Were There.* New York: Penguin, 1972.

Whitman, Walt. *Complete Poetry and Selected Prose.* Boston: Houghton Mifflin, 1959.

Whittemore, Charles. "John Sullivan: Luckless Irishman." In Billias, ed., *George Washington's Generals and Opponents,* pp. 137–62.

Wilkenfeld, Bruce M. "Revolutionary New York, 1776." In Milton Klein, ed., *New York: The Centennial Years, 1676–1976.* Port Washington, N.Y.: Kennikat Press, 1976.

Willcox, William B. "Arbuthnot, Gambier, and Graves: 'Old Women' of the Navy." In Billias, ed., *George Washington's Generals and Opponents,* pp. 260–90.

———. *Portrait of a General: Sir Henry Clinton in the War for Independence.* New York: Knopf, 1964.

Wolfe, Gerard. *New York: A Guide to the Metropolis.* New York: McGraw-Hill, 1994.

WPA New York City Guide. New York: Random House, 1939.

Young, Philip. *Revolutionary Ladies: Being the Surprising True Histories of Some Forgotten American Women—All Beautiful, Rich, and Loyalist—Whose Lives Were Shaped by Scandal and Turned Upside Down by the War for Independence.* New York: Knopf, 1977.

Index

~

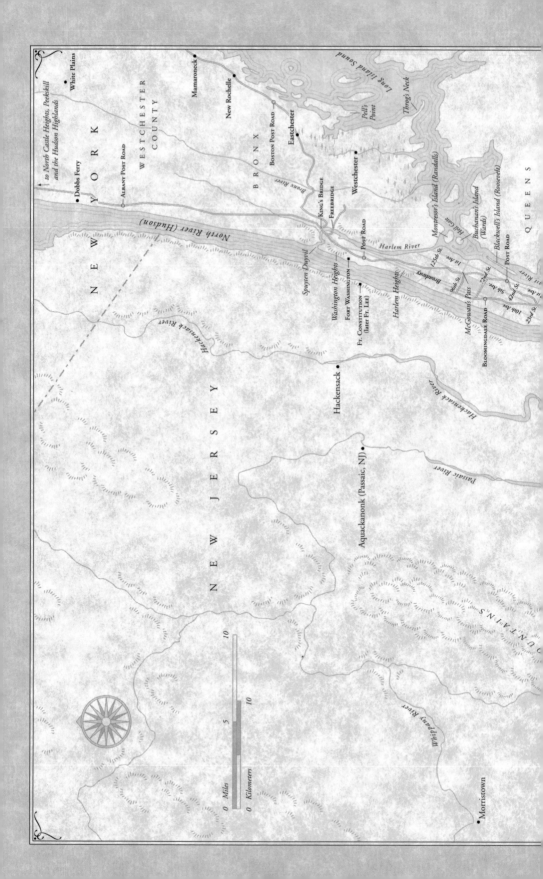